The Small Business Marketing Han

By the same author

How to Buy and Run a Shop
Franchising
The Business Planner
Successful Business Plans in a Week
Budgeting for Non-financial Managers
How to Recruit
Recruiting – How to Do It
The Barclays Guide to Managing Staff for the Small Business
Managing Staff
Managing Human Resources
Motivating People
Managing Your Time
Getting a Result
Running a Successful Advertising Campaign
How to Plan Press Advertising
How to Plan Radio Advertising
How to Plan Direct Mail
How to Plan Exhibitions
The Perfect Conference
How to Organize a Conference
Perfect PR
Correct Letters
Instant Business Letters
Write That Letter!
Make That Call!
Tricky Business Forms
How to Win at Job Hunting
How to Win at Interviews
Answer the Question, Get the Job!
Passing Interviews
How to Win at Aptitude Tests
Your Mid-career Shift
The Business Environment

The Small Business Marketing Handbook

Iain Maitland

CASSELL

Cassell
Wellington House, 125 Strand, London WC2R 0BB
370 Lexington Avenue, New York, NY 10017-6550

www.cassell.co.uk

British Library Cataloguing-in-Publication Data
A catalogue record for this book is available from the British Library.

ISBN 0-304-70419-9

Designed and typeset by Kenneth Burnley, Wirral, Cheshire.
Printed and bound in Great Britain by Redwood Books, Trowbridge, Wiltshire.

To Tracey, Michael and Sophie

Contents

Acknowledgements

I WISH TO THANK the following organizations and individuals who provided information or assistance in the compilation of *The Small Business Marketing Handbook*. Special thanks to those who allowed me to reproduce their material in the text.

Abbot Mead Vickers-BBDO Ltd; and Malcolm Duffy
Advertising Association; and Philip Spink
Advertising Standards Authority Ltd; and Patrick O'Dee and Chris Reed
Agricultural Show Exhibitors Association
Association of Exhibition Organisers; and Blanche Hunter
Association of Independent Radio Companies Ltd
Association of Media Independents Ltd
Audit Bureau of Circulations Ltd; and Austen Hawkins
Batiste Publications Ltd
Blue Cross; and Sarah Allcock
British Exhibition Contractors Association
British Telecom; and Ian Ash
Broadcasting Standards Council
Capital Radio
Classic FM
Committee of Advertising Practice
Conference and Travel Publications Ltd
Direct Mail Information Service
Direct Marketing Association (UK) Ltd
Directory Publishers Association
East Anglian Daily Times Company Ltd
Exhibition Audience Audits
Exhibition Surveys Ltd
Exhibition Venues Association
Express Newspapers plc; and Michael Moore
Franchise Development Services Ltd; and Roy Seaman

Incorporated Society of British Advertisers Ltd
Institute of Direct Marketing
Institute of Practitioners in Advertising
Inter Garden Promotions Ltd
International League for the Protection of Horses; and Sarah Bligh
IPC Magazines Ltd
League Against Cruel Sports Ltd; and Anita Cole
Leo Burnett
Maclean Hunter Ltd; and Clare Thomas
Mailing Preference Scheme
Marketing Guild; and Nick Robinson
Media Audits Ltd
National Exhibitors Association; and Peter Cotterell
National Society for the Prevention of Cruelty to Children; and
    Allison MacDowell
Office of the Data Protection Registrar; and Sue Lawrence
Periodical Publishers Association
Radio Advertising Bureau Ltd
Radio Authority; and Tony Stoller
Radio Sales Company
Radio Trent
Scottish and Irish Radio Sales
Suffolk Group Radio; and Robb Young
Target Response
TAS Exhibitions Ltd
Themetree Ltd; and John Charlton
Vision Technology Ltd; and Jan Murray
Williams and Harmer Partnership; and Mark Aspinall
York Publishing Ltd
Young and Rubicam Ltd

Preface

THE SMALL BUSINESS MARKETING HANDBOOK is written for you – the owner or manager of a prospective, new or established small firm who is planning to advertise, probably for the first time. This book takes you through the whole process, explaining in clear terms, supporting with action checklists and illustrating with classic examples of hugely successful advertisements and other documents from recent years. It is a step-by-step guide to success.

It begins by introducing the key media to you – the press, the radio, direct mail and exhibitions. These are the four media that are most likely to be used by small businesses, and with the greatest success. You'll also need and want to know who's who in the media, and the key players and their roles within each medium and the advertising industry are detailed here.

Next, the book highlights the importance of doing your groundwork: analysing yourself, knowing your market, establishing your overall budget, and calculating the costs of direct mail and exhibition activities in particular. You may even want to consider bringing in experts at this stage. This preparatory work is absolutely essential if you intend to go on and make a success of your advertising campaign.

Moving ahead, you're shown how to plan your activities – press advertising, radio advertising, direct mailing and exhibitions – in the build-up to a campaign. You'll want to pull these diverse activities together and co-ordinate them successfully. The book also explains how to put over your message to the audience, creating press and radio advertisements, mailshots and exhibition stands that are most effective. You'll need to know the tricks of the trade if your advertising is to be successful here.

Then, the book looks at running an advertising campaign – buying press space, purchasing radio time, producing mailshots and having a successful exhibition. It is crucial that you approach this campaign cautiously and carefully, testing, making changes and amending your approach on that all-important, step-by-step basis. In the Conclusion, you'll find four checklists – for the press, the radio, direct mail and exhibitions – which will enable you to assess your understanding of each of the key media, and how well you are using them in your advertising campaign.

Appendices are included towards the end of the book – and should be studied closely. A media pack, rate cards, the British Code of Advertising Practice, the Code of Advertising Standards and Practice, the British Code of Sales Promotion Practice, the Data Protection Act and the Code of Practice covering the Use of Personal Data for Advertising and Direct Marketing Purposes – these all combine to give an instant ready-reference source for all advertisers. Useful contacts, Recommended reading and a Glossary complete the book and help to make it an essential, hands-on manual throughout each and every advertising campaign.

Iain Maitland

1 Introducing the key media

TO BEGIN WITH, YOU SHOULD LOOK at the four main media that form the basis of most small business advertisers' activities: the press, the radio, direct mail, and exhibitions. You should be familiar with what they can offer, and how best to make the most of them in an advertising campaign. Only then can you decide which are right for you to use in your individual circumstances.

The press

'The press' is an all-embracing term which covers a wide and extremely diverse range of newspapers, magazines and miscellaneous publications such as directories, programmes and brochures. Each offers its own distinctive mix of characteristics, advantages and disadvantages to the prospective advertiser. Initially, you need to possess a broad, overall knowledge and understanding of their key features as well as the similarities and differences that exist between them if you are to move on to preparing for, launching and running a winning advertising campaign.

Newspapers

Newspapers may be divided up into various categories. There are national dailies such as the *Daily Star*, *The Sun*, and *The Times*, and national Sundays including *The People*, *Sunday Express* and the *News of the World*. There are regional dailies incorporating the *East Anglian Daily Times* and the *Yorkshire Post*, regional Sundays such as Avon's *Sunday Independent* and the West Midlands' *Sunday Mercury*, plus paid-for weeklies and bi-weeklies including the *Burnley Express* and *The Cornishman*, and free weeklies and bi-weeklies incorporating the *Bucks Advertiser* and the *Trent Valley Journal*. Many newspapers, whether regional or national, have several editions. For example, the *Daily Express* and *Sunday Express* print three – for Scotland, the North and the South.

Every regional and national newspaper is as different in its approach to news coverage and reporting as the *Daily Mirror* is to the *Daily Mail,* and *The Sun* is to *The Times*, and are thus more or less attractive to people of either

sex, varying ages and social grades – that is, the classes into which the population is grouped according to the occupation of the head of each household
(A: upper middle class; B: middle class; C1: lower middle class; C2: skilled
working class; D: working class; E: those on subsistence levels). Regionally,
newspapers have a relatively widespread and in-depth appeal across and into
all sections, developing a close and personal relationship with local people.
Nationally, newspapers are more likely to be taken by certain groups, with ABs
favouring *The Times*, C1C2s preferring *The Sun,* and so on. Love-hate feelings
tend to exist towards many national titles.

The circulation of a newspaper – the number of copies of each issue sold,
delivered or handed out – differs enormously according to its individual type.
The regionals are circulated to a local area and have much lower figures than the
nationals which sell across the country. An average regional newspaper – so far
as any publication can be described in such a manner – may have a circulation
of perhaps 15,000 to 150,000. *The Cornishman* sells around 20,000 copies each
week, the *East Anglian Daily Times* about 50,000 per day and the *Sunday Mercury* approximately 150,000 every weekend. A typical national newspaper – if
such a title exists – could achieve a circulation of possibly 500,000 to five million. The *Daily Star* is purchased by around 900,000 people each day and the
News of the World by over five million every Sunday. As a rule of thumb, Sunday papers – whether regional or national – tend to have larger circulations than
dailies because people buy several rather than one title at the weekend for
leisure reading.

The 'pass-on' readership of a newspaper – the number of people who
look at or read a copy of a publication – is always higher than its circulation, as
dailies may be handed to friends and colleagues at lunchtimes or after work, and
Sunday papers could be seen by other family members. Weeklies might be left
in the office or about the home for a week or so and are usually perused by other
people during this period. The readership of any given title might be three to six
times more than its circulation, which is of some considerable interest and relevance to the prospective advertiser.

Advertising costs within regional and national newspapers are closely
related to individual circulation and readership figures. Classified advertising
– whereby line-by-line advertisements are placed under assorted headings such
as 'Goods for Sale' and 'Business Services' – may cost from perhaps £1 to £3 per
line in regional papers and from possibly £5 to £20 per line in national papers.
The *West Suffolk Mercury* – a free weekly – requires £1.65 for each line and has
a circulation of 45,000-plus. The *Sunday Express* charges £16 for its linage with
a circulation of two million. Display advertising – where bordered and often
illustrated advertisements are located almost anywhere in the newspaper, subject to availability – could vary in price from about £2 to £12 per single column

centimetre in the regionals to around £30 to £120 for each single column centimetre in the nationals. An 'SCC' measures one column wide by one centimetre deep. The *West Suffolk Mercury* requests £3.25 upwards per SCC and the *Sunday Express* charges £80 or more per SCC.

There are numerous benefits to newspaper advertising. You can advertise to a broad, cross section of a local population and/or to scattered groups across the country, depending on your requirements. Advertisements may be put under those headings or in the sections or supplements where you believe they will be most effective, subject to availability. The theme, layout and copy of your advertisements can change from one newspaper or edition to another to test the effectiveness of alternative approaches or to pass on a revised message in some areas. Advertisements may be printed on a given weekday or Sunday, allowing you to be topical and/or to convey a sense of 'act now' urgency. You can advertise day after day (or at least week after week) to increase exposure and reinforce your advertising message. Advertisements may be taken at short notice from perhaps two to four days prior to publication so you can quickly place new ones or make amendments to existing ones, according to changing circumstances.

However, various drawbacks exist regarding newspaper advertising. Most people do not read a newspaper from cover to cover nor for any length of time: they flick through and dip into it for about ten to twenty minutes and may therefore miss your advertisement. A significant proportion of readers are probably not interested in your message, so you could effectively be wasting much of your money. The mood of those readers who see and are potentially receptive to your advertisements can vary from harassed and edgy on a crowded train to relaxed and mellow in a warm bath. It is difficult to compose advertisements that are appropriate and equally appealing in all circumstances. Many newspapers have a fairly short lifespan, often left behind on the train after the journey or discarded after the bathwater has drained away, so those advertisements which are not seen immediately and absorbed rarely have a second chance to succeed. The general absence of colour may affect the quality of your message, especially if you want to highlight the appearance of your goods.

Magazines

These can be separated into consumer and business titles. Consumer magazines may be broken down further into general consumer titles of widespread, popular appeal and consumer-specific titles for special-interest groups. *Candis*, *The Listener* and *Time Out* may be called general consumer magazines, *Practical Parenting*, *Slimming* and *Waterski International* might be termed consumer-specific magazines. Business titles are usually related to particular products and services, jobs and careers or trades and industries. Hence, *Engineering*

Lasers and *Frozen and Chilled Foods* are product associated, *Dairy Farmer and Dairy Beef Producer* and *Teleflorist News* are job related and *Retail Week* and *Sheet Metal Industries* are trade associated. As with newspapers, some magazines have several editions, perhaps for the north, south, east and west of their circulation areas.

Each magazine addresses its own unique mix of topics which attracts various individuals and assorted groups into purchasing and/or reading it. General interest subjects draw in people of both sexes, all ages and social grades, albeit in varying proportions. Special interest topics appeal to those people who share common hobbies, pursuits and/or concerns regardless of sex, age or social grade. Business matters may attract individuals and groups from a sector of a certain trade or from across a number of industries. Each magazine also tackles its blend of subjects in an individual way so that even those titles which appear to appeal to and be bought and/or seen by the same people have slightly different readerships. For example, parentcraft magazines are most popular with expectant women and mothers. *Practical Parenting*'s female readership comprises 76 per cent under-35s, 23 per cent over-35s, 57 per cent ABC1s and 44 per cent C2DEs. *Parents* consists of 74 per cent under-35s, 26 per cent over-35s, 33 per cent ABC1s and 67 per cent C2DEs, which could be of key significance to a prospective advertiser.

A magazine's circulation may be based upon the number of copies sold over the counter, posted to subscribers, handed out to passers-by, pushed through letterboxes or sent free of charge to named individuals (which is more commonly known as controlled circulation). Generally, business titles have relatively low but extremely well-defined circulations, typically ranging from perhaps 2,000 to 50,000. *Sheet Metal Industries*' is approximately 1,700 per issue, *Dairy Farmer and Dairy Beef Producer*'s is close to 26,000. Consumer titles usually have far higher circulations, averaging from possibly 50,000 upwards. *Slimming* sells around 120,000 per issue, compared to 145,000 for *Practical Parenting* and 520,000 for *Candis*. As a rough and ready guide, the wider a magazine's interests are, the higher its circulation is.

On average, a magazine, whether it is a consumer or a business title, has a readership figure which is ten times more substantial than its basic circulation. As examples, *Parents* has a pass-on readership of 6.6 people, *Vogue*'s is close to the norm at 9.8 whilst *Film Review*'s is well above the average at 18.6. Most magazines are kept until the next one is issued the following week, fortnight, month or quarter. They can be re-read between four to six times by each person during this period.

Advertising rates in magazines are associated with circulation and readership types and numbers. Normally, these titles sell their space by the page – sixteenth, eighth, quarter, half, full-page or double-page spread (two side-by-side pages). Business titles may charge from £200 to £2,000 per page. *Frozen and Chilled Foods'* rate is £725 for a page with a circulation of nearly 4,000 and *Retail Week's* is £1,980 and has a circulation of approximately 15,000. Consumer titles could demand from £500 upwards for a full page. *Slimming's* and *Marie Claire's* rates are £1,230 and £3,100-plus with 120,000 and 155,000 circulations respectively. Hopefully, line and single column centimetre rates may be quoted as well, or need to be calculated for simpler comparisons between each other's and newspapers' standard rates.

Magazine advertising offers many advantages. You can address clearly defined, small and compact, or large and extensive groups of people who tend to be well informed and interested in your subject. Varied advertisements may be printed in different places within magazines (subject to availability) to maximize potential sightings by the right readers. People often consider 'their' titles to be friends, which gives added credence to any associated advertisements. They also look at magazines in a leisurely and receptive mood which makes it easier to compile appropriate advertisements; and they read titles in more detail and for longer than newspapers thus raising their opportunities to see your advertisements. Magazines have a lengthy lifespan, being retained and re-read numerous times; this increases the chances of your advertising message being absorbed. Colour is widely available, allowing your advertisements to be more creative, lifelike and appealing.

However, there are several disadvantages to magazine advertising. As many titles are published at fortnightly, monthly or longer intervals, you cannot advertise day after day or week after week to rapidly build up exposure and awareness of your advertising amongst your potential customers. With advertisements needing to be submitted between one week and a month prior to publication, it is difficult to react swiftly and make changes in response to ever-developing scenarios. Given their lifespans – which go some way to compensating for these drawbacks – it is hard to predict the exact day or even the week in which your advertisement may be spotted, making it almost impossible to create a highly topical advertising message or mood of 'act quickly' urgency which might suit your particular needs.

Miscellaneous publications

The press does not consist simply of newspapers and magazines: it is also made up of directories and yearbooks, programmes and brochures, in-house journals, timetables, maps and guidebooks. The sensible small business advertiser contemplates and, where relevant, makes the most of this hotch-potch of assorted, complementary publications.

Directories and yearbooks – *Carpet Annual, Chemist and Druggist Directory* and the *United Kingdom Franchise Directory* amongst them – are reference works covering different trades and industries, and may sometimes double up as advertising media as well. Published regularly on an annual basis in most instances, circulation is relatively low, ranging from perhaps a few hundred to several thousand copies which are distributed to organizations and individuals who are extremely interested in the specific topic. Kept in shops, factories, offices, libraries and about the home for twelve months or more, they may be perused by many people during that time.

In their favour, the majority of directories and yearbooks have status and respectability in their field, giving credibility to those firms which are listed or are advertising in them. You can address a specialized group of readers who are receptive to your message. Knowing your audience and their likely attitudes it is easier to create suitably appropriate advertisements that appeal to them. Being retained for a lengthy period, your advertisements may continue to be seen time and again, hopefully reaping enquiries and even sales for as long as five years or more.

However, bear in mind that limited choices exist concerning the size, position, design and contents of advertisements, which might not tally with your personal requirements. Colour is rarely available, which can hinder creativity. Readers dip in and out of these media and are unlikely to spot every business, product or service mentioned within them. Given their longevity, it is unwise to be topical and impossible to promptly amend your advertisements if unsuccessful. Copy deadlines may be six months or so ahead of publication, so advertisements must be planned well in advance as part of an overall campaign.

Programmes and brochures are published for sporting fixtures, leisure events, fund-raising activities and so forth, on a weekly, monthly, quarterly, occasional or one-off basis, as relevant. Their circulation differs enormously depending on circumstances – perhaps from a hundred or so at a village fête to 2,000 at a touring company's week-long run at a theatre or 50,000-plus at a cup final. Buyers are usually involved closely with the associated topic, whether rugby, athletics, a town carnival or cancer research. Programmes and brochures may be kept as long-term souvenirs of the particular event.

There are benefits in promoting yourself via such media. Varied advertisements – sizes, positions, styles – can be placed, and often in colour for maximum impact. Knowing when and where they will be published and probably read, your advertising message may be up-to-date and highly relevant. Readers are familiar with and knowledgeable in the topic, making the creation and design of advertisements simpler for you. Nevertheless, there are drawbacks too. It is not always easy to remedy unsuccessful advertising as quickly as you might wish, as deadlines may be long and publication only semi-regular or occasional. Although the immediate response to your advertisements may be impressive it tends to drop off rapidly as programmes and brochures are some-times thrown away soon after being purchased.

In-house journals such as *Barclays News* and *British Airways News* can take the form of newspapers, magazines, newsletters or news-sheets, depending upon the company and its attitude towards internal communications. They may be prepared within the organization or by outside agencies. There are an esti-mated 25,000-plus house journals in the United Kingdom, with an overall cir-culation assessed at approximately twenty-five million. Typically published once a month, they are seen by employees at all levels within the firm, and some-times by customers and other business contacts as well.

On a positive note, those journals normally accept advertisements of dif-ferent sizes, shapes and even colours, positioning them according to the adver-tiser's wishes. You can sell your ideas, products and services to a well-defined, identified audience, and employees tend to assume that advertisers in their title have been approved, and view them as being trustworthy and reputable. Adver-tisements can also be adjusted at short notice in numerous journals. On the neg-ative side, many titles are of very dubious quality – badly designed, edited and printed – which could reflect upon your concern. Some employees do not read them or do so sparingly, therefore missing your advertisement. Most titles have a fairly short lifespan, being discarded after a brief read.

Timetables are printed for buses, trains, boats, planes and so forth, while maps and guidebooks are published for certain localities and regions. Many of them accept advertisements perhaps from complementary businesses for inclu-sion alongside of or to the rear of the main material. Circulation is typically in the hundreds or low thousands, and normally limited to readers who are very interested in the topic related to the publication. Timetables, maps and guide-books may be passed around and looked at by numerous people and are often retained for at least a year, if not for much longer.

The key advantage of advertising in these media is that the authority they possess can rub off onto the advertisements inside them. You may promote your concern to a hands-on readership, who are directly involved with the associat-ed subject matter. A lengthy, active life, often of many years, should ensure the advertisements are seen continually over and again. The main disadvantages are that the restrictions upon your advertisements – positions and so forth – may hinder their success; and with long deadlines and lifetimes, it is hard to be top-ical, make changes or remedy mistakes.

Always contemplate using miscellaneous publications as part of your advertising campaign: more money is spent on advertising within them each year than on consumer magazines. However, they are a very mixed bag: some are worthy media, others are not. Consider all of them, weighing up the benefits against the drawbacks but don't use them if you feel that the minuses equal or outweigh the pluses. It's not worth risking your money when the traditional and often more reliable media of newspapers and magazines are available.

The radio

There are more than three hundred independent radio stations in the United Kingdom, ranging from Plymouth Sound in England to Heartland FM in Scotland, Downtown Radio in Northern Ireland and Swansea Sound in Wales. As an advertising medium, commercial radio offers a unique blend of characteristics, advantages and disadvantages to its advertisers. You should be broadly familiar with these key features before going on to decide whether radio advertising is right for your firm and – if it is – to incorporate it within your advertising activities.

Characteristics of radio stations

Local radio stations are traditionally a mix of music, news, phone-ins, competitions, sports, traffic, travel, weather and other reports, all geared up to meet the requirements of their individual audiences, whether rural or urban. Devon Air in the South West has a different flavour to Capital FM in London. They both reflect their own particular communities, and do it well. Regional and national stations are distinct from local stations and usually concentrate on particular forms of music: Classic FM's classical music, Virgin's rock music and so on.

The burgeoning numbers and types of radio stations are transmitted on FM and AM wavebands, or 'VHF' and 'medium wave' as they were once more commonly known. The FM band extends in frequency from 87.7 MHz to 108.0 MHz. FM 87.5 to 94.6 MHz is used mainly by BBC regional and national radio; 94.6 to 96.1 MHz by BBC local radio and BBC Radio 4 in places; 96.1 to 97.6 MHz by independent local radio; 97.6 to 99.8 MHz by BBC Radio 4; 99.8 to 102.0 MHz by independent local and national radio;102.0 to 103.5 MHz by independent local radio; and 103.5 to 105.0 MHz by BBC local radio. The AM band spans 531 kHz to 1602 kHz, comprising BBC and independent local and regional transmissions with some BBC national services too.

Audience numbers for radio stations vary significantly. In terms of total population, a local station such as Classic Trax in Belfast can be heard by up to 540,000 people, whereas Kiss 100 FM in London covers 9,700,000, which is likely to be on a par with some regional radio stations. Independent national stations may be picked up by all (or almost all) of the UK population. Most reputable radio stations will provide (independently audited) figures of their estimated weekly audience, or 'reach'. As examples, Classic Trax 'reaches' 32,000 or 6 per cent of its target population and Kiss 100 FM 'reaches' 1,091,000 or 11 per cent.

The types of people who listen to commercial radio stations differ considerably too; the long-held belief that only 15- to 24-year-olds tune in is no longer sustainable and audiences are changing as rapidly as independent radio itself. Most quality radio stations supply independently verified figures breaking down their audience into various groupings, typically by sex, age (5 to 14 years, 15 to 24 years, 25 to 34 years, 35 to 54 years, 55 years plus) and social class (A: upper middle class, B: middle class, C1: lower middle class, C2: skilled working class, D: working class, E: those on lowest subsistence levels such as pensioners). As a general rule, commercial radio now appeals to a broader cross-section of the population. For example Southern FM on the Sussex coast plays classic hits, and its audience make-up or 'profile' is 50 per cent male, 50 per cent female, 23 per cent 15 to 24 years, 57 per cent 25 to 54 years and 20 per cent 55 years plus. 53 per cent are ABC1s and 47 per cent are C2DEs .

Listening habits follow similar patterns in many respects. The typical household – so far as one exists – has some three to four radios around the home, which are usually tuned in to just one or two favoured stations. The radio audience normally peaks at breakfast time with all types of people listening around the house and then falls steadily away throughout the day, as listeners go to work, do the shopping, see friends, or whatever. The stay-at-home audience of housewives, young children, students, the unemployed, pensioners and the like is boosted briefly at teatime as people return home from work before reducing again into the evening. Saturday and Sunday listening patterns, perhaps surprisingly, follow closely matching trends. On average, the radio listener tunes in for between seven and twelve hours per week.

So far as radio advertising is concerned, airtime is sold on a 'spot' basis, typically of 30 seconds' duration. The cost of each spot varies according to when it is transmitted, with the day divided into segments and priced in relation to the audience during that period. As an example, SGR FM in Suffolk charges £54 per 30-second spot between 6 a.m. and noon, £32 between noon and 6 p.m. and £14 between 6 p.m. and midnight. Shorter and longer spots are available, on request. 10- and 20-second spots on SGR FM are respectively 50 and 20 per cent less than the equivalent thirty-second spot. 40-, 50- and 60-second spots are 30, 65 and 80 per cent more than the relevant 30-second spot. Advertisements which are longer than 60 seconds are charged pro rata to the 60-second rate.

Normally, a package of advertisements is purchased, perhaps 28 over one week, 112 over four weeks, 196 over seven weeks, 364 over thirteen weeks and so forth. Obviously, the more airtime bought, the lower the average price per spot. Volume, advance booking, first-time and other assorted discounts – ranging between 5 and 25 per cent according to circumstances – are nearly always on offer to entice advertisers. Spots are usually distributed evenly throughout each week and day unless otherwise agreed. Early-week discounts of 20 to 30 per cent may be given for advertising only on Sundays, Mondays and Tuesdays, with end-of-week surcharges of the same amounts applying for Thursday, Friday and Saturday advertising. Limiting transmissions to a particular day might increase costs by 10 per cent, to a specific hour by 20 per cent, to a day *and* hour by 30 per cent and to a given break by 50 per cent.

Independent radio stations – small or large, in the country or in the city – provide in-house production facilities, whereby advertisements are scripted and produced by them for a set fee, subject to advertisers' suggestions and requests. For example, Orchard FM based in Taunton in Somerset charges £85 for a basic commercial, comprising one voice-over plus a piece of music or sound effect. Each additional voice – perhaps as heard in a so-called customers' conversation about the merits of a business or a product – costs £23.50. Extra music and/or sound effects are charged at £25 and £15 respectively, per piece or per effect. Whether a small business or a multinational, advertisers receive the same service.

Advantages of radio advertising

Radio is a varied and diverse advertising medium, offering considerable choice to its advertisers, who may advertise on a local, regional or national basis and alongside jazz, the classics or middle-of-the-road music. They can advertise at different times of the year, month, week, day or night, and as frequently or as infrequently as they wish. Advertisements may differ from one station to another, from morning to night or even from transmission to transmission – all of which helps advertisers to ensure that the right numbers and types of listeners receive the right messages at the right times and places.

Radio is also both immediate and responsive to advertisers' needs. It usually broadcasts live amid potentially changing circumstances with news being made and events unfolding on air. It therefore has a fresh and topical feel which may rub off on those businesses advertising on it. Similarly, radio stations can react quickly to their advertisers' requirements with advertisements written, cleared, recorded and transmitted in hours when necessary, allowing advertisers to respond to changes in the marketplace, keeping abreast of the competition and remaining up to date.

Commercial radio is still – and will probably stay for some time yet – a predominantly local medium, identifying with and moulding itself to the needs and wants of its specific audience, whether in the Welsh Valleys or the Scottish Highlands. It is often regarded as a companion by many listeners, and as being friendly and approachable. Again, those small firms which advertise via this medium – perhaps promoting themselves as on-the-spot businesses with similar qualities to those believed to be possessed by the radio station – may find that they are perceived in the same way by the audience.

Radio is also compact and portable, unlike other media such as television. It can be heard in the home, whether in the bedroom, bathroom, kitchen or lounge. It may be listened to in the car or on the train, when travelling to work. It can be carried out into the garden, to break up the monotony of mowing the lawn or the drudgery of weeding the flowerbeds. Whenever one chooses to advertise, wherever the listeners are and whatever they are doing when advertisements are transmitted, they can potentially be reached at all times and in all situations.

With 30 seconds of airtime purchased for as little as £10 to £15 and an advertisement created for under £100, radio is an inexpensive advertising medium to use, in terms of both airtime costs and production expenses. Thus, small firms can not only afford to advertise on it but are able to do so extensively and regularly. As important, it allows smaller concerns to compete on a relatively equal footing with their national rivals, without being priced out of the most popular spots and outclassed by glossy production techniques as happens in some other media, most notably television.

Disadvantages of radio advertising

As an advertising medium, radio has several, significant drawbacks that need to be considered carefully, and which could even dissuade small business advertisers from conducting a campaign over the airwaves. It is one-dimensional, wholly dependent upon sound for its success. Obviously, text, pictures, colours and so on – the key ingredients of most winning advertisements – do not exist in this medium, and advertisers must convey their messages through speech, music and sound effects. Clearly, this might not suit certain firms, goods, services. Even if it does, creating quality advertisements to be heard but not seen is a hard task.

Radio is also a transient medium, with advertisements going into one ear and out of the other within 10, 20, 30 seconds or so. It is difficult to put across any message, let alone a complex or detailed one, in such a short time. Lengthening the advertisement to perhaps 40, 50 or 60 seconds, or broadcasting it more frequently may bore or irritate listeners, as well as increasing costs. Even if the message does register, other advertisements, a news update, traffic and travel information or another classic hit is then transmitted, demanding the listener's attention and interest.

Of course, radio is often little more than a background noise anyway, to be half-heard when boring tasks are being carried out, whether writing an essay, doing household chores, driving to work or filling in forms at the office. It may be listened to now and then for a news headline or favourite song but rarely has the listener's total concentration on an ongoing basis. When it does – for a lively phone-in or a chart show – listeners do not really want to hear the advertisements, which are tolerated until the next caller comes on the line or song is played. It is not unusual for some listeners to station-hop during advertisements, trying to find more music.

An unavoidable disadvantage to be faced is that the number of listeners tuning in to a radio station is usually fairly low in relation to the population covered by its transmission area. Consequently, the right types of listeners and potential customers reached are that much lower too. This drawback is becoming more significant as more and more local, regional and national stations start broadcasting. The numbers of listeners and hours listened will not increase in the same proportions which means that advertisers will find themselves advertising to a shrinking audience per station.

Radio is also a hard-to-measure medium. It is difficult to know exactly who heard which advertisements and how they reacted to them. People responding to a newspaper advertisement may return a coupon or quote a reference number. Customers replying to a sales letter from a firm will mention the letter or return an easily identified reply-paid card. Visitors to an exhibition stand might fill out an enquiry form, or be logged by stand staff. Radio listeners will most likely just telephone through an order or walk in and buy a product without indicating that they listened to and acted upon an advertisement. Advertisers will have to work hard to find out if their radio advertising activities were effective.

Direct mail

Direct mail may be defined as personal messages sent to named customers and/or prospects, either at work or at home. To begin with, you ought to know about the basic characteristics of direct mail and be conscious of the main benefits and drawbacks of promoting your firm, products and services via this particular medium. Such an initial understanding should enable you to decide if it is worthwhile investigating the industry in more detail with a view to running advertising activities in this way.

Features of direct mail

Direct mail can be classified into two, broad categories: business-to-business and consumer mail. Business-to-business mail involves mailshots that are sent to fellow concerns. Consumer mail is delivered to members of the public at their homes. Whatever their type, all mailshots ought to be addressed to a specific person, whether the owner or purchasing manager of a firm, the head of the household or whoever. It is this personalization which distinguishes it from unnamed and unaddressed junk mail, and which contributes so much to its success.

A typical mailshot – so far as one exists – may consist of an envelope, a letter and a reply device to encourage the recipient to respond to the message. The envelope could vary from a plain manilla, with or without a window and a printed business symbol or phrase, to a highly individual and colourful one designed specially for this mailshot. The letter can vary from short and concise to long and explanatory, but will seek to attract attention, retain interest, instil desire and initiate action, whether to make an enquiry or place an order for a product or service. The reply device might be a pre-paid, addressed postcard or envelope, either first or second class.

Additional material may be inserted into the envelope alongside the sales letter and reply device to support and enhance the message, and to increase the prospects of the recipient responding in the desired manner. These inserts might incorporate product samples or sales literature such as brochures, leaflets and accompanying price lists and order forms. Money-off, discount vouchers and coupons and novelties such as bingo and scratch-and-sniff cards are increasingly popular additions too. All of these items could form part of the sender's current sales and promotional materials or might be designed and produced specifically for the mailshot.

Benefits of direct mailing

Direct mail is a highly versatile medium. It may be used to address businesses and/or individuals, at work and/or at home, in the north, south, east or west, hundreds, thousands or tens of thousands at a time. Using this medium, you can contact customers and prospects when you want to, timing mailshots to arrive on almost any day of the year. You are able to send out whatever you like, from the basic envelope, letter and reply-paid card to a package bursting with a plethora of additional material such as sales literature and gimmicks. You can be as creative as you wish, using plain or dazzlingly colourful envelopes, writing short or long letters full of sharp, pithy comments or long, wordy arguments. It is up to you.

The medium is extremely targetable. If you possess accurate contacts lists built up from your own resources or rented or purchased from other organizations, you can pinpoint and put across your message to a very precise audience identified by name, address, occupation, income, interests or however you wish to categorize them. Unlike some media such as newspapers, magazines and the radio, which reach large numbers of unknown scattered groups, you know exactly who you are reaching *and* that they are existing or would-be customers, potentially interested in what you have to say to them. Every single letter counts, and is seen by the right business executive or individual with relatively little waste.

Direct mail is very personal, with its one-to-one contact between the writer and the recipient. Your letters are, or certainly ought to be, personalized with the envelope, letter and accompanying material being addressed to Mr Reynolds, Mrs Platek or whoever. Not surprisingly, this helps to overcome many people's resistance towards advertising in general, and unaddressed junk mail in particular. It gains their attention immediately and puts them in a positive mood towards the person who has written personally to them. Assuming the contents are of interest, they will read on and hopefully react as they are expected to do. This personalized message is also hidden from competitors in the marketplace, unlike press and radio advertisements which anyone and everyone can see and hear.

As the name implies, this is also a very direct medium. It allows you to cut straight through wholesalers and retailers to deliver your message directly to the end buyers and users. You may choose to offer discounts to these existing and prospective customers which are less than you need to give to intermediaries to persuade them to stock your goods, thus saving you money. These discounts are likely to represent savings for customers too, who might consequently choose to buy direct from you in future rather than from a shop.

Direct mail is a relatively easy-to-measure medium. You know precisely who have been sent mailshots, when they would have received them and how many were delivered in total. You will also be able to tell exactly who and how many have or have not responded. Similarly, you will be in a position to work out when those respondents replied and how much they ordered in terms of the number and total value of goods. If you keep careful account of all of the costs involved with the mailings, you can then evaluate whether your activities were successful or unsuccessful in financial terms.

Direct mail is generally considered to be a cost-effective medium for advertisers. Envelopes, letters and reply material can be printed and posted at modest expense, perhaps for as little as 50 pence per mailshot depending on the size and nature of the total mailing. Other media may boast that they can reach 1,000 people or whatever at a lower price per person, but fail to mention that only a handful of these are likely to be existing or prospective customers. Thus it is misleading: calculate the cost of reaching an actual customer and/or prospect, and the figure will often be much higher than for this medium.

Drawbacks of direct mailing

Several disadvantages exist with regard to direct mail, and these ought to be recognized by every would-be mailer. It takes time to prepare for, test and run even the most modest mailing campaign. You need to know the industry well, and learn about the trade, regulatory and advertising bodies within it, and how they may help and can affect your activities. It is necessary to understand your business and market inside out, to ensure that the medium is suitable in your circumstances. You have to build up, rent or purchase lists of customers and prospects, keeping them up-to-date. Winning envelopes, letters and inserts need to be designed and created. Your campaign has to be tested, measured and amended, as appropriate. It all takes time, and you cannot cut corners. An incomplete list, untested mailings and inadequate monitoring of responses may mean your activities are less successful than they ought to be.

As a highly specialized medium, direct mail also needs to be tackled with skill and expertise to produce quality results. It is not always easy to obtain and maintain accurate mailing lists, free of the names of businesses that have closed down and people who have changed jobs or moved homes. It is hard to put together a mailshot, produce an eye-catching envelope, write a persuasive sales letter and decide what else should be tucked into the envelope as well. Testing various aspects of your mailing activities – one mailshot alongside another, one offer or the next and so on – is often a subjective rather than an objective matter, based as much upon experience as on immediate short-term results. The more versatile a medium is, the more opportunities exist for errors, due to a lack of know-how and expertise.

Of course, direct mail may simply be an unsuitable medium in your situation, with its particular features just not appropriate to your firm, goods, services and customers. Perhaps your small business does not have the in-house resources to build customer and prospect lists, and produce mailshots; and cannot afford to bring in specialists to work on your behalf. Possibly, you may feel that your bulky, complicated goods are best sold by demonstrating them face-to-face at an exhibition, allowing prospective customers to examine them and ask questions, receiving instant responses. Your products and services might be available to a mass consumer market, and it is extremely difficult to obtain the names and addresses of such a huge and diverse group of people.

Exhibitions

Several types of exhibition can be readily identified from the many thousands of events which are held in the United Kingdom and overseas each year. They may be grouped together loosely into three broad categories: consumer, trade and private shows. Initially, you should be aware of their basic characteristics as well as the possible advantages and disadvantages of exhibiting at them. Only then can you expect to press ahead to successfully plan, prepare for and attend those exhibitions which are most suited to your specific circumstances.

Types of exhibition

Consumer shows are usually associated with products and services of widespread appeal as at the Holidays and Leisure Exhibition and the Which

Computer?' Show. Anyone can attend – members of the public and tradespeople – so large numbers and diverse types of visitors are commonplace, the attendance of which is often audited at bigger, well-organized events. Admission may be free or, more likely, by ticket purchased in advance or on arrival. Such exhibitions can be held outdoors or indoors, from the grounds of a small hotel to the huge purpose-built exhibition centres in Birmingham, Glasgow and London.

Public shows may be local, with interest restricted to nearby residents; regional when people are drawn from up to 100 miles away; national with visitors coming from all areas of the country; or international when 20 per cent or more of exhibitors or visitors are from overseas. These events can be run by trade associations and/or professional exhibition organizers, such as Blenheim Events Limited and Nationwide Exhibitions Limited. Sometimes they are sponsored by another body as with the *Daily Mail*'s British Ski Show and Ideal Home Exhibition.

Trade exhibitions – often called business or technical events – are aimed typically at either everyone within a particular trade or industry or a specific group (or groups) across a range of different industries. The Hospitality Exhibition and the Softworld in Personnel and Human Resources Exhibition are examples of such shows. Admission is often by invitation only so that a quality rather than a quantity attendance is assured, and strict registration and entry procedures are enforced vigorously so that this is achieved.

As with public exhibitions, these events can be held inside or outside, and may be referred to as local, regional, national or international. They are normally set up and administered by the appropriate trade body, perhaps in association with an experienced, professional exhibition organizer. Many shows have close links with a trade newspaper or magazine. As an example, the British International Toy and Hobby Fair is well publicized in the trade journal *Toy Trader*.

Sadly overlooked or at best ill-considered, private shows may be arranged for either public and/or trade visitors, depending upon the individual situation. All may be welcome, or admission could be strictly limited to a carefully chosen number of people such as trade buyers within the locality or region. Held outdoors or indoors in a tent, a mobile showroom or a hotel suite, these exhibitions are self-organized, perhaps in collaboration with other, complementary firms. Sometimes they are run close to related, national or international events in order to attract visitors from them.

Advantages of exhibitions

There are many benefits from exhibiting at a show. Typically held on an annual or bi-annual basis, it is an exciting, looked-forward-to event: everyone is wondering what it will be like, who will be there, what will be different and new, what may happen and so on. Just by being there, you can help to establish, change or maintain your reputation and status in the field. In many instances, you almost have to be present to 'keep up with the Joneses'. Your absence could be viewed – correctly or incorrectly – as a bad sign, possibly even of impending business failure.

Depending on the size of your stand, you can display a fuller range of goods than your sales team can take out on the road. Larger items – everything from an office photocopier to a mocked-up, one-bedroom starter home – may be shown too. Your products can be displayed as you want them to be seen, under controlled conditions. They may also be demonstrated, touched, tested, examined and operated by visitors. Supporting material from pattern swatches to promotional literature is readily available to hand. You can create the perfect sales environment.

Usually, a relaxed and informal show atmosphere exists at an event. For visitors, going to an exhibition is seen as an enjoyable, social occasion, or at least as a working holiday. They want to be there, are in a positive mood and are potentially interested in you and your goods and services. They have time to concentrate on you and what you have to show and say, without having other work to do, meetings to attend or telephone calls to take or make. You have a captive and attentive audience.

An exhibition is a direct, face-to-face medium. You can meet past, present and prospective customers and talk, discuss products and services, ask and answer questions, negotiate, judge reactions and establish relationships with them. Leads may be generated, contact lists built up, orders taken and sales made. Staff other than sales representatives can greet customers to exchange views and get to know each other better. If it is a busy show visited by the right people, you may meet more customers in one day than in weeks on the road.

Attending an exhibition also gives you the opportunity to research your market. You can discover what manufacturers, wholesalers, retailers, trade and statutory bodies are doing and planning, keep up-to-date with rivals and customers and identify changes, developments and trends in your area. In addition, you may find out what your customers think of you and – as important – your competitors and their products and services. In many ways, a show enables you to learn all about your trade in a short space of time.

Not surprisingly, each particular type of exhibition has its own individual benefits to offer to exhibitors. Consumer shows can be extremely busy, with a wide cross section of visitors, which may be what you want from an event. Trade exhibitions generally tend to have a smaller, tighter attendance containing a higher percentage of potential customers, assuming you have picked an appropriate show. Private events provide the greatest flexibility with regard to location, approach and price. Your customers are not distracted by other stands, nor can your rivals see what you are doing, as long as you carefully control and monitor entry to the exhibition.

Disadvantages of exhibitions

Various drawbacks can be attributed to exhibiting at an event and these need to be contemplated before going any further. A show may be set up for the wrong reasons. It could be organized simply because the owners of a hotel, hall or whatever want to promote their property as a would-be exhibition venue. It might be arranged to fill a venue during a seasonal lull. A trade association could launch a show to compete with a well-established and popular rival event. If an exhibition is not put on for the right reason – because there is a genuine demand for buyers and sellers to meet – then it is likely to fail, with insufficient numbers of exhibitors, visitors and so forth.

As in every industry, there are large numbers of 'cowboys' operating in the field. Some venue owners have totally unsuitable properties for the shows that they stage, perhaps being too small and with a complicated layout. Various organizers appear, take bookings and payments for events that never run, disappear and then re-appear at a later date in a different guise to begin the fraudulent process again. Numerous contractors – employed to bring the exhibition and exhibitors' stands to fruition – are qualified only in their desire to make money quickly at everyone else's expense. These people steer clear of trade associations' codes of conduct and recommended conditions of contract, and prey on naïve exhibitors.

In many cases, exhibitions are a wholly irrelevant medium for exhibiting firms. These exhibitors attend because it has not been tried before, a substantial discount has been offered to them and so on, rather than because it fits into their overall strategy and will help them to achieve their business objectives. Even if exhibiting is appropriate, it is hard to do well. You will find it difficult to choose the best exhibitions, book a quality site, create and design a winning stand. You are also very dependent upon others for your success – the venue owner, the organizer, contractors and even other exhibitors who must attend in the right numbers and mix to attract the necessary visitors.

The costs of exhibiting at any show are high. It is expensive to rent space, build a stand, arrange services, transport exhibits, book staff accommodation, promote your business before and after the event, and so on. Attending an exhibition also takes up the time and energies of senior, sales and other staff prior to, during and following the show, which might be better spent on alternative projects. Your routine may be disrupted for a significant period as well. As an example, sales representatives' visits to customers could be postponed with the possibility that orders might be delayed or even lost.

Being on display hour after hour, day after day can be both a blessing and a curse. If your products begin to look tatty and staff start to lounge around then a negative impression will be conveyed and potential custom lost. Other stands can be an attraction too, with many exhibitors fighting to appeal to the same customers. Typically, visitors are also unwilling to place orders on site, preferring to see several stands and gather their thoughts together before making decisions. Unless you are ready to follow through with letters, phone calls and visits, business can simply drift away once the excitement of the moment has passed.

Each specific type of show has its own particular drawbacks for exhibiting firms. Sometimes, both consumer and trade exhibitions become too large, having so many exhibitors that visitors cannot see all of the stands in one day. If there are large numbers of visitors, it is likely that only a very small percentage of them will be interested in you. Also, more popular stands and surrounding gangways can become busy, rapidly destroying the relaxed atmosphere. Private shows may be especially difficult to set up as you invariably have to take charge of everything yourself and must stand or fall by your own experience and abilities. It may also be hard to attract visitors, unless a rival event is being staged nearby.

Summary

- The press is an all-embracing title that encompasses newspapers, magazines and miscellaneous publications such as directories, programmes and brochures.

- Various types of newspaper exist – national dailies and Sundays, regional dailies and Sundays, paid-for and free (bi-)weeklies amongst them. It is sensible to be aware of their approaches to news coverage, readership, circulation, pass-on readership, advertising costs, benefits and drawbacks for advertisers.

- Magazines can be grouped into consumer and business titles. It is wise to know about their subject matter, readerships, circulations, pass-on readerships, advertising rates, advantages and disadvantages for advertisers.

- Numerous, miscellaneous publications are often available for advertising purposes, including directories, yearbooks, programmes, brochures, in-house journals, timetables, maps and gradebooks. Potential advertisers should be conscious of their individual features, specific pluses and minuses for advertising purposes, and their possible role within an advertising campaign.

- Radio has certain, identifiable characteristics that would-be advertisers should know about. It also offers particular advantages and disadvantages to advertisers.

- Direct mail can be defined as 'personal messages sent to named customers and/or prospects, either at work or at home'. 'Business-to-business mail' is sent to business organizations; 'consumer mail' to homes. Prospective advertisers should be furnished with the various benefits and drawbacks of this medium.

- Exhibitions can be characterized as 'consumer shows', 'trade exhibitions' and 'private events'. It is wise to consider the pros and cons of exhibiting at these often very different types of exhibition.

Notes

Notes

2 Who's who in the media

MANY MEDIA ARE STRUCTURED along similar lines, with departments and employees performing comparable functions within each of them. They are represented by numerous trade bodies and liaise with various advertising organizations that monitor and regulate their activities. You ought to know who's who inside and outside of the press, radio stations, and the direct mail and exhibition industries, and be familiar with the other advertising organizations that exist. You'll then be better able to handle them properly, and to maximize the success of your advertising campaign.

Inside a publication

As a would-be advertiser within the press, it is useful for you to possess a brief understanding of the workings of:

- The Editorial Department
- The Advertisement Department
- The Marketing Department
- The Subscriptions Department
- The Production Department
- The Circulation Department.

The Editorial Department

This department is responsible for the contents of the publication – its precise mix of news, features, pictures and advertisements, its attitudes and approaches towards specific topics and so on. It is headed by an Editor-in-Chief who normally has overall responsibility for its success or failure, with assistance from news editors who seek up-to-date news, features editors who co-ordinate occasional and regular articles, and art editors who illustrate news stories and feature articles. Beneath them, staff and freelance journalists, illustrators and photographers write copy, produce illustrations and take photographs. Hopefully, they create an attractive and appealing publication to readers and prospective readers, thus boosting circulation and raising sales income, and increasing revenue as a higher circulation usually allows for more substantial advertising rates to be set.

The Advertisement Department

The purpose of this department, and the classified and display advertisement managers and representatives working within it, is to sell all of the advertising space for every issue of the publication, at the best possible prices. It works closely with the editorial department, and will have determined the amount, positions, sizes and rates of the spaces available. A difficult and sometimes tense relationship may exist between editorial and advertisement departments, with editorial staff usually preferring to have less advertising in the publication and advertisement employees requesting additional spaces in improved positions and wanting favourable editorial mentions for advertisers. In theory, if not always in practice, you should receive help from this department when drafting your press advertising schedule and designing advertisements. Do ask for advice.

The Marketing Department

Also known as the promotions or advertising department, this performs the key role of publicizing the newspaper, magazine or publication to advertisers and their advertising agencies who may buy space in it, wholesalers and retailers which could stock it and customers who might purchase, subscribe to or take it. The marketing (promotions or advertising) manager and his or her assistants may carry out various, related tasks of particular interest and relevance to you. They could accumulate research data, either from readily available sources, their own findings or specially commissioned surveys about their markets and customers, other media and current and anticipated trends, all of which may be made available to you. They might then promote their publication and services via press advertisements, direct mail shots, exhibitions, guided tours around the premises, and brochures and leaflets, which could enable you to find out if these are suitable titles for your purposes. Get information from here.

The Subscriptions Department

Many publications – most notably magazines and especially business titles – have a subscriptions department, although some may incorporate it within their marketing or another appropriately named department. Its role in handling readers' subscriptions falls – sometimes uneasily because it occasionally overlaps – midway between the duties of the marketing department which tries to attract buyers and readers and those of the circulation department which distributes copies of the publication. The people who subscribe to a title, probably on a yearly, renewable basis, are not only a regular source of up-front income but are a fount of accessible information too. The subscriptions manager and his or her staff can ask them about themselves and their likes and dislikes and so forth, and can pass these important details to you. Ask for data.

The Production Department

Some newspapers and magazines are conceived, designed and printed on the same premises, with editorial, advertisement and production staff all sharing a work environment. Others – including innumerable miscellaneous publications such as directories – are passed to an independent printer who runs off the required copies of the latest issue. Whether in-house or external production facilities are used, the aim is to produce the publication in the way in which it has been visualized and pieced together by the editorial and advertisement departments, making certain that text, photographs and illustrations are in the correct places and are legible, clear and free of errors.

The Circulation Department

The function of this department, which may be merged into the subscriptions department, is to co-ordinate the tasks of addressing, bundling up and transporting copies of each issue of the publication, whether these total a thousand or a million. The circulation manager and his or her team have to ensure that the appropriate number of copies are sent out, by post, vans, trains, boats or planes and arrive at the right wholesalers, retailers and/or individuals on time. In all probability you will have little or even no contact at all with the circulation (nor the editorial and production) departments although it is sensible to be broadly familiar with what they do: you may find it beneficial for when you negotiate and deal with the publications that you plan to use in an advertising campaign.

Press bodies

There are various trade organizations which represent newspapers, magazines and miscellaneous publications. It is helpful to know about the roles, and their relevance to you and your possible press advertising activities, of the following bodies. Refer to 'Useful contacts', page 385, for addresses and telephone numbers.

- The British Business Press
- The Directory Publishers Association
- The Newspaper Publishers Association
- The Newspaper Society
- The Periodical Publishers Association.

The British Business Press

The BPP – which operates within the Periodical Publishers Association – acts on behalf of the publishers of professional, trade and technical journals within the British Isles. Its over-riding objective is to promote the main features and benefits of advertising within this specialized medium to advertisers, advertising agencies and the business world. You will find it worthwhile to contact this organization which will answer any queries and give you assorted data about these particular publications.

The Directory Publishers Association

The DPA offers full membership to bona fide directory publishers in the United Kingdom, with associate membership available to their consultants and agents, directory printers, compilers and distributors, title owners and overseas directory publishers. The Association's aims include advancing its members' interests, raising the standards and status of directory publishing throughout the country, maintaining a code of professional conduct which members must follow, protecting the public against disreputable and fraudulent practices, and marketing directories as an ideal advertising medium. It is sensible to advertise only in those directories which are issued by publishers belonging to this organization, and are therefore trustworthy and reliable. On request, the DPA will provide a booklet containing its members' names, addresses and telephone numbers along with details of their various publications.

The Newspaper Publishers Association

Representing national newspaper publishers, the NPA seeks to forward their economic and social causes, co-ordinate their activities and supply advice and guidance to them as and where required: training and development, management and staff relations, marketing and advertising and so on. As a consequence, it may be wise to get in touch with this body if you have any questions concerning national dailies or Sundays – answers and supportive material ought to be made available to you.

The Newspaper Society

Acting for regional newspaper publishers, the NS tries to upkeep their reputations, increase co-operation between them on all matters of mutual interest, investigate and report on topics of key significance, and provide information and assistance on major areas of concern such as industrial relations, employment affairs, advertising controls and legislation, training and so forth. For the small business advertiser, the Society is a useful contact because it handles general advertising enquiries, has a database of regional newspaper titles and their circulations, and offers a central production service whereby a single piece of artwork can be converted into different sizes for various newspapers.

The Periodical Publishers Association

The PPA represents consumer and business magazine publishers – in liaison with the British Business Press – regardless of whether their publications are distributed across the counter, by post, subscription or controlled circulation. Its many goals incorporate helping and supporting members and their particular causes, encouraging high standards of media and market research, improving distribution networks, and achieving more advertising and sales for magazine titles. As with the BPP, it is sensible to approach the Association should you want to know more about these publications.

Inside a radio station

If you are thinking of advertising on the radio, you should know about the various departments and employees inside a radio station as well as the radio bodies and advertising organizations which you might come across during your activities. It is sensible to be conscious of their roles and what they can do for you as a would-be radio advertiser.

It is useful to start by learning something about those particular departments and employees with whom you are most likely to come into contact at some stage of your advertising campaign. Naturally, each and every radio station is different in terms of size and structure, but most will contain the following, in one guise or another:

- The Programming Department
- The Sales Department
- The Production Department
- The Marketing Department
- The Accounts Department.

The Progamming Department

Programming is responsible for interpreting and giving the listening audience what it wants to hear. It decides upon the mix of programmes that are transmitted, the presenters who front these programmes, the range of music played whether from the 1960s and 1970s or the latest chart sounds, and the overall blend of programmes, music, news and so on that actually goes on air. In practice, control may rest in the hands of the station owner – consequently known as the 'programme controller' – or a board of directors in larger concerns, perhaps representing each of the departments or functions involved within the station. In all probability, you will have little or nothing to do with these controllers, nor the presenters, journalists and secretaries working for them.

The Sales Department

The role of this department is to sell all of the advertising time available for each day, week and month, and for the best prices. The sales – or 'advertisement' – director, manager and executives usually work closely with programming to ensure that programmes, music and advertisements are well matched. For example, if programming is planning to broadcast a special, week-long feature on job hunting, executives would be despatched to attract suitable recruitment advertisers for that period. Similarly, a one-off programme on environmental issues might mean that firms with an interest in this subject would be approached for advertising. Usually, a sales or advertisement executive will act as a go-between, in your day-to-day dealings with the station.

Many radio stations are also represented by independently owned sales houses which sell advertising time on their behalf, on a fee or commission basis. These sales – or 'rep' – houses are based in London and other big cities where larger advertisers and their advertising agencies are located, so that negotiations can be conducted more easily. As examples, Independent Radio Sales, and Media Sales and Marketing are based in London and Manchester. You may liaise with a representative of a sales house if you are sited in or near to a big city and wish to advertise via a distant, provincial station. Addresses and telephone numbers of leading sales houses are given in 'Useful contacts', page 385.

The Production Department

A production team – of sound engineers, technicians and the like – is responsible for putting the programmes, presenters and music on air, to be heard by the listening audience. Although you will almost certainly not deal directly with production staff, they will play a significant role in your advertising activities. As a small-business owner or manager without expertise in this field, they will inevitably transfer the thoughts and ideas that you have for your advertisements onto tape for transmission. Voice-overs will be done by a nucleus of actors used regularly, with music and sound effects being added from the station's library, built up over the years.

The Marketing Department

Equally likely to be known as the promotions or advertising department – and incorporating market research and merchandizing functions – this has the key responsibility of publicizing the station in order to increase and expand its audience and advertisers, in terms of both numbers and types. The marketing manager and his or her team of assistants may do this in various ways. They will carry out market research into the station's transmission area and audience which will be made available to prospective advertisers. They may use direct mail shots and trade press advertisements to attract advertisers, and local and national press advertisements, sponsorship of events and the merchandizing of pens, pencils, cups and so on to increase awareness of the station amongst its potential audience. Various facts and figures will be given to you either through the station's rate card or via a sales executive, when you eventually meet one.

The Accounts Department

As with all organizations, a radio station has an accounts department to handle financial and associated administrative matters, issuing invoices, paying bills and so forth. Since most of your advertising activities will be dealt with by a sales executive acting for you, it is likely that you will not come across this department or its staff until later on in your campaign when invoices are issued. You would be advised to check these carefully, as mistakes can and often do arise at this stage.

Radio organizations

Various trade bodies exist which represent, monitor and/or regulate the different organizations working within the radio industry. You should be aware of these, what they do and how they can help you to become a more successful advertiser within this particular medium. See 'Useful contacts', page 385 for relevant addresses and telephone numbers:

- The Association of Independent Radio Companies Limited
- The Broadcasting Standards Council
- The Radio Advertising Bureau Limited
- The Radio Authority
- Radio Joint Audience Research.

The Association of Independent Radio Companies Limited

AIRC is the trade association of commercial radio stations in the United Kingdom, with a membership of all but a handful of the smaller stations. Widely recognized as one of the most active and effective bodies in the media world, it represents its members in dealings with the government and the regulatory organization known as the Radio Authority as well as maintaining close and constructive links with fellow trade and advertising associations, other broadcasting bodies such as the BBC and overseas radio stations. Of prime interest to advertisers, it manages research on behalf of Radio Joint Audience Research, provides a script clearance and advisory system for what can and cannot be included in radio advertisements, and is the central source of radio information in the country.

The Broadcasting Standards Council

The Council is an independent body acting on behalf of consumers in the United Kingdom. Its brief is to deal with the range of issues arising from the portrayal of sexual conduct and violence, and matters of taste and decency relating to television and radio programmes and advertisements. It monitors programmes and advertisements on an ongoing basis, conducts research into audience opinions and attitudes, provides a forum for consumer discussions through public meetings and correspondence, and considers complaints from consumers. It prefers to adopt an advisory role – of relevance to would-be advertisers – rather than a regulatory one, although it does possess certain statutory powers, such as compelling offending programmes to broadcast its findings.

The Radio Advertising Bureau Limited

The RAB is a small company supported financially by all of the independent radio stations in the United Kingdom, with a board of directors drawn from just six leading stations in order to shorten decision-making processes. Its aims are to mount studies into how radio advertising works, to correct widely held prejudices about the medium, to build up a database of radio advertising experiences to share with potential advertisers, and to promote radio as an advertising medium. Along with AIRC, this is probably your best source of advice and guidance on all aspects of your radio advertising activities, from start to finish.

The Radio Authority

This authority licenses and regulates the independent radio industry in the United Kingdom. Its over-riding aim is to help to develop a successful and diverse radio network throughout the country which offers a wide listening choice to the whole population. It plans frequencies, awards licences to radio stations, regulates programmes and advertising as necessary, and plays a key role in discussing and formulating policies which affect the independent radio world and its listeners. Of significance to prospective advertisers, it publishes the Code of Advertising Standards and Practice (and Programme Sponsorship) that sets the standards to which stations and advertisers must adhere at all times. See Appendix D: 'Code of Advertising Standards and Practice', page 331, for further details.

Radio Joint Audience Research

RAJAR is a limited company owned jointly by the BBC and AIRC with a management committee made up of representatives of other radio and advertising organizations that is responsible for supervising research into the listening habits of audiences tuning in to BBC and independent radio stations. A representative sample of households throughout the country completes weekly diaries showing its listening habits in quarter-hour periods. From these diaries, projections are made to show total numbers and types of audience per station and at different times, cumulative weekly audiences, total and average listening hours and so on, the key details of which are given in radio stations' promotional literature.

Direct mail participants

As a prospective direct mail user, you ought to have a basic knowledge of:

- List owners
- List brokers
- Direct mail advertisers
- Mailing houses
- The Royal Mail
- Direct mail recipients
- Fulfilment houses
- Miscellaneous suppliers.

List owners

Any organization or individual who holds and uses lists of customers and/or prospects can be called a list owner, from the biggest multinational company with its lists of worldwide customers to the sole trader with a list of people who have enquired about his or her services. These lists – of customers and prospects, hundreds or thousands of names long and classified by job title, interests, location, trade, industry and in a hundred and one different ways – may be rented out to direct mail advertisers on a one-off or regular basis or could be sold outright for an appropriate fee. Although you might use your own customer records as the basis for your mailing list on this occasion, you may have to approach list owners in some instances, such as when you are expanding into a new, unknown market.

List brokers

These are specialist firms or independent experts who act as intermediaries between list owners and direct mail users who wish to hire or buy mailing lists. Highly experienced in their field, they may deal with specific types of list, whether for a particular trade or industry, business-to-business mailings, consumer mailshots or for the United Kingdom or overseas markets. They usually have access to a wide range of lists and can help direct mailers to research, choose and evaluate the most suitable ones for their circumstances. Some also act as list compilers, collecting data from existing lists and other published material such as directories to piece together highly individualized lists for their clients. Should you need to rent or purchase mailing lists – perhaps for an unfamiliar marketplace – it may be sensible to approach a broker.

Direct mail advertisers

All types of firms use direct mail, both large and small and across all trades and industries. Mail order firms, insurance companies and banks are the leading senders of consumer mail with 18, 10 and 8.2 per cent of the total, respectively. Retailers, charities and manufacturers are next with 7.9, 7.2 and 6.5 per cent, followed by credit card companies, book clubs and gas/electricity boards on 4.6, 4 and 3.2 per cent. The remaining 30.4 per cent of mailshots is spread out between miscellaneous businesses and sectors. It is important that you are aware that direct mail is not just for big companies: it can be used with equal success by sole proprietors and partnerships doing all of the work themselves and mailing only a hundred or so mailshots to their existing customer base.

Mailing houses

These houses, or 'lettershops' as they are also referred to, are firms which concentrate on receiving mailshot items from direct mailers, packaging them into complete mailings and delivering them to the Royal Mail for distribution to the appropriate businesses and/or members of the public. They take care of much of the laborious, nitty-gritty work for direct mail advertisers, obtaining envelopes for them, folding letters and packing inserts into the envelopes in the correct manner and order and physically handing over a sackful of mailshots to the post office. As a first-time mailer probably undertaking a limited, initial campaign, you may not wish to use a lettershop this time, but might find it economical to employ one later on as your activities become more ambitious.

The Royal Mail

In most circumstances the Royal Mail will deliver your mailshots. It offers a wide range of postal services to direct mail users which can save time and money. For outgoing mail, you can simply affix stamps to envelopes, and will invariably do this for small quantities. For larger volumes, more economical alternatives are available. You can buy or lease a franking machine from an authorized company and postmark any number of letters up to a pre-paid, agreed total. A selection of pre-paid envelopes for standard first- and second-class mail can also be purchased.

For bigger direct mail advertisers, postage paid symbols may be used instead of stamping or franking letters or packets. You order envelopes that are pre-printed with a 'postage paid' symbol along with your corporate logo and any message. These are available in most sizes, but a minimum order of 25,000 is required. You pay a printer for printing the envelopes and pay the Royal Mail for the postage – at the same rate as ordinary stamped mail – when you draw envelopes from the stocks held on your behalf (and without charge) by the Royal Mail.

'Mailsort' is a range of services for large volume mailings of at least 4,000 letters (or 1,000 packets) at any one time. You have to sort your items into post-coded districts before passing them over in relevant bundles to the Royal Mail. Discounts of between 13 and 32 per cent are given according to the numbers sent, how you have sorted the mailings and whether you require delivery in one, three or seven working days. In exceptional circumstances, a minimum of 2,000 letters may be accepted if they are all to be delivered within one postcode area *and* are all posted within that same postcode area.

Direct mail recipients

Clearly, these may comprise firms and/or members of the public, with mailshots being sent to managers at their workplaces or the public in their homes. You can contact sole traders, partnerships, private or public limited companies and multinationals, husbands, wives, sons and daughters, or whoever you wish. Your key concern now and throughout any campaign is that the names and details on your mailing lists match your target audience as precisely as possible. For example, there is little point in sending information about baby products to a middle-aged, single man when your audience is made up of young, married women in their 20s and 30s.

Fulfilment houses

These businesses deal with the responses to mailing activities, storing products, collecting and recording enquiries and orders, processing payments, despatching goods and so forth on behalf of direct mail advertisers. This allows the direct mailer to continue with normal tasks and duties. Often, fulfilment houses and mailing houses are one and the same, saving the direct mail user both time and money. As you are possibly planning a relatively small and self-contained campaign on this first occasion, you may feel able to handle responses yourself, to stay in touch as a hands-on operator.

Miscellaneous suppliers

There is always a host of other, miscellaneous suppliers which provide various products and services to direct mail advertisers. Advertising agencies may supply advice on planning advertising activities, the creation and design of envelopes, letters and additional materials, and running a campaign. More likely, you will probably turn to local stationers and printers – the most common source of guidance and technical information for small direct mailers – who can be surprisingly helpful when selecting envelopes, letters and inserts.

Direct mail bodies

Influential trade organizations exist in the direct mail industry. You ought to know about the following, what they do and how they can help you to become a first-rate, direct mail user. Addresses and telephone numbers are given in 'Useful contacts', page 385.

- The Direct Mail Accreditation and Recognition Centre
- The Direct Mail Information Service
- The Direct Marketing Association (UK) Limited
- The Institute of Direct Marketing
- The Advertising Standards Authority Limited
- The Committee of Advertising Practice
- The Data Protection Registrar
- The Mailing Preference Service.

The Direct Mail Accreditation and Recognition Centre

DMARC is an unincorporated association serviced administratively by the Direct Marketing Association and funded by the Royal Mail. It aims to encourage the highest possible standards of direct mail practice and conduct and works closely with other bodies in and around the industry to achieve and sustain these standards. Of particular interest to you, it administers and operates a recognition scheme for those companies such as list brokers and mailing houses that provide services for direct mailers. To be accredited, organizations must be financially stable, committed to high business ethics, willing to uphold the industry's various codes of practice and deal fairly, honestly and competently with clients.

The Direct Mail Information Service

Financed by the Royal Mail, this information service channels through facts and figures about direct mail to other media, the advertising industry and the public at large. Its research generates a wealth of statistics on such topics as expenditure on direct mail and other advertising media, expenditure on direct mail production and postage, the volume of business-to-business and consumer direct mail, the senders of direct mail and the treatment of direct mail by its recipients. Consider getting in touch with the DMIS if you wish to receive broad, background details about the industry, although you will probably find that the statistical information provided is of interest to you rather than of essential help.

The Direct Marketing Association (UK) Limited

The DMA is the trade body that represents everyone involved with the direct marketing industry, including direct mail advertisers, list brokers, mailing houses and service suppliers. It seeks to raise standards of practice through education, training and self-regulation, to tackle legislative threats and opportunities and to communicate the nature, breadth and positive image of direct marketing to the outside world. Hence, it offers the DMA Diploma in Direct Marketing and various other courses through the educational establishment known as the Institute of Direct Marketing. It lobbies policymakers and legislators in the United Kingdom and overseas and liaises with the Government, media owners and relevant institutions as necessary.

Membership of the Association is open to businesses but not to individuals. To join, organizations must agree to adhere to the DMA Code of Practice, whereby they have to promise to abide by the industry's two self-regulatory Codes of Practice; see Appendix C: 'The British Code of Advertising Practice', page 317, and Appendix E: 'The British Code of Sales Promotion Practice', page 363. They must also accept the rulings of the Association and the regulatory body that administers the Codes, the Advertising Standards Authority Limited. Furthermore, they have to observe any other codes of practice that are relevant to their own trade or industry, act in accordance with the law at all times, maintain the highest ethical standards in dealings, and handle any queries and complaints in a prompt and courteous manner.

As a would-be direct mailer, it is wise to trade only with those concerns which belong to the DMA so that you can be sure of their integrity throughout your transactions with them. You may even wish to put your own firm forward for membership of this leading body. In addition to the acquired status and credibility, you will become eligible to receive advice and guidance on direct mail subjects, a monthly newsletter with issue briefs on current legislative matters, an annual membership directory listing all members by category, as well as access to research findings, statistics, conciliatory and arbitration services plus discounts on training courses, seminars and conferences.

The Institute of Direct Marketing

Established in London, this is a library and archive source of direct marketing information, a facility for research and consultancy and an educational and training centre providing courses in direct marketing and related topics. Of its many courses, the best known and most important is the IDM Diploma in Direct Marketing – the officially recognized qualification for direct marketers in the country. Run over 30 weeks, two evenings per week, this mix of theory and practice provides a comprehensive grounding for all serious direct mail users, and covers such major subjects as marketing systems and strategy, media communications and planning, and industry application. Research projects and a residential course are also integral features of the IDM Diploma.

The Advertising Standards Authority Limited

The ASA is an independent organization funded by a levy on advertising in the United Kingdom. Its main role is to oversee the two codes of practice which provide the self-regulatory framework for the advertising industry in general: the British Code of Advertising Practice and the British Code of Sales Promotion Practice, or BCAP and BCSPP for short. Direct mailers ought to know these inside out, as they suggest guidelines for high quality, direct mail standards and procedures. See Appendix C: 'The British Code of Advertising Practice', page 317 and Appendix E: 'The British Code of Sales Promotion Practice', page 363 for further details.

In brief, the British Code of Advertising Practice states that all advertisements, including leaflets and brochures mailed or delivered directly, must be legal, decent, honest and truthful. In addition, they should be prepared with a sense of responsibility to the consumer and to society. They also ought to conform to the principles of fair competition as generally accepted in business. Specific rules apply to particular categories of advertisement – alcoholic drinks, children, motoring, environmental claims, health and beauty products, slimming, employment and business opportunities and financial services and products. You must be aware of these too if they are of relevance to your particular business, products and services.

There are also specific rules relating to distance selling and database practice, and these are reproduced at the end of Appendix C: 'The British Code of Advertising Practice'. Required reading for each and every direct mail advertiser, these rules cover the do's and don'ts of advertisements and list and database practice, and incorporate detailed guidelines on such topics as the conformity of goods to relevant standards, goods sent on approval, obtaining personal data and list maintenance.

The British Code of Sales Promotion Practice – of equal if not of more significance to many direct mailers – covers marketing techniques such as reduced price and free offers, sampling and price promotions of all types. Like its sister code, it states that promotions should be legal, decent, honest and truthful and must adhere to the principles of fair competition as generally accepted in business. Various general guidelines, concerning topics such as the protection of privacy to ensuring the availability of promotional products, apply to all forms of sales promotion and are of key concern in particular cases such as free offers, promotions with prizes and charity-linked promotions.

The ASA seeks to make certain that these two all-important Codes are maintained at all times by continually monitoring the advertising industry, making some 150,000 random spot checks each year and handling complaints raised by members of the public. Those firms which breach the Codes' guidelines are asked to amend or withdraw the offending material, as appropriate. If they do not, they may receive negative publicity in the Authority's widely read monthly report, could find that the media refuse to handle this and subsequent material and might even jeopardize membership of professional organizations such as the Direct Marketing Association (UK) Limited.

The Committee of Advertising Practice

The CAP is made up of representatives of trade and other organizations acting on behalf of advertisers, agencies and media within the advertising industry. Part of the Advertising Standards Authority Limited, this committee is responsible for drawing up the British Code of Advertising Practice, the British Code of Sales Promotion Practice and the various specific rules including List and Database Practice. Its other functions include co-ordinating its members' activities to achieve compliance with the Codes, continually reviewing and amending the Codes, investigating complaints made by commercially interested parties and providing a free and confidential pre-publication advisory service, as relevant to direct mailers as it is to advertisers in other media.

The Data Protection Registrar

The Registrar is an independent officer who exists as a direct consequence of the Data Protection Act of 1984 which was passed to protect individuals against the misuse of personal information that is held about them on computer systems. His role incorporates publicizing the Act and its workings, building up a public register of data users and ensuring compliance with the Act at all times. With a very few exceptions, those businesses and/or people who control the contents and use of a collection of personal data – which includes direct mailing lists – have to register with the Office of the Data Protection Registrar and comply with the terms and conditions of the Act.

In essence, this involves abiding by certain key principles. Personal data must be obtained and processed fairly and lawfully and should be held and used only for the lawful purposes described in the register entry. Furthermore, it ought to be disclosed only to those people described in the register entry. All data has to be adequate, relevant and not excessive in relation to the purposes for which it is held, and needs to be accurate and kept up-to-date. Also, it should be held for no longer than is necessary for the required purposes and has to be surrounded by proper security during that time. Individuals must be allowed access to data about themselves and to have this corrected or deleted, as and when appropriate.

Those data users who are obliged to register but who choose not to are committing a criminal offence and may be prosecuted and fined. The Registrar has successfully prosecuted offenders on numerous occasions amid substantial adverse publicity for the firms concerned. Similarly, registered users who fail to adhere to the principles of the Act may be served with an enforcement notice requiring actions to be taken to achieve compliance, could receive a deregistration notice cancelling all or part of their register entry or might be sent a transfer prohibition notice preventing personal data held from being transferred. Failure to comply with the terms of these notices is a criminal offence. Again, the Registrar does act to bring offenders into line. As a direct mailer, you must be aware of this Act and be prepared to register and follow its principles, as relevant. See Appendix F: 'The Data Protection Act 1984', page 371.

The Mailing Preference Service

The MPS is a non-profit-making, regulatory body financed by a levy attached to volume mailings handled by the Royal Mail. It works for the direct mail industry, with its members ranging from list owners and brokers through computer bureaux and mailing houses to advertising agencies. Its aims are to foster quality relations between direct mail users and the public and to promote high ethical standards throughout the industry. It does this by giving consumers (but *not* businesses) the opportunity to have their names added to or deleted from mailing lists, thus increasing or decreasing the amount of direct mail received by them. Members of the public register their wishes with the MPS which puts the information into its computer; this information is then distributed to its licenced direct mailers each quarter for appropriate action to be taken. You should register with the Service to increase your credibility as a direct mail advertiser and to maintain more up-to-date lists.

At an exhibition

As a potential exhibitor, it is sensible to possess some background knowledge of:

- venue owners
- exhibition organizers
- designers
- contractors
- exhibitors
- visitors.

Venue owners

The individuals or company which owns the purpose-built centre, hall or showground will usually deal exclusively with the organizer of the show and will not come into contact with anyone exhibiting there at all. Clearly, they will have firm ideas about how the venue is and is not to be used though, and these will tend to be incorporated into the organizer's rules and regulations which exhibitors must adhere to in every way. Some venue owners belong to the trade body known as the British Exhibition Venues Association, page 41.

Exhibition organizers

Many events are organized and run by the leading trade organization within a particular industry, such as the Building Societies Association and the Camping and Outdoor Leisure Association. They are well established, trustworthy and reliable and often have years of experience in the field. If you are a member of the association, you may obtain useful, hands-on advice and guidance as well as discounts on and first choice of the stands available at the venue.

Other events are administered by professional, exhibition management specialists. Larger, reputable ones are members of the trade body called the Association of Exhibition Organizers (see page 40). Smaller, less reputable ones tend to come and go, even conning money from would-be exhibitors with contracts for events which are never staged. All exhibition organizers need to be investigated carefully before money is handed over.

Designers

Professional designers – either freelance or employees of design groups – are commissioned by inexperienced but sensible exhibitors to design stands, advise on exhibits and display materials, and supervise their construction and installation at and removal from the exhibition floor. Care needs to be taken when choosing a designer and entering into a contractual obligation. Many first-rate designers belong to the Chartered Society of Designers. Refer to 'Useful contacts', page 385.

Contractors

Contractors – often nominated by the organizer or chosen individually by each exhibitor according to circumstances – are responsible for building stands under the supervision of the designers. They may also be responsible for other, associated services such as signwriting, painting and cleaning. Care has to be taken when selecting a contractor and signing a legally binding agreement. Some contractors are members of the trade body known as the British Exhibition Contractors Association. See 'Useful contacts', page 385.

Exhibitors

Not surprisingly, the majority of exhibitors will be in your industry, and many of them will be known to you; some may even be your direct rivals. Whether large or small, experienced or inexperienced, you will want to be sure that a good number and mix of exhibitors are present to draw in the right quantity *and* quality of visitors. You may also find that some exhibitors will be very open and helpful to you if approached, giving you useful information about their experiences. A small but growing number of exhibitors belong to the trade bodies called the Agricultural Show Exhibitors Association and National Exhibitors Association. Refer to 'Useful contacts', page 385.

Visitors

The people coming to the show will hopefully include a significant proportion of your existing and potential customers; there is little point in exhibiting if they will not be there. The media will also be present, looking to report on the event, new products and services and any happenings of interest to their readers and listeners. You may want to tell them about yourself and your news.

Exhibition organizations

There are numerous trade bodies which represent those organizations and people that are involved with exhibitions. You should be familiar with the following and the ways in which they can help you to become a successful exhibitor. Refer to 'Useful contacts', page 385, for addresses and telephone numbers.

- Agricultural Show Exhibitors Association
- Association of Exhibition Organizers
- British Exhibition Contractors Association

- British Exhibition Venues Association
- Exhibition Venues Association
- National Exhibitors Association
- Audit Bureau of Circulations Limited
- Exhibition Audience Audits
- Exhibition Surveys Limited
- Incorporated Society of British Advertisers Limited.

Agricultural Show Exhibitors Association

ASEA exists to serve the interests of its members at agricultural events, whether they are sole traders or multinational companies exhibiting in a shed or at a large pavilion. It is committed to maintaining the agricultural nature and content of shows as it believes that this type of event provides the best trade opportunity or public relations advantage for exhibitors. ASEA is constantly in contact with exhibition organizers, is represented on the committees of most major shows at county and national level, has representatives attending these events to aid members, and can offer advice and guidance based on a wide pool of knowledge and experience of agricultural shows.

Association of Exhibition Organisers

AEO has several key objectives. It seeks to protect the interests of exhibition organizers in the United Kingdom by influencing venue owners on prices and developments and through liaising with the Government and European Union bodies on show issues. Also, it wants to increase awareness of exhibitions, promoting their value through research, publicity and training. The AEO wishes to raise exhibition management standards in the United Kingdom by ensuring that its members adhere to its code of practice.

The Association deals with enquiries about exhibitions, holds seminars and conducts training in show matters, all of which can be of considerable benefit to the would-be exhibitor. Its members also have to follow its code of practice and in most instances have to audit the attendance figures of the exhibitions to provide evidence of their professionalism and honesty. Clearly, these are reassuring signs for any firm thinking of exhibiting at an AEO member's event.

British Exhibition Contractors Association

BECA acts on behalf of contractors and suppliers who build and equip exhibition stands in the United Kingdom and overseas. Its main role is to protect its members' interests and to upkeep good standards of business practice, workmanship and service in the industry. As with most representative bodies, it will provide a list of its members on request, divided into operating areas such as signwriting, standfitting and so on. Also of interest to potential exhibitors,

BECA members have to follow a code of practice and should issue contracts which match the Association's recommended conditions of contract.

British Exhibition Venues Association

BEVA is a trade body that represents venue owners and tries to protect and enhance their image whilst furthering their interests within the exhibition industry. The Association offers free information and advice on its members and their facilities and services to those requiring suitable venues for exhibitions, and to would-be exhibitors as well.

Exhibition Venues Association

EIF was created by venue owners, show organizers and contractors to improve communication within and increase business for the exhibition industry in the United Kingdom. Membership is restricted to trade bodies rather than companies or individuals. Of particular interest to the potential exhibitor, the Association commissions research and publishes an annual report on exhibition statistics, covering volume, expenditure and effectiveness. In co-operation with the Department of Trade and Industry, it publishes an annual calendar of major United Kingdom trade fairs. Also, it organizes and promotes seminars and conferences on exhibition practice.

National Exhibitors Association

NEA is run by exhibitors *for* exhibitors and has one overriding aim which is to increase the profitability of its members' exhibitions. It fights and campaigns for exhibitors on all fronts. For its members, it offers a helpline for impartial advice and guidance plus a low-cost, in-house consultancy service. Members are also entitled to substantial discounts on training courses dealing with subjects such as marketing strategies and stand design. Copies of a monthly newsletter *Exhibition File* are supplied free of charge.

Audit Bureau of Circulations Limited

ABC is an independent, non-profit making company whose members include publishers, advertisers and advertising agencies. Its main role is to audit and certify the circulations of publications, such as newspapers and magazines. However, it also has an Exhibition Data Division which administers the auditing of exhibition attendance data in terms of quantity and quality. The auditing system produces what is known as a 'Certificate of Attendance' (COA) for the exhibition.

To achieve an ABC audit, members have to retain auditable records proving the attendance and demographic make-up of exhibition visitors. Audits are conducted to ABC rules and procedures by ABC's staff auditors or by chartered/certified audit firms, approved by ABC. The stringency of the audit is based on a full count of attendance and associated demographic data, and various checks being carried out to establish their accuracy such as reconciling registration cards with registered attendance and contacting a sample of claimed visitors to confirm they attended the event.

The results of each ABC exhibition audit are published as a 'Certificate of Attendance' (COA) which provides verification of the attendance at that exhibition and visitors' demographic details – in particular, their geographical locations, job titles and areas of company activity. The certificate also identifies the organizer, the sponsor (if appropriate), the date and venue of the show, the number of stands and space occupied, the date and venue of the next event, association membership (if applicable), target audience and products and services exhibited. An example of a Certificate of Attendance is shown on pages 44 to 57. Potential exhibitors ought to be wary of exhibiting at events which do not supply them with independently audited and verified figures.

Exhibition Audience Audits

EAA is an independent research consultancy specializing in the control of market research on behalf of exhibition organizers and exhibitors. In particular, it authenticates the total number of visitors to shows and produces audited attendance figures to standards approved by the Exhibition Industry Federation. Visitor research undertaken covers such areas as a detailed audience profile, audience interests, the overlap with competing shows and trends in the industry served by the exhibition. Research is also undertaken in exhibition development and management and the value of any special features and services.

Exhibition Surveys Limited

This company specializes in industrial market research and aims to provide businesses with low-risk decision-making and marketing solutions. It is totally independent and has no connection with exhibition organizers, trade associations, publishers or exhibitors other than on a consultant/client basis. Working for small firms or multinational companies, it evaluates events for both organizers and exhibitors and supplies pre- and post-show information and advice on exhibition potential, audience quality, stand performance and so forth, customized to the individual client's requirements.

Incorporated Society of British Advertisers Limited

ISBA represents national and international advertisers and seeks to promote quality advertising in all its many forms and at all times. It tries to help the exhibition industry to maintain and better its standards for the benefit of everyone involved. For example, it took the lead in improving the availability of reliable exhibition data by initiating the Certificate of Attendance administered by ABC. It also conducts an annual Exhibition Expenditure Survey based on a postal survey sent to exhibiting members and a selection of other exhibitors plus data collected from industry-wide sources. It attempts to assist would-be exhibitors to exhibit successfully by offering information and advice on request.

Other advertising organizations

Various organizations in the advertising industry are relevant to all media: the press, radio, direct mail and exhibitions among them. Some of the following have been referred to already, but it is wise to look at them again now in their wider, advertising context. See 'Useful contacts', page 385, for addresses and telephone numbers:

- The Advertising Association
- The Advertising Standards Authority Limited
- The Association of Media Independents Limited
- The Audit Bureau of Circulations Limited
- The Committee of Advertising Practice
- The Incorporated Society of British Advertisers Limited
- The Institute of Practitioners in Advertising
- The Joint Industry Committee for National Readership Surveys
- Media Audits Limited
- Verified Free Distribution Limited.

The Advertising Association

With its membership made up of many different organizations such as the Incorporated Society of British Advertisers Limited, the Newspaper Publishers Association and the Institute of Practitioners in Advertising, the AA acts on behalf of advertisers, media, agencies and other companies which provide associated advertising services. The Association's main purpose is to champion advertising: to maximize standards at all times, to safeguard its interests, to inform and educate everyone about its role in society and the economy, and to promote universal confidence in it. Of particular relevance to you, the AA can supply information on all aspects of advertising, putting you in contact with specialists when necessary. It also publishes various publications, some of which may be of significance to small-business advertisers.

The Advertising Standards Authority Limited

The ASA is an independent company which oversees the British Code of Advertising Practice – the industry's self-regulatory control system that covers

Exhibition News

CERTIFICATE OF ATTENDANCE

Exhibition News '96

ORGANISER	ATTENDANCE	
Audit Bureau of Circulations	Registered Free	6804
Black Prince Yard	Registered Paid	691
207-209 High Street	*Prior Year Registrations	432
Berkhamsted, Herts HP4 1AD	Total Attendance	7927

		%	
Tel No: 01442 870800	*Prior Year Age Of Registration		
Fax No: 01442 877998	Under 1 year	92	396
email: abcpost@abc.org.uk	1-2 years	8	36
Net: http://www.abc.org.uk	2-3 years	0	0
	Total Prior Year Attendance	100	432

SPONSOR	STAND SPACE OCCUPIED: sq m 1843
ISBA	NUMBER OF STANDS: 194

ORGANISERS ASSOCIATION MEMBERSHIP	DATE OF EVENT: 6-8 March 1996
Association of Exhibition Organisers	VENUE: Royal Horticultural Halls

YEAR SHOW ESTABLISHED: 1976	DATE OF NEXT EVENT: 4-6 March 1997
FREQUENCY: Annual	NEXT VENUE: Royal Horticultural Halls

MAIN PRODUCT GROUPS/SERVICES EXHIBITED

Organisers, exhibitors, contractors and caterers involved in the exhibition industry. Also trade media, training, marketing, research and allied services.

TARGET AUDIENCE

Managing Directors, Directors, Managers, Purchasers, Sales Executives, Advertising Agency and Media Personnel.

Page 1 of 4

AUDITED ANALYSIS OF REGISTERED ATTENDANCE

Visitor Analysis by Geographical Area

DESCRIPTION	%	TOTAL
Northern	15.0	1189
Yorkshire & Humberside	7.5	592
North West	22.5	1784
East Midlands	5.1	402
Midlands	6.7	534
East Anglia	11.9	943
London	1.3	104
South East	0.5	38
South West	1.2	97
Wales	3.5	277
Scotland	0.3	24
Northern Ireland	0.5	38
TOTAL UK	76.0	6022
OVERSEAS		
Europe - EU	8.9	704
Europe - Non EU	1.1	89
North America	7.5	592
Central & South America	0.0	2
Australasia & The Pacific	2.3	184
Asia	1.2	94
South East Asia & Pacific Rim	1.0	84
Africa	1.6	127
Middle East & North Africa	0.4	29
TOTAL OVERSEAS	24.0	1905
TOTAL REGISTERED ATTENDANCE	100.0	7927

AUDITED ANALYSIS OF REGISTERED ATTENDANCE

Visitor Analysis by Job Function

DESCRIPTION	%	TOTAL
Chairman/Chief Executive	4.8	383
Managing Director	14.4	1143
Sales/Marketing Director	8.6	682
Director	11.9	943
Financial Director	5.8	456
Exhibition Manager	10.2	809
Other Manager	19.0	1506
Sales Executive	7.2	572
Consultant	7.6	601
Agency Personnel	2.2	169
Student	1.1	87
Other	4.7	374
Unspecified	2.5	202
	100.0	7927

Visitor Analysis by Company Activity

DESCRIPTION	%	TOTAL
Exhibition Organiser	37.9	3004
Stand Design	37.0	2930
Contractor	22.5	1784
Caterer	4.1	327
Sales/Marketing Agency	6.0	479
Consultant	9.3	740
Other	4.3	342
Unspecified	1.3	104
		9710

Note: Analysis allows for multiple responses by the attendee

AUDITED ANALYSIS OF REGISTERED ATTENDANCE

Visitor Analysis by Company Size

NUMBER OF EMPLOYEES	%	TOTAL
Under 10	12.4	984
11 - 20	24.6	1948
21 - 50	31.1	2462
51 - 100	15.8	1248
101 - 250	2.9	231
251 - 500	2.8	222
501 - 1000	2.1	169
1001 +	5.0	400
Unspecified	3.3	263
	100.0	7927

EXAMPLE

ABC Reference Number: 001

All data published in this Certificate of Attendance has been audited to the standards laid down
by the ABC Exhibition Industry Working Party and is authorised for issue by the Exhibition
Division of the Audit Bureau of Circulations Ltd (by Guarantee).
No figures may be published without the permission of the copyright holders.
Although every care is taken to ensure that the information published is correct
the Audit Bureau of Circulations cannot accept responsibility for mistakes or omissions.

Published by ABC, Black Prince Yard,
207-209 High Street, Berkhamsted,
Herts, HP4 1AD
Phone (01442) 870800 Fax (01442) 877998
email: abcpost@abc.org.uk Net: http://www.abc.org.uk

ABC
AUDIT BUREAU OF CIRCULATIONS
EXHIBITIONS

Authorised for issue by the ABC   **1st March 1996**

Page 4 of 4

1. INTRODUCTION

1.1   The purpose of the ABC Exhibition audit is to give prospective exhibitors, advertisers, sponsors and other interested parties an independent and comparable guide of the past performance of an exhibition to enable them to gauge its likely future performance.

1.2   The Audit Bureau of Circulations (ABC) was founded in 1931 as a non profit making organisation by advertisers who wanted an independent standard for the validation of circulation and attendance data. ABC now provides, to the highest standards in the world, accurate, objective and comparable figures on over 3,000 member titles and exhibitions.

1.3   ABC is managed by a full-time staff governed by a general council of members representing advertisers, agencies, organisers and publishers. Working Parties and ABC staff representing each category of membership, continually monitor the rules and procedures appropriate to each category to ensure that they reflect the needs of members and the industry at large.

1.4   The audits are conducted to ABC rules and procedures by ABC's own staff who are responsible for certifying audit returns, visiting organisers and their registration bureaux to check the audit rules and procedures are fully adhered to.

1.5   ABC has been certifying trade exhibition attendance since 1976. In 1993 the two previous audit schemes were consolidated into the Certificate of Attendance (COA). The COA has quickly become the industry standard for the provision of quantitative and qualitative trade exhibition attendance data.

1.6   The Exhibition Organiser is responsible for producing the attendance data, maintaining proper records and completing the ABC Certificate of Attendance return and has a duty of care to the Bureau.

1.7   ABC must have full and free access to all relevant financial and other records connected with the audit of the exhibition, as far as may be necessary to conduct the audit in accordance with notes and instructions herein.

2. REGISTRATION

2.1   Registration for a Consumer Event Certificate of Attendance (hereafter referred to as the COA) must take place before the start of the exhibition and should, ideally, take place 6 months in advance of the exhibition.

2.2   Registration of the exhibition must be approved by the Bureau in writing.

2.3   The exhibitor pack detailing stand space costs should be submitted with the registration form or as soon as it is available.

2.4   The exhibition catalogue should be sent with the registration form or as soon as it is available.

2.5   The complimentary ticket (if applicable) should be approved by the Bureau. They must be submitted with the registration form as soon as it is available.

ABC audit rules – consumer events

2.6   A Stand Plan detailing the length and width of each stand should be submitted with the registration form or as soon as it is available.

2.7   Having registered an exhibition for a COA, the Organiser is committed to the audit and completion of the certificate unless the show is cancelled or the show attendance is affected by circumstances outside the organisers' control. Non completion will result in the exhibition registration being formally terminated by ABC.

However Organisers registering for their first audit may elect for a 'Trial Audit' which will not commit them to publishing their registration for the audit or the results.

2.8   Once an exhibition is registered with ABC, the registration stands until the Organiser specifically resigns that registration (i.e. subsequent equivalent events are committed to completing COA's unless a resignation is properly effected). The resignation must for, Annual shows be tendered at least 6 calendar months before the first day of the next show and for bienniel shows 12 months in advance of the show.

2.8.1 For all subsequent events the Organiser must submit a completed Permanent Information Form 6 months before the first day of the show. The event catalogue and stand plan detailing the length and width of the stands must be submitted with this Permanent Information Form or as soon as they are available.

2.9   An exhibition which has had its registration terminated, may not, even after reapplication for an exhibition audit use the ABC logo in pre-show publicity until a new certificate has been issued.

3.   CERTIFICATION

The Certificate will analyse the attendance by different entrance fee levels as follows:

Full Price	Visitors who gain access to the show via payment of the advertised full price admission fees.
Concessions	Visitors who gain access to the show at a reduced rate to those advertised.
Bulk Sales	A sale of two or more tickets resulting in such tickets being given, free of charge, to the visitor.
Complimentary	Visitors who gain access to the show free of charge.
Exhibitor personnel	Exhibition staff who man the stands may, as an option, be reported on the certificate. Exhibitor personnel will be included in the total net attendance.

4.   INSPECTION

4.1   An Exhibition Organiser must, on application by the Bureau, allow any authorised representative of the Bureau access within seven days to all or any records necessary to check the accuracy of a COA.

4.2   The Bureau reserves the right to visit a registered exhibition at any time to observe entry and recording procedures. The Organiser, at this time, must grant free access to the authorised representative of the Bureau to the exhibition and all relevant records

5.   PUBLICITY/REPRODUCTION OF THE COA

5.1   ABC strongly recommends the earliest possible registration of the exhibition as this allows maximum use of promotional opportunities.

5.2   ALL promotional material that makes reference to ABC must be approved by ABC, in writing, prior to release.

5.3   Any figures quoted near the ABC logo, on any material, must be the latest figures certified by ABC and the dates of the show must be stated. The attendance total must also show the breakdown between free and paid attendees.

5.4   Any attendance figures or statements which are made in publicity material that include the ABC logo must be presented in such a way that it is clear which information has and which information has not been certified by ABC.

5.5   Following successful completion of the COA audit, ABC will produce the original COA from the audited data provided. Copies may be reproduced by the Organiser from the aforementioned original or ABC can provide copies at cost. All copies must be reproduced in the format of the original certificate produced by ABC.

6.   TIME LIMIT FOR SUBMISSION OF THE COA

6.1   The completed COA return must be received by the Bureau within 45 days of the last day of the exhibition. Late submissions will be subject to a surcharge of £100.

6.2   The surcharge must be paid and the COA must be submitted within 14 days of the date of issue of the late submission invoice, otherwise the exhibition registration will be formally terminated by ABC. Any such termination will be entered in the ABC newsletter, Update.

7.   QUALIFIED PAID ATTENDANCE

Qualified Paid Attendance will be the number of visitors who gain access to the show by paying an admission charge only. The Paid attendance will be evaluated by reconciling the cash collected against the counted attendance. To facilitate this reconciliation the following financial/attendance records, audit rules and procedures must be adhered to.

Paid attendance is split into two main categories, visitors who purchase their entrance ticket at the exhibition (on-site) and visitors who purchase their ticket before the start of the exhibition (advance). To allow ABC to audit the counted paid attendance, and the cash collected for on-site and advance/attendance ticket sales, the following audit rules and procedures will apply:

7.1   ON-SITE TICKET SALES

The following audit rules apply to tickets purchased at the show.

7.1.1   **Ticket Books/Fan Tickets**

Ticket books or fan tickets **must** be used to count the paid attendance.

7.1.2   All claimed on-site paid attendees **must** purchase an entrance ticket from the ticket box office at the show.

7.1.3   The attendee will surrender the ticket to gain entrance to the show. The Organiser will either collect the whole ticket from the visitor or tear the ticket, retaining one portion and returning the other portion to the visitor.

7.1.4 ABC does **NOT** require on-site tickets to be retained by the Organiser, however if they are, they must be stored separately from advance tickets.

7.1.5 Each ticket book must have its own unique sequential number range printed on the tickets.

7.1.6 Separate identifiable ticket books with unique number ranges must be used for each payment rate available to gain access to the exhibition (i.e. full rate (adult), 75% of full rate (student), 50% of full rate (child/OAP) etc.).

7.1.7 Each cashier should be given a specific number of ticket books. The unique ticket number range should be recorded and signed for by the cashier and the Organiser's accountant/supervisor. The cashiers should only sell the batch of tickets they signed for.

7.1.8 Unsold tickets must be returned to and retained by the Organiser. The number of returned tickets and their unique number range must be recorded and signed for by the cashier and the Organiser's accountant/supervisor.

7.1.9 The unique ticket numbers of the first ticket and the last ticket sold in the period **must** be recorded on the relevant cashier sheet. See audit rule 7.5 and sample cashier sheet A1.

7.1.10 **"The Period"** referred to in these rules relates to the life span of a cashiers sheet. A cashiers sheet is completed and a new one started each time the organiser's supervisor or accountant collects cash from the cashier.

7.1.11 The counted paid attendance, for ABC purposes, can be calculated using ticket books only. However, as an option, Organiser may wish to use any or all of the listed below, in conjunction with ticket books, to count the paid attendance.

7.2 TICKETING MACHINES

7.2.1 The machines used to dispense and count the on-site entrance tickets issued to visitors **should** be used in conjunction with ticket books to count the paid attendance.

7.2.2 All on-site entrance tickets will be sold through the ticket box office and should be despatched via a ticketing machine.

7.2.3 The counters on the ticketing machine will be read at the start and the finish of the period and recorded together with the unique ticket numbers on the relevant cashiers sheet.

7.3. TILL ROLLS

7.3.1 As an option Organisers **may** elect to use Till rolls in conjunction with ticket books to count the paid attendance.

7.3.2 If so, all sales of entrance tickets must be cashed via a till which can record the transactions on a till roll.

7.3.3 The number of ticket sales on the till must be recorded on the cashier sheet and all the till rolls attached to the relevant cashiers sheets.

7.4 TURNSTILE

7.4.1 As an option Organisers **may** elect to use turnstiles in conjunction with ticket books to count the paid attendance.

7.4.2 If so, all visitors must pass through a turnstile when entering the exhibition. The counters must be read at least at the start and finish of each day.

7.4.3 The counter reading must be recorded and signed as correct by the reader.

7.5   CASH SHEETS

7.5.1   For each cashier, a cash sheet recording and reconciling the cash collected against the counted attendance must be maintained. A cash sheet must be completed and a new one started each time cash is collected by the organisers from the cashier and passed for banking.

7.5.2   The cash sheet must, as a minimum, make provision for the capture of the data listed below. Please see sample enclosed cashier sheet reference Al. If you wish to use this form please contact the Bureau for copies or photocopy the attached.

- Exhibition title and date
- Cashier's name and window position
- Float
- Opening number, closing number and total number of tickets issued for each payment rate available to gain access to the show. If all the tickets are sold, a 2nd batch of tickets will be issued to the cashier. The opening and closing numbers and total number of tickets issued must be recorded separately on the cash sheet. Please see column headings "1st batch ticket book" and "2nd batch ticket book" as an example on attached cash sheets reference A1.
- Opening number, closing number and total number of tickets dispensed per the ticket machine (if applicable).
- Till Rolls (if applicable).
- Value of tickets sold
- Cash collected, cheques collected, voucher value, credit card total.
- Cashier's signature and supervisor's signature.
- Cash analysis, voucher analysis.

7.5.3   Obviously the frequency of completion of the cash sheets will be dependent upon the visitor flow at the show. Some shows may require several cash sheets to be completed per cashier per day, whereas other shows will only require 1 or 2. However, as a minimum, each cashier must complete one cash sheet per day.

7.5.4   Where multiple cash sheets are completed each day, a daily cash sheet summary form should be completed. This summary sheet must, as a minimum, include the data listed below. Please see sample enclosed cash sheet summary form reference A2. If you wish to use this form, please contact the Bureau for copies or photocopy the attached.

- Exhibition title and date
- Cashier's name and window position
- Type of ticket, payment rate, number of tickets sold.
- Each cash sheet (A1) must be given a unique reference number. This number or range of numbers (if multiple cash sheets are completed each day) will be recorded on the Daily Cash summary form (A2).

7.6   BANKING SHEETS

7.6.1   A banking sheet must be completed each time ticket money is banked. The sheet must, as a minimum, include the data listed below. Please see sample enclosed banking sheet form reference B 1. If you wish to use the form please contact the Bureau or photocopy the attached.

- Exhibition title and date
- Cashier's name and window position
- Cash collected per cashier and total amount banked

7.6.2   ABC strongly recommends that ticket sales are banked separately from catalogue sales and other miscellaneous income. However if this is not the case then the above banking sheet must include a breakdown of the cash banked, for example:

Ticket sales	£
Catalogue sales	£
Poster sales	£
Miscellaneous	£

7.6.3   Where multiple banking sheets are completed each day, a daily banking sheet summary form should be completed. This summary sheet should, as a minimum, include the data listed below. Please see sample enclosed banking sheet summary form reference B2. If you require copies of this form please contact the Bureau or photocopy the attached form.

- Exhibition name and date
- Cashiers' names and window positions
- Banking sheet Reference number(s)
- Value of tickets sold per cashier, revenue collected per cashier
- Total value of tickets sold, total revenue
- Total banked, time of banking, revenue analysis.

7.7   VOUCHERS

7.7.1   To facilitate the audit of visitors who gain entrance to the show at a reduced rate via submission of a voucher, the following will apply.

7.7.2   The visitor must surrender the voucher to the cashier when purchasing the entrance ticket.

7.7.3   If multiple types of vouchers are available to gain reduced rate entrance, they must be separated and counted on a daily basis. The number of vouchers collected will be recorded and analysed on the cash sheet. The vouchers must be kept in their counted bundles with a note detailing the number of vouchers held in the bundle. ABC will sample check the voucher count.

7.7.4   With the exception of a family voucher, a single voucher may only allow one reduced payment entry. One voucher CANNOT allow multiple visitors reduced rate entrance.

A family voucher may only allow a set discount for a set number of Adult and Child visitors, i.e. Two Adults and Two Children may gain entrance at X reduced rate fee with submission of the voucher. The number of adult and child visitors who gain reduced rate entrance on a family voucher will be set by the Organiser.

The number of reduced rate visitors who gain entrance via submission of a family voucher ticket will exactly match the number of reduced rate visitors per the family vouchers collected from the visitors on entrance to the show. ABC will sample count these vouchers.

7.7.5   A single voucher may only give one rate of discount. It CANNOT give one discount for an adult visitor and a different rate for a child visitor.

7.7.6   Daily voucher sheets should also be completed. The sheet should, as a minimum, include the data listed below. Please see sample enclosed daily vouchers sheet reference C1. If you require copies of this form please contact the Bureau or photocopy attached.

- Exhibition name and date
- Source of voucher (i.e. Daily Mail, News magazine)
- Value of each type of voucher
- Total number of each type of voucher

7.8   ADVANCE TICKET SALES

The following audit rules apply to entrance tickets purchased in advance of the show.

Ticket Books

7.8.1   Ticket books **must** be used to count the advance paid attendance.

7.8.2   All claimed advance paid attendees **must** purchase an entrance ticket from an official outlet, e.g. Organiser box office, ticket agency, British Rail, etc.

7.8.3   The attendee must surrender the ticket to gain entrance to the show. The Organiser must collect and retain the whole or the stubb of the ticket from the visitor. If the Organiser collects the stubb of the ticket only that section of the ticket may be counted towards the attendance. If the wrong section of the ticket is collected it will be excluded from the counted attendance.

7.8.4   Each sales outlet must have a separately identifiable ticket. If variable entrance rates are available from a single ticket outlet, the entrance rate must be printed on each ticket.

7.8.5   Advance tickets must be retained and stored separately from on-site tickets.

7.8.6   The various ticket types and payment rates must be separated and counted on a daily basis. The number of advance tickets collected will be recorded and analysed on the advance ticket sales sheet.

7.8.7   The advance tickets must be kept in their counted daily bundles with a note detailing the number of tickets held in the bundle. ABC will sample check the ticket counts.

7.9   Advance Ticket Sales Sheet

An advance ticket sales sheet detailing the number of tickets sold by each ticket outlet must be maintained. The advance ticket sales sheet must, as a minimum, include the data listed below. Please see attached sample enclosed advance ticket sales sheet reference DI. If you require copies of this form please contact the Bureau or photocopy attached.

- Exhibition name and date
- Ticket sales outlets
- Ticket type and payment rate
- Total number of tickets collected
- Total value of tickets collected

7.10   Bulk Ticket Sales

A sale of two or more tickets resulting in such tickets being given, free of charge, to the visitor.

Examples include sales to exhibitor, airlines, hotels, business, etc.

8.   QUALIFIED FREE ATTENDANCE

Qualified free attendance will be the number of visitors who gain access to the show free of charge and adhere to the audit rules below:

8.1   **Ticket Books/Registration Cards**

8.1.1   Ticket books/registration cards must be used to count the free attendance.

8.1.2   The attendee must surrender a ticket to gain access to the show. The Organiser must collect and retain the whole ticket from the visitor. The complimentary tickets must be stored separately from on-site and advance tickets.

8.1.3   The collected complimentary tickets must, as a minimum, be counted on a daily basis. The counts must be recorded on the advance ticket sales sheet. The tickets must be stored in their counted daily bundles with a note detailing the number of tickets in the bundle. ABC will sample check the ticket counts.

8.1.4   The Organiser must also comply with ONE of the following two criteria listed below:

- The complimentary entry ticket must include the name of the show and make provision for the capture of the visitor's name, address, postcode and telephone number.

- Only complimentary entry tickets surrendered by the visitor to gain access to the show which have captured the name and address will be included on the certificate.

   OR

- Each ticket book must have its own unique sequential number range printed on the tickets.

- The Organiser maintains a record of who the complimentary tickets were sent to. The record will include the name, company name, address, telephone number, number of tickets, and the tickets unique reference number or range of numbers. ABC will, on a sample basis, cross reference the unique number held on those complimentary tickets (collected from free visitors on entrance to the show) to unique reference numbers recorded by the Organiser. ABC will also contact a random sample of the companies held on the list to seek their verification of receipt of the complimentary tickets.

8.2   **Exhibitor Personnel**

The Exhibition Organiser may, as an option, report the number of attending exhibitor personnel, providing auditable records are held to support inclusion of the data (i.e. exhibitor registration cards). Exhibitor personnel will be included in the total net attendance.

9.   TOTAL ATTENDANCE & REVENUE SUMMARY SHEETS

9.1   To allow ABC to reconcile the total attendance against the total cash/vouchers collected, the Organiser must collate the various sheets maintained for the duration of the show into a accurate summary of the visitor attendance and the revenue generated from ticket sales.

9.2   The attendance summary must, as a minimum, include the data listed below. Please see enclosed sample attendance summary sheet reference E1. If you require copies of this sheet please contact the Bureau or photocopy attached.

- Exhibition name and date
- Number of visitors per day analysed by type of attendance ticket

9.3   The ticket revenue summary must, as a minimum, include the data listed below. Please see enclosed revenue summary sheet reference F1. If you require copies of this form please contact the Bureau for copies or photocopy attached.

- Exhibition name and date
- Type of ticket and payment rate
- Number of tickets sold
- Revenue collected
- Revenue invoiced

10.   RECORDS TO BE HELD

10.1   All records listed and any further records financial or otherwise needed to ensure the accuracy of the ABC Certificate must be held until the ABC certificate for the subsequent show has been audited by ABC. All records must be available for audit or inspection at any time and within 7 days of request by ABC or its appointed representatives.

10.2   All financial records relating to ticket sales and stand sales including invoices, credit notes, paying in books and bank statements must be made available to ABC for inspection at any time within 7 days of ABC's request. If there is any doubt as to what should be held, the Organiser should contact ABC. The aim of the rule is to ensure that the audit can be conducted from the retained records.

10.3   All vouchers, advance and complimentary tickets must be separated by ticket design and stored with a record of the number of tickets held in each batch and on what day the tickets were collected.

10.4   All records maintained to count and record the counted paid attendance and cash collected, i.e. cash sheets, banking sheets, etc.

11.   NUMBER OF STANDS AND STANDS SPACE OCCUPIED

11.1   The COA will certify the Total Stand Space Occupied.

11.2   Stand Space Occupied will include all exhibition stands available to all attendees, whether paid, free or obtained via a contra deal. It shall NOT include rest areas, restaurants, conference rooms, exhibitor lounges etc.

11.3   The COA will certify the Total Number of Stands. The Organiser must hold auditable contractual evidence for each stand shown on the COA.

11.4   The Stand Plan submitted with the registration form (see Audit Rule 2.5) should be coded to indicate which stands have been sublet and the number of sublessees.

11.5   Any stands that have been divided by sub-letting by the original contracted exhibitor may only be included as additional stands on the COA under the following circumstances:

11.6   The catalogue reflects entries for those on the shared stand area or the original contracted exhibitor provides written evidence of the division of the stand.

11.7   The Bureau is satisfied that the stand space clearly allows the individual exhibitors to be identified and located within the divided area. In any cases of doubt the Bureau will decide.

11.8   The Organiser must submit, with the return, an exhibitor list detailing the exhibitor's company name, stand number, stand dimension and stand space occupied.

11.9   **Feature Area Stand Space** may, as an option, be included on the certificate as a separate figure, i.e. feature areas stand space will not be included in the mandatory exhibitor stand space figure.

12.   COMPLAINTS PROCEDURES

12.1.   Any complaint made against an Organiser shall be in writing addressed to the ABC Chief Executive.

12.2.   The Chief Executive shall, if he considers that a prima facie case for complaint exists, refer the complaint to the Exhibition Organiser complained of who shall have the right to make a written statement in answer within fourteen days.

12.3.   If the ABC Chief Executive finds a complaint against an Organiser well founded, he may withdraw any ABC COA already issued and/or that Exhibition Organiser may be censured, suspended temporarily and/or subject to the fulfilment of such conditions as the Bureau may impose or may terminate the exhibition registration. Such decisions of the Chief Executive shall be notified to all ABC members and such other parties as the ABC sees fit in the interest of protecting the reputation of the ABC.

12.4.   If, in the opinion of the Chief Executive, a complaint is well founded, the Bureau will pay the costs of any re-audit incurred in connection with the complaint. The Bureau will recover such costs from the offending Organiser unless otherwise agreed by the Chief Executive. If in the opinion of the Chief Executive a complaint is not well founded, the complainant will pay the costs of re-audit plus 20% thereof to cover the Bureau's expenses.

advertisements in printed media and which is based on the precepts that they should be legal, decent, honest, truthful and prepared with a sense of responsibility to consumers, society and competitors. It seeks to ensure that standards are maintained by monitoring the trade, making approximately 150,000 random checks each year and dealing with complaints raised by the public. Those advertisers whose advertisements breach the Code are asked to amend or withdraw them, as appropriate. Failing this, advertisers will find few – if any – publications which are willing to accept the offending, unaltered material. Refer to Appendix C: 'The British Code of Advertising Practice', see page 317.

The Association of Media Independents Limited

The AMI is the trade body for specialist agencies which deal solely with the planning and purchase of media space and time. They do not offer creative services concerning the style, layout and text of advertisements as traditional advertising agencies do. For small-sized concerns which might employ a media independent, it is sensible to pick one who belongs to this organization. To provide safeguards for advertisers, the Association insists that its members are in the business of media buying, of good professional and sound financial standing as well as being wholly independent of any advertiser, advertising agency or media owner.

These agencies have to demonstrate from client lists and billings that they have capabilities across all media. They must give a written undertaking to supply customers with copy invoices from the media showing the costs of space and time purchased by them. They need to be recognized by the Independent Television Companies Association, the Newspaper Publishers Association and the Periodical Publishers Association and agree to abide by the British Code of Advertising Practice. Copies of their six-monthly and annual accounts have to be filed as proof of their financial status.

The Audit Bureau of Circulations Limited

An independent and non-profit-making company, ABC has a membership of leading publishers, advertisers and advertising agencies. Its purpose so far as the press advertiser is concerned is to certify the circulations of members' publications. It does this by forwarding forms to each publication which must be completed by an independent auditor who is normally the publisher's accountants. On their return to the Bureau, these are checked and if correct an ABC certificate is issued, usually stating the average number of copies sold and/or freely circulated as appropriate each day, week, fortnight or month over the preceding six months. Regular spot checks are made on publishers' records to ensure that auditing procedures are being carried out in the proper manner. It is sensible to be wary of any publications whose circulations are not independently certified, since self-certified statements could be incorrect.

The Committee of Advertising Practice

The CAP – with its members drawn from all major advertising trade bodies such as the Newspaper Publishers Association, the Newspaper Society and the Periodical Publishers Association – drafts and implements the British Code of Advertising Practice. Its functions include constantly reviewing and amending this Code, investigating complaints made by commercially interested parties (with the Advertising Standards Authority handling the public's grievances) and co-ordinating its members' activities to uphold standards. It gives free, confidential advice to advertisers who wish to know how to correctly interpret the Code's detailed and occasionally complex guidelines. See Appendix C: 'The British Code of Advertising Practice', page 317.

The Incorporated Society of British Advertisers Limited

Representing national and international advertisers such as British Airways, British Gas and Guinness, the ISBA seeks to advance their causes and promote first-class advertising practices by maintaining an ongoing dialogue with the government, media, advertising agencies and the public. Of special significance to you, it offers advice across a range of subjects including budgets, agency agreements, schedules, costs and so on. Also, it regularly conducts one-day training workshops on topics such as 'Press Media – saving money by effective planning and buying', 'Negotiating with Agencies' and 'Basic Copywriting Skills'. Various, useful books, directories and pamphlets are available as well.

The Institute of Practitioners in Advertising

The IPA is the representative organization of advertising agencies within the United Kingdom, giving its members a broad mix of specialist and information services and highlighting their views in discussions with the Government, media and advertising industry. Any small-business person who may consider using an agency ought to choose one which belongs to this body. To join, the Institute stipulates that a would-be member must prove that they can plan and carry out an advertising campaign from start to finish. Consequently, only traditional, full service agencies capable of putting together business and media buying plans, creating advertisements and so forth are eligible, not media independents who simply deal in space and time purchasing.

Accordingly, the IPA checks out the agency's experience – its client base and the type, number and variety of different accounts which are and have previously been handled. Its financial standing and creditworthiness are studied and recognition by other trade organizations is taken into account as well – all of which provide a sense of security for those ventures selecting one of the Institute's members to help them with their advertising.

The Joint Industry Committee for National Readership Surveys

JICNARS acts for the Newspaper Publishers Association, the Periodical Publishers Association, the Incorporated Society of British Advertisers Limited and the Institute of Practitioners in Advertising. It controls a national readership survey conducted on a continuing basis among a random sample of approximately 28,000 members of the public. This generates up-to-date information about the press (plus television, cinema and radio) including the readership of various publications by types of people (analysed by sex, age and social grade), reading frequency and the like. Various reports and bulletins are regularly produced for subscribers which are of particular help to advertisers wishing to promote themselves to the general public.

Media Audits Limited

This independent company offers a consultancy service regarding the best use of advertising media, primarily television and the press. Of key interest to you, advertisers may submit a detailed schedule – type and number of insertions, costs and so on – of their planned advertising within national newspapers and magazines. This is then broken down and analysed with individual positions and prices paid being compared alongside pooled data. An overall assessment of the advertiser's planning and buying performance is then made, for subsequent discussion and future improvements.

Verified Free Distribution Limited

VFD – and Bulk Verified Services (BVS) which is part of it – is a self-supporting subsidiary of the Audit Bureau of Circulations Limited that certifies the distribution of free publications. Those newspapers, magazines and directories which are delivered to homes are eligible for a Verified Free Distribution certification. Others – distributed in bulk to hotels, stores and miscellaneous pickup points – may receive a BVS certification. Should you subsequently decide to incorporate the free press within your advertising activities, it is advisable to use only the publications which have VFD or BVS certificates as the uncertified claims of other publications may be unrepresentative and potentially misleading.

Summary

- Many publications are structured along similar lines and incorporate editorial, advertisement, marketing, subscriptions, production and circulation departments.

- Various trade bodies exist in the press industry. Among them are the British Business Press, the Directory Publishers Association, the Newspaper Publishers Association, the Newspaper Society, and the Periodical Publishers Association.

- Most radio stations will have programming, sales, production, marketing and accounts departments or sections within their organization.

- Leading radio bodies include the Association of Independent Radio Companies Limited, the Broadcasting Standards Council, the Radio Advertising Bureau Limited, the Radio Authority, and Radio Joint Audience Research.

- The direct mail industry is made up of list owners and brokers, direct mail advertisers, mailing houses, the Royal Mail, direct mail recipients, fulfilment houses and miscellaneous suppliers of goods and services.

- Influential trade organizations exist within the direct mail industry. In particular, these include the Direct Mail Accreditation and Recognition Centre, the Direct Mail Information Service, the Direct Marketing Association (UK) Limited, the Institute of Direct Marketing, the Advertising Standards Authority Limited, the Committee of Advertising Practice, the Data Protection Register and the Mailing Preference Service.

- The exhibition industry comprises venue owners, exhibition organizers, designers, contractors and exhibitors.

- Industry participants are represented by various bodies – the Agricultural Show Exhibitors Association, the Association of Exhibition Organisers, the British Exhibition Contractors Association, The British Exhibition Venues Association, the Exhibition Venues Association, Audit Bureau of Circulations Limited, Exhibition Audience Audits, Exhibition Surveys Limited, and the Incorporated Society of British Advertisers Limited.

- Key players in the advertising industry are the Advertising Association, the Advertising Standards Authority Limited, the Association of Media Independents, the Audit Bureau of Circulations Limited, the Committee of Advertising Practice, the Incorporated Society of British Advertisers Limited, the Institute of Practitioners in Advertising, the Joint Industry Committee for National Readership Surveys, Media Audits Limited, and Verified Free Distribution Limited.

Notes

3 **Doing your groundwork**

BEFORE YOU START TO PLAN your advertising activities for the press, radio, direct mail and exhibitions, you need to carry out extensive preparatory work, looking at your business, the marketplace, and the costs of advertising. You may wish to bring in some specialist assistance at this stage too. It is this groundwork that underpins a successful advertising campaign; you cannot succeed without it.

Analysing yourself

Your initial preparation for an advertising campaign must begin with a vigorous investigation into your business, products, services and objectives. This thorough self-appraisal, when subsequently combined with a detailed knowledge of your market and the establishment of a budget, will enable you to make a preliminary assessment of the types of media which are most likely to be suitable in your individual circumstances. Also, all of this background work ought to allow you to build up sufficient information to move on to commence and administer highly successful advertising activities.

Assessing your business

It is sensible to conduct a wide-ranging, in-depth analysis of your firm, considering its organization, structure and operations. Think about factors such as location with regard to amenities, suppliers, customers and competitors. Contemplate its premises, especially their size, facilities, image and the like. In turn, visit each department – production, finance, personnel, sales – to observe and talk to colleagues and employees about policies, work methods and techniques. Discover everything there is to possibly know, both good and bad, so that you possess a broad and wholly comprehensive understanding of all aspects of your concern.

List the firm's strengths as you see them. Your notes – which will prove absolutely invaluable when you go on to launch your advertising campaign – might typically include comments such as: 'Being my own boss, I can make immediate decisions as I do not have to consult other people; therefore, I am able to run a flexible venture, swiftly introducing new goods, changing suppliers when deliveries are late and varying payment terms to suit customers' needs; the business is well sited close to the industrial estate where most of my clients work, thus I am assured of a high number of quality passers-by; my property is spacious and roomy allowing me to have an extensive product range which draws would-be customers onto the premises; I employ a friendly and knowledgeable team who handle enquiries in an engaging manner, persuasively converting them into sales.'

Detail any weaknesses that you are aware of and calculate how to remedy them, if possible. Your records might incorporate statements similar to these: 'Working alone, I do not have the financial resources to bulk buy for quantity discounts; as I cannot always compete on price with larger firms I concentrate instead on offering a prompt, personal service for clients; three months ago, a national competitor opened a unit which is located only two streets away from me; in comparison with the same period during last year, my income has fallen by 35 per cent, largely as a result of this increased competition; I intend to bring in new lines to compensate for these losses; operating in a seasonal trade, my fluctuating turnover creates cash flow difficulties for me; I shall have stock clearance sales at appropriate times to solve these problems.'

Linking together your knowledge of the firm with your appreciation of the key media should mean that you are now able to think about where you might advertise. Read back over your uniquely individual notes, contemplating the significance of your business and its particular favourable and unfavourable features so far as your advertising activities are concerned. Wishing to notify prompt decisions to customers, perhaps about new stock and changing prices, might point to the use of the radio or daily or weekly rather than monthly or quarterly publications. Being based near to clients' workplaces may suggest the suitability of advertising within in-house journals so that those people who drive rather than walk to work are reached. Trading locally could indicate the viability of regional rather than national radio stations, as might modest financial limits. Completing 'Assessing your business: an action checklist', page 65, may be helpful at this stage.

Studying your products and services

Examine closely whatever you offer or are planning to offer to your customers. Look at your products and services in terms of age, varieties, colours, sizes, shapes, packaging, uses, prices, quality, safety, reliability, availability, guarantees and after-sales service, as relevant in your circumstances. Your products and services are of critical importance as most of your advertisements will probably concentrate on them. Hence, they have to be good: meeting customers' needs, doing the job properly, being readily available, well-priced and so on.

THE BUSINESS: A SELF-ASSESSMENT		Campaign:			Number:	
		Media:			Date:	
The firm	**Press**	**Radio**	**Direct mail**	**Exhibitions**	**Comments**
Characteristics:	Features:	Features:	Features:	Features:	
Strengths:	Advantages:	Advantages:	Advantages:	Advantages:	
Weaknesses:	Disadvantages:	Disadvantages:	Disadvantages:	Disadvantages:	

Assessing your business: an action checklist

However excellent your advertisements may be, they will not be able to sell unwanted or poor quality items (or at least not more than once).

Separate each product's characteristics into pluses and minuses. Consider the benefits – the lowest price, the most reliable performance, two years parts and labour guarantee – from the customers' viewpoint. You will want to promote these in your subsequent advertisements to encourage customers to buy from you. To coin a phrase, you're selling the sizzle not the sausage. Contemplate any drawbacks that exist as well, seeking to remedy them so far as you possibly can. That sausage needs to taste as good as the sizzle suggests it will do!

Reviewing your detailed product and service notes should help you to revise your initial list of possible media to use and can be referred to again later on when you start work on your advertisements. As an example, wanting to illustrate a product's breadth of colours and innovative features would highlight the use of direct mail, magazines and some miscellaneous publications such as brochures rather than newspapers where colour is less widely available, and certainly not the radio where they can't be seen at all. 'Studying your products and services: an action checklist' on page 67 may be of interest to you now.

Looking at your objectives

It is wise to set out your precise short-, medium- and long-term business goals in as much depth as you can. These will provide you with the clearest indicators yet of the media that you may eventually select and, when you move ahead to launch your advertising activities, the ways in which you might successfully run your campaign. They will give you, along with any professional advisers whom you may subsequently commission, a framework to work within and targets to work towards.

Your slightly generalized short-term objectives, some of which could be equally well placed below later headings, might typically include: to promote awareness of our new goods, their key features and uses amongst independent retailers and consumers in the county; to develop a contacts list of potential retail stockists for follow-up mail shots and visits by our sales team; to build up a customer base of 100–125 accounts within the next 12 to 18 months; to introduce this innovative product range into the region, generating an annual turnover in excess of £200,000 by the close of the second trading year.

In the medium term, goals may be: to recruit appropriate numbers and types of managerial and shop floor staff in readiness for anticipated market expansion; to increase product recognition and understanding amongst all multiple and independent retailers and users across the country; to distribute our goods via as many reputable stockists as possible throughout the United Kingdom; to sell direct to consumers via mail order; to regularly adjust demand when uneconomic sales peaks and troughs occur; to constantly reassure previous and

PRODUCTS AND SERVICES: A SELF-ASSESSMENT

| Campaign: | | | | Number: | |
| Media: | | | | Date: | |
Products/ services	Press	Radio	Direct mail	Exhibitions	Comments
Characteristics:	Features:	Features:	Features:	Features:	
Pluses:	Benefits:	Benefits:	Benefits:	Benefits:	
Minuses:	Drawbacks:	Drawbacks:	Drawbacks:	Drawbacks:	

Studying your products and services: an action checklist

current customers that they bought a winning product or range; to compete against all rivals, gaining and sustaining revenue of £500,000 per annum and a 20 per cent market share by the end of the fifth operating year.

Your long-term targets, which may be just as relevant if located under earlier headings, could incorporate: to continually remind existing and potential stockists and users of the existence and special qualities of our goods; to notify relevant company and product changes and developments to the market; to uphold the respected name of the firm and the reputation of our goods at all times; to steadily clear out slower-selling products at discount prices; to replace existing goods with equally successful new products before demand for the original range has entered into a permanent decline.

Checking back over your list of objectives will enable you to start thinking about using various media at different stages, according to what you want to achieve at a particular time. Initially wishing to make local shopkeepers and customers fully aware of your new products may point to the maximization of regional press advertising, with some additional activities within business magazines to draw in enquiries from would-be stockists. Then seeking to recruit shopfloor employees might indicate the further use of regional newspapers, either weeklies and/or dailies especially if they have a separate section devoted to job advertisements on the same day of each week. National newspapers and/or business magazines may be needed if specialized or managerial positions are to be advertised, which could perhaps be difficult to fill locally. Expanding distribution and sales across the country suggests the possibility of the national press, perhaps backed by the regionals in resisting areas and when new products are again launched, later on. Filling in 'Looking at your objectives: an action checklist' on page 69 may be beneficial at this point.

Knowing your market

Moving on with your preparatory work in anticipation of advertising activities, you ought to carry out a study of your existing and/or potential customers, competitors and the marketplace. You need to discover as much as possible about all of them so that you have sufficient knowledge to allow you to further assess the types of media which may be ideal in your particular situation. The accumulated market data that you will have gathered together will also consequently help you to approach your imminent advertising campaign in the most relevant and rewarding manner.

Contemplating your customers

Whether you sell to businesses or to the public, you must seek to obtain a broad understanding of them. You cannot expect to develop a detailed knowledge

| OBJECTIVES: A SELF-ASSESSMENT | | Campaign: | | | Number: | |
The firm	Press	Media:	Radio	Direct mail	Date: Exhibitions	Comments
Short-term:	Features:		Features:	Features:	Features:	
Medium-term:	Advantages:		Advantages:	Advantages:	Advantages:	
Long-term:	Disadvantages:		Disadvantages:	Disadvantages:	Disadvantages:	

Looking at your objectives: an action checklist

unless you deal with very limited numbers. With regard to traders, try to find out what you can about their present and future numbers, current and anticipated sizes, locations and activities. For the public, it would be useful to know something about their numbers, locations, sexes, ages, marital status, children, social grades, occupations, incomes and interests, as appropriate. Have a mind's-eye picture of your target customer. For example, 'She is probably a 25–35-year-old housewife, with two children', and so on.

It can also be helpful to check out your customers' habits, so far as you can. Knowing what products and services they buy and when, how often and where they purchase them can be revealing. Understanding which media they read, listen to, when, how often, for how long and what they do afterwards could be beneficial too. Their opinions of your organization and products and services (especially the perceived benefits) may be highly relevant to the direction and style of your advertising activities. Attempting to unravel their views of your competitors could be worthwhile as well.

Possessing such background information about your present and/or would-be customers' characteristics, habits and opinions – much of which can be obtained from your own records plus regular correspondence and discussions with them – ought to enable you to think again about the types of media you might subsequently use. Look back through your notes to see if they indicate whether you ought to use the national or regional press, newspapers, magazines or other miscellaneous publications as examples. Selling to traders rather than members of the public points to business magazines rather than consumer magazines, and vice versa. Having all of your customers living in a little village perhaps suggests it would be worthwhile to advertise in the church and/or women's institute newsletter, with the regional press being used if they are spread across the county and the national press being used should they be dotted about the country. See 'Contemplating your customers: an action checklist' on page 71 for further help.

Evaluating your competitors

It is sensible to familiarize yourself with your current and prospective rivals, appraising them in as much depth as you analysed your own firm, so far as this is possible. You certainly should be able to assess their respective organizations, contemplating their operations, locations, properties and so on and separating these out into plus and minus points. Similarly, their products and services ought to be easy to investigate, viewing them in terms of age, varieties, colours and so forth and grouping these into benefits and drawbacks.

You must also study and evaluate carefully your competitors' past and present advertising activities within the various media, as far as you can, but obviously you cannot realistically expect to spot or hear each and every

CUSTOMERS: AN ASSESSMENT

Campaign: Number:

Media: Date:

Customers	Press	Radio	Direct mail	Exhibitions	Comments
Characteristics:					
Purchasing habits:					
Media habits:					
Opinions:					
Other:					

Contemplating your customers: an action checklist

COMPETITORS: AN ANALYSIS

Campaign: Number:

Media: Date:

Competitors	Press	Radio	Direct mail	Exhibitions	Comments
Characteristics:					
Products and services:					
Advertising schedules:					
Advertisements:					
Other:					

Evaluating your competitors: an action checklist

advertisement. Look at the publications used as well as when, how often and for how long they advertised. Check out their advertisements too, perusing sizes and positions, the themes and approaches adopted and the various contents. Listen to the radio, try to see their mailshots – perhaps by registering with them as a customer from your home address – and visit their stands at exhibitions.

Knowing all about your competitors – an understanding which should have developed gradually through many years of reading about and talking to them and other individuals and firms in the trade – will allow you to work further upon your list of possible types of media to use. As an example, you may be aware that a national rival advertises its products in newspapers but never (so far as you can see) in magazines or miscellaneous publications. There must be sound reasons for this and if you correctly assume that a large competitor is experienced and knows what it is doing, you would be wise to think about following rather than bucking the trend. 'Evaluating your competitors: an action checklist' on page 72 may be helpful.

Appraising the marketplace

It is advisable to build up a broad and detailed appreciation of the main features of the market in which you trade now, as well as of those which you may be planning to enter or diversify into at a later stage. Discover the total turnover and overall size of each market in the past, in the present and anticipated in the future. Find out what you can about manufacturers, wholesalers and retailers and their former, current and estimated future market shares. Study the ways in which the market is structured and administered by representative bodies and how its key individuals and companies interact, co-operate and conflict with each other.

You should also look outside of the market, becoming aware and remaining mindful of the external influences upon it. Political or legal changes such as new government initiatives or statutes may have favourable or adverse effects. So too could social or demographic developments including shifting public opinions, population movements and unemployment. Do not forget the economic situation, especially rising or falling inflation and interest rates. Technological advances with rapidly improving worldwide communication methods and techniques plus environmental issues such as a shortage of natural resources and pollution could be of relevance as well. You ought to be able to calculate the ways in which these and any other external events will affect your particular marketplace.

By reading back over your lengthy list of internal features and external influences – which will have been relatively easy for you to piece together after years of experience and trading in your chosen field – you ought to crystallize your ideas concerning the assorted media available to you. In an optimistic market – perhaps encouraged by the prospects of falling interest rates and lower unemployment figures – you may decide to branch out from regional to national media so that you are ready to take a larger share of the expected, increasing sales when they arise. Technological advances which allow newspapers to be printed in a wider range of more realistic colours at a lower price may persuade you to use them instead of magazines in forthcoming campaigns. 'Appraising the marketplace: an action checklist' on page 75 is worth completing now.

Carrying out additional research

Most of the information that you want to accumulate and write down about your customers, competitors and the marketplace will already be known to you or be easily accessible via sales, financial and miscellaneous records plus formal and informal communication networks. However, there will inevitably be odd gaps in your knowledge and existing details which will leave you with unanswered questions and incomplete notes. Although these spaces may not affect adversely your hopefully correct choice of media, they could be detrimental later on when the real significance and true value of all of this work and built-up material becomes fully apparent. If you are to go on to plan a schedule, create appropriate advertisements, mailshots and/or exhibition stands, and administer successful activities – all developing from these original records – then it is wise to carry out any additional research which is necessary to finalize your notes.

Innumerable local, national and specialist organizations conduct and commission surveys, collect and publish reports and statistics which may contain snippets or even masses of information that could be of relevance and interest to you. Depending on your circumstances, gather up and sift through any material which may be kept by Chambers of Commerce – contact names and details can be obtained from the Association of British Chambers of Commerce. It may be worthwhile visiting libraries too, particularly specialized business ones. The *ASLIB Directory* and *The Guide to Government Departments and Other Libraries* which list these are available from the London Business School Library and the Science Reference Library respectively. Think about getting in touch with local authorities as well – these are much overlooked and underrated sources of substantial reference materials. See 'Useful contacts', page 385, for addresses and telephone numbers.

Your professional or trade association should be of considerable help to you. *The Directory of British Associations* published by CBD Research Limited and detailing over 6,500 trade organizations in the United Kingdom ought to be referred to in your nearest library if you do not know who or where your representative body is. It is sensible to contact media and other advertising organizations such as the Advertising Association and the Incorporated Society of British Advertisers Limited as they will often reveal their research findings to would-be advertisers. The government with its multitude of departments is

THE MARKETPLACE: AN APPRAISAL	Campaign:			Number:	
	Media:			Date:	
The market	**Press**	**Radio**	**Direct mail**	**Exhibitions**	**Comments**
Characteristics:					
Internal features:					
External features:					
Likely effects:					

Appraising the marketplace: an action checklist

probably the biggest producer of useful reports and statistics, which it sells through Her Majesty's Stationery Office. A guide to all government publications can be sent out on request from its Central Statistical Office. Refer to 'Useful contacts', page 385, for addresses and telephone numbers.

Consider approaching specialist market research agencies, which exist for the sole or primary purpose of pulling together often exclusive information about customers, competitors and the marketplace on behalf of their clients, many of which are small businesses. The Association of Market Survey Organisations Limited and the Market Research Society – highly respected and reputable trade bodies representing organizations within this industry – can provide you with useful general material as well as recommending a number of agencies which are likely to assist you with your specific requirements. Check out 'Useful contacts', page 385, for key addresses and telephone numbers.

Establishing a budget

Concluding your initial preparations for an advertising campaign, you must review the past, consider the present and anticipate the future before moving on to allocate funds for your planned activities. Having completed a comprehensive self-analysis and market study as well as setting your appropriation – as the budget is also known – you should be able to go on to launch a suitable, winning campaign.

Reviewing the past

If appropriate, consider how much you have spent on advertising in previous years along with the range, number and type of advertisements purchased and their effectiveness, whether in terms of increased enquiries, sales and so forth. Those firms with a limited capacity – perhaps a self-employed painter and decorator or a family-run hotel – and which operate in a constant environment often spend the same sum each year, with allowances made for inflation and higher media costs. From hard-earned experience, they know that it will generate sufficient but not too much business for them. Other concerns trading amidst ever-changing internal and external circumstances should simply use this figure as the starting point from which a suitable budget can be calculated.

Some businesses base their advertising appropriation for the coming year on a percentage of their last annual turnover. The chosen figure, which is typically between 2 and 5 per cent, would be based upon the trade or industry averages uncovered during research. Although it is wise to take this into account when reaching a decision, it is important to bear in mind that last year's turnover might have been especially high or low. High, and it may lead to increased expenditure for this year when it is not necessarily needed; low, and it could result in less money being spent when it is most required, perhaps to reverse or slow a decline in sales.

Contemplate any profits that may remain from last year's trading activities, as part of this can be used for advertising purposes during the forthcoming year. Most firms limit their budget according to what they can actually afford to spend. Realistically, smaller concerns which are restricted by credit terms, overdraft limits and cash flow problems cannot afford to overspend, buying their way out of financial difficulties through extensive advertising. They are unlikely to survive long enough to reap the eventual rewards.

Considering the present

Taking your total sales and deducting production and distribution costs leaves you with your gross profit. Consider setting aside a proportion of this sum for your advertising needs. Sensible though it is to link together profits and advertising monies, be mindful that higher sales and the more economic spread of costs leads to a larger gross profit and advertising appropriation with lower sales having corresponding, knock-on effects. Thus, your newly allocated budget may either be excessive or too restrictive for your requirements at this particular time.

Numerous small firms calculate their advertising expenditure by working out the selling price of each individual unit sold, subsequently breaking this amount down between materials, labour, advertising and so on. Planning to sell perhaps 1,000 units in a given period, they then multiply the advertising costs within a single unit by 1,000 to finalize the appropriation. Analysing this method, you need to recognize that it may be worthwhile in the short term, but less so later on. Internal and external costs rarely remain constant and in line with each other for long, so they have to be monitored on an ongoing basis, and revised time and again.

Difficult though it is to assess your rivals' advertising budgets, you ought to attempt to estimate what they are. Of course, you cannot know for sure because it is unlikely that you can check each and every medium and identify and add up the cost of every advertisement, mail-shot or exhibition stand. Nevertheless, from the promotional activities which you have seen, you may be able to hazard approximate minimum and maximum figures. Clearly, such information is more useful than having nothing at all. You may then decide to set an appropriate, high appropriation if you are seeking to seize a larger share of the market.

Anticipating the future

Forecasting your sales for the upcoming quarter, six months or year, you may choose to put by a percentage of this to pay for your advertising campaign. Selecting a figure which is close to the across-the-board, trade average is wise. Nevertheless, the success or failure of this budgeting method is largely dependent upon the accuracy of your forecast. Also, more advertising is likely to take place in boom times when sales are at a peak rather than during lean periods when it might be most needed.

Many concerns estimate the profits that may be generated in their next accounting period and then allocate some of this amount for their advertising during this time. Relating the appropriation to future profits is a sound approach in principle, but not always in practice. If profits are overestimated and too much money is spent on advertising, cash flow problems can result, especially for smaller ventures which are running on limited finances. It is therefore advisable to continually review sales, costs and profits, adjusting advertising expenditure as and where necessary.

Setting your short-, medium- and long-term business goals – whether to attract 5,000 enquiries, sell 1,000 units or clear out all of your remaining stock at cost prices – you will naturally wish to set a budget which is substantial enough to achieve these objectives. Naturally, it is hard to calculate the minimum sum which needs to be spent to fulfil your targets. It is tempting to spend excessively to try to ensure success with money wasted on more and more frequent advertising and for longer periods for few additional enquiries or sales.

Allocating advertising funds

Whatever your favoured approach, always budget well in advance – typically for the next twelve months – and establish a flexible, financial framework in which you can consequently plan an advertising schedule and activities for the same period. For some advertisers, the approximate amount which ought to be allocated will be readily apparent, based on a calculating method – a percentage of earlier sales, a proportion of previous profits and so on – that seems to be most relevant in the circumstances. The craftsman who works alone manufacturing handmade goods knows he can only produce so many models and that advertising in a certain publication at given times will generate enough orders for his business.

More likely though, you will be unable to decide how much or how little money should be made available for your advertising needs. It is sensible to work out the respective sums which would be budgeted if you followed each of the main methods, subsequently comparing and contrasting the resultant figures. Taking the lowest and highest amounts, you could then set minimum and maximum financial limits for your advertising activities, perhaps pencilling in various proportions between departments, products and services, types of media, times of the year and so forth. Plan initially to spend a sum which is close to your lower limit, thus keeping funds in reserve for appropriate special offers which may unexpectedly arise for advertising at short notice in one-off or seasonal supplements or for taking space left free as a result of last-minute cancellations by other advertisers.

Ask or instruct your colleagues and employees, if relevant, to keep you informed on a continuing basis of possible developments and changes which may occur both inside and outside your firm, with particular regard to your production capabilities, overheads and costs, selling prices, sales levels, profits, sales targets and expectations, the trading environment, competitors' (estimated) budgets and customers' responses to your advertising. All of these factors could influence your appropriation to varying degrees. Be prepared to review each and every one of them in successive quarters and if necessary update your minimum and maximum figures for the next year. Completing 'Allocating advertising funds: an action checklist' on page 80 is a good idea at this stage.

Costing direct mail activities

If you have concluded that direct mail is an appropriate medium in which to advertise yourself and your goods and services to existing and would-be customers in the marketplace, you should look at the costs involved with a mailing campaign. You need to try to recognize all of the potential costs, subsequently appraising those which appear to be most relevant to you. Then you can go on to establish the total expenditure that is likely to be incurred during your mailing activities, thereby calculating whether or not such an outlay is viable, or not.

Recognizing direct mail costs

Initially, you ought to aim to piece together a comprehensive picture of the prospective key costs, without making any attempt to identify those that are most significant to you, or to estimate and add up any of the actual sums that may be incurred. At this stage you should simply attempt to build a broad, overall image of what your finances may need to be spent on, before pressing ahead with these other, equally important tasks. It is sensible to make a note of would-be expenses beneath different headings, such as 'mailing lists', 'mailshots' and 'the campaign'. The time and effort tied up with your various activities should also be taken into account.

Mailing lists of customers and prospects are the foundations of a successful mailshot campaign, hopefully representing some or even all of your target audience. You will need to spend time building your own lists from in-house

ADVERTISING BUDGET: AN ASSESSMENT		Campaign:		Number:	
		Media:		Date:	
Method	Relevance	Minimum figure	Maximum figure	Target figure	Comments
Previous budget					
% past sales:					
% past profits:					
% cost price:					
% selling price:					
Rivals' budgets					
% future sales					
% future profits					
% by objectives					
Combination:					
Combination:					
Combination:					

Allocating advertising funds: an action checklist

sources, and perhaps money on adding information to them from external sources. It could be necessary to rent or buy mailing lists from list owners, possibly working through brokers who will charge for their services. More time and money may need to be spent on updating and maintaining accurate, first-class mailing lists. You might have to subscribe to the Mailing Preference Service and/or register with the Data Protection Registrar.

Mailshots need to be created, designed and produced, ready to be sent to the existing and would-be customers on those lists. Envelopes have to be chosen, whether plain manilla or highly colourful ones. They need to be rubberstamped with a logo or phrase, stamped or franked for posting and handwritten or addressed with sticky labels. The envelopes, rubber stamps and inks, postage stamps or franking machine and labels all have to be paid for. Letters have to be written to convey your sales message to customers and prospects, and paper has to be selected and purchased. Inserts may need to be added. Reply-paid cards or envelopes, product samples, catalogues, brochures, leaflets, price lists, proposal, order, membership or subscription forms, discount vouchers, money-off coupons, bingo and scratch-and-sniff cards – whatever you use has to be bought.

The campaign itself may prove to be costly. Stationers and printers need to be selected and briefed to supply the envelopes, letters and inserts that you want, and all at the right prices. Letters have to be folded and inserts packed into envelopes which are then addressed, stamped or franked, either by you or a mailing house acting on your behalf. Mailshots need to be delivered to the Royal Mail for distribution. Mailing lists, your message, the timing and other aspects of your activities have to be tested and responses recorded and assessed, by yourself or a fulfilment house working for you. It all costs money; more if you bring in outside help to assist you.

Never overlook the time and effort involved with direct mail activities, both before *and* after the campaign. You will have spent considerable time learning about the characteristics, pros and cons of direct mail and the key participants in the industry. You will have approached and taken advice from trade bodies and regulatory and advertising organizations. Money may even have been spent on joining the Direct Marketing Association (UK) Limited and on attending courses at the Institute of Direct Marketing. Your business, goods, services and objectives will have been investigated and evaluated, as will your customers, competitors and the marketplace. Codes of practice will have been studied and understood so that a lawful campaign is run. Afterwards, your activities will be reviewed and changes made for the future. Cost out your time and effort, and bear in mind that these could have been directed towards alternative, more profitable activities. You may find it helpful at this stage to fill in the first column of 'Calculating mailing costs: an action checklist', page 82.

MAILING COSTS: A BREAKDOWN		Campaign:		Number:	
		Media:		Date:	
Categories	Possible costs	Likely costs	Minimum costs	Maximum costs	Estimated costs
Mailing lists:					
Mailshots:					
The campaign:					
Title and effort:					
TOTALS:					

Calculating mailing costs: an action checklist

Investigating the costs

Following on from this broad overview, you should work through the many costs in sequence to calculate which ones are likely to be especially relevant to you, and to then contemplate the possible sums involved. Not surprisingly, the costs that will be incurred will depend upon numerous factors, not least the size of your campaign, your approach and what you can and cannot do for yourself. As a first-time mailer, your initial activities will probably be of a limited nature, possibly being sent to just a hundred or so customers who are well known to you. Obviously, this will restrict your expenditure as you can use in-house rather than externally rented or purchased lists, may need to spend less on updating them, and so on.

As a small-business owner or manager, you will inevitably be used to taking a do-it-yourself approach to most activities and will adopt a similar stance on this occasion. Again, costs will be reduced because you will choose your own envelopes, write your own letters and add existing sales literature and material to your mailshots. Likewise, you will be familiar with doing everything that needs to be done for yourself, to minimize expenditure as far as possible. Therefore you will take responsibility for putting letters and inserts into envelopes, delivering them to the local post office and receiving and responding to replies rather than handing over these tasks – and your hard-earned money – to a mailing or fulfilment house.

Mindful of your particular circumstances, sketch out those costs that you feel are most likely to apply to you and your specific campaign. Typically, this list may include the costs of composing in-house lists and adding to them from outside sources, updating them, subscribing to the Mailing Preference Service and registering with the Data Protection Registrar. It would also incorporate buying envelopes, paper, rubber stamps, inks and postage stamps, writing letters and adding existing sales literature. It could conclude with preparing mailshots, taking them to the Royal Mail and noting the replies. Clearly, this is very much a hands-on direct mail campaign. The second column of 'Calculating mailing costs: an action checklist' on page 82 can be completed at this point.

Establishing direct mail expenditure

You should be able to draw upon your own existing business knowledge and experiences to ascertain some of these costs for yourself. For example, you will inevitably have purchased stationery for your concern before and will have paid a printer to produce sales brochures, catalogues and price lists on your behalf. Assessing their costs for your direct mail activities should therefore be relatively straightforward. Similarly, it ought not to be too difficult to work out how long it will take for you and your colleagues or employees to fold letters and tuck them into the envelopes, and to cost out the overall time spent on fulfilling this task. Other, less familiar costs, such as those concerned with compiling lists, joining the MPS and registering with the Office of the Data Protection Registrar, may need to be researched.

It is sensible to approach the various trade and regulatory bodies within the direct mail industry for advice and guidance. The Direct Marketing Association (UK) Limited and the Direct Mail Accreditation and Registration Centre can provide industry-wide information and assistance. The Advertising Standards Authority Limited, the Data Protection Registrar and the Mailing Preference Service are particularly helpful on legal and associated matters. See 'Useful contacts', page 385.

By using your own expertise and seeking opinions from a variety of other organizations, many of which will put you in touch with their members for quotations, you should be in a position to sketch out low and high figures for each and every expense, and an overall, minimum and maximum sum for your proposed direct mail activities. You can then decide whether budgeting to spend such an amount is reasonable and is likely to prove worthwhile, weighing up the expense alongside the likelihood of achieving the responses you require through this medium. You should now be able to fill in the rest of 'Calculating mailing costs: an action checklist' on page 82.

Budgeting for an exhibition

If you have decided that exhibitions may be a relevant medium for your firm, you need to go on to identify and analyse all of the possible costs that can be involved with attending a show, deciding which ones are likely to be incurred by you if you proceed. Then you can move ahead to estimate your potential expenditure and conclude whether the outlay required is acceptable to you. Only when these tasks have been completed can you set about choosing exhibitions that are appropriate for your firm.

Identifying exhibition costs

At this stage, you should simply be looking to compile a full and complete list of prospective costs, without trying to calculate which will be most significant to you or assessing how much each of them might actually cost. These two difficult tasks follow on afterwards. For convenience, you can group possible expenses together under headings such as the stand, exhibits, staff and promotion. Indirect costs – especially the time and efforts associated with successful exhibiting – ought to be noted down as well.

Start off by writing out stand-associated costs: stand design; space rental; stand construction; furniture such as desks and chairs; telephone installation and usage; stationery including notepads and enquiry forms; flowers; carpets; catering equipment such as coffee-making facilities; display materials and mountings; security and safety items, such as mirrors and fire extinguishers; electricity, gas, compressed air, water and waste installation and usage; cleaning arrangements; insurance; and stand removal.

With regard to exhibits, expenses will be related to: products; product mountings; assembly, testing and packing; technical literature, including specifications; transportation and storage; installation, perhaps incorporating the use of cranes; withdrawal and return of products. Concerning staff, costs may be linked to: briefings and training courses; uniforms and badges; travel, car parking, accommodation and subsistence; usage of existing staff and additional, hired employees, such as interpreters.

Then move on to set down those costs involved with publicizing yourself, your stand and your goods and services to visitors and the outside world. Promotional expenses could be attributed to: advertising, perhaps via direct mail, show catalogues and trade journals; press releases and kits; company literature, such as brochures, catalogues and price lists; entertainment, possibly including invitations to a dinner dance; refreshments such as light snacks; gifts, incorporating pens, pencils, balloons and key fobs.

Do not forget to jot down any indirect costs that may be involved with exhibiting at a show, and which are often ill-considered. The time devoted to planning an exhibition, finding out about shows, who's who in the industry and so on ought to be thought about. Perhaps that time could have been spent to the detriment of other work; similarly, the efforts of turning ideas into reality, carrying out some activities and overseeing others might be best directed towards different, more lucrative projects. Fill in the first column of 'Estimating exhibition expenditure: an action checklist' on page 86 at this point.

Analysing the costs

Next, you have to consider all of these costs to ascertain which ones are particularly relevant to you and to mull over the likely figures involved with each of them. Of course, the expenses which will be incurred and the total monies that need to be spent are affected by many factors. In particular, much will depend upon the type of stand chosen, the approach adopted and what you can and cannot do for yourself.

Usually, you will choose between a shell scheme and free-build stand. With a shell scheme, you rent one (or more) of a series of standard, box-like units with a ceiling, walls and floor. A sign, strip-lights and spotlights, power points, furniture, carpet tiles, display mountings and other, miscellaneous items may

EXHIBITION EXPENSES: A BREAKDOWN

Campaign: Number:

Media: Date:

Categories	Possible costs	Probable costs	Minimum figure	Maximum figure	Estimated figure
The stand:					
Exhibits:					
Staff:					
Promotion:					
Indirect costs:					
Other costs:					

Estimating exhibition expenditure: an action checklist

be included within the price, or could be available for additional, set charges. You are simply responsible for personalizing the basic shell and adding individual exhibits and display materials. With a free-build stand, you rent floor space from the show organizer and are wholly responsible for designing and constructing your stand from scratch, subject to the organizer's approval.

Obviously, shell schemes are cheaper at about half the total price of designing and building your own stand. These standardized units are quick and easy to assemble and erect with workmanlike, at-hand materials. However, they are sometimes rather nondescript, may be unsuitable for large and bulky exhibits and could be sited on the edges of the exhibition, away from busy gangways. Freebuilds are more expensive, typically involving larger design fees and longer assembly and erection times with specially purchased materials being used. Nevertheless, they offer greater choice and flexibility, with the opportunity to stand out in a crowd and to incorporate unusual ideas and exhibits.

Clearly, your approach to exhibiting will be a contributory factor towards the costs incurred, and your final bill. To begin with, you may choose to adopt a low-key attitude to feel your way forward – taking a shell scheme, personalizing it with items hired from the organizer and so on. Later, with a track record behind you and more exhibitions planned, you could decide to have a free-build stand designed, furniture and display materials and mountings purchased for long-term, regular use and so forth.

Not least, the total bill will depend upon your own experiences and abilities within this field. Working through your list of would-be costs, you may feel that you possess sufficient, in-house expertise to carry out some tasks yourself such as preparing and transporting exhibits, briefing and training staff, advertising, writing press releases and so on. Other prospective exhibitors – without the expertise or unwilling to commit their time and energies to such activities – may bring in outsiders to attend to these tasks. Complete the second column of 'Estimating exhibition expenditure: an action checklist' on page 86 now.

Estimating exhibition expenditure

With a clearer idea of the direct and indirect expenses that you may possibly incur under the headings of the stand, exhibits, staff and promotions, you can then set about adding up all of the probable costs of exhibiting in an attempt to reach a total, minimum to maximum figure. Drawing on your own background knowledge, you should be able to sketch out estimates of many costs, perhaps including printing and producing technical literature, brochures, catalogues and price lists, booking hotel accommodation for your staff, advertising in trade journals, purchasing promotional gifts for giveaways and so on.

Other, more specialized areas – stand design, construction and so forth – will require further research, and representative bodies within the industry should be able to offer some guidance with regard to the likely outlay involved. In particular, the Association of Exhibition Organisers and the British Exhibition Contractors Association can advise on stand and related costs, such as the storage and installation of exhibits, advertising in show catalogues and associated entertainments. The Agricultural Show Exhibitors Association, National Exhibitors Association and the Incorporated Society of British Advertisers Limited can provide general, across-the-board assistance. Refer to 'Useful contacts', page 385.

By obtaining such a wide range of views and opinions from a number of sources, you should be able to piece together low and high estimates for each possible expense and an overall minimum and maximum figure for exhibiting at an event. Not surprisingly, there are huge differences between what can be spent depending upon your intentions. A small, private event held in a local hall or on your own premises will cost very little, if anything, in purely financial terms; a large, independently-designed stand at a major exhibition can cost thousands of pounds. It is useful to find where your own figures fall within these approximate limits.

Whatever your top and bottom figures, you must then decide whether exhibiting at a show is likely to be a worthwhile activity for your firm. Typically, your main aim in attending an exhibition will be to obtain a certain volume and value of new or additional business and clearly you need to weigh up the costs of exhibiting alongside the likelihood of achieving this aim via this medium (and indeed in comparison to other approaches, such as sales visits). Also, the total expenses have to be set alongside other, difficult-to-measure goals, such as increasing awareness in the market and finding out more about customers and rivals. Fill in the rest of 'Estimating exhibition expenditure: an action checklist' on page 86 now. This will help you clarify your thoughts.

Bringing in experts

At this stage, you ought to consider commissioning an advertising agency and think about employing other specialists, such as a market research agency, an illustrator, a photographer, a copywriter and a typesetter who may be able to help you to maximize the success of an advertising campaign. Although most small-business advertisers conduct their own activities by mixing together in-house knowledge and experience with some assistance from the various departments within each medium, it is useful to be aware of these independent experts and their roles, the services that they can provide and the ways in which they should be assessed and subsequently chosen by you, if relevant.

Commissioning an advertising agency

There are several, rather generalized types of advertising agency which can assist you with your activities. A 'full service' agency offers a broad and diverse range of different services, typically including market research, marketing, media scheduling, advertisement design and creation plus media buying. An 'à la carte', or 'creative', agency usually concentrates on pulling together winning advertisements instead of becoming involved in media planning, negotiating and purchasing. Some à la carte agencies work in tandem with a 'media independent' – another type of agency – which does not provide creative services but devotes itself to buying the best space and time available from a variety of media at the most advantageous prices. Numerous agencies – whether full service, à la carte or media independent – specialize in certain trades (financial, recruitment and so on), products and services (such as newly developed items and industrial goods) and individual media (television, posters and the like).

If you are considering the possibility of hiring an agency to help with or even take control of your advertising activities, you need initially to decide which type (if any) is likely to be most suitable for you in your specific circumstances. Having comprehensively assessed already the key strengths and weaknesses of your own venture and being aware of the support which may be offered to you by assorted departments within different media, you should be able to conclude swiftly whether you ought to have either the whole campaign run by an independent agency, part of it such as creative or space buying services or none of it at all.

Conscious of the type of agency which you wish to employ and the work that you expect to be carried out on your behalf, think about the main characteristics which you want to see in your chosen agency. You may believe that it must be reputable, with an ethical approach to business and financial stability so that it shall not handle competing accounts, will disclose conflicting interests to you, shall offer impartial advice, will maintain your confidentiality, and shall not suddenly collapse taking any of your deposited funds with it. Belonging to and/or being recognized by respected trade bodies and supplying sound references should be sufficient proof of this. Previous knowledge and experience of your type of concern, goods and services, customers, competitors and/or markets could be a requirement too, in order that its team knows how to piece together an appropriate schedule for you, is familiar with what succeeds and fails in your field and has tackled and hopefully overcome common problems before. Finding out about its years in business, key executives and personnel, former and existing clients and past and present campaigns should provide enough evidence for you.

Creativity may be an important quality to look for in an advertising agency so that advertisements which are designed by its staff convey your message in a fresh and original way, rather than simply rehashing old and oft-used ideas. Learning about the agency's creative team – their backgrounds, qualifications, earlier work, thoughts and opinions – ought to reveal the answers to you. Compatibility is another, often overlooked attribute which is worth seeking, with you, your employees, agency personnel, in-house and agency tasks all needing to dovetail and pull in the same direction if your campaign is to be a winner. Sharing common ground – perhaps similar-sized firms trading in the same region – and being able to establish quickly a warm, working relationship, swiftly understanding what each party wants and expects from the other are all favourable signs for the future.

You have to be sure that the agency offers you value for money and does not exploit your inexperience in certain areas by overcharging you for its services. It is wise to familiarize yourself with the ways in which agencies are paid, just before going on to shortlist them and meet their employees. Not surprisingly, no hard and fast rules exist. Some agencies receive commission at around 15 per cent from the media in which advertisements are placed, and are satisfied with that sum. Effectively, you are receiving the agency's expertise free of charge, as that commission would not be deducted from your total bill even if you had dealt direct with the titles or stations. Others require an additional amount for their services if this revenue does not cover their workload, perhaps when commissions are below 15 per cent as they are from various titles and stations. Numerous agencies ask for a flat annual fee and/or submit invoices for their work, based on hourly or daily rates. Make certain that you are aware of an agency's policy and are happy that it is fair to you before asking them to act.

Draw up a shortlist of potentially suitable agencies by contacting the Institute of Practitioners in Advertising and the Association of Media Independents Limited. These leading trade organizations will supply you with lists of their trustworthy and reputable members as well as providing other, miscellaneous information and advice about making the right choice of agency for you. Reading through the brief notes about each individual agency, pick out those which appear to have the qualities that suggest they may fulfil your criteria – perhaps small but growing concerns which are near to you and so on. Write to or telephone each one in turn, arranging to meet an accounts executive – the person who is responsible for dealing with clients and acting as an intermediary between them and the agency – to discuss a possible commission. Hopefully, you will have at least one meeting with accounts executives, or directors in smaller businesses, of perhaps three to six agencies from which you will eventually make your final choice.

At a first meeting with an accounts executive – which should ideally be on your premises – you ought to tell him or her all about yourself so that ideas can be formulated accurately and valid suggestions subsequently made about a proposed advertising schedule and/or prospective advertisements for you. Discuss your business and hand over accompanying notes and documentary data such as sales and financial records concerning your business, its products and services, your objectives and advertising appropriation. Be as open and detailed as possible so that the agency has the raw materials needed from which to develop quality plans and proposals on your behalf. Talk – and back up your comments with supplementary notes and supporting evidence such as research findings – about your customers, competitors and the marketplace.

To convey a fuller and more precise impression of yourself, show the accounts executive around your property and/or various outlets so that he or she can see how it is organized and run, look at its location and facilities, sit in on discussions and meetings (perhaps about goals and budgets), watch different departments operating and liaising with each other and chat to your colleagues and employees, especially to those who will be involved with advertising in some capacity. Encourage the accounts executive to examine and use your products and to see services being performed. Allow the executive to meet and talk to your customers, perhaps by standing behind a counter with an experienced member of staff or by spending time on the road with sales representatives or agents. Explain where your competitors are based (if relevant), so that the executive has the opportunity to visit and assess them, which may be of some assistance when the agency puts together advertising proposals for your approval.

Naturally, you also wish to discover more about the advertising agency in order that you can decide whether it possesses the key characteristics which you are seeking and if its staff are able to carry out the work that you want them to do for you. During your meeting, ask questions such as: How long have you been trading for? When did you join your representative body? Do you act on behalf of any of my competitors? Will you have conflicting interests by working for me? Are you recognized by other trade organizations? How is your agency structured? Who are your directors? What are their backgrounds, qualifications and areas of expertise? How many people work for the agency? What are their career histories? What exactly do each of them do? Who do you represent, and who have you represented, particularly in my field? What campaigns are you, and have you been, working upon? Do you have any examples of your recent and present work with you? May I have the names and addresses of the companies which you are currently acting for? What are your terms and conditions of work? The answers to these queries – drawn subtly into an amiable conversation – will enable you to start taking the agencies in order of preference.

Work through all of the responsibilities and tasks which you hope to hand over to your selected agency – space planning and/or buying, advertisement creation and design and so on – making certain that both parties are wholly familiar with what the other side seeks and needs from them, to avoid overlapping activities, confusion and possible ill-feeling later on. Providing written confirmation of verbal requests and expectations, offering assistance without interference, supplying up-to-date information on any relevant developments, changes and problems, and delivering work and paying bills on time are likely to be mutually agreed requirements for working together well. Ask the executives of your favoured agencies if they would like to prepare outline proposals for presentation and analysis at a second meeting and whether you may obtain references from your choice of its past and present clients. The remaining executives – who will probably concur with you in your decision that the two parties are ill-matched – need to be thanked and rejected graciously.

Follow up meetings with the account executives or directors of your first and second choice agencies ought to be conducted at their offices so that you can further assess them in their own working environment. Ask to be shown around the property, paying a visit to the market research, marketing, media planning, media buying and creative departments in turn (although these may be amalgamated or even merged into one within smaller agencies). Look at the overall appearance of the premises and equipment, ranging from old and tatty to new and in mint condition. Listen to the comings and goings; hopefully the agency is constantly busy, with telephones ringing and an air of controlled chaos. Learn from the atmosphere, whether cold and frosty or friendly and co-operative. Seeing the agency at work can help you to decide how reputable, financially stable, compatible and so on it really is.

Talk to the agency's staff, especially the media planner and buyer, copywriters and artists who are mainly responsible for preparing your provisional advertising schedule and proposed advertisements. Still wishing to know more about them, you ought to raise queries such as: What do you do? What work and advertising experience do you have? What are you working upon at the present time? How is that progressing? Why did you choose to draft this schedule? How did you think of these advertising ideas? What have you previously worked on in my particular field? How successful were those campaigns? What are the do's and don'ts of advertising in my given territory? What suggestions do you have for my advertising activities? The replies to these questions – which will need to be timed and phrased carefully – should give you the necessary insights into the team's characters and qualities.

Your visit should then conclude with a brief presentation by the agency's team, setting out their thoughts about and proposals for your potential schedule and advertisements. Typically, they would discuss and explain their views on the media they believe should be used; the sizes, positions, approaches, layouts and contents of your advertisements; the timing, frequency and duration of your activities; as well as the total costs which would be incurred. Contemplate and respond to their comments, trying to appraise whether their plans are realistic, original and viable, showing an appreciation and understanding of your business situation, wants and needs and financial circumstances. Take away a written copy of their ideas for later, quiet consideration and assessment.

Having attended various meetings and studied your first and reserve choice agencies' proposals at length, you now should be able to settle on which one is most reputable, experienced, creative, compatible, cost-effective and so on. Confirm your decision by taking up references for your probable choice, telephoning rather than writing to the referee to increase the likelihood of more realistic, off-the-record opinions being made. These questions should be posed: Has the agency always acted in a reputable and ethical manner? – if 'No', what happened? How relevant have its suggested schedules been to your particular situation? How successful have its advertisements been for you? How well do you get along with its staff on a personal level? Have you had value for money from the agency? Have you experienced any problems with the agency or its team? – if 'Yes', what happened? Will you use the agency again? In the light of these answers, you ought to be in a position to commission the best agency for you, whilst politely declining the services of the others.

Employing other specialists

If you prefer not to work with an advertising agency, you may instead refer to numerous other experts either now or at an appropriate later date to assist in some capacity with your campaign. A market research company could seek out additional data concerning your customers, competitors and marketplace which you were unable to uncover. An illustrator might design attractive artwork, a photographer could produce eye-catching photographs, a copywriter may draft interesting text, and a typesetter could provide distinctive typefaces to choose from if they have not already been specified by the illustrator (as sometimes happens). All of these people can help to make your advertisements more effective.

Consider which of these specialists (if any) may be of value and of active assistance to you. Gaps in your knowledge of the market could prove to be damaging, if not fatal, to the quality of your forthcoming schedule and advertisements. For example, being unaware of your customers' readership habits and their perceptions of your goods might lead to inadequately detailed advertisements in unread publications. You may not have the in-house facilities to create appealing advertisements and could suspect that staff working for the innumerable titles in which you might advertise do not possess the flair or inclination to produce fresh and distinctive ones on your behalf. Even if you can handle all of your advertising activities yourself, it is still wise to liaise with experts so that you can derive a broader and more complete understanding of the ways in which advertising works.

Obtain the names, addresses and brief details of regional market research agencies from their leading trade organizations – the Association of Market Survey Organisations Limited and the Market Research Society. Build up a localized list of other specialists by contacting the Association of Illustrators, the British Institute of Professional Photography, the British Printing Industries Federation and the Society of Typographic Designers. See 'Useful contacts', page 385 for addresses and telephone numbers. More data and personal recommendations should be forthcoming from well-informed business colleagues and associates which ought to enable you to shortlist half a dozen experts who are worth talking to.

Your discussions with candidates – on the telephone and at face-to-face meetings at each other's offices – should unfold along similar lines to your earlier negotiations with advertising agencies. You will sketch out the key qualities that you wish to recognize in them, more often than not expecting respectability, a working knowledge of your field, a lively imagination, an understanding of your individual traits and problems plus fair and reasonable charges. Then, you will want to get to know each of them as well as you possibly can, seeing how far they match your set criteria by asking gently probing questions, looking around their premises, talking to their employees, studying their work and so on.

At the same time, these experts – whether market researchers, illustrators, photographers, copywriters or typesetters – may (or certainly ought to) wish to know more about you in addition to the various tasks that you want them to carry out on your behalf. Accordingly, you will need to chat, and could be questioned, about your firm, goods, short-, medium- and long-term targets and budget, as well as your customers, main rivals and markets, as relevant to the particular specialists. Obviously, a copywriter may need to possess an in-depth, working knowledge of all of these aspects if he or she is to produce the right approach and copy for your advertisements, whereas a typesetter could simply seek to find out how you wish your venture to be perceived in the marketplace so that appropriate typefaces can be recommended. Walk them around your property or units, supplying products for examination, introducing customers and handing over market details where necessary.

Clarify and discuss the work that you intend to allocate to them, possibly to ascertain what your present customers really think of your services, to photograph you and your management team or to set out advertisements in a variety of ways so that you can finalize a house style. Explain precisely what you are looking for from them, by when and for how much money. Check out what they want from you – no amateur interference, regularly updated data and so forth.

Go through their ideas and suggestions to see which are likely to be most fitting in your situation. Ask for the names, addresses and telephone numbers of their former and current clients, requesting permission to approach two or three for references. Contact these referees to substantiate your thoughts, consequently commissioning the most suitable expert to work alongside you, and rejecting the others in a polite and amicable manner.

Summary

- Preparations for a prospective advertising campaign should involve an analysis of the would-be advertiser's business, market and budgetary considerations. These preparations enable preliminary assessments to be made about potentially suitable media and provide information to be used during any subsequent advertising activities.

- Analysing the business should comprise four, key steps – an overall analysis of all areas, a list of its strengths, a list of its weaknesses, and an assessment of possible advertising media. Particular attention should be paid to its products and services and its short-, medium- and long-term objectives.

- Evaluating the market should involve obtaining a broad understanding of customers, appraising competitors' strengths, weaknesses and advertising activities, and assessing the present marketplace and the internal and external influences upon it. Additional, local, regional and national research may be needed to accumulate all necessary information.

- Establishing an advertising budget should consist of considering past, present and future budgets, sales and various techniques before allocating minimum and maximum figures based on these considerations.

- Direct mail costs should be estimated under the headings of 'mailing lists', 'mailshots' and 'the campaign'. Again, minimum and maximum sums should be allocated to these activities.

- Exhibition expenses should be categorized in terms of 'stand', 'exhibits', 'staff', 'promotion'. Minimum and maximum figures should be identified for these activities.

- Advertising agencies and other specialists such as market research agencies may need to be brought in if prospective advertisers fail to complete the all-important groundwork and/or if they are wholly inexperienced in this field.

Notes

Notes

4 Planning your advertising activities

YOU ARE NOW READY to start planning your press, radio, direct mail and exhibition activities. Typically, you will start by using press advertising, as most small business advertisers do, subsequently including radio advertising and direct mailing into your campaign. Exhibitions will probably feature as well, with all four media eventually playing their part in a successful campaign.

Using press advertising

To launch press advertising activities, you need to list the publications which you might use, subsequently comparing your audience, thinking about timing, and checking out costs prior to drafting them into a schedule. It is now that all of your extensive and detailed preparatory work – analysing yourself, getting to know the market and establishing a budget – will prove invaluable to you. Always refer back to any previous notes which you have made, whilst piecing together your preliminary schedule.

Listing publications

Begin by setting down the different types of publication, from national daily newspapers through business magazines to house journals, which may conceivably be appropriate advertising media in your particular situation. Reflect again upon your own venture, its goods and services and your goals to convince yourself that these publications really seem to be relevant to you. Similarly, think about your customers, competitors and the marketplace for the same reason. Contemplate your advertising appropriation as well, since some publications may simply be too expensive for your financial circumstances.

Beneath the varied headings of national dailies, national Sundays, regional daily newspapers and the like, you then have to discover and write out all of the many titles which exist within each category. To draw up a full and comprehensive list, refer to *British Rate and Data* – or BRAD as it is more commonly known – which is a 600-plus-page directory that provides extensive details of the widest possible range of newspapers, consumer and business publications, as well as broadcast, electronic and outdoor media, within the United Kingdom. Published each month by Maclean Hunter Limited, a typical entry would include information about publication and copy dates, advertising rates, mechanical data, circulation and key executives. See 'Useful contacts', page 385 for the address and telephone number.

Additional data about these titles and other, miscellaneous publications – directories, yearbooks, house journals and the like – may be derived from your friends, colleagues and/or advertising contacts. Contact press representative bodies such as the Directory Publishers Association, Newspaper Publishers Association and Periodical Publishers Association, plus other press organizations including the Audit Bureau of Circulation Limited, Joint Industry Committee for National Readership Surveys, and Verified Free Distribution Limited – all will supply useful background material to you.

Moving ahead, you should contact the advertisement director or manager of each title requesting a media pack, rate card and a copy of the most recent issue if you have not seen it. A media pack, or marketing or media guide as it may be called, is a brochure or booklet which is published by many leading newspapers and magazines, setting out detailed information about the publication (its price, regular columns, features, supplements and so on), its circulation (including the total number, sexes, ages, social grades, occupations, activities and interests of the population) and its readership (incorporating the total number, sexes, ages, plus readership habits and opinions of the title). Look at Appendix A: 'Media pack', page 261, for an example.

A rate card – sometimes incorporated within a media pack – is a double-sided sheet or pamphlet which is available from all reputable publications. It lists data such as display, classified and special position advertising rates, circulation and readership figures, perhaps including demographic and/or regional breakdowns, copy deadlines, on-sale dates, the names, telephone extension numbers of key personnel, technical and mechanical information and the conditions of acceptance of advertisements. See Appendix B: 'Rate cards', page 279, for examples from various publications.

Possessing a copy of the latest edition of the title will enable you to study and assess its editorial and advertising matter. It may be sensible to obtain several issues, possibly over a number of months, to appreciate fully its individual style and approach and to see how it changes during this period of time. Such a hands-on knowledge of each publication when linked with the information available in the media packs and the rate cards will allow you to go on to analyse fully the titles you want to use. It will also be particularly helpful to you when you begin to sketch out prospective advertisements.

Comparing audiences

In turn, you must check through the assorted media guides and rate cards, noting the circulation and readership figures and breakdowns of every publication on your list. Hopefully, this in-depth information will have been confirmed by the Audit Bureau of Circulation Limited, Verified Free Distribution Limited or Bulk Verified Services so that it can be and relied upon. Next to each individual set of facts, write out the business and/or personal characteristics of your customers. These details ought to be available from your previous analysis. Having side-by-side data in front of you about your customers and the respective audiences will enable you to compare and contrast them in a thorough manner.

Study the profile of each newspaper's, magazine's and miscellaneous publication's audience alongside your own, working through all of the twin subheadings to assess how closely the overall make-up of one matches or clashes with the other. Clearly, you are looking to retain titles on your list which are purchased and read by those people who match your customer profile whilst deleting the rest. Also evaluate how far each publication penetrates into your audience, calculating the number and percentage of your customers that it will reach. Naturally, you are seeking to advertise only in those titles which are perused by the highest possible proportion of your target market, and will exclude the remaining ones from your plans.

It is important that you appraise individual publications strictly on the grounds of profile and penetration rather than on high or low circulation and readership figures alone, as so many first-time advertisers do. No matter how many copies of a title are sold or how many times they are seen, they have to be read by the right type and number of customers if your advertising activities are to be successful. It is a waste of your time, money and efforts to direct a message towards people whose response is to ignore it. Having completed profile and penetration assessments and reduced your original lengthy list of publications, you should then be able to move ahead to look at the timing of your press advertising campaign. Fill in 'Comparing your audience: an action checklist' on page 101 at this stage.

Thinking about timing

You must consider when you should advertise, perhaps before and/or during a particular week, month or quarter. Obviously, your timing depends mainly upon your business, products and services and objectives. Referring back to your earlier notes will help you to make the right choice. Regularly introducing new lines, holding stock clearance sales, preparing to launch an updated product, selling seasonal goods and wishing to adjust sales peaks and troughs may indicate certain times to you. Timing will also be influenced strongly by your customers, competitors and the marketplace. Looking through those previous

PRESS AUDIENCE ANALYSIS FORM	Campaign:	Number:
	Media:	Date:

Press audience:	Target audience:
Characteristics	Characteristics
Purchasing habits	Purchasing habits
Reading habits	Reading habits
Opinions	Opinions
Other	Other
Other	Other
Other	Other
Other	Other

Comparing your audience: an action checklist

records will provide you with some answers. Dealing with customers who spend most of their money at the end of a month, knowing that large and experienced national rivals advertise at given times, and being aware of imminent legislation which might affect demand all point towards specific periods which are fitting in your circumstances.

It is sensible to think about how often you ought to advertise, possibly daily, weekly or fortnightly. The frequency of your advertising should be affected by your specific situation – firm, goods, goals and so on – as summarized in those accumulated notes. New ideas and developments whether in your concern, products or services usually indicate that rapid promotion is needed if they are to be absorbed and accepted by customers who are generally slow to become accustomed to innovations of any kind. Oft-purchased goods normally require more repetitive advertising than slower-selling products so that customers are reminded continually of them and their benefits just before or when the buying decision is being made. Seasonal and fashionable goods which are available or popular for only a short time before entering a sudden and sharp decline have to be promoted vigorously if they are to make and sustain a sales impact. Ever-changing customers and market conditions suggest the need for increased advertising if recognition and understanding of your business and its products are to be maintained.

You have to contemplate for how long you should advertise. The duration of the advertising activities again ought to be decided by your individual circumstances as outlined in your thorough records. You may feel that short, quick-fire bursts of advertising are appropriate for you, perhaps to coincide with your brief clearance sales, the availability of a seasonal or fashionable range of goods and services, or the necessity to boost sales for a limited period of time. Alternatively, you could think that long-term, steady advertising is more relevant, possibly if you are always adding to your stock on an ongoing basis, and are seeking and are happy with constant turnover throughout the year.

It is then necessary to check the copy deadlines of the various titles, as set out in the rate cards in front of you. Bearing in mind how far in advance you must submit material to some publications, especially glossy magazines and directories, you may discover that you have insufficient time in which to prepare your advertisements and could have to delete numerous titles from your steadily shortening list. Get in touch with the advertisement departments of the publications left to make certain that you will be able to advertise when, as often and for as long as you want to. Many newspapers, magazines and miscellaneous publications have some advertising space booked on a semi-permanent basis, with others taken promptly, especially at the most popular times. You may find it difficult to pick and choose titles and spaces.

Checking out costs

You must consider the sizes of your press advertisements, making sure that you book advertising spaces which are big enough to carry your message and to be seen by your customers, whilst still incurring acceptable costs. Reviewing your various notes should provide some clear pointers for you. Running a certain type of business may indicate that a particular size is most appropriate in the situation – you could believe that a large advertisement is required to convey the correct image of your prestigious business. Perhaps you wish your goods to be illustrated to highlight their key features or want to explain their many uses, all of which needs substantial room if the advertisements are to be effective. Your customers' readership habits should reveal which sizes are seen and not seen, as relevant. Your competitors' advertisements – small or large – could influence you as well, especially as you are trying to keep pace with or ahead of them in the marketplace.

It is wise to think about the positions of your advertisements, seeking to maximize their chances of being spotted and read by customers, whilst minimizing their prices. Those detailed records ought to be of further assistance to you. Owning a garden centre may suggest that advertisements on or near to a regular horticultural page would be successful, a nightclub could be promoted in a 'What's On' supplement and so on. Similarly, your goods may be best advertised in or close to various sections – a fashion column, business news, television and radio pages, as examples. Your goals should provide some ideas too, with new staff being sought via advertisements in special recruitment features. Your findings concerning the readership habits of your customers may be decisive factors in your choice of positions. Typically, they would indicate that advertisements towards the front, rather than the back of a publication, alone instead of alongside other advertisements and at the top in preference to the bottom, to the right instead of to the left, and on the outside rather than on the inside of a page are seen and studied most often. The advertising positions selected by your competitors ought to be taken into account as well.

You then have to work out, either from the rate cards or by contacting the various advertisement departments, the respective costs of placing these advertisements within the remaining titles on your list. A precise 'value for money' comparison between each publication is difficult as their advertising rates will all differ according to circulation and readership figures, advertisement sizes and positions as well as discounts that are available for repeated advertising and at quiet times of the year. Nevertheless, making comparisons, rough and ready though they may be, is worthwhile so that those titles which seem to reach the correct type and number of customers at the best prices are kept and perhaps ranked in order of preference and those that appear to be less cost-effective are eliminated from your thoughts.

The traditional method of comparing prices – which can equally well be applied to different types of publications and advertisements – is to calculate the cost of reaching every thousand people within each title's circulation. Simply take the price of the advertisement (unit), dividing it by one-thousandth of the circulation to discover the 'cost per thousand'. As an example, one publication charges £3 per single column centimetre and has a 60,000 circulation. Its cost per thousand – £3 divided by 60 (60,000 divided by 1,000) – is 5 pence. Another title sells advertising space at £5 per single column centimetre and is circulated to 90,000 people. Its cost per thousand – £5 divided by 90 (90,000 divided by 1,000) – is 5.5 pence. Of course, the sensible advertiser recalls that high or low circulation, and therefore comparisons between publications solely on this basis, is less relevant than a title's readership and its profile in relation to and penetration into the target audience. Increasingly valid assessments may then be made by appraising the cost of reaching every thousand readers *and* targeted customers.

Drafting your press schedule

Having composed a list of potentially suitable titles, compared their audiences with your own, thought about the timing of your advertising activities and checked out the costs involved, you are now ready and able to pull together all of your knowledge and information and draft a provisional schedule for your press advertising activities. This should consist of the names of the newspapers, magazines and miscellaneous publications which you plan to use with their circulation, readership, profile and penetration figures and copy deadlines. Also include the number of advertisements within each title plus their sizes, positions, costs and insertion dates. Spell out the duration of your proposed press campaign and the total estimated expenses which will be incurred.

Realistically, your first attempt at sketching out a schedule is unlikely to tally with your appropriation for press advertising, more often than not substantially exceeding it. You should consider revising it by reducing or increasing the range of titles in which you might advertise, looking back over the publications that you have included to see if your audience will be contacted fully and whether certain sections might be covered excessively or inadequately. Consider cutting out those titles with profiles which do not match as well nor penetrate as far as others, in addition to those which largely address the same, identical people. Similarly, it would be wise to study the number of advertisements which you intend to place, making sure that all of your customers see them enough times for your message to be absorbed, but not so often that they become bored and ignore it. You may choose to advertise on alternate days rather than every day to save money and decide to vary the layout and copy of advertisements to retain interest.

Contemplate taking smaller or larger advertisements, possibly in different positions within the newspapers, magazines and/or miscellaneous publications. You may be able to reduce the size and cost of your advertisements without detracting from the overall message or you could relocate them on to other, less expensive pages whilst still being seen by the same, basic audience. It is sensible to reflect upon the duration of your planned press campaign too, shortening or lengthening it, as relevant. Be wary of pumping money into more advertising once you have achieved your goals. Going back over the preliminary schedule and its blend of key ingredients is a worthy and valid exercise. You will gain an increased awareness of the advertising mix and will – after several or even innumerable revisions – be able to match it to your appropriation. Filling in the 'Media schedule' form on page 106 may then be beneficial.

Including radio advertising

Having completed the groundwork and established an appropriate budget for your advertising activities, you can begin to approach radio stations, peruse rate cards, assess audiences and calculate costs before preparing your schedule for your radio advertising campaign. It is at this point that all of your careful and occasionally tedious preparatory work really begins to pay dividends, with those copious notes helping you to make the correct choices about various aspects of your approaching campaign.

Approaching radio stations

Initially, it is important to obtain a full and complete list of commercial radio stations in the United Kingdom. It is advisable to obtain this information by referring again to *British Rate and Data* which provides data about radio stations including broadcasting frequencies, addresses, telephone numbers and contact names, audience figures, advertising rates and trading terms and conditions. Check it out in your local library rather than buying it as a one-off purchase or by annual subscription, both of which are costly.

It should be a relatively straightforward task to reduce this comprehensive list to a shortlist, simply by referring to your back-up notes, as and where necessary. If you own a small business seeking to sell to nearby customers, you need to make a note of the handful of stations that broadcast in your area. Similarly, should you be aiming to expand distribution and sales into surrounding areas or across a region or the whole country, you should write down the details of those radio stations that transmit over the relevant areas. When you have worked through each radio station on the original lengthy list, you may find that you are left with perhaps three to six stations which are worth contacting.

You can then write to or telephone one station after another, asking them

MEDIA SCHEDULE	Campaign:		Number:	
	Media:		Date:	
Medium	Week beginning			

Media schedule form

to forward information to you, as a prospective advertiser. At this stage, avoid arranging to meet any sales executives, as is often suggested, as you really need to analyse the radio stations and what they can do for you as an advertising medium, prior to discussing your advertising, negotiating terms and ordering your first package of advertisements. If you are thinking of using several stations and subsequently find it easier to book all your advertising through one central source, you may prefer to approach the relevant sales house(s), whether Independent Radio Sales, Media Sales and Marketing, the Radio Sales Company or whoever. *British Rate and Data* gives guidance on which sales houses act for the various stations. Refer to 'Useful contacts', page 385.

Perusing rate cards

Each radio station and/or sales house approached should send a rate card (or cards) to you, on request. Within these glossy pamphlets, you will discover key facts about its transmission area, probably with a map showing how far afield the station can be heard and the population in that region, perhaps broken down demographically by sex, age and social grade. Alongside this, there should be details about the total audience reached, divided up demographically into sexes, ages and social grades, and in their thousands and percentage terms too. Average, half-hourly audience figures may also be given, highlighting how these rise and fall through the day and week. Hopefully, these data will have been audited independently.

Advertising rates will be set out per 30-second spots – and for other 10-, 20-, 40-, 50-, 60-second spots – at different times of the day. Various segments will be identified – perhaps 6 a.m. to noon, noon to 6 p.m., 6 p.m. to midnight and midnight to 6 a.m. – with rates set according to listening figures during those times. Details of surcharges and discounts offered will be explained, albeit under a variety of names. Not surprisingly, surcharges will apply at peak listening times earlier in the day and later in the week, whereas discounts are applicable at quieter times towards the end of the day and at the beginning of the week. Surcharges or 'fixing charges' as they are also popularly known, are added if you wish your advertisements to be transmitted during specific periods or in special positions, perhaps between 9 a.m. and 11 a.m. or after news breaks instead of being run out evenly across the station's schedule.

Discounts crop up in many guises on the rate card. 'Volume', 'contract' or 'expenditure' discounts are extremely commonplace and are made available if you guarantee to spend a certain sum with the station over a given period. Advertisements will be re-invoiced at the higher rate at the end of that time if you fail to spend the agreed amount. 'Advance booking' discounts, or 'incentives', may apply to orders placed perhaps a month or so ahead of transmission. 'Combination' discounts exist if your advertisements are broadcast over two transmission areas, which happens when a radio station has split frequencies, broadcasting over AM and FM wavebands. 'First time' or 'test market', discounts could be on offer too, for advertisers using this medium on a trial basis.

The basic terms and conditions involved with buying a package of advertisements will be set out in the rate card. In particular, airtime is generally booked according to the availability level in force at the time the booking is taken. Obviously, only a limited amount of advertising airtime is available and is usually offered on a first-come, first-served basis. If you book late, you will not only pay a higher rate, but will find the best spots have already been allocated elsewhere. All new customers will be expected to pay for their advertising in advance, perhaps seven days or more ahead of transmission. Advertisements may be cancelled without charge if written notice is received by the station at least twenty-eight days prior to being broadcast. A sliding scale of charges will apply thereafter – perhaps 10 per cent of the bill for fourteen working days written notice, 20 per cent for seven working days and 40 per cent for three working days.

Brief details may also be provided about the production of advertisements, which are invariably put together by the radio station on behalf of its advertisers, especially small businesses which simply do not possess the in-house resources and expertise required to produce quality advertisements themselves. The cost of a basic commercial consisting of one voice with one piece of music or a sound effect will be stated. Data about additional voices, music, sound effects and copies of the advertisements made available to you on cassette will be noted as well.

Other miscellaneous information will be incorporated within the rate card. Facts and figures may be supplied about the station's history, programme schedules and presenters, music and associated services, and overall aims. The advantages of radio advertising could be promoted heavily along with details of major advertisers who have used the radio station, and their opinions of it. See the rate card for what it is – sales literature containing a mix of data and sales hype which is exaggerated as far as possible to make you want to spend money with that particular station. You need to recognize this, and be able to sort out the relevant details – audience figures, advertising rates, terms and conditions, production facilities – from the less important sales blurb. Peruse the rate cards on pages 109 to 116 to distinguish the key details from the sales hype, which will help you later on when you have to do it. Then take a look at 'Perusing rate cards: an action checklist' on page 117.

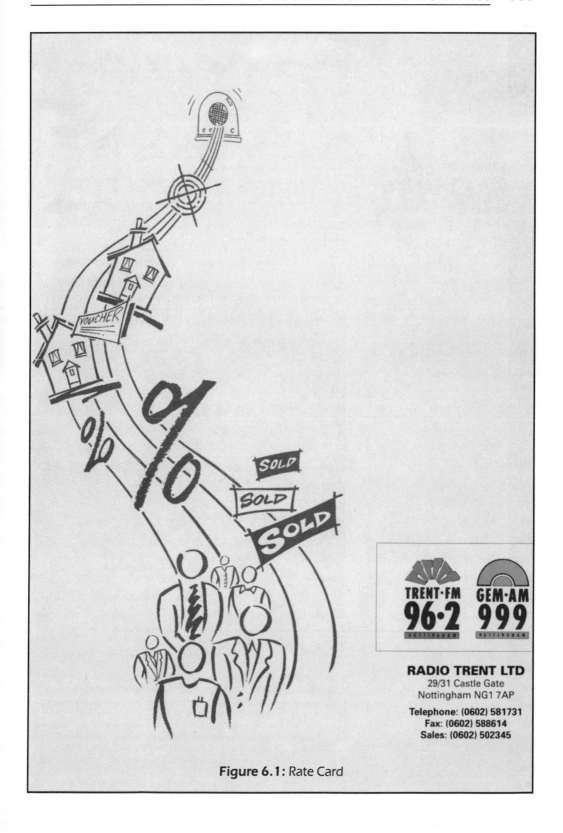

Figure 6.1: Rate Card

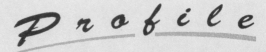

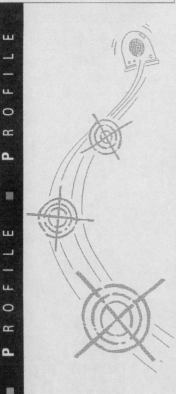

Radio Trent began broadcasting from its historic Georgian building in the heart of Nottingham in July 1975 and quickly established itself as a radio station in tune with the City and County. In October 1988 it became one of the first radio stations in Britain to create two separate twenty four hour a day programme outputs with TRENT-FM and GEM-AM.

The station has won many awards including the coveted Sony Award for Programming and twice, the equally prestigious award for Locally Made commercials. The station has always been at the forefront of development in the radio industry. Innovative programming and technical developments have contributed to Radio Trent's success and high reputation amongst professional broadcasters and listeners alike.

Trent runs the industry's only full-time Training School. The Radio Training Unit trains broadcasters, engineers and journalists. The school is also becoming increasingly involved in business courses for the public and private sector. Recent clients have included Texaco, British Telecom, Boots, Local Authorities and the DSS.

Radio Trent's programming is designed to appeal to a wide cross section of listeners throughout the diverse and dynamic transmission area stretching from Mansfield and the mining communities of North Nottinghamshire to the rich

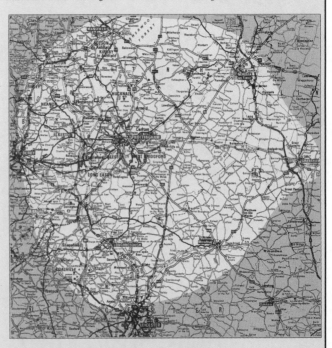

agricultural areas of Grantham and the Vale of Belvoir, from historic Newark on Trent in the East to the Erewash Valley in the West. It is an area which includes a wide range of industries, many of which have common household names, including Boots, Raleigh, Pedigree Pet Foods, Plessey, Wrangler and Speedo.

The programming reflects this buoyant and confident area with a wide range of music, comprehensive news and sports coverage, and special programmes focussing on business, the arts and fashion. TRENT-FM and GEM-AM with their individual sound and style complement each other perfectly, winning an ever increasing audience.

Figures represent £'s Sterling

SEGMENTS		60 SEC	50 SEC	40 SEC	30 SEC	20 SEC	10 SEC
P1	0600-0900 MON-FRI 0900-1200 SAT-SUN	202	185	146	112	90	56
P2	0900-1200 MON-FRI 0600-0900 SAT-SUN	171	157	124	95	76	48
P3	1200-1500 MON-SUN	97	89	70	54	43	27
P4	1500-1800 MON-SUN	104	96	75	58	46	29
P5	1800-2400 MON-SUN	41	38	30	23	18	12

DAYTIME PACKAGE MON-SUN 0600-1800						
SPOT LENGTH	60 SEC	50 SEC	40 SEC	30 SEC	20 SEC	10 SEC
COST	144	132	104	80	64	40

TOTAL AUDIENCE PACKAGE MON-SUN 0000-2400hrs						
SPOT LENGTH	60 SEC	50 SEC	40 SEC	30 SEC	20 SEC	10 SEC
COST	106	97	77	59	47	30

NIGHT TIME PACKAGE 35 SPOTS MON-SUN 2400-0600hrs						
SPOT LENGTH	60 SEC	50 SEC	40 SEC	30 SEC	20 SEC	10 SEC
COST	270	248	195	150	120	75

RATINGS PACKAGE COST £1090				
	ADULTS	MEN	H/WIVES	15-34 ADULTS
UNIVERSE (000)	1090	531	525	411
TOTAL HOURS	6897	3837	3040	2232

AMOUNT OF EXPENDITURE REQUIRED	DISCOUNT
£10,000+	10%
£15,000+	15%
£20,000+	20%
£30,000+	25%
£40,000+	30%

LOCAL ADVERTISING RATES
Are only available to companies whose businesses are predominantly confined to the Trent-FM and GEM-AM broadcast area.

ACCOUNTS
Accounts shall normally be paid not later than seven clear working days before scheduled broadcast date unless by prior agreement. When an agreement has been reached, accounts must be paid within 28 days of the date of invoice. The existence of a query on an individual item on an account will not affect the due date of payment of the balance.

CASH WITH ORDER DISCOUNT
A discount of 5% will be made available for payments at the same time as an order is placed. This discount only applies to air-time orders placed by account customers and is not a pre-payment discount.

PRODUCTION AND RECORDING FACILITIES
A fully equipped studio and an experienced creative team are available to produce commercials tailored to specific needs. Prices on request.

FIXED SPOTS
Subject to availability, advertisers may fix their basic rate spots at a surcharge of 10%.

CANCELLATION PERIOD
Air time is cancellable by either party provided that notice is received 28 days prior to the scheduled broadcast date. In the event of a cancellation, the advertiser will be charged at the appropriate rate to the number of commercials broadcast or scheduled to be broadcast within that period.

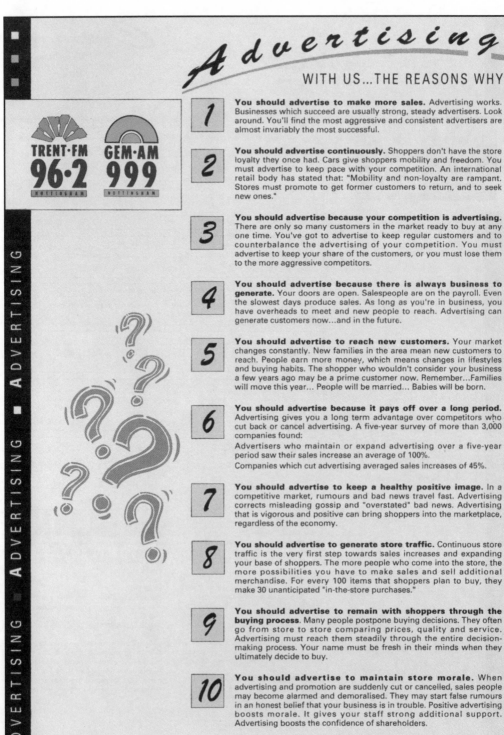

Advertising

WITH US...THE REASONS WHY

1 **You should advertise to make more sales.** Advertising works. Businesses which succeed are usually strong, steady advertisers. Look around. You'll find the most aggressive and consistent advertisers are almost invariably the most successful.

2 **You should advertise continuously.** Shoppers don't have the store loyalty they once had. Cars give shoppers mobility and freedom. You must advertise to keep pace with your competition. An international retail body has stated that: "Mobility and non-loyalty are rampant. Stores must promote to get former customers to return, and to seek new ones."

3 **You should advertise because your competition is advertising.** There are only so many customers in the market ready to buy at any one time. You've got to advertise to keep regular customers and to counterbalance the advertising of your competition. You must advertise to keep your share of the customers, or you must lose them to the more aggressive competitors.

4 **You should advertise because there is always business to generate.** Your doors are open. Salespeople are on the payroll. Even the slowest days produce sales. As long as you're in business, you have overheads to meet and new people to reach. Advertising can generate customers now...and in the future.

5 **You should advertise to reach new customers.** Your market changes constantly. New families in the area mean new customers to reach. People earn more money, which means changes in lifestyles and buying habits. The shopper who wouldn't consider your business a few years ago may be a prime customer now. Remember...Families will move this year... People will be married... Babies will be born.

6 **You should advertise because it pays off over a long period.** Advertising gives you a long term advantage over competitors who cut back or cancel advertising. A five-year survey of more than 3,000 companies found:
Advertisers who maintain or expand advertising over a five-year period saw their sales increase an average of 100%.
Companies which cut advertising averaged sales increases of 45%.

7 **You should advertise to keep a healthy positive image.** In a competitive market, rumours and bad news travel fast. Advertising corrects misleading gossip and "overstated" bad news. Advertising that is vigorous and positive can bring shoppers into the marketplace, regardless of the economy.

8 **You should advertise to generate store traffic.** Continuous store traffic is the very first step towards sales increases and expanding your base of shoppers. The more people who come into the store, the more possibilities you have to make sales and sell additional merchandise. For every 100 items that shoppers plan to buy, they make 30 unanticipated "in-the-store purchases."

9 **You should advertise to remain with shoppers through the buying process.** Many people postpone buying decisions. They often go from store to store comparing prices, quality and service. Advertising must reach them steadily through the entire decision-making process. Your name must be fresh in their minds when they ultimately decide to buy.

10 **You should advertise to maintain store morale.** When advertising and promotion are suddenly cut or cancelled, sales people may become alarmed and demoralised. They may start false rumours in an honest belief that your business is in trouble. Positive advertising boosts morale. It gives your staff strong additional support. Advertising boosts the confidence of shareholders.

TRENT·FM 96·2 NOTTINGHAM
GEM·AM 999 NOTTINGHAM

ADVERTISING ■ ADVERTISING ■ ADVERTISING ■ ADVERTISING ■ ADVERTISING

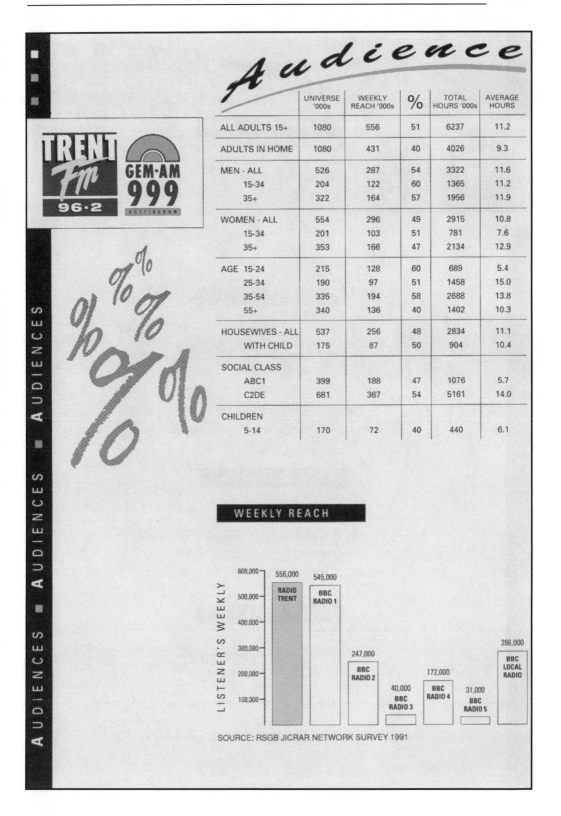

Audience

	UNIVERSE '000s	WEEKLY REACH '000s	%	TOTAL HOURS '000s	AVERAGE HOURS
ALL ADULTS 15+	1080	556	51	6237	11.2
ADULTS IN HOME	1080	431	40	4026	9.3
MEN - ALL	526	287	54	3322	11.6
15-34	204	122	60	1365	11.2
35+	322	164	57	1956	11.9
WOMEN - ALL	554	296	49	2915	10.8
15-34	201	103	51	781	7.6
35+	353	166	47	2134	12.9
AGE 15-24	215	128	60	689	5.4
25-34	190	97	51	1458	15.0
35-54	335	194	58	2688	13.8
55+	340	136	40	1402	10.3
HOUSEWIVES - ALL	537	256	48	2834	11.1
WITH CHILD	175	87	50	904	10.4
SOCIAL CLASS					
ABC1	399	188	47	1076	5.7
C2DE	681	367	54	5161	14.0
CHILDREN					
5-14	170	72	40	440	6.1

WEEKLY REACH

LISTENER'S WEEKLY

- 556,000 RADIO TRENT
- 545,000 BBC RADIO 1
- 247,000 BBC RADIO 2
- 40,000 BBC RADIO 3
- 172,000 BBC RADIO 4
- 31,000 BBC RADIO 5
- 286,000 BBC LOCAL RADIO

SOURCE: RSGB JICRAR NETWORK SURVEY 1991

TRENT FM 96·2   GEM·AM 999 NOTTINGHAM

AUDIENCES ■ AUDIENCES ■ AUDIENCES ■ AUDIENCES ■ AUDIENCES

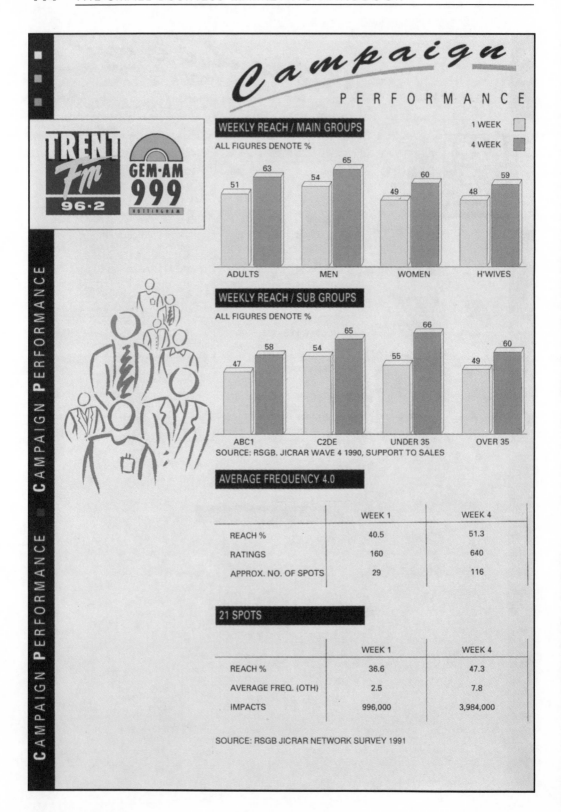

Campaign PERFORMANCE

WEEKLY REACH / MAIN GROUPS

ALL FIGURES DENOTE %

1 WEEK
4 WEEK

	ADULTS	MEN	WOMEN	H'WIVES
1 WEEK	51	54	49	48
4 WEEK	63	65	60	59

WEEKLY REACH / SUB GROUPS

ALL FIGURES DENOTE %

	ABC1	C2DE	UNDER 35	OVER 35
1 WEEK	47	54	55	49
4 WEEK	58	65	66	60

SOURCE: RSGB. JICRAR WAVE 4 1990, SUPPORT TO SALES

AVERAGE FREQUENCY 4.0

	WEEK 1	WEEK 4
REACH %	40.5	51.3
RATINGS	160	640
APPROX. NO. OF SPOTS	29	116

21 SPOTS

	WEEK 1	WEEK 4
REACH %	36.6	47.3
AVERAGE FREQ. (OTH)	2.5	7.8
IMPACTS	996,000	3,984,000

SOURCE: RSGB JICRAR NETWORK SURVEY 1991

SCHEDULES

Broadcasting contemporary hit music, album tracks and great oldies with hourly news and weather, and frequent local information, keeping you in touch 24 hours a day.

MON/FRI

06.00-09.30	Gary Burton with The Breakfast Show
09.30-13.00	Rob Wagstaff with The Morning Show
13.00-14.00	The Music Jam - Continuous Hit Music
14.00-18.00	Andy Miller with The Afternoon Show

18.00-20.00 **Monday: The Eurochart**-Europe's favourites with Pat Sharpe.
Tuesday: The Trent FM weekly Top Thirty with Gary Burton - A second chance to hear Nottinghamshire's most popular singles.
Wednesday: Electric Wednesday with Craig Strong.
Thursday: 18.00-18.45: The Business Programme with Ann Marie Minhall - Weekly update of news and discussion for Nottinghamshire's business community.
18.45-19.00: The Look with Louise Moore - Fashion Programme.
19.00-20.00: The Break - Neil Fox talks to the music headliners.
Friday: America's Choice - Benny Brown with the American Top Forty.

| 20.00-00.00 | Mon/Thurs: Tim Disney with The Late Show |

Friday: Phil McKenzie with The Late Show

00.00-01.00	Midnight Love Affair with Viv Evans - Music for Late Night Lovers
01.00-03.00	Greatest Songs with Viv Evans
03.00-06.00	The Early Show with Mark Burrows

SATURDAY

06.00-09.00	Danny Cox with The Breakfast Show
09.00-12.00	Tim Disney with The Morning Show
12.00-15.00	Andy Miller with The Lunchtime Show
15.00-18.00	Craig Strong with The Afternoon Show
18.00-22.00	Phil McKenzie
22.00-01.00	Get on the Good Foot with Mark Spivey - Playing the Latest Dance Music
01.00-06.00	Greatest Songs with Graham Wright

SUNDAY

06.00-09.00	Tim Disney with The Breakfast Show
09.00-12.00	Rob Wagstaff with The Morning Show
12.00-14.00	The Trent FM weekly Top Thirty with Gary Burton - unveiling Nottinghamshire's most popular singles
14.00-16.00	Craig Strong with The Afternoon Show
16.00-19.00	The Network Chart - David Jensen counts down the Nations Top Thirty
19.00-20.00	The Break with Neil Fox
20.00-00.00	Adrian Air
00.00-01.00	Midnight Love Affair with Viv Evans - Music for late night lovers.
01.00-06.00	Greatest Songs with Viv Evans

News and Weather on the hour 24 hours a day

Trent FM's Careline broadcasts throughout the day Monday to Friday.

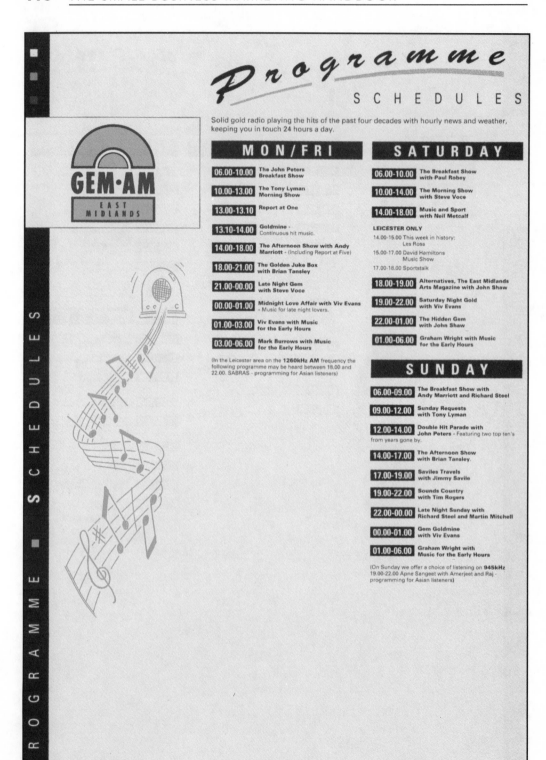

Programme

S C H E D U L E S

Solid gold radio playing the hits of the past four decades with hourly news and weather, keeping you in touch 24 hours a day.

GEM·AM
EAST MIDLANDS

MON/FRI

06.00-10.00	The John Peters Breakfast Show
10.00-13.00	The Tony Lyman Morning Show
13.00-13.10	Report at One
13.10-14.00	Goldmine - Continuous hit music.
14.00-18.00	The Afternoon Show with Andy Marriott - (including Report at Five)
18.00-21.00	The Golden Juke Box with Brian Tansley
21.00-00.00	Late Night Gem with Steve Voce
00.00-01.00	Midnight Love Affair with Viv Evans - Music for late night lovers.
01.00-03.00	Viv Evans with Music for the Early Hours
03.00-06.00	Mark Burrows with Music for the Early Hours

(In the Leicester area on the **1260kHz AM** frequency the following programme may be heard between 19.00 and 22.00. SABRAS - programming for Asian listeners)

SATURDAY

06.00-10.00	The Breakfast Show with Paul Robey
10.00-14.00	The Morning Show with Steve Voce
14.00-18.00	Music and Sport with Neil Metcalf

LEICESTER ONLY
14.00-15.00 This week in history: Les Ross
15.00-17.00 David Hamiltons Music Show
17.00-18.00 Sportstalk

18.00-19.00	Alternatives, The East Midlands Arts Magazine with John Shaw
19.00-22.00	Saturday Night Gold with Viv Evans
22.00-01.00	The Hidden Gem with John Shaw
01.00-06.00	Graham Wright with Music for the Early Hours

SUNDAY

06.00-09.00	The Breakfast Show with Andy Marriott and Richard Steel
09.00-12.00	Sunday Requests with Tony Lyman
12.00-14.00	Double Hit Parade with John Peters - Featuring two top ten's from years gone by.
14.00-17.00	The Afternoon Show with Brian Tansley.
17.00-19.00	Saviles Travels with Jimmy Savile
19.00-22.00	Sounds Country with Tim Rogers
22.00-00.00	Late Night Sunday with Richard Steel and Martin Mitchell
00.00-01.00	Gem Goldmine with Viv Evans
01.00-06.00	Graham Wright with Music for the Early Hours

(On Sunday we offer a choice of listening on **945kHz** 19.00-22.00 Apne Sangeet with Amerjeet and Raj - programming for Asian listeners)

P R O G R A M M E ■ S C H E D U L E S

To ensure that you have studied each rate card properly, ask yourself whether or not you have read about the following points. You ought to be able to say 'Yes' to every question.

	Yes	No
The transmission area	❑	❑
Population, numbers and types	❑	❑
Audience, numbers and types	❑	❑
Half-hourly audience figures	❑	❑
Advertising rates	❑	❑
Advertising segments	❑	❑
Surcharges	❑	❑
Discounts	❑	❑
Terms and conditions	❑	❑
Production facilities	❑	❑
Miscellaneous data	❑	❑

Perusing rate cards: an action checklist

Assessing audiences

Your first consideration when studying the key information on the rate cards must be to compare and contrast each station's audience alongside of your own targeted one. Do not be concerned about the breadth of a radio station's transmission area, nor the total numbers and types of people which it can potentially be heard by. Hyped up though these superficially impressive facts may be by the rate card and the station's employees, they are almost wholly irrelevant to you. However wide a territory is covered and whoever has the chance to tune in, it does not necessarily mean that those people in the area will listen any more than everyone who has an opportunity to buy a newspaper, visit an exhibition or go to the cinema actually does.

Pay closer attention to the radio station's weekly reach, in terms of numbers and types. These figures should be audited independently either by Radio Joint Audience Research or a reputable research company such as National Opinion Polls so that you can feel confident that they have been calculated in an honest and straightforward manner. Even so, do be aware that the figures quoted are only estimates based on limited samples, and findings for the same stations have in the past been at odds with each other which suggests discrepancies exist somewhere. Also, these figures may be up to a year or so old. Bear in mind that this is a rapidly developing industry in which new radio stations are being launched regularly, taking away listeners from older, established stations – so numbers are more likely to fall than rise.

Taking the material that you have (which despite its flaws is still likely to possess a broad semblance of accuracy), write out each radio station's audience, broken down in numbers and types by sex, age, social grade and so forth. From your notes, set out your own (prospective) customer base in the same manner. Taking sex, age and so on at a time, compare their make-ups – or 'profiles' – together, section by section to see how far each division and the overall groups match or differ from the other. Obviously, you are looking to retain those stations whose audiences resemble your own as closely as possible. There is little sense, for example, in advertising to a predominantly male audience if your customers are mostly female, to young listeners when you wish to reach older ones.

Similarly, ascertain how far each radio station's audience penetrates into your customer base, again evaluating and comparing one at a time and section by section. For example, perhaps you are trying to promote your business, products and services to the 100,000 young people between 15 and 24 years in a region and can see that one station reaches 25,000 or 25 per cent of them whereas another reaches 50,000 or 50 per cent. Likewise, you are attempting to appeal to an ABC1 audience which totals 200,000 in number and a radio station reaches 100,000 or 50 per cent of them whilst the next reaches 120,000 or 60 per cent. Clearly, you can then rank remaining stations into an order of preference. See 'Assessing audiences: an action checklist' on page 119 for more help in this area.

RADIO AUDIENCE ANALYSIS FORM	Campaign:	Number:
	Media:	Date:

Radio audience:	Target audience:
Numbers:	Numbers:
Sexes:	Sexes:
Ages:	Ages:
Social grades:	Social grades:
Location:	Location:
Other:	Other:
Other:	Other:
Other:	Other:
Assessing audiences: an action checklist	

Calculating costs

Having shortened and prioritized your list of radio stations on the basis of how many and who they reach, you should then set about calculating and comparing the costs of advertising yourself and your goods and services via each of these stations. This is not an easy task given the range of packages on offer, the diversity of rates, surcharges and discounts available and the different numbers and types of people who tune in to the respective radio stations. Nonetheless, it is worthwhile making some comparisons, however approximate they may be, in order to identify those stations which look as though they will be the most cost-effective for your firm.

To make value-for-money comparisons between the remaining stations, work out the cost of reaching every 1,000 people within each station's audience. You can take the cost of a standard 30-second spot – free of surcharges, discounts and the like – and divide it by one thousandth of the weekly reach to obtain a 'cost per thousand figure'. For example, one station charges £50 for 30 seconds and has an audience of 200,000. Thus, £50 is divided by 200 (200,000 ÷ 1,000) which equals 25 pence. Another radio station charges £80 per 30-second spot and possesses an audience of 350,000. Hence, £80 is divided by 350 (350,000 ÷ 1,000) which represents 23 pence, and so on.

Naturally, you are aware that although this method of evaluating media alongside each other is sound, it is inappropriate to simply compare and contrast each radio station's total audience – as some naive advertisers do – since these do not precisely match your own audience in terms of types and numbers. Superficially, the station with a 23 pence figure seems to offer better value than the other at 25 pence, but perhaps the first radio station's audience resembles your own more closely. If that first station charges £50 and reaches 50,000 of your audience and the second charges £80 and contacts 75,000, then the first represents better value, at £1 per thousand compared to £1.07 per thousand.

Again, you must also be conscious that you will not be buying one, 30-second spot on its own, but will be purchasing a package of advertisements. Some will be shorter at 20 seconds, others longer at 40 seconds. Some will be broadcast in the morning, others in the afternoon. You may have your advertisements rotated evenly through the schedule, or transmitted at specific times. Your campaign of 28, 112 advertisements or whatever could last for a week or a month or more. All radio stations have different pricing structures to reflect these many and varied alternatives so it is wise to keep recalculating and recomparing costs as far as you can, seeing which station is most cost-effective for 20- and 40-second advertisements, morning and afternoon broadcasts and so on, until you are wholly confident of your conclusions.

Preparing your radio schedule

Having concluded which stations to use because they seem most likely to reach the right numbers and types of your targeted audience at the right price, you then need to go on to piece together a preliminary schedule of radio advertisements. Initially, you must decide exactly when you should promote your goods and services – which time of the day, what part of the week, which month, what quarter and so on. Your gut reaction, which will be the same as many other first-time radio advertisers, is to choose those times of the day, week and so forth that attract the most listeners, whether between 6 a.m. and 9 a.m., Thursdays and Fridays rather than Mondays and Tuesdays, or whatever. This is unwise as these times may not necessarily be best in *your* circumstances.

The timing of your advertisements must derive from your own unique situation, as highlighted in your notes on your business, products, services and goals, those concerning your customers, competitors and the budget available to you. Base your decisions on these, and these alone. Your firm may open from 5 p.m. until midnight so it might not be appropriate to advertise in the mornings when customers cannot telephone immediately or visit you in response to your advertisements. Goods and services may be seasonal, which could suggest certain weeks or months to you. It would be more sensible to promote romantic gifts in the week before Valentine's Day than the week after, and school uniforms in August before the new academic year rather than in October. Your goal might be to increase sales in spring instead of autumn, summer rather than winter.

All of the background research which provided you with these notes may have informed you that your existing and would-be customers listen to the chosen radio station in the mornings instead of the afternoons, during weekdays rather than at weekends. Successful national rivals might promote themselves in certain months or quarters, giving you a lead which you may be wise to follow. Aware of imminent political changes or legislation that might adversely affect your marketplace, you could decide to advertise sooner rather than later. Your budget may restrict you to advertising at less instead of more expensive times.

Then, you need to work out how long your advertisements should be, whether 10, 20, 30, 40, 50, 60 seconds or even longer. Although 30 seconds is the norm and the length quoted in most rate cards, it should not be an automatic choice. Again, you ought to reach a decision suited to your own circumstances. You may prefer longer, more detailed advertisements to give status to your business, to explain the main functions of your goods and to achieve your objective of maintaining a high profile. You could select shorter advertisements because your customers are busy people and your budget is limited. You will need to take account of creative considerations too, when making a choice.

Moving on, you should consider how often you ought to advertise –

whether every hour or other hour, day after day or alternate days, 28 times in a week, a fortnight or whatever. Go through your accumulated notes once again, to enable you to decide. A new concern usually needs to be promoted more often than an established one if it is to become as well known. Seasonal goods ought to be advertised rapidly before they are unavailable. Regularly used services should be promoted steadily to remind customers of their many benefits just before the next purchase is made or order placed. Your goal might be to boost sales which points to more frequent advertising, not less, and so on.

Similarly, you have to contemplate how long your advertising campaign ought to last, whether for a short, sharp month or a slow and steady quarter. Perhaps your customer base is constantly changing and evolving, with new people coming into the marketplace and others leaving. This might suggest an ongoing, steady level of advertising. Possibly a new rival is opening, and a short burst of rapid, quick-fire advertising at and around that time may be fitting. Of course, the market in which you operate could have trading peaks and troughs which might indicate advertising times and durations to you.

Aware of the most appropriate timing, length and frequency of your advertisements and the duration of your planned radio activities, you can draft out a proposed schedule for your radio advertising campaign. Make a note of the stations you intend to use, the number of advertisements to be transmitted for each one, their lengths, preferred dates and times, the costs incorporating surcharges and discounts and the total, estimated expenditure which ought to fall somewhere between your minimum and maximum budget figures. You are then ready to translate this possible schedule into practice, composing advertisements and getting in touch with radio stations and/or sales houses to conduct your campaign. Add the details to the 'Media schedule' form on page 106.

Incorporating direct mailing

If you are going to use direct mail, you should now turn your attention to mailing lists, knowing how to build up your own lists, obtain other lists, maintain accurate and up-to-date lists and comply with the law in this area. Mailing lists will play a pivotal role in your direct mail activities, hopefully enabling you to send your messages to the right people, whether customers or prospects. No matter how skilful and persuasive your mailshots may be, they will meet with little or no success if they are received by the wrong recipients. Do not underestimate the value of quality mailing lists to your campaign. They are essential.

Building your own lists

Many small-business owners and managers can piece together mailing lists for themselves, from within their own organizations and activities. You should already possess the basic information that you need to know about existing and would-be customers from various in-house sources. Names, addresses, sexes and other data can be obtained easily from membership and subscription files, attendance records at seminars, conferences and exhibitions, competition entry forms, enquiry, sales and accounts records and completed product guarantee forms and questionnaires. Even conversations between you and your customers and prospects can generate useful details which may be noted down and referred to later on.

You can broaden and build upon this information by studying the masses of existing, published material that are available all around you, and which are easily accessible through simple research. As examples, business prospects may be selected from yearbooks, journals and directories as diverse as *Yellow Pages* and *The Times* top 1,000, which categorize firms in many ways whether by size, location, activity or whatever. If you are a member, professional and trade associations, chambers of commerce and chambers of trade could supply you with their membership lists on request. Similarly, consumer prospects can be picked from readily available clubs' and societies' lists, telephone directories and even electoral registers. Other sources – from a fellow small-business owner or manager to the Government and its multitude of departments – might be willing to provide you with snippets or reams of information, on businesses and consumers alike, and without charge.

In many instances, your existing and easy-to-find data will be more than enough for you to compile an appropriate, first-rate mailing list that is suited to your individual needs. For example, if you are aiming to generate a certain number of enquiries about a new and highly specialized trade product for your sales representatives to follow up, you might select the names of those firms which have enquired previously about or purchased similar or related goods from you. Enquiry and sales records and the like would be checked. Your list could then be extended by adding on the names and details of other concerns which might conceivably be interested in the product because of their size, type of operation, activities etc. You might refer to a trade yearbook, or a professional association here.

Never undervalue your own, self-composed lists, and do not believe the view that you must rent or buy externally produced lists to be a successful direct mailer: this is simply not true. As a rough-and-ready rule of thumb, a self-generated mailing list will produce three times as many responses as one that is hired or bought from an outside source. Previous buyers, users and enquirers know you and your products and services, they probably like you, are interested in your goods and are more likely to respond to your letters than those firms and individuals who have never dealt with or even heard of you before. Your own additional research will have been conducted carefully and thoroughly and will be absolutely relevant to your circumstances, which is not necessarily true when other parties do it on your behalf. In-house lists are also cheaper to compile than those purchased from elsewhere, taking your time rather than your money.

Obtaining other lists

There may be situations when you need to rent or buy lists from other organizations or individuals. Perhaps you have not maintained complete and accurate books and records of enquiries, sales and the like, or simply cannot uncover sufficient data about a new business, consumer or geographical marketplace. Therefore you will have to approach either a list owner or broker. You should be able to obtain numerous contact names and addresses by getting in touch with the Direct Marketing Association (UK) Limited and the Direct Mail Accreditation and Recognition Centre which will provide you with data about their members. Also, study trade magazines such as *Direct Response* and *Precision Marketing* in which list owners and brokers advertise themselves and their lists. See 'Useful contacts', page 385.

When contacting list owners and brokers who appear, from the details provided by the trade associations and magazine advertisements, to possess lists of potential use to you, a number of questions need to be raised and answered before you proceed to hire or purchase any mailing list. See 'Questioning list owners: an action checklist' on page 125. You need to be sure that your suppliers are reputable organizations or individuals who have acquired the mailing lists in a thorough and honest manner, keep them accurate and up-to-date and use them in a professional and ethical way. Deal only with those owners or brokers who belong to the DMA and/or DMARC and who are obliged to adhere to the guidelines of good practice issued by these bodies. As in all walks of life, disreputable people exist in this trade and operate outside these professional organizations in order to exploit naive, first-time mailers.

Ask yourself, from the information supplied to you about the mailing lists on offer, how well they cover your particular market. Your background research into your customers – who they are, where they are, their likes, dislikes and so on – has given you a hands-on understanding of the numbers and types of firms and people you want to reach to generate enquiries and produce sales. You ought to compare and contrast the lists with your target audience to see how closely matched they are. You must seek to ensure that as many names on those lists as possible are potential respondents.

These are the key questions you should ask a list owner or broker when arranging to rent a mailing list. You need to receive satisfactory answers to all of them if you are to proceed with confidence.

Do you belong to the DMA?

Are you recognized by DMARC?

Can I approach these trade bodies for confirmation?

Does the list match my target market, and closely?

How was the list compiled originally?

How old is the list?

Is it fully postcoded?

Is it divided up logically, perhaps by demographics?

When is the list updated?

How is this done?

How often is it updated?

What are the costs involved in renting the list?

What other terms and conditions are imposed?

Are these negotiable?

Is the list available in my preferred format?

Can I test it before renting?

Who used the list last time?

How successful was it then?

Can I contact the previous user?

Will you refund a proportion of the rental charge if the response rate is poor?

Questioning list owners: an action checklist

Find out as much as you can about how the lists were created, and their sources. It may be that one list owner built up a mailing list from his or her membership records whereas another pieced one together from a variety of published sources. As a rule, those mailing lists which are based on actual responses – people joining and buying from a book club, video club and so on – are far more successful than ones that have been compiled 'cold' from other sources such as telephone directories and electoral registers. Those concerns and individuals who have shown themselves to be active in your particular field, by sending off application forms and placing orders, are much more likely to respond than unknown prospects.

Discover everything possible about the ages of the lists, how they are recorded and looked after. Not surprisingly, lists of recent respondents will be more productive than earlier ones, with lists based on this year's directories being better than those derived from previous years. All lists ought to be fully postcoded for convenience and registered with the Data Protection Registrar by law, if appropriate. Consumer lists should be divided up demographically into sexes, ages and so on for easy comparisons and amended according to data provided regularly by the Mailing Preference Service. Check when, how, and how often lists are updated: the more often, the better they are likely to be. See who last used the lists and check their success rates.

Deciding upon a list/or lists which seems satisfactory, you then need to ascertain the costs, terms and conditions of using it. Normally, you will rent a mailing list on a once-only basis, perhaps at a cost of £80 per 1,000 or so names. The list must not be passed on, copied or used again without authorization from the list owner, plus the payment of another, appropriate fee. You should be entitled to, or inevitably will in practice, retain the names and details of respondents to your mailings for subsequent use during further mailshot campaigns. Be wary of buying a list outright at a cost of thousands of pounds, as 95 per cent or more of the names on it will not respond, and thus represent wasted time and considerable expense. Concentrate instead on building your own lists in combination with the names of those firms and people responding from a rented list – the best of the rest!

The list owner will also want to know exactly what you intend to use the hired list for, to make certain that you are going to use it legally, that mailshots adhere to accepted standards and – most significant of all – that you are not in direct competition with each other. Not surprisingly, a rival firm is hardly likely to provide you with a detailed list of its past and present customers if you are planning to distribute a mailshot promoting your own similar products and services. You will be expected to submit samples of your mailings well in advance, for approval by the list owner. A number of unidentified names of businesses and/or people who will feed back information to the list owner about your activities will be incorporated into the list to ensure that you use it in the agreed manner.

As the prospective list user, you must be sure that it is available in a suitable manner for your firm, whether on computer disk, sheets of paper or pre-printed sticky labels to be stuck onto envelopes. Almost all list owners and brokers retain data on computer systems nowadays for easy access and updating, but can supply printouts of details for small-business owners and managers upon request. Do not feel that your concern cannot rent a particular list because you run your activities on a manual basis. Many smaller firms continue to operate in this manner, and will do so for some time yet.

Also ensure that the list owner will agree to allow you to test a portion of the list before renting all of it. You need to conduct a trial run, sending mailings to a sufficient number and representative cross-section of the entire list to enable you to calculate whether the whole list is likely to produce the overall response required, whether 100 enquiries, 50,000 sales or whatever. Finding out who used the list previously and approaching them for their comments on its success rate is a sensible step to take as well. Clearly, it would be astonishingly naive to simply rent any list without such precautionary checks.

Should you be satisfied with your test findings, and your projections show that you will probably achieve the desired response if you use the full list – and it is wise to err on the cautious side when reaching a decision – then you will proceed to hire the list at the agreed price and on the negotiated terms and conditions. Do not try and force the owner to promise to refund a fair proportion of the cost if mailings are returned unopened because the firms and people have moved away, or even if you fail to achieve an acceptable response rate.

Maintaining lists

Whatever lists you choose, you must work through them yourself to remove duplicated names before using them. It is surprisingly common to discover lists with some names repeated several times, especially for members of the public called Smith, Jones and so on. From your internal sources, you may find that Mrs Tracey Jones is on your membership list, crops up as Mrs T. L. Jones in a batch of competition entries and as Ms T. Jones in a list of visitors to your exhibition stand. Hence, she could appear three times in your pieced-together list of would-be users of a new and improved service. Other organizations' lists – usually merged from many sources – are notoriously repetitive, duplicating the names of businesses and individuals who were perhaps originally listed under several, diverse categories in a directory. Check everything carefully, even if you have to do it manually, one after another. To send out repeated, identical mailings to the same recipient will irritate and alienate them – *and* increase your costs too.

It is crucially important that you keep your mailing lists up-to-date at all times, ever mindful that your business, products and services, goals, customers, competitors and marketplace are constantly changing and developing. A list which is relevant and produces a good response today will generate successively poorer results each time it is used, unless and until it is amended regularly according to evolving circumstances. As examples, some businesses on an original mailing list may diversify into different product and service areas, could relocate to distant regions or might even cease trading. Similarly, people change jobs, move homes, develop other interests and eventually die. Obviously, these firms and individuals will no longer want your goods and services, so it is pointless to continue mailing to them.

You can help maintain accurate and valid lists by constantly attending to numerous, commonsense tasks. In-house, check membership and subscription renewal forms, making a note of any changed details. Watch competition entry forms, enquiry, sales and accounts records plus product guarantee forms and questionnaires for altered data. Follow up lapsed memberships and subscriptions and non-attendance at subsequent seminars, conferences and exhibitions to discover the reasons and consider deleting names from your lists, if appropriate. Be ready to add to, amend and remove duplications from your books and records, day by day, week by week: a tedious process perhaps, but one which needs to be done.

Externally, there is much that can be done as well. Study quarterly updates and new editions of yearbooks, journals and directories to spot and record changes. Keep in touch with professional and trade bodies, chambers of commerce, chambers of trade, clubs and societies to remain aware of developments. Look through telephone directories and electoral registers as and when new ones are published. Keep your eyes and ears open at all times, talking to people, reading the national, local and trade press and so on. Again, do anything and everything you can think of to build up, adjust and keep lists free from duplications – and do it on a continuous basis.

If your mailshots are directed to members of the public rather than businesses, subscribe to the Mailing Preference Service (or MPS for short), which will forward information to you every three months about those consumers who have registered with it. The Service will tell you which members of the public do not want mailings of a particular type, and about those who wish to receive more. This is an especially valuable service for all consumer-orientated direct mail users, as it helps to ensure that you do not waste time and money on mailing items to disinterested or hostile members of the public, concentrating instead on those people who are keen to receive mailshots from you and fellow organizations. See 'Useful contacts', page 385.

Not least of your activities, keep scrupulous records of all mailings sent, being aware of those who do respond, what they buy, how much they spend, when they spend it and so forth. Clearly, these concerns and people may move to the top of your mailing lists of probable and/or possible buyers next time around. Likewise, those who do not reply might shift down your lists accordingly. Make a special point of looking out for those mailshots which are returned by the Royal Mail marked 'Addressee has gone away' and the like, so that you can delete them from your books and records.

Complying with the law

It is important that you are aware of the Data Protection Act of 1984 which places legal obligations upon organizations and individuals who record and use personal data. The Act applies only to computer rather than manually processed information and to that data which concerns living individuals, not businesses. If you record and use computerized data about people, you must register with the Data Protection Registrar. There are one or two exceptions – if the information is used just for calculating and paying wages, keeping accounts and so forth – but these are unlikely to apply to you. Registration simply involves completing a form (DPR4) which is the basis of your register entry, and paying a modest fee.

From the details that are stated in your completed application form, the Registrar then draws up your register entry. This sets out your name and address along with broad descriptions of the personal data which you hold, the purposes for which it is used, the sources from which it was obtained, the people to whom it may be disclosed and any overseas countries or territories to which you might wish to transfer it, now or in the future. Your entry is kept in the register and is available for public inspection. You can apply to alter or cancel your entry at any time should your circumstances change.

As a registered data user, you must adhere to the Data Protection Principles of the 1984 Act which state that you have to act in a fair and open manner, obtaining data lawfully, keeping it accurate and up-to-date, allowing access to it, correcting it where appropriate and so on. It is sensible to read and follow the Advertising Association's Code of Practice Covering the use of Personal Data for Advertising and Direct Marketing Purposes which takes each of the broad and rather generalized principles in sequence, and explains how they can be maintained on a practical, day-to-day basis.

If you are obliged to register and abide by the Data Protection Act, then you would be well advised to do so. To attempt to avoid your legal responsibilities – as some direct mailers do – leaves you open to prosecution and associated, adverse publicity in the marketplace. The Office of the Data Protection Registrar is not a powerless body. It can and frequently does take legal action against tardy direct mail advertisers to force them to fulfil their obligations.

Even if the Act is not relevant to you – perhaps because your data is processed manually and relates to businesses only – it is still worthwhile knowing about the law in this field. The Data Protection Principles are a guide to good business practice for every data user, large or small, computerized or not. See Appendix F: 'The Data Protection Act 1984', page 371, and Appendix G: 'The Code of Practice Covering the use of Personal Data for Advertising and Direct Marketing Purposes', page 377.

Making the most of exhibitions

If you are planning to include exhibitions in your advertising campaign, you should now go on to shortlist the exhibitions that you might attend, contact organizers to learn more about these shows, make choices about which ones are suitable for you, book spaces and draft a timetable leading up to your first planned event. It is at this stage that all of your earlier, background research into your firm, market and budget will prove once more to be most useful to you. Be ready to refer to any notes made to help you to reach the right decisions in your circumstances.

Shortlisting exhibitions

To begin, you need to obtain a list of exhibitions for the coming year, or for a longer period, if possible. You can buy or subscribe on a regular basis to a publication such as *Conferences and Exhibitions Diary* which supplies extensive information in this field. 'Recommended reading', page 393, describes this and other titles in more depth.

Having already concluded whether you should be exhibiting at either consumer and/or trade shows, it should be relatively easy to read carefully through lists to pick out those events which could be of potential interest to you. Of course, there are many exhibitions to consider and only brief details are provided – usually topic, date, title, venue and organizer – so if in doubt about the relevance of some, add them to your list of 'possibles' for the moment. It is obviously better to investigate one or two more than to risk missing a potentially ideal show.

Taking each event in turn, work through your accumulated notes to whittle down your lengthy list to a shortlist of 'probables'. Compare every show alongside your accumulated notes on your firm, products, services and goals. Decide which should remain, and which ought to be deleted. As examples, one show may be too early for your production schedules to gear up to meet the increased, consequent demand; another could be too late for your seasonal goods. Perhaps your objective of increasing awareness of your products in the international arena sounds as though it is unlikely to be fulfilled at an exhibition held in a muddy field in Suffolk.

Next, think about each show in relation to your customers, rivals and marketplace. For example, conclude if the event is likely to be visited by the right people, whether tradespeople, members of the general public or both, if appropriate. Also think about whether your leading competitors will be there, and if this is a good or bad sign for you. Naturally, you can still only reach tentative conclusions, and if you are uncertain about a particular exhibition it is wise to keep it in your list for subsequent, further analysis.

Contacting organizers

Working through your shortlist, you must get in touch with the organizers of each of the events to ask for further information. Not surprisingly, the material sent to you will vary, depending upon whether the organizer is small or large, professional or unprofessional, reputable or disreputable and so on. Hopefully, you should receive a sales brochure, floor plan, booking form and details of the organizer's rules and regulations. It is also sensible to request previous exhibition catalogues, if any are still available. This material and your existing notes will enable you to select the best exhibitions for your situation.

The sales brochure is usually a glossy publication which hypes up the show as best as it can. Although it should be read with a jaundiced eye and a suspicious mind, it does contain some useful information (albeit requiring verification). Typically, it will supply general details about the sponsor, the organizer and its services, the venue, the purpose of the exhibition, show dates and opening hours, the numbers and types of exhibitors and visitors at earlier events and those who are expected on the following occasion. A classic example of a sales brochure is reproduced on pages 141 to 147.

A large and reputable organizer will provide would-be exhibitors with a copy of the ABC 'Certificate of Attendance' as issued by the Audit Bureau of Circulations Limited. It gives you detailed and independently audited data about the attendance at the last show, which is helpful and reliable. It does not mean that this will be repeated at the next show, but is a relatively good indicator and is certainly better than unaudited, hollow claims.

The floor plan, which may need to be requested before it is made available, sets out the scale of the show, the sizes and locations of the stands that are available plus information about the exhibitors who have already booked sites, and their positions. It is wise to check that the exhibitors listed have made firm bookings rather than provisional reservations only, which do not guarantee that they will definitely attend, especially in recessionary times. An example of a floor – or 'hall' – plan is laid out on page 148.

You will be supplied with a booking form. Normally, this gives further brief data about the show, the venue, dates and times, the types of stand available as well as details of how and when to apply. Your attention should be drawn to the contractual obligations which come into effect once the form is completed, signed and returned to the organizer with the appropriate deposit. A booking – or 'space application' – form is reproduced on pages 149 to 151.

The organizer's rules and regulations list the terms and conditions of the contract that apply between the exhibition organizer and the exhibitor on payment and acceptance of the deposit. It covers such topics as the respective rights and responsibilities of the two parties along with specific information on areas such as payments of fees, cancellations, withdrawals and so on. These details – typically set out in microscopic, easy-to-overlook print – need to be read in their entirety, by you *and* a solicitor with experience in this field. An example of an organizer's rules and regulations is set out on pages 152 to 157.

Do ask for show catalogues from earlier events and it is probable that one or two will be forwarded to you in due course. These will encompass much of the information set out in the sales brochure and other material, and more besides. It will provide you with fuller details of the sponsor, organizer, venue, exhibitors, visitors and the exhibition industry in general. Peruse it from cover to cover. It is a worthwhile read, conveying a 'feel' for the event.

Making choices

Armed with your original notes, organizers' material and being ready to seek advice from other organizations and people as and when necessary, you are now in a position to choose between the various events on your shortlist. You may perhaps wish to nominate one exhibition that you will work towards, with others pencilled in for later on, if all goes well at this first show. Picking out each event in sequence, you need to consider the event itself, the organizer, the venue and the likely exhibitors and visitors in some depth.

Start off by contemplating the show itself. You can probably think of many questions that need to be answered, such as what is its size and status in the field? You may not wish your small, specialist firm to be swallowed up in a huge, sprawling event nor to be associated with an exhibition that gives the impression of being a shoddy, fly-by-night operation. What is its range? You need to know if it is local, regional, national or international in nature, and whether this suits you. If you are aiming to appeal to overseas buyers, you will want to select international events where 20 per cent or more of the visitors are from abroad. Some shows simply have the prefix 'International' attached to their title to puff up a parochial, second-rate event.

Is it a new or well-established show? If it is a new one, you have to be certain that a genuine demand exists and that it has not been set up just to promote a venue, or whatever. Discover if it is replacing another event and whether that one failed. If this is the case, find out how the situation has changed or what is different about this exhibition to make it a success. Should it be a well-established event, check how long it has run for. Long-running shows tend to be better choices for new exhibitors as errors have been rectified, everyone knows what they are doing and so on. What competing shows exist? Be wary of attending an event which is close in time or location to another, possibly set up by a rival organizer trying to draw away custom. Usually, exhibitors and visitors split in two, with both exhibitions being less successful than they might otherwise have been.

Next, turn your sights to the organizer, whether this is a trade association, professional exhibition organizer or whoever. Again, you will find that certain queries spring to mind: two are most pressing. First: Is is reputable? Not surprisingly, you need to convince yourself that it is not going to take your money and disappear without staging the event. Check its reputation in the trade, how long it has been operating for, what other shows it arranges and whether it belongs to the Association of Exhibition Organizers and/or other representative bodies. Do be especially wary of becoming involved with new, small organizers setting up one-off, solitary events. Some are perfectly respectable, but others have a habit of coming and going under different names, pocketing deposits at every twist and turn.

Second: Is it capable? Equally important, you want to feel confident that it will not only stage the exhibition, but do it well, drawing in the right kinds and numbers of exhibitors and visitors. Obviously, experienced trade associations and well-known exhibition organizers have built up years of know-how and expertise (although past achievements do not necessarily guarantee future success, especially in recessionary times). Even the best organizers can make mistakes and misjudgements, consequently experiencing failure. Find out as much as you can about its plans for the show, with particular emphasis on how it intends to attract exhibitors and promote the event to the desired audience.

Moving on, consider the venue, which many new exhibitors overlook until they arrive prior to the show and find it to be totally unsuitable. Several questions need to be posed and answered satisfactorily: Is it easily reached? You need to be sure that both exhibitors and visitors can get to the site conveniently and on time, so check its proximity to good roads, parking facilities and transport networks, whether buses, trains or planes. Is it large enough? You also want to be certain that the venue is sufficiently spacious for the anticipated numbers to congregate in a relaxed and comfortable atmosphere without being so big that it seems half-empty all of the time, which can cast a downbeat mood on the proceedings.

Is it well structured for exhibitors? Take time to contemplate the large and bulky items that you might show at the event. Decide whether you can deliver, unload and place them on display without difficulty. Investigate access arrangements, lengths and widths, ceiling heights and strengths, possible obstructions and so on. See if there is adequate, controllable light and services such as electricity, gas, water and so forth. Is it laid out well for visitors? Discover if they can walk around it easily, reaching the stands they want to visit and whether restaurant, toilet and other facilities are close at hand.

Then consider the other organizations and individuals who may exhibit at the show. Ascertain the answers to two specific questions: How many exhibitors will be there? You want to see a satisfactory number have booked so that the exhibition is staged. An adequate quantity must be present so that visitors are drawn to it. What types of exhibitor will be at the event? You have to be sure that the mix of exhibitors is appropriate too. As an example, a show which is designed to attract trade and public visitors in equal numbers should perhaps have exhibitors who will deal with fellow businesses *and* direct with the general public as well.

Last – but most definitely not least – turn your attention towards the visitors who are expected to come to the event. Two key queries will be most prominent in your mind: How many visitors will attend the show? Of greater significance, what types of visitor will come along to the exhibition? You need to feel confident that both the quantity *and* the quality of the potential visitors are comparable with your own target audience. Do not be swayed into picking events that promise huge numbers of visitors. Unless they are current or prospective customers, they are largely irrelevant to you.

All of these questions – and you can probably add more which are as relevant to you – do need to be answered fully and accurately before you can even think about booking space at any event. Of course, some organizers are scrupulously honest professionals and the material submitted to you is comprehensive and correct, as with the ABC form. Others are untrustworthy, and the information provided is a mixture of hyped-up and deceitful nonsense. Unfortunately, it is sometimes difficult to distinguish reputable organizers from disreputable ones. Therefore, it is always sensible to obtain an extensive and substantiating answer from second and other sources for every question raised.

Contact anyone and everyone who you can think of that might help you by supplying independent and reliable advice and guidance. Get in touch with each of the representative and other bodies involved in the exhibition industry for their views and opinions. In particular, the Association of Exhibition Organisers may offer especially useful assistance concerning organizers, as might the British Exhibition Venues Association with regard to venues. Talk to the Audit Bureau of Circulations Limited about visitors. Consider joining the

Agricultural Show Exhibitors Association and/or the National Exhibitors Association to benefit from their help on all aspects of exhibiting. Contemplate employing Exhibition Surveys Limited to conduct a full evaluation.

Perhaps most important of all, chat to exhibitors at the last show and to those who plan to attend the next one. Find out about them and their thoughts on the exhibition, the organizer and so on. Did they match your expectations? Will you exhibit again? If not, why not? Similarly, speak to any visitors who have been to the show, and discover what they have to say about it. Was the venue easy to find? Was there a relaxed atmosphere? Of crucial significance, go out on the road yourself. Visit as many events as you can. See them in action, judge the organizer, appraise the venue and so forth for yourself. Build up your hands-on experience. Know what you are doing before going any further on.

Booking space

Continuing with your step-by-step approach, you will want to progress to focus on one initial exhibition, deciding which type of stand you want as well as its size and position before returning your booking form with a deposit. Other potentially suitable shows which are due to be staged thereafter can be pencilled in, with firm bookings being made when – or if – this first exhibition helps you to achieve your goals.

You will have found out about the types of stand that are available and have thought about their pros and cons when you contemplated budgetary considerations earlier on. Whether you favour a shell scheme or an independently designed stand, it is now time to select which one is right for you. If in doubt, refer to those notes again. Perhaps your goal of maintaining your status as the premier manufacturer in your trade might tip the balance towards a unique, designed stand rather than the standardized, shell scheme format. Alternatively, a limited budget may nudge you towards booking a basic shell, albeit with the intention of personalizing it so far as you can.

Selecting the right size and site depends largely upon your specific situation. The dimensions and weight of your goods may mean that a larger stand is needed, whilst various areas could be out of bounds because these items cannot be manoeuvred and placed there safely. If you are trying to appeal to, and expect to have to accommodate, a large number and variety of visitors, you will want to take a big stand where you can be seen by passers-by – perhaps near to the entrance, main gangways and wherever people tend to flow and/or congregate. Steer clear of obstructions, secondary routes and dead-ends unless you expect to meet a small number of hand-picked, personally invited customers who know where to find you and will relish the relatively peaceful environment.

As a general rule of thumb, you will probably not want to draw your customers' attention to your direct rivals by being next to or opposite their stands. However, some newly established, small firms base themselves close to a huge competitor in an attempt to siphon off customers who are milling about, waiting to be seen by busy staff. Such a brazen policy can be successful, assuming the small exhibitor approaches the job in a professional manner.

Some sites may be of limited or even no interest to you if you are operating within a budget, as many exhibitors are. Other positions could be unavailable to you because they have already been booked by fellow-exhibitors. It is not unusual for exhibiting firms to reserve space for the next show as soon as the current one has ended, even if it is planned for one or two years' time. Realistically, your choices – of type, size and site – are always restricted for one reason or another and you should be prepared to be flexible, working within your constraints.

Having settled upon the type, size and site of the stand that you require, you need to fill in and return the booking form with your deposit. Prior to doing this though, do scrutinize the organizer's rules and regulations again. Study each clause in turn, making sure that you understand and approve of all of them. Then take legal advice to clarify and confirm your thoughts and opinions. To all intents and purposes, you are about to enter a legally binding contract and should treat it with due respect, in the same manner that you would approach signing any legal document. To take it lightly would be an error of judgement that could prove to be an expensive mistake.

There are numerous, identifiable areas of concern which you can look for. Pose several questions as you read through the clauses. What payments am I committed to make, and when? Usually, you will have to send a 10 per cent deposit with your completed form, with staggered payments spread out perhaps at quarterly intervals up to the show. Try to avoid paying out too much too soon, to maintain your cash flow and to reduce the risks of substantial losses in the event of unforeseen circumstances. Also, check to see what can happen if you are late with a payment – sadly, it is not uncommon to discover you are liable to have your booking cancelled, stand re-sold, monies retained and any remaining balance demanded. Not surprisingly, you will want to avoid exposing yourself to such a scenario.

What changes can the organizer make with regard to the event? Often, you will find that it is legally entitled to alter anything in certain, exceptional situations – from the scope and layout of the show down to the size and position of your individual stand. Clearly, this is not unreasonable as the organizer should be entitled to the final say on how its exhibition is run. Nevertheless, you ought to try to ensure that if changes occur, you retain the right to withdraw and to receive a refund of monies paid, perhaps depending on the extent and effects of the amendments.

What happens if you want to withdraw from the show? Some organizers will demand that you pay the full cost of the space booked before they will release you from your contract with them. You may feel that this is unfair, especially if you give notice in good time, and should therefore seek to have a sliding scale of charges incorporated into the rules and regulations – such as 10 per cent with six months' notice, 25 per cent with three months' notice and so on.

What happens if the exhibition is postponed or cancelled? Hopefully, this will not affect you, although it is not an uncommon occurrence. Should it be postponed, you must attempt to make certain that you can pull out of your agreement and retrieve any monies handed over to the organizer to date. Similarly, if it is cancelled, you ought to be looking for a full refund, and indeed compensation for your time, efforts and expenses so far (although this is unlikely to be an achievable aim).

Does the organizer disclaim responsibility for any damages or losses, whenever and howsoever caused? This is a relatively common clause inserted into most if not all of the rules and regulations drawn up by exhibition organizers, and is not wholly unreasonable (although you may wish to try to limit the overall breadth of such a disclaimer). If it is included in your organizer's terms and conditions, you are advised to take out appropriate insurance to protect yourself against damages or losses.

If you or your solicitor come across clauses that you are unhappy with, do not hesitate to haggle over them, seeking amendments, as relevant. Whatever may be stated in public, these rules and regulations are not cast in stone and many organizers will be ready to negotiate to a certain degree rather than risk losing a prospective exhibitor (and his or her money). As a last resort though, be prepared to walk away from a show rather than committing yourself to a contract that is not in your interests, and might even be detrimental to you. Only sign and return the form and deposit when you are totally satisfied with the agreement.

Planning a timetable

Your next step is to note down a list of activities which have to be carried out up to and beyond your first show, followed by the dates by which they must be completed. You need to make absolutely sure that everything is ready and in place before the doors open to visitors. Sketch out all of the tasks which have to be attended to, perhaps grouping them together under the loose (and often interchangeable) headings of the stand, exhibits, staff, promotional and other activities.

With regard to your stand, you will have to do most, if not all, of the following: pick a theme; select contents; tackle presentation; compose a brief for a designer; commission a designer, working to your (amended) brief; submit your stand design to the organizer for approval; alter the stand design, if necessary; employ a contractor to build the stand; order workers' passes from the organizer; supervise erection of the stand; and arrange for the stand to be dismantled and removed after the event. You may be able to add some more tasks which are fitting in your situation, and others could arise as you proceed.

Concerning the exhibits, you will need to carry out these actions, and probably in this (or a similar) order: prepare relevant, existing and new products for display; examine and test goods for faults; gather up technical literature about the products; transport goods to the contractor or exhibition, as appropriate; arrange for the products to be lifted into place, assembled and installed on the stand, under supervision; and attend to the removal and return of the goods after the show. Again, other activities may be identified now, or at a later date.

Turning to the all-important topic of staff, various duties must be overseen, some of vital significance, others apparently mundane. These will include; appointing a stand manager (if not you); selecting the right numbers and types of staff; drawing up a rota; administering a briefing; arranging training; measuring up for uniforms, if appropriate; ordering badges and passes from the organizer; booking accommodation; making travel arrangements; ordering car park tickets; and setting up a debriefing. More tasks will possibly unfold as you set about your workload.

Going on to promotional activities, you should take the following steps, probably in this sequence: compile a prospects list; arrange direct mail shots to customers; submit an entry to the show catalogue, with accompanying advertisement, if relevant; write press releases and complete press kits for distribution; obtain sales literature about yourself; make entertainment arrangements; order giveaways; attend to general advertising campaigns; arrange more direct mail shots to contacts; and write further press releases for the media. Of course, you may also have your own ideas about worthwhile advertising actions, to add to these.

Looking at a final, catch-all heading, you might incorporate these activities: book electrical, gas, compressed air, water and other services; order telephone service, if relevant; order stationery; attend to refreshments arrangements; ensure stand safety and security; take out necessary insurance; and organize stand cleaning. Numerous additional tasks will also spring to mind here, depending on your specific circumstances. More will crop up at later stages.

In many instances, the exhibition organizer will effectively dictate the dates by which tasks have to be finished. As examples, the proposed stand design and your entry for the catalogue have to be submitted at certain times, exhibits have to be on site so many days before the show begins and so on.

Thus, most activities can be rearranged into a logical sequence, in order of dates. You will then find that the remaining actions which need to be taken tend to slot into place. For example, you will perhaps want to start work on your catalogue entry and associated advertisement (if appropriate) a month or so before the delivery date, allowing you time to consult with colleagues and take advice, if relevant. When timetabling activities, you may find it helpful to use the project planner on page 140.

PROJECT PLANNER

Project:

Number:

Completion:

Date:

Task	Week beginning													

Project planner form

A long tradition of gardening

Last year's GLEE, the International Garden & Leisure Exhibition, was the largest ever held with over 750 exhibiting companies and a record-breaking attendance of over 15,000 buyers; this being achieved in what was widely considered to be a recessionary period!
But this is a trend that GLEE has established - consistent growth over the past ten years in line with the

continued expansion of the UK garden and leisure market - and a trend that is likely to continue as we move into the mid-90's with the full impact of the single European Market. Any company, whether UK based or overseas, involved in the manufacture and supply of garden and leisure products should seriously consider the advantages of exhibiting at GLEE. The show is the shop window for the industry covering all aspects of gardening and one that delivers the buyers from garden centres to high street multiples to the DIY

superstores; three types of retail outlet that account for 80% of the estimated total UK garden product sales of £2,000 million each year.
Analysts forecast that sales will continue to grow during the next decade, pointing to good long term prospects for sustained real growth. Among reasons given are more spending on the home, environment issues, expanding market potential from convenience products aimed at the younger gardener, and the growth of the over-55's market as the early retirement trend continues.

THE VISITORS:
Attendance at GLEE 1991 was: Sunday 5,064, Monday 5,678, Tuesday 5,752. Of these visitors, retailers from garden centres, garden shops and florists

accounted for over one in three visitors. Hardware and DIY Stores accounted for just over 5%, major buyers from Department Stores, Multiple shops and Mail Order companies amounted to just under 5%. Machinery Dealers 2.3%. Wholesalers 10.7 %, Press 1.9% and Overseas Visitors 7.4%.

Analysis of product interest categories indicated by visitors, not surprisingly, showed a very high level of interest in the visitors main product area, e.g. virtually all garden machinery dealers indicated an interest in garden machinery and wholesale nurseries

showed a high level of interest in plants. There was also, however, a high level of interest by the majority of visitors in other product categories, e.g. over a third of all machinery dealers indicated an interest in 'outdoor living' primarily garden furniture and nearly a third of DIY Stores were interested in 'nursery products' primarily plants.

TRADE SPONSORSHIP:
GLEE is sponsored by major UK trade associations, including The British Hardware and Housewares Manufacturers Association, The Federation of Garden & Leisure Manufacturers, The Horticultural Trades Association and the Leisure and Outdoor Furniture Association.

Comprehensive service for exhibitors

Any advice that may be needed, especially for a company exhibiting for the first time can be obtained from the GLEE Sales Office. Their first concern is that exhibiting at GLEE should be as smooth running as possible and they are happy to help with any query that may arise however big or small.

They can advise on position and size of stand, contractors, furniture hire, signwriting, catering arrangements - right through to hotel accommodation and travel arrangements.

MODULAR SHELL STAND

Many exhibitors find it convenient to make use of the modular shell scheme stands. Complete with walling where appropriate, carpet, fascia and name panel, they are ideal for exhibitors who do not wish to be involved with stand design and construction. Sizes start as small as 9 square metres (3m x 3m) and are particularly suitable for the first time exhibitor.

PUBLICITY MATERIAL

Each year promotional material including invitation cards that can be personalised, and correspondence stickers are produced and supplied free of charge to exhibitors. They form an essential part of the promotional programme for the exhibitor and GLEE.

THE GLEE CATALOGUE

Produced in an easy to handle A5 size format, the catalogue contains exhibitor entries, combined with product and trade name indices, (entries are free of charge to exhibitors), which act as an invaluable reference for purchases throughout the year. Advertising by exhibitors is also available at competitive rates.

NEW PRODUCTS AND PACKAGING

The New Product and Packaging Stand at GLEE has gained so much significance over the years that most major companies plan their product launches around the exhibition. The massive stand is purpose designed for easy viewing, enabling buyers to assess all that is new in the industry at a glance. Each exhibit

carries the company's stand number where the product can be discussed in greater depth. For the exhibitor, prestigious GLEE DESIGN AWARDS combined with the Stand offer unrivalled benefits in promotional activity.

GLEE '91 CATEGORIES OF VISITOR

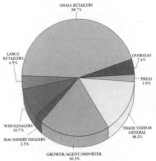

Judged by leading experts in the industry, a product acclaimed at GL can truly be regarded as the best in the field.

REGISTRATION AND PRE-REGISTRATION

The computerised registration syste at GLEE is one of the most sophisticated ever produced for an exhibition.

On completion of a registration car prior to the show, the visitor will receive an entry badge, advance information on the show, and detail of new products and special offers available. Additionally a pre-show guide with colour coded plans of th halls, enables pre-registered buyers plan their visit well in advance, saving valuable time. Visitors unable to pre-register will find entry to the exhibition smoothed by the use of a fast computerised badging system.

PUBLICITY
THE GLEE promotional activity is revised annually to achieve maximum publicity for the exhibition and the exhibitors; its aim is to ensure that every potential visitor is fully aware of the importance of GLEE in the home and international calendar. The budget for this world-wide campaign is considerable.
An extensive advertising campaign is carried out in the major garden, hardware, leisure, and ancillary trade press throughout Great Britain and leading European publications, whilst direct mail is targetted at specific retail sectors at home and overseas.
The wide coverage of the press relations programme results in GLEE editorial being published throughout the world. Nearly 200 journalists representing major trade and consumer publications attend GLEE, ensuring considerable publicity for both GLEE and exhibiting companies.

THE PRESS OFFICE
The Press Office distributes information concerning GLEE to the trade media throughout the year, commencing immediately after the show with reviews, followed by general exhibition and market data. Leading up to the exhibition, the releases cover the individual exhibitors and particularly any new products that are being launched. To gain maximum publicity from exhibiting at GLEE, exhibitors need to ensure that customers are fully aware of their plans. Promotion assistance is

available from the GLEE Press Office, as well as advice on how exhibitors can best promote themselves at the exhibition through the trade magazines.
All the major trade magazines produce extensive editorial previews of GLEE and the exhibitors, and in addition there is a daily newspaper at the show.

OVERSEAS BUYERS AND JOURNALISTS
Each year, in conjunction with the DTI, GLEE organises an official group of overseas buyers to visit the show. Different countries are targetted each year, with the buyers representing

major retail and wholesale outlets. Overseas buyers have a separate registration point at the show, which leads into an overseas visitor's lounge where interpreters, export/import advice, refreshments and a range of office facilities are available.
In addition, a group of journalists is organised each year, who come from leading garden trade magazines throughout Europe and North America. This results in some excellent editorial coverage for the exhibitor and GLEE.

The vast range of products on display

NURSERY PRODUCTS & FLORISTRY
Plants, Trees & Shrubs,
Seeds & Bulbs,
Cacti & Succulents,
Bonsai,
Cut Flowers,
Landscaping,
Florists Sundries,
Pot Covers & Jardinieres,
Vases & Baskets.

GARDEN BUILDINGS
Coldframes,
Conservatories,
Greenhouses,
Sheds,
Summerhouses,
Walling, Fencing & Paving.

GARDEN CARE PRODUCTS
Chemicals & Fertilisers,
Compost & Peat,
Non-decorative Plant Pots &

Containers,
Netting & Trellis,
Hosereels & Accessories,
Watering & Irrigation
Equipment,
Wheelbarrows & Rollers.

GARDEN MACHINERY & TOOLS
Chain Saws,
Garden Tractors,
Hand Tools,
Lawn Mowers & Equipment,
Power Tools,
Ride-Ons,
Rotary Cultivators.

OUTDOOR LIVING
Barbecues & Accessories,
Beach Equipment,
Camping & Caravanning
Equipment,
Furniture for Conservatory,
Garden, Pool & Patio,
Garden Lighting,
Garden Ornaments &
Statues,
Picnic Equipment,
Saunas,
Sports Equipment,
Swimming Pools &
Equipment,
Synthetic Grass & Playing
Surfaces.

POOLS & PETS
Fish and Aquaria,
Pets & Cages,
Pet Foods,
Pet Care Products,
Garden Ponds & Water
Plants,
Fountains & Pumps,
Pool Lights.

GIFTWARE
Artificial & Dried Flowers,
Christmas Decorations,
Confectionery,
Decorative Pots & Jars,
Hanging Baskets,
Garden Ornaments,
Pot Pourri.

ANCILLARY PRODUCTS & SERVICES
Books & Consumer
Magazines,
Computer Equipment &
Software,
Shopfitting & Display
Equipment Signs,
Trade Magazines,
Garden Centre Trollies &
Baskets,
EPOS,
Security Systems &
Equipment,
Heating, Ventilation,
Humidifiers.

FOR FURTHER INFORMATION
OR ANY QUERY, PLEASE CONTACT
CHRIS O'HEA OR STEVE BRYANT
ON 081-390-1601/2211
FAX NO: 081-390-2027.

GLEE IS ORGANISED BY
INTERGARDEN PROMOTIONS LTD
60, CLAREMONT ROAD,
SURBITON, SURREY KT6 4RH.

GLEE 1992 SEPTEMBER 13-15
GLEE 1993 SEPTEMBER 26-28
GLEE 1994 SEPTEMBER 11-13

GLEE
THE HOME
OF BRITISH
GARDENING

How to get to the NEC

The National Exhibition Centre is a purpose built complex including the exhibition halls, restaurants and banking facilities, railway station, airport, and the Metropole Hotel, and is easily accessible by all means of transport.

By road, there are direct links with a motorway network providing access from all the major cities in the UK, Parking is free for visitors to GLEE, with space for 15,000 vehicles, and a free shuttlebus service links the car parks and the main entrance.

British Rail's Birmingham International Station, alongside the halls, is served by the Inter-City network with travel time from London Euston, being 80 minutes, with Birmingham New Street Station a 10 minute journey. Birmingham International Airport, adjoining the NEC, greatly increases accessibility to the NEC. It provides scheduled service links with 10 UK airports and 19 overseas destinations, and is ideal for day visits to the exhibition. A fast monorail links the airport and the National Exhibition Centre complex.

ACCOMMODATION
The organisers arrange discounted rates at a variety of hotels close to the exhibition. Full details will be sent to all exhibitors on booking.

GLEE

**THE INTERNATIONAL
GARDEN & LEISURE EXHIBITION
NATIONAL EXHIBITION CENTRE
BIRMINGHAM, ENGLAND
13-15 SEPTEMBER 1992**

GLEE is organised by Inter Garden Promotions Ltd., 60 Claremont Road, Surbiton, Surrey KT6 4RH. Telephone: 081-390 1601/2211. Fax 081-390 2027.

NEXT YEAR'S GLEE TAKES PLACE FROM 26-28 SEPTEMBER 1993.

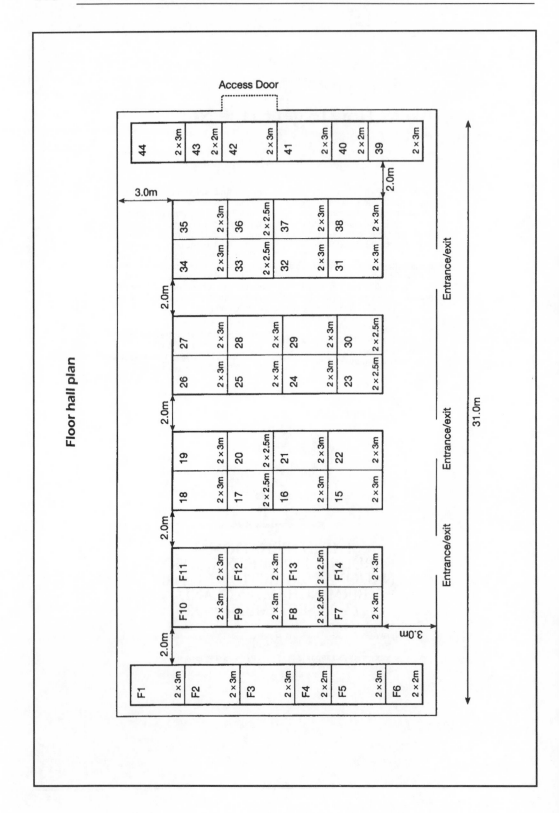

Floor hall plan

Information and Space Application Form for the
CHILD AND NURSERY FAIR 1992

Organised by TAS Exhibitions Limited
60 Claremont Road, Surbiton, Surrey KT6 4RH.
Telephone: 081-390 2211/1601
Fax: 081-390 2027

Venue and Dates

The 1992 Child and Nursery Fair will be held from Sunday 4 October to Tuesday 6 October 1992 inclusive at Earls Court Exhibition Centre, London. Opening times will be 9.30 a.m. to 7.00 p.m. on the Sunday, 9.30 a.m. to 6.00 p.m. on the Monday and 9.30 a.m. to 4.00 p.m. on the Tuesday.

Space Applications

Companies wishing to exhibit at the 1992 Child and Nursery Fair should complete and return the application form as soon as possible. The application form, together with a cheque for the appropriate deposit including V.A.T., should be made payable to TAS EXHIBITIONS LTD. No applications for space will be considered unless the space application form is completed and signed and accompanied by the appropriate deposit.

Before 1 March 1992 the deposit due is 10% of the total stand rental together with V.A.T. On or after 1 March 1992 but before 1 June 1992 the deposit due is 55% of the stand rental together with V.A.T. On or after 1 June 1992 the full cost of the stand together with V.A.T. must be paid on application.

Types of Stand

Two main types of stand are available. Firstly Space Only sites where exhibitors arrange for the design and building of their own stands. The cost is £68.00 per square metre. Secondly, Shell Scheme stands, these are constructed from a modular shell scheme by the official contractor. The cost, including space rental is £97.50 per square metre. Full details of both types of stand are in the Rules, regulations and Conditions Note 5a.

Contractural Obligations

The attention of potential exhibitors is drawn to the fact that once their application has been accepted by the Organisers, or a stand has been allocated to them, then the application will form the basis of a binding contract. Once a site has been chosen a confirmation letter will be sent to the exhibitor, detailing any changes to the original application. This letter will modify the terms of the contract.

N.B. Space Only Sites

Where more than one exhibitor occupies an island site, the organisers will provide a traditional dividing wall painted white. No charge will be made for this service. The exhibitors contractor will be permitted to use this wall as part of any stand construction and exhibitors should ensure that any specification provided by their contractor does not include provision of this walling. This ensures that all dividing walls conform to a common standard improving the overall appearance of the adjoining stands. Walling will not be provided for perimeter sites and these should be provided by the exhibitors own contractors.

Return this form to
TAS EXHIBITIONS LTD
60 CLAREMONT ROAD, SURBITON
SURREY KT6 4RH
Tel: 081-390 2211 Fax: 081-390 2027

APPLICATION FORM

CHILD AND NURSERY
FAIR 1992

Sunday 4 October to Tuesday 6 October 1992
Earls Court Exhibition Centre, London, England

FOR ORGANISERS USE ONLY
Deposit Paid ....
Date Paid ....
Space/Shell ☐ BPA Member
Stand No. ....
Width .... Depth ....
Deductions .... Area ....

Company Name ....

Address ....

....

Telephone: .... Fax:...

Name of contact responsible for stand ....

I/We apply for a stand at the 1992 Child and Nursery Fair.

I/We agree to abide by Rules, Regulations and Conditions overleaf and further agree that a binding contract will exist on acceptance of this application by the Organisers or by allocation of a stand.

I/We require .... m² of * space only/* shell scheme (*delete as appropriate - see note 1).

NOTE 1
1992 charges are as follows:

Space Only Stands ..... £68.00 per m²   Shell Stands .... £97.50 per m².

I/We agree to pay the total sum applicable to this stand, plus V.A.T. at the prevailing rate, in the instalments shown in the Conditions overleaf, not later than the due dates.

I/We enclose a cheque for the appropriate deposit for the stand applied for, together with V.A.T. thereon.

I/We understand that time will be of the essence with regard to all payments as set out in Clause 11 of the Conditions overleaf.

I/We agree the terms of the discount available to members of the Baby Products Association as detailed below:-
Members of the Baby Products Association are entitled to a 10% discount on stands, provided they are fully paid up members of the Association at 1st June 1992.
By agreement, half of the 10% discount is paid direct to the Baby Products Associationt by the Organisers and the eligible exhibitor will be credited with the remaining 5% in accordance with the conditions printed opposite.
To qualify for the discount, payment of the final invoice and any other balance outstanding must be made by 30th June 1992.
The discount will be deducted from the final invoice for eligible exhibitors, previous invoices will be calculated on the full cost of the stand.
No discount is available to exhibitors booking after 1st June 1992.

I/We confirm that our major activity is (tick one box):-
Manufacturer .... ☐   Sole Importer/Sole Distributor .... ☐

Products to be Exhibited
I/We have ticked below the main types of products to be exhibited on my/our stand.

(1) Baby Care Products	....	(2) Baby Clothing	....
(3) Baby Food	....	(4) Baby Walkers/Bouncers	....
(5) Boys Clothing	....	(6) Carry Cots	....
(7) Christening Wear	....	(8) Component and Material Supplies	....
(9) Co-ordinated Bedding	....	(10) Cots	....
(11) Feeding Items	....	(12) Girls Clothing	....
(13) High Chairs	....	(14) Mattresses	....
(15) Nursery Furniture	....	(16) Prams & Accessories	....
(17) Pre School Toys	....	(18) Publications	....
(19) Pushchairs & Accessories	....	(20) Safety Products	....
(21) Soft Toys	....	(22) Other (please state)	....
....	....	....	....

Sole Importers/Sole Distributors
This section is to be completed only by exhibitors who are importers or distributors of the goods concerned.
I/We list below all companies whose goods I/We will be exhibiting:-

1   Manufacturers Name ....
    Address ....
    ....

2   Manufacturers Name ....
    Address ....
    ....

3   Manufacturers Name ....
    Address ....
    ....

4   Manufacturers Name ....
    Address ....
    ....

5   Manufacturers Name ....
    Address ....
    ....

(list further manufacturers on separate sheet if necessary).
No application for space will be considered unless properly signed and accompanied by the appropriate deposit. Overseas exhibitors should pay by sterling draft on a London clearing bank.

Signed .... Date..................................

Position ....
Note:- If a limited company, this form must be signed by a director of the company, if a firm by a partner and if a sole trader by the proprietor.

DEFINITIONS

In the Conditions and in any Rules and Regulations from time to time made by the Management the following expression shall (unless inconsistent with the particular context thereof) have the following meanings:

Exhibition – International Garden and Leisure Exhibition ('GLEE')

Exhibition Days and Hours – Sunday 13 September 1992, Monday 14 September 1992 and Tuesday 15 September 1992 from 9.00 a.m – 6.00 p.m.

Exhibitor – Any person firm company or other body corporate to whom a Stand Licence is granted.

Management – Inter Garden Promotions Limited.

Exhibition Site – National Exhibition Centre.

Premises – That part of the Exhibition Site allocated for the holding of the Exhibition.

Stand Licence – The Licence granted by the Management to an Exhibitor to erect and use a stand on the Premises during the Exhibition Period for the purposes of the Exhibition which licence shall be deemed to be granted on and subject to the Conditions and any Rules and Regulations from time to time in force thereunder.

NEC – The National Exhibition Centre Limited.

NEC Rules and Regulations – All Rules and Regulations made by the NEC concerning the use and occupation of the Premises and Exhibition Site from time to time in force.

Relevant Authorities – NEC the Management all Authorities as defined in the NEC Rules and Regulations and the Electricity Board and Gas Board and the Water Authority as herein defined and their respective servants and agents.

Licence Fee – The fee for a Stand Licence for a stand of the size and type alloted to an Exhibitor and Value Added Tax thereon.

Special Services – All gas, compressed air, electricity, water or other services supplied to any stand and all connections to each stand for the supply of the same and for telephones and the removal of waste (in the case of connections for electricity being such connections up to but not beyond the distribution point or points on each stand).

Special Service Charge – All or any charges for the supply or connection to each stand of any Special Services.

Setting-up Period – 8.00 a.m. Tuesday 8 September to 12.00 noon Saturday 12 September.

Stand Dressing – 12.00 noon Saturday 12 September to 8.00 a.m. Sunday 13 September.

Pulling-down Period – 6.15 p.m. Tuesday 15 September to 4.00 p.m. Thursday 17 September. Or such other periods as the Management may notify Exhibitors as the respective times for the erection and dressing of the respective stands and the dismantling and removal of the same.

Exhibition Period – The Setting Up Period the Exhibition Days and the Pulling Down Period.

RULES AND REGULATIONS

In these Rules and Regulations words and expressions used shall where appropriate and unless inconsistent in the particular context have the same meanings as are respectively ascribed thereto in the Conditions.

A Each Exhibitor will observe and will procure the observance by his employees agents contractors sub-licencees and invitees of the NEC Rules and Regulations and any directions given by any relevant authority concerning the use and occupation of the Exhibition Site or any part or parts of it. In particular (but without limitation) each Exhibitor will ensure that each of his employees is fully conversant with precautions to be taken against, and procedures to be followed in the event of, fire. The Management will on request supply or make available for inspection copies of the NEC Rules and Regulations.

Organizer's Conditions, Rules and Regulations

B Subject thereto and to the intent that in the event of any inconsistency the NEC Rules and Regulations shall override the rules and regulations set out below each Exhibitor will observe and procure the observance by his employees agents contractors sub-licencees and invitees of the following rules and regulations:

1 Each stand shall be used solely for the purposes of the Exhibition.

2 Each Exhibitor will ensure that his stand is open to view and adequately staffed throughout the Opening Hours on Exhibition Days. In the event of failure on the part of any Exhibitor so to do the Management shall be at liberty at the Exhibitor's expense in each case and without being liable for any resultant loss or damage to take all or any reasonable steps to ensure that such stand is so open and staffed.

3 The Management reserves the right to refuse admission to any person without assigning any reason therefor.

4 Each Exhibitor will procure that his stand or other temporary structure erected by him is erected and maintained to reasonable and proper standards of construction having particular regard to the planning fire and other regulations of the relevant authorities and will ensure that all items displayed on or about the stand shall so conform.

5 Each Exhibitor will procure that his stand is properly managed and that he his employees agents contractors sub-licencees and invitees conduct themselves in a proper and unobjectionable manner and no Exhibitor will display or permit to be displayed any offensive or obscene material. The Management reserves the right to expel any person from the Premises who does not so conduct himself and to close any stand which is not so managed or on which such material is displayed or if in the reasonable opinion of the Management he or it is or may become a nuisance or annoyance to the NEC or Management or to other Exhibitors or their respective employees agents contractors sub-licencees or invitees as the case may be.

6 No Exhibitor will place or keep or permit or suffer to be placed or kept on in under or over the Premises or any part thereof any substance which is in the opinion of the Management of a dangerous explosive or objectionable nature.

7 Each Exhibitor shall make good all and any damage to the Exhibition site or the premises suffered or caused by any act or default of himself his employees agents contractors sub-licencees or invitees (damage by risks insured against pursuant to Condition 3(1) only excepted).

8 No Exhibitor will interfere with or make any alterations attachments or additions to the Premises and will not place any unusual load on any beam pillar or other part of the premises or allow any such load to be so placed.

9 No Exhibitor will park on or otherwise obstruct and will ensure that none of his servants or agents shall park on or otherwise obstruct any part of the Exhibition Site save as may be permitted by NEC.

10 Each Exhibitor will take all or any Special Services required for his stand only from NEC. In the event that NEC shall not be able to provide the supplies needed by the Exhibitors only such mode of generation or supply as shall first be approved by NEC or by the Management shall be used. Charges for any Special Services requested by an Exhibitor will be additional to the Licence Fee and such charges must be paid direct to the NEC or their appointed agents. The Management can accept no responsibility in relation to the provision of Special Services.

11 Exhibitors must ensure that all work on the construction, assembly, erection, decoration and dismantling of exhibition stands is carried out by contractors who are either members of The British Exhibition Contractors Association or have been specifically approved by the Organisers. The Organisers reserve the right to stop work on any stand construction and, if necessary, to employ approved contractors at the exhibitor's expense to complete any work on the stand if these conditions are not complied with.

12 Each Exhibitor will procure that all beverages alcoholic drinks food ice cream sweets confectionery and (except as regards personal requisites) tobacco and other consumable refreshment of any nature whatsoever which are to be consumed on the Premises by themselves and their employees and invitees respectively are obtained from the NEC.

13 Each Exhibitor will only deliver and remove stands and any equipment or fixtures and fittings therefor, exhibits and other goods of whatsoever nature during such reasonable hours as the Management may from time to time notify that Exhibitor. The Management can accept no responsibility therefor.

14 Each Exhibitor will procure the immediate removal from the Premises of all his packing cases packaging material and rubbish or waste of any description and will not store or permit the same to be stored thereon and in the event of any default the Management shall be at liberty to remove the same at the cost of the Exhibitor.

CONDITIONS

1 Payment of Licence Fee
(1) The Licence Fee shall be payable
(a) as to 10% of the Licence Fee for the size and type of stand applied for on making an application for a Stand Licence.
(b) as to 35% of the Licence Fee for the size and type of stand allocated or (in the event that the Stand Licence actually granted shall be for a stand of a different size and/or type from that applied for by the Exhibitor) an amount equal to the outstanding balance of 45% of the Licence Fee for the Stand Licence actually granted on or before 1st December 1991.
(c) as to 30% of the Licence Fee on or before 1 March 1992.
(d) as to the outstanding balance of the Licence Fee on or before 1 June 1992.
(2) In the case of each instalment of the Licence Fee payable as hereinbefore mentioned each Exhibitor will pay an amount equal to the Value Added Tax thereon at the appropriate rate
(3) Without prejudice to the provisions of Condition 6 hereof if an Exhibitor shall fail to pay the Licence Fee or any Value Added Tax in respect thereof in accordance with these Conditions then that Exhibitor shall in addition to the sums above specified pay the Management interest at the rate of 1.5% per month on the outstanding balance.
(4) Any Exhibitor resident or incorporated outside the United Kingdom shall make payment of all monies due or to become due under these Conditions by means of a sterling draft drawn on a London Clearing Bank.
(5) If any instalment of the Licence Fee referred to in paragraph (1) of Condition 1 or any Value Added Tax or interest payable under these conditions shall be unpaid for 14 days after the due dates for payment thereof (whether the same shall have been demanded or not) or if any Exhibitor shall fail substantially to observe or fulfil all or any of these Conditions, Rules or Regulations, then the Stand Licence may be determined immediately by the Management. In this case the Management may retain any monies already paid under the Stand Licence and any remaining balance due under the Stand Licence shall immediately become payable by the Exhibitor.

2 Cancellation or Interruption
(1) If by reason or force majeure fire tempest explosions of any kind failure or neglect of anybody supplying electricity power gas or water strikes or workmen labour difficulties or shortage of materials or other cause (whether ejusdem generis or not) beyond the control of the Management and whether occurring before or during the Exhibition Period the Management is prevented or hindered from holding the Exhibition on the Exhibition Days or any of them or the use of the whole or any part of the Premises during the Exhibition Period or any part thereof for or in connection with

the Exhibition is prevented or inhibited then the Management shall be entitled to cancel or suspend the holding of the Exhibition or the use of any part of the Premises for those purposes and in particular (but without limitation) shall be entitled to cancel or suspend any Stand Licence granted to any Exhibitor or make such alterations in the terms thereof as it shall in its absolute discretion think fit.

(2) In the event of cancellation or suspension of the Exhibition or the cancellation or suspension or alteration of any Stand Licence pursuant to paragraph (1) above the Management shall be under no liability to any Exhibitor for any damage or loss which such Exhibitor may sustain in consequence of any such cancellation suspension or alteration.

(3) Such cancellation or suspension shall not affect the liability of any Exhibitor to make any payment of the Licence Fee or any Value Added Tax or interest provided for by these Conditions and the Management shall in its absolute discretion be entitled to retain or recover payment of any such monies.

(4) In the event of the cancellation or suspension of the Exhibition as a whole the Management (but without being liable in any way for any failure so to do) will endeavour to make arrangements for the holding of a similar exhibition.

3 Insurance and Indemnity

(1) The Management will use all reasonable endeavour to procure that the NEC shall insure in the names of the NEC the Management and each Exhibitor and their contractors and such other persons as NEC and the Management may agree (hereinafter called 'the insured') against public liability on the part of the insured or any of them with an indemnity limit of £10,000,000 (or such other limit as NEC and the Management may agree) on any one claim or series of claims arising from any one event and causing death bodily injury illness disease or loss of or damage to property during the Exhibition Period and happening upon the

Exhibition Site including the Premises provided always that there shall be excluded from the risks so insured such risks as NEC and the Management may from time to time in their absolute discretion agree including (but without limitation)

(i) employers' liability claims

(ii) in the case of the Management Exhibitors and their respective contractors any liability arising from goods, products or samples supplied sold or distributed

(iii) damage to the Exhibition Site fixtures and fittings caused by fire explosion aircraft riot and civil commotion malicious damage storm and tempest burst pipes flood impact and consequential loss.

(iv) occurrences at the Warwick and Metropole Hotels

(v) property belonging to an individual insured and damaged by an act of that individual insured his employees or contractors

(vi) the use of the premises for activities other than trade exhibitions

(vii) any vehicle licensed for road use or otherwise subject to compulsory insurance.

(2) No Exhibitor will omit or do or cause to be done any act, matter or thing whereby the policy referred to in the preceding subparagraph or any material damage or other policies from time to time effected by NEC or the Management shall be rendered void or voidable or whereby any moneys payable thereunder shall be withheld or the amount of any moneys so payable shall be reduced.

(3) Save and subject as aforesaid all public liability insurance all insurance against loss of or damage to the property and effects of Exhibitors and their respective employees agents contractors and invitees or against injury loss or damage suffered by Exhibitors or any agent of or any persons employed by any of them or by their invitees or to their respective property and effects or against consequential loss suffered by them or any of them shall be the responsibility of the Exhibitor or other persons affected and each Exhibitor shall indemnify and save harmless the Management against all claims which may be made against the

Management in respect of any such matter save only injury loss or damage caused by the act default or negligence of the Management or its employees or agents and in respect of any material damage to the Premises (including buildings and Landlord's fixtures and fittings thereon) and any consequential loss to NEC or any other person or body resulting from any act or default of such Exhibitor or any of his employees agents contractors or invitees.

4 Rules and Regulations

Each Exhibitor shall during the Exhibition Period observe and perform the Rules and Regulations hereinbefore set out and any further or amended or modified Rules and regulations which the Management shall from time to time during the Exhibition Period think fit to impose including all Rules and Regulations concerning the use and occupation of the Premises and the Exhibition Site for the time being imposed by the NEC.

5 Overseas National Stands

Organisers of Overseas National Stands are responsible for ensuring that all Exhibitors on their stands are fully aware of and agree to abide by all the current Rules and Regulations and Conditions.

6 Bankruptcy

If an Exhibitor (being an individual) shall become bankrupt or (being a Company) shall enter into liquidation whether compulsory or voluntary (save for the purpose of amalgamation or reconstruction of a solvent Company) or if a Receiver shall be appointed of its undertaking or if an Exhibitor shall enter into an arrangement or composition for the benefit of that Exhibitor's creditors or shall suffer any distress or execution to be levied on that Exhibitor's goods then and in any such case it shall be lawful for the Management forthwith to give Notice determining his or its Stand Licence. Payments made hereunder shall be absolutely forfeited to the Management but without prejudice to any of the

Management's rights or remedies in respect of such default breach or omission.

7 Withdrawal of Exhibitors

(i) Once an application for a Stand Licence has been accepted in writing by the Management and a site has been allocated, the Exhibitor cannot be released from his contractual obligations. If in exceptional circumstances (force majeure etc.), release from the Stand Licence is granted by the Management then the following scale of cancellation charges will apply:

Cancellation before 1 March 1992. 10% of total cost of stand together with V.A.T. thereon.

Cancellation on or after 1 March 1992, but before 1 June 1992. 45% of total cost of stand together with V.A.T. thereon.

Cancellation on or after I June 1992 but more than 60 days before the opening of the Exhibition. 75% of total cost of the stand together with V.A.T. thereon.

Cancellation within 60 days of the opening of the Exhibition. 100% of the total cost of the stand together with V.A.T. thereon.

(ii) The above conditions and cancellation charges will also apply pro-rata to any reduction in stand size requested by an Exhibitor once a stand has been allocated.

8 Variation of Opening Hours

The Management reserves the right in its absolute discretion to alter or vary the Opening Hours.

9 Literature

The Management will use all reasonable care in the preparation of any literature issued by it in connection with the Exhibition but it will not be responsible for any error therein contained and no such error shall entitle an Exhibitor to any remedy whether by way of rescision of the Licence or damages or otherwise howsoever.

10 Assignment

The benefit of a Stand Licence is personal to the Exhibitor to whom it is granted and no Exhibitor shall or shall purport to assign deal with or otherwise dispose in any manner whatsoever with his interest thereunder or any part thereof.

11 Promotional Events
In order that attendance by buyers and/or press will not be adversely affected each exhibitor agrees that he will not organise or participate in any form of event or promotional activity, within 25 miles of the NEC, during the open hours of the exhibition unless that event or activity takes place within the premises.

12 Variation of Conditions
Only the Management has authority to vary all or any of the above Conditions or alter all or any of the Rules and Regulations made by the Management and from time to time in force.

Summary

- Prospective press advertisers should list all 'possible' publications; and then shortlist 'probables' by comparing media and target audiences by referring to their groundwork notes and media publicity material, such as rate cards.

- Thought needs to be given to the frequency and duration of press advertising, and the sizes, positions and costs of advertisements. A draft schedule should be drawn up, ready for testing.

- Would-be radio advertisers should obtain a list of radio stations from 'British Rate and Data' (BRAD), consequently shortlisting by comparing the profile and penetration of each station's audience with the target customer base.

- The timing and length of radio advertisements needs to be considered carefully and a provisional schedule should be composed; to be tested in due course.

- Potential direct mailers should produce mailing lists based on their own records and research, renting or buying externally produced and supplied lists as and when necessary. Any external lists should be tested before committing time and money to them.

- The accuracy and validity of internal and external lists relies upon constant maintenance; checking sources and updating changes on a regular basis. All direct mailers should also ensure that they comply with the law; mainly the Data Protection Act of 1984.

- Likely exhibitors should list 'possible' exhibitions by referring to 'Conferences and Exhibitions Diary'; subsequently shortlisting by assessing each show alongside their groundwork notes; and evaluating the show's status, the organiser's reputation, the venue's suitability, fellow-exhibitor's nature and the types of visitor attending.

- Attention needs to be given to the type and image of stand to be taken, and its site. It is sensible to have a contract checked by a suitably experienced solicitor. A preliminary schedule should be devised, subject to amendments and improvements.

Notes

Notes

5 Putting over your message

To ADVERTISE SUCCESSFULLY, you must be able to put over your message – 'We're the cheapest!', 'We've the widest range of stock!', or whatever – to your audience. Often, your message will be the same, but your approach will need to be different, depending on whether you are creating press advertisments, recording radio advertisements, writing mailshots, or designing exhibition stands.

Creating press advertisements

You need to know about the different types of press advertisement that are available to you as well as how to choose an appropriate approach, decide upon the layout and select the correct copy for them. Despite the creativity involved in designing advertisements – which almost demands that you break suggested rules – a number of broad guidelines do exist that ought to be loosely adhered to. It is also sensible to find out about staying within the law when compiling your advertisements.

Types of advertisement

You will already have given some thought to display and classified advertisements when you were sketching out a schedule. Nevertheless, you should now pay further attention to these two alternatives and the particular advantages and disadvantages that they offer, before going on to create or approve the approach, layout and copy of your own advertisements. You may even wish to amend your schedule in the light of your additional thoughts.

A display advertisement – mixing perhaps a headline, illustration and text together inside of its own borders – is distinctive and set apart from other, rival advertisements. With space for creative and design skills to be developed fully, it can be eye-catching and appealing to readers. In many instances, it may be placed on any page within a title – depending upon availability – thus ensuring that it is likely to be seen mostly by the right types and number of people. On the minus side, display advertising rates are usually relatively high and this could restrict the breadth and depth of your activities. Also, having more than sufficient room in which to work can be a drawback in the hands of an inexperienced or amateurish advertiser, serving simply to highlight his or her inadequacies and lack of imagination.

A classified advertisement, running on line by line beneath a heading such as 'Miscellaneous Sales' or 'Recruitment', is fairly inexpensive in comparison with displays. Only those dedicated readers who are especially interested in the field and whom you probably wish to address will scan through the classifieds, which are normally tucked away in the back pages of a title. Of course, there may be tens if not hundreds of classified advertisements to read, and yours could be easier to overlook than to see, effectively wasting your money.

A semi-display advertisement is a display that is incorporated under a classified heading: 'Accountancy Services', 'Business Equipment' and so on. Such an advertisement, which is rarely considered as fully as it ought to be by advertisers, can combine the qualities of the two main types of advertisement. It may be attractive, separated from others around it, charged at a reasonable cost and looked at by readers who are keen to peruse it. At the same time, those negative aspects which are often attributed to display and classified advertisements can be avoided. Judging displays, classifieds and semi-displays alongside of each other, you may decide to bring more semi-display advertisements into your schedule.

Choosing your approach

Many varied approaches can be adopted towards advertisements, especially displays and semi-displays. Humour may be very effective if it is handled professionally. An amusing headline and/or illustration can draw readers' attention to an advertisement, whilst witty text may help to put across a message in a warm and friendly manner to people in a relaxed and responsive mood. These advertisements can leave a lasting, memorable impression on readers long after they have turned the page and discarded the title. The classic Volvic advertisement on page 164 provides an excellent example of a humorous headline linked with an illustration. The hugely successful Perrier and PC World advertisements on pages 165 and 166 highlight the clever use of word-plays, closely related to the products being sold by the advertisers.

In some instances, you may appeal to people's emotions – such as their ego, machismo, desire for status, paternal or maternal instincts and feelings of nostalgia – or could employ shock tactics to convey information. The memorable Heinz and Blue Cross advertisements on pages 167 and 168 both play on the 'aah factor' amongst readers, to considerable effect. Those for the International League for the Protection of Horses, the League Against Cruel Sports and the National Society for the Prevention of Cruelty to Children on pages 169, 170 and 171 almost demand to be read and acted upon. In other situations, logic may prevail. The Kwik Save advertisements on pages 172 and 173 set out clearly the reasons why people ought to shop at *their* stores in preference to others.

Incorporating a well-known personality into an advertisement with his or her permission – whether a local or national celebrity, cartoon or puppet character or a renowned expert in the field – gives status and adds credibility to your firm, goods and services, and can remind readers of you when he or she (or it) are seen elsewhere, possibly on television. Demonstrating a product – its appearance, in action or the results of using it – may be extremely effective, particularly if colour is available to you. Kodak's unforgettable advertisement on page 174 combines two approaches – the use of a famous face and a demonstration of the quality of the product. Sometimes, comparisons are made between one company and its rivals, in terms of the respective strengths, weaknesses and so on. Those Kwik Save advertisements on pages 172 and 173 adopt this technique, to good effect.

The approach which you select – whether using humour, emotion, logic, a personality, demonstration, comparison or a combination – must depend upon your own individual situation. You have to compare and contrast the numerous approaches alongside your business, goods and services, goals, customers, competitors, market and budget. One or more techniques may stand out as being potentially ideal for you, whilst others could be obviously unsuitable in the circumstances. Your concern – perhaps a funeral parlour – may be ill-suited to humour, but well matched with emotion. Your products could need to be demonstrated – the tanning effects of a sun lotion – to maximize their benefits. Possibly your budget, limited by a poor cash flow, does not stretch to commissioning a personality, which may run into hundreds or even thousands of pounds for a well-known local or national personality.

Deciding upon layout

Aware of the types of advertisement and the approach that you will be using, consider exactly what your advertising message will be. Naturally, this will be tied in with your forthcoming goals – perhaps you will decide to stress the key consumer benefits of your product if you are trying to increase sales, possibly you will promote the advantages of shopping by post if you are seeking to sell goods direct to customers, and so on. (Never forget that customers want to know what's in it for them.) Although advertisements may vary slightly – from one region to another, to test them and so forth – the same basic message ought to run throughout the campaign or at least until the objective has been achieved, constantly hammering home the points that you are attempting to make. It should be reflected in and supported by the headline, illustration and text which make up the layout of your display and semi-display advertisements.

Your headline is vitally important, catching the readers' attention and sparking off sufficient interest to make them study all of the advertisement and take in its message. You need to ask yourself what heading will force your target customers to stop, concentrate and read carefully. You may choose a headline that is interrogative (the National Society for the Prevention of Cruelty to Children advertisement on page 171), dramatic (the International League for the Protection of Horses advertisement on page 169), declarative (the League Against Cruel Sports advertisement on page 170) or humorous (the PC World advertisement on page 166), according to your situation. Whatever you decide to put – such as the job title for a recruitment advertisement, the discounts offered for a seasonal sale advertisement and so on – it should encapsulate and sum up the main thrust of your message in one succinct word, phrase or line.

An illustration – whether a sketch, photograph or cartoon supplied by a specialist – can also serve to capture and retain readers' thoughts, complementing or sometimes even replacing the headline. You must question which picture will be looked at by your audience and will convey and strengthen your advertising message. The illustrative material used ought to be simple, relevant and self-explanatory; see the Blue Cross advertisement on page 168 which is clear, to the point and cries out 'Help Me!' at first sight. The other illustrated examples, especially those of the International League for the Protection of Horses and the League Against Cruel Sports on pages 169 and 170 respectively, are equally effective. A busy or obscure drawing or photograph will succeed only in blurring and detracting from what you are trying to say.

The appearance of the text – whether ten or a hundred words – can be attractive or unappealing, persuading or dissuading people from reading the advertisement. You may choose from a number of type designs – or 'faces' as they are more widely known – which should build on or could lessen the impact of your advertisement. For example, to further put across the image of a long-established, traditional family business in order to uphold its reputation you might pick an old-fashioned typeface. Other, popular tricks of the trade include varying the shades of the faces, alternating bold typefaces with italics and having white faces on a black background. A range of typefaces have been used in the PC World and other advertisements, and these should be studied. Whatever you choose, make sure that it is both appealing and easy to read.

You have to think about how to lay out the headline, illustration and text in the most attractive way. By studying all of the examples on pages 164 to 174, you can see there are no hard and fast rules. Headlines are at the top of the advertisements, halfway down, below photographs or even replaced by them. Different types of illustration are used in various places and text is scattered from left to right and from top to bottom. It is wise to discuss your ideas with the production department of the titles in which you will advertise.

This year, he's going to keep his Volvic on court.

Still, natural mineral water.

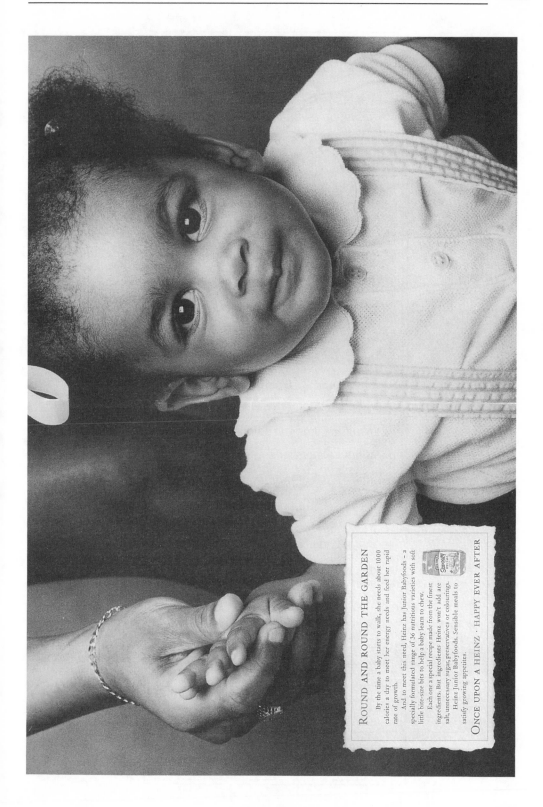

ROUND AND ROUND THE GARDEN

By the time a baby starts to walk, she needs about 1000 calories a day to meet her energy needs and feed her rapid rate of growth.

And to meet this need, Heinz has Junior Babyfoods – a specially formulated range of 36 nutritious varieties with soft little bite-size bits to help a baby learn to chew.

Each one a special recipe made from the finest ingredients. But ingredients Heinz won't add are salt, unnecessary sugar, preservatives or colourings.

Heinz Junior Babyfoods. Sensible meals to satisfy growing appetites.

ONCE UPON A HEINZ · HAPPY EVER AFTER

THE BLUE CROSS
NEEDS YOU.

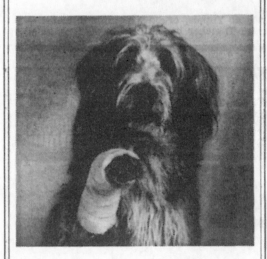

Every year the Blue Cross cares for thousands of animals, from kittens to horses.

Many are strays who not only need treatment but a loving home as well.

Others are brought to us for free treatment by owners who just can't afford vet fees.

And they all need you.

For the Blue Cross is a charity and relies solely on donations to survive.

So please help by filling in the coupon.

I enclose a cheque for £10 ☐ £20 ☐ £50 ☐ Other £_____
I'd like more information on The Blue Cross ☐

Name_____

Address_____

_____

_____Postcode_____

To: The Blue Cross,
Room 54A, Shilton Road,
Burford, Oxon OX8 4PE

BLUE ✚ CROSS

If you can't look at the picture, please help us face the problem.

July 1990, Bari, S. Italy
A horse is winched up through the decks by its hind legs. It is still alive, but only just.
Its body, covered in wounds, was then dumped on the deck where it lay shaking until its death.
That was just one of 900 equines shipped from Argentina to Italy.
Five died en route, many others were injured.
This cruel, barbaric treatment of horses in transport is commonplace on the continent.
The ILPH is the largest international equine charity and we are fighting to stop it.
Please help us by lending your support now. **Thank you.**

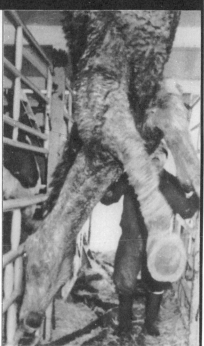

I wish to lend my support by; Making a donation towards your **'General Fund'** of £100 ☐, £50 ☐, £25 ☐, £10 ☐, OTHER ☐. £5 of any donation will be used for your membership, or you may elect Life Membership (£50). Please send me your brochure.

Name_____

Address_____

Postcode _____ Signature _____

I enclose cheque/P.O. made payable to I.L.P.H., to the

sum of £_____ or please debit my Access/Visa/Amex card no.

☐☐☐☐☐☐☐☐☐☐☐☐☐☐☐☐

to the sum of £_____ Expiry date _____

I. L. P. H.
Founded 1927

REGISTERED CHARITY NO.206658.

INTERNATIONAL LEAGUE FOR THE PROTECTION OF HORSES

Dept.   , I.L.P.H. H.Q., Anne Colvin House, Snetterton, Norwich, Norfolk, NR16 2LR. Tel. 0953 498682

Fox-hunting is a sickening bloodsport.

Every year from November 1st, this horrific scene is repeated thousands of times across Britain.

Defenceless foxes run for their lives, chased by mounted hunters and 40 baying hounds.

When they are caught, they suffer a savage death.

Killed for fun.

The League Against Cruel Sports' campaign to ban this outrage is funded entirely by donations.

So if fox-hunting tears you apart, please part with as much as you can.

IF FOX-HUNTING TEARS YOU APART, TEAR THIS OUT.

Yes, I want to help stop fox-hunting. You have my full support.

Please accept my donation of: £100 ☐ £50 ☐ £25 ☐ £15 ☐ Other £ _____

(Please make cheques/postal orders payable to the League Against Cruel Sports)

Name (Mr/Mrs/Ms/Miss) _____

Address _____

_____ Postcode _____

LEAGUE AGAINST CRUEL SPORTS

I wish to donate by Access/Visa

Card No. ☐☐☐☐☐☐☐☐☐☐☐☐☐☐☐☐

Expiry Date / / Signature _____

WORKING FOR WILDLIFE

Or phone our Hotline number on **071 378 6697** to make your credit card donation.

☐ Please send details of how I can make regular contributions by Standing Order.

☐ Please send more information about the League's campaigns to protect wildlife.

To: League Against Cruel Sports, Room 157 FREEPOST, 83-87 Union St, London SE1 1BT

DON'T LET BRITAIN'S WILDLIFE GO TO THE DOGS.

If you kept hearing the child next door screaming, is this how you'd stop it?

IT'S THAT NOISE again. The same one that you heard last night, and two nights ago.

It sounds like a child screaming, but you'd rather not think about it. So you turn the TV up, or do the hoovering. Anything to blot it out.

No matter what you do though, it doesn't stop you thinking. Countless thoughts race through your mind.

You try to persuade yourself it's something else. A hungry cat for instance. Or a whistling kettle.

And even if it is the child, he's probably a right little handful, and deserves to be taught a lesson.

Though he doesn't seem like a naughty kid. Maybe he is being ill-treated. But it's nothing to do with you what people get up to in their own houses, is it?

The fact of the matter is, it is your business. You could be the child's only chance of being saved from the horrors of physical abuse. Ignoring the screams can't stop the child's suffering. Calling the NSPCC Child Protection Helpline can.

We realise reporting a neighbour is a difficult decision to make. But don't be put off by thinking that you'll split up the family. Children only get taken into care in very few cases.

When a case is reported to us, first we listen closely to what is said and then decide on the best course of action.

An NSPCC Child Protection Officer or Local Authority social worker may then visit the child's home.

After this, we then make a careful assessment of the family to identify why the parents have been mistreating their child. In a lot of cases, they don't even realise they've been doing wrong. A period of counselling may then follow which can often involve helping the parents learn how to love and understand their children.

We always prefer it if you give your name, but the most important thing to us is to stop a child being at further risk from abuse.

Maybe you think it can't be going on next door to you. But unfortunately, that's what most people think.

Reporting a case isn't the only way you can help, however. We're always crying out for donations. 80% of our funding relies on the generosity of the public.

And please remember, if you keep hearing a child scream, picking up the TV remote control can't stop it. Picking up the phone can.

For further information on the work of the NSPCC, or to make a donation, write to: NSPCC, 67 Saffron Hill, London, EC1N 8RS or call 071-242 1626.

To report a suspected case of abuse, call the NSPCC Child Protection Helpline on 0800 800 500.

NSPCC
Act Now For Children.

LOOK AT THESE SAVINGS -AND SEE HOW LOW YOUR SHOPPING BILL CAN GO.

In a price survey carried out on 14th November, the following items were purchased from Budgens, Milton Keynes and Kwik Save, Dunstable. The columns below show how much less was paid by shopping at Kwik Save compared with Budgens.

	KWIK SAVE	BUDGENS	YOU SAVE
ST. IVEL GOLD 250gm	38p	39p	1p
LURPAK Butter 250gm	68p	69p	1p
MR KIPLING 6 Apple Pies	79p	£1.03	24p
GOLDEN SHRED Marmalade 454gm	69p	72p	3p
HELLMANS Mayonnaise 400gm	£1.09	£1.13	4p
KIT KAT 7 pack	57p	61p	4p
WALKERS Handy Size Crisps 30gm	18p	21p	3p
COCA COLA 330ml can	24p	26p	2p
CHUNKY Dog Food Large 412gm	31p	32p	1p
McVITIES Digestive Biscuits 400gm	49p	51p	2p
McVITIES Penguin 7 pack	55p	58p	3p
COMFORT Fabric Conditioner 1 ltr	89p	91p	2p
ANDREX Toilet Rolls 4 pack	£1.52	£1.56	4p
MIGHTY WHITE Sliced Loaf 800gm	54p	61p	7p
CADBURYS Dairy Milk 200gm	79p	82p	3p
HEINZ Sponge Pudding 300gm	66p	72p	6p
POLO MINTS 5 pack	49p	53p	4p
SMARTIES 3 pack	55p	65p	10p
CADBURYS Twirl 5 pack	53p	55p	2p

*Own label/specially packed for Budgens

CHAMPION PRICE FIGHTERS

As well as our usual top brands, we have selected a range of quality products that we are able to offer at exceptionally low prices – even by our standards.

SHOPPER'S CHAMPION

KWIK SAVE

NO NONSENSE/FOODSTORES

	KWIK SAVE	BUDGENS	YOU SAVE
MARS BARS Snack Size 8 pack	£1.05	£1.25	20p
CELEBRITY/OLDE OAK Round Ham 454gm	85p	95p PRINCES	10p
UNCLE BENS Stir Fry Sauce 350gm	95p	99p	4p
TOLLY BOY/WHITWORTHS Long Grain Rice 1kg	79p	£1.19 TILDA	40p
TYPHOO QT Instant White Tea 150gm	£1.25	£1.29	4p
CADBURYS/ROWNTREES Cocoa 125gm	65p	78p	13p
TETLEY Tea Bags 240 pack	£4.47	£4.55	8p
LYONS Original Ground Coffee 227gm	£1.25	£1.39	14p
PRINCES Spaghetti in Tomato Sauce 411gm	21p	*26p (440gm)	5p
Q-MATIC Automatic Liquid 2 ltr	£1.97	*£2.75	78p
PAMPERS Disposable Nappies all sizes	£6.15	£8.49	£2.34
ROSS Value Garden Peas 2 lbs	47p	*69p	22p
PERRIER Water 75cl	57p	59p	2p
JACOBS Club 6 pack	49p	56p	7p
ROWNTREES Jelly assorted 1 pint	26p	29p	3p
HORLICKS Instant Low Fat 500gm	£1.89	£1.95	6p
TYPHOO Tea 125gm	67p	70p	3p
NESCAFÉ 200gm	£2.63	£2.69	6p
MARS Ice Cream Bars 4 pack	£1.89	£1.99	10p

Kwik Save's policy is to offer the best value shopping basket in town. Due to localised 'price wars' prices on products shown above may therefore be lower in certain Kwik Save stores

NOW CELEBRATING OUR 750th STORE OPENING

COMPARE THESE PRICES

BUDGENS

KELLOGGS Cornflakes 500gm	£1.15
WEETABIX 24 pack	94p
PG TIPS 160 Tea Bags	£3.15
PASTEURISED MILK 4 Pts	£1.09
GRANULATED SUGAR 1 kg	66p
TIZER 2 Ltr	91p
DOLMIO 475gm	£1.18
BUDGENS Baked Beans 440gm	27p
McVITIES Milk Chocolate Homewheat 300gm	74p
McVITIES Cheddars 150gm	43p
PHILADELPHIA 200gm	£1.12
BUDGENS Pink Salmon 213gm	82p
SKI Fruit Yoghurt x1	28p
WHITE SLICED LOAF	49p
GOLDEN WONDER Pot Noodle	69p

TOTAL   £13.92

KWIK SAVE

KELLOGGS Cornflakes 500gm	92p
WEETABIX 24 pack	83p
PG TIPS 160 Tea Bags	£3.09
PASTEURISED MILK 4 Pts	98p
GRANULATED SUGAR 1 kg	59p
TIZER 2 Ltr	82p
DOLMIO 475gm	£1.09
PRINCES Baked Beans 425gm	17p
McVITIES Milk Chocolate Homewheat 300gm	69p
McVITIES Cheddars 150gm	36p
PHILADELPHIA 200gm	89p
JOHN WEST/PRINCES Pink Salmon 213gm	53p
SKI Fruit Yoghurt x1	26p
WHITE SLICED LOAF	29p
GOLDEN WONDER Pot Noodle	65p

TOTAL   £12.16

AT THE END OF THE DAY YOU'LL APPRECIATE WHY OUR STORES HAVE NO FRILLS

OUR CHARTER

For over 25 years Kwik Save's charter has been to bring you Britain's favourite brands at Britain's favourite prices.

We've done so by sticking with some basic business beliefs from which over 4 million customers a week now benefit at 750 stores.

——— BELIEF 1 ———
The more efficiently we operate, the more you benefit from the best prices.

——— BELIEF 2 ———
We only sell top brands and top sellers, and never compromise on quality.

——— BELIEF 3 ———
We will always use our buying power to keep costs to a minimum, and pass on the savings through our everyday low prices.

——— BELIEF 4 ———
We will operate smaller, efficient stores that are easy to shop at and easy to get to.

——— BELIEF 5 ———
We will not insult you with frills or gimmicks that you the customer end up paying for.

We believe that all this adds up to the best value grocery shopping in the country.

SHOPPER'S CHAMPION

KWIK SAVE

NO NONSENSE/FOODSTORES

"I've been shopping at Kwik Save for about six years now. The prices are cheaper than at other stores and there's plenty of choice. It's perfect for me and my family"

Mrs. K. Lewis

"We prefer brands we know and at Kwik Save we can get them cheaper than anywhere else"

Mr & Mrs Baker

NOW CELEBRATING OUR 750th STORE OPENING

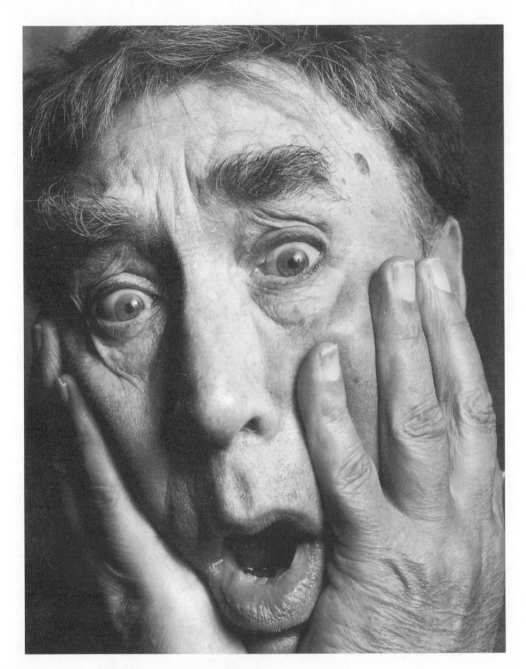

EKTAR RESOLUTION: A FRANK EXPOSÉ.

 When you've tittered as much as Frankie Howerd, you can expect a few laughter lines. As is revealed by the candid sharpness of EKTAR film.

Whether you choose 25, 125 or 1000 speed, Kodak EKTAR film will give you superbly clear enlargements. This is because it has 'T' Grain technology, tabular shaped grains in the emulsion that catch the light more effectively. Resulting in photographs that are visibly more detailed and virtually grain-free.

Though not, unfortunately for Frankie, wrinkle-free.

TOO SHARP FOR SOME.

Selecting copy

You need to think further about the words, phrases and expressions you are going to put into advertisements. As a rule, copy should be clear and to the point, using everyday words in simple sentences and short paragraphs – like those in the Blue Cross and the League Against Cruel Sports advertisements on pages 168 and 170. Relatively few readers take in complex ideas and detailed explanations. Generally, avoid lengthy text, however clearly written it may be. Unnecessary words and sentences can obscure the sales message. Even the fuller PC World and Kwik Save advertisements on pages 166 and 172–3 are still brief and direct, and easy to absorb.

Often, it is sensible to set out copy in a logical order, perhaps stressing the one key benefit so far as the reader is concerned, or several selling points in turn. Take another look at that Kodak advertisement on page 174, noting the main benefit that it is emphasizing over and again to great effect. Similarly, the Kwik Save advertisements on pages 172 and 173 are equally effective, really driving home to the reader what's in it for them. Constantly repeating the same basic message: 'It's sharper!', 'We're cheaper!' or whatever, is a successful tactic, helping to instal it in the back of the reader's mind.

Hopefully, your advertisements will be stylish and distinctive, and the copy can enable you to achieve this. Make sure it flows and is readable, paying attention to grammar, spelling and punctuation. See the National Society for the Prevention of Cruelty to Children advertisement on page 171 as a good example of this. Try to be original, steering away from clichés, corny expressions and trite phrases. Sound positive and enthusiastic, to encourage the reader to act now, otherwise the moment will pass and they will move on to the next page of the newspaper, magazine or miscellaneous publication.

Staying within the law

It is essential that your advertisements comply with the British Code of Advertising Practice, which is the advertising industry's self-regulatory control system. Those advertisements which fail to reach acceptable standards will not be taken by reputable publications. The Advertising Standards Authority and the Committee of Advertising Practice also regularly monitor and deal with complaints about press advertising, seeking to have offending advertisements changed, withdrawn or dropped, if necessary. Look at Appendix C: 'The British Code of Advertising Practice', page 317.

To adhere to the Code, you need to check back to ensure that your advertisements are: legal, with their contents neither breaching the law, bringing it into disrepute nor omitting anything which needs to be incorporated within them; decent, by not including any matter which might cause grave or widespread distaste or offence; honest, by not exploiting consumers' vulnerabilities such as a lack of knowledge or experience and by making certain that the advertising message and any points which are made are easy to grasp and understand; and truthful, by not trying to mislead consumers through inaccuracies, ambiguities, exaggerations or omissions.

Advertisements then have to be prepared with a sense of responsibility to consumers and society. They must not: play on fear nor excite distress without good cause; condone nor incite violence or anti-social behaviour; portray or refer to any living person unless prior permission has been obtained from them; cause offence to those connected in any way with deceased persons depicted or referred to; show or advocate dangerous behaviour or unsafe practices unless in the context of promoting safety; or contain anything which may lead to physical, mental or moral harm to children or might exploit their credulity, lack of experience or sense of loyalty.

You should further make sure that your advertisements conform to the principles of fair competition which are generally accepted in business. Hence: comparisons ought to deal fairly with rivals and be set out in such a way that there is no likelihood of a consumer being misled on any matter; competitors' products should not be described or shown to be broken, defaced, inoperative or ineffective, nor discredited by any other unfair means; inaccurate or irrelevant comments concerning the persons, characters or actions of rivals ought to be excluded; and advertisements should not resemble others to a degree whereby they might mislead or confuse. If or when your advertisements meet *all* of these terms and conditions, you are ready to move on to purchase advertising spaces.

Recording radio advertisements

You now need to think about your radio advertisements, selecting your approach, choosing their contents and making sure that they too comply with the law and are acceptable to radio stations and the listening public. Realistically, you will leave the actual creation and production of the advertisements to the stations' production teams. As a small-business owner or manager, you simply do not have the in-house skills and expertise needed to plan and record advertisements which are good enough to be transmitted on air. Nevertheless, you will have various thoughts and ideas that you can put in writing or on tape for submission to the radio stations to ensure they produce the advertisements that you want.

Picking your approach

Various approaches may be taken towards radio advertisements, and humour is probably the most popular. A funny situation, catchphrase or jingle, voices, music or sound effects can capture the listeners' attention, so that they hear the advertisements and what you are trying to say to them. Handled properly, humour may be very effective and can leave a lasting impression. However, it is hard to be truly funny. An idea which seems hilarious to you now may be less so to the listener struggling out of bed bleary-eyed at 6 a.m. in the morning. In-house jokes and silly voices – side-splittingly funny though they may be to colleagues – could appear nonsensical to the outside world. Sometimes, really humorous advertisements can detract from your message. The catchphrase or jingle is recalled, instead of the concern, products or services. The popular 'Cracker' radio script on page 178 shows an example of a funny *and* successful radio advertisement.

You could seek to appeal to listeners' emotions, using a mix of different voices, music and sound effects to play upon their maternal or paternal instincts, desire for status, nostalgia for times gone by, or whatever. These may attract and retain the listeners' interest, helping them to absorb your message. For example, a gentle caring voice, soothing music and the sound of a baby gurgling in the background may be attractive to young mothers who would then listen to what you were telling them. Alternatively, you might adopt a more logical approach, winning over listeners with sensible, reasoned arguments. As an example, a firm but friendly voice may spell out the key selling points of a new, executive car to convince businessmen and women that it is worth buying. Look at the 'Mr Dobie' radio script on page 179 to see how this particular advertisement plays on listeners' emotions.

Using a well-known personality to praise your firm, products and services on air is another, increasingly popular technique, which can give status and credibility. When that person is seen or heard again elsewhere on television or radio, listeners may be reminded of your products once more. Of course, it is important that he or she is perceived to have the same qualities – honesty, reliability, integrity and the like – that your business has and also possesses an appropriate and instantly recognizable voice. Bear in mind that employing a personality is costly, often running into thousands of pounds for just a few hours' work. It can be risky too, if he or she becomes involved with other activities which may be racier than the image you want to convey, or is mixed up in a scandal. The 'Box' radio script on page 180 and the 'Wind' radio script on page 181 were read by Miranda Richardson and Donald Sutherland respectively. In both cases, the personalities and their recognizable voices were considered to have played a key role in the success of the advertisements.

Bullish small-business owners and managers advertising on the radio can sometimes be drawn into a comparative approach, comparing and contrasting their firms, goods and services with those of their rivals. Typically, the prices of their products are quoted and direct or indirect, knocking references

'Cracker'

SFX: (Cracker being pulled, rustling of paper)

MVO: Doctor, doctor, I feel like a pair of curtains.
(without emotion)   Pull yourself together man.

SFX: (Cracker pulled)

                    What shakes on the sea bed?
                    A nervous wreck.

SFX: (Cracker pulled)
(authoritative)

                    What animal is it best to be on a cold day?
                    A little otter.

                    (Sigh)

MVO: If you want something a little more
                    stimulating to read this Christmas, the
                    bumper edition of 'The Economist' is out
                    tomorrow/out now.

'Cracker' radio script

'Mr Dobie'

Mr Dobie: My name's Paul Dobie, and this is what hap-pened to me last March.

I was feeling sick whilst driving along the M6 and decided to pull on to the hard shoulder in my Volvo Estate.

After a short while I felt better, and put my safety belt on to continue my journey.

But it wasn't just nausea that hit me that day.

I looked in the mirror and to my horror saw a lorry speeding towards me on the hard shoul-der.

I was hit from behind with incredible force. My Volvo was spun around, tipped onto its side, and pushed 200 yards up the motorway into a ditch.

I climbed out of the car and discovered I'd been struck by a 40-ton articulated lorry with a JCB Earth Mover on the back.

I reckon if it hadn't been for the Volvo's pas-senger safety cell I'd never have known what hit me.

MVO: Volvo. A car you can believe in.

'Mr Dobie' radio script

'Box'

Miranda Richardson:	Famous Names liqueur chocolates come in a box.
	They have no sugary layer which makes them deliciously smooth.
	At Christmas I asked my husband Nigel to buy me some Famous Names liqueur chocolates.
	Nigel bought me a tin of scented talcum powder.
SFX:	Gun-shot.
	Now Nigel comes in a box.
	Deliciously smooth Famous Names liqueur chocolates.
	The perfect present for discerning palates.

'Box' radio script

'Wind'

SFX:	Irish country music throughout.
Donald Sutherland:	It was a Friday evening and Joe found himself on the way to the bar. He also found his brother Michael with him, and his friend Eddie. Joe and Michael but not forgetting Eddie turned the corner and the wind fair sandpapered their cheeks.
SFX:	(music)
	'Why,' thought Joe 'was this enjoyable?' Was it perhaps because if he felt his eyes watering and his ears burning cold he must be alive? Or maybe it was because he liked the wind. It was so . . . bracing! Or was it simply because there was a glass of Beamish with his name written on it that would soon be slipping and sliding down, in the lovely warm bar?
SFX:	(music)
	'Answer C' thought Joe, who had always been so good at multiple choice.
SFX:	(music)
MVO: (sensual)	Beamish Stout. Just slips away.

'Wind' radio script

are then made about the prices of competitors' goods. This may seem to be a sensible and successful approach, especially if you are genuinely better than your rivals in some respects. Nonetheless, it is a dangerous attitude to adopt. You are drawing the listeners' attention to your competitors, and giving them free advertising time. Knocking rivals is also regarded as being in poor taste and a sign that you are worried about your competitors. Customers may visit them to see why you are so concerned, and buy from them. Also, you have to be absolutely sure of your facts, to avoid legal action being taken against you by outraged rivals.

Whatever your favoured approach – and you will probably have some ideas of your own on the subject – always be mindful of the particular benefits and drawbacks of this highly individual medium. For example, the radio is live and immediate, with advertisements being recorded and transmitted very quickly if necessary. Price cuts could be notified to existing and would-be customers within a few hours. Similarly, this is a localized medium, so a humorous and well-known local incident might be referred to in an amusing and topical manner.

Do not overlook the drawbacks of radio though. As an example, it is one-dimensional, with advertisers dependent upon sound only. You cannot show the products you are trying to sell, their colours and varieties and so on, and are unable to demonstrate them. You need to conjure up the required image by voices, music and sound effects alone. You may find it hard to make listeners feel nostalgic for your products and services simply by describing them. It is a shortlived medium too, with advertisements lasting for seconds rather than minutes. It is difficult to work through reasoned arguments in such a limited period of time.

Not surprisingly, your selected approach must also reflect your specific situation. Humour may be appropriate for a joke shop, but not for a funeral parlour. Playing on listeners' emotions could be relevant for baby goods, but not if financial services are being offered. Obtaining an endorsement from a popular personality may be more suited to a large, national firm than a small business operating on a restricted budget. Comparing yourself with competitors might (just) be worth considering if you are that much better than them in *all* respects, but not if you are closely matched. Work through your background notes to finally conclude which approach is right for you.

Choosing contents

Aware of the type of approach that is correct for the medium *and* your particular circumstances, you then have to decide upon your sales message. Be clear about what you want to say, and why you wish to state it. Perhaps you want to stress the enormous numbers and types of products stocked by your shop, in order to attract customers and boost sales. Possibly, you wish to outline a job vacancy to appeal to suitable applicants and to enable you to pick the right person. Whatever your aim and reasons are, be fully familiar with them prior to writing down or recording any of your ideas. Each voice and every statement, piece of music and sound effect used must be chosen with these in mind.

Start advertisements by trying immediately to seize the listeners' attention and to make them tune in to what you are about to tell them. A clear and commanding voice may achieve this, as could a funny, cartoon-like one or an instantly recognized voice, perhaps quoting a famous catchphrase. Soft and sentimental music, a rousing burst of song or a well-known, much-loved jingle might be equally effective. Sound effects – as diverse as an opening door or the rat-tat-tat of gunfire – could be used too, in order to draw the listeners into your world. Whatever you pick – and there are hundreds and thousands of voices, snatches of music and sound effects to choose from at a radio station – attempt to separate the listeners from the last song or advertisement in a definite manner, to turn their attention onto your advertisement. Take another look at the 'Cracker' radio script on page 178 to see how this advertisement begins.

Sketch out the main part of your advertisements by noting down your sales message and the points that you wish to put across to substantiate and enhance it, whether the name of your shop and a list of the main types of goods stocked or details of your firm, the job and the person required to fill it. Keep your notes as simple as you can. Bear in mind that you are advertising via an unseen medium, and for only 30 seconds or so. Elaborate descriptions and endlessly repeated points will not convey and support your message – they will just confuse and obscure it. Make sure that your points are brief and wholly relevant, and are sorted into a sensible order. The 'Mr Dobie' radio script on page 179 is a good example of this.

Contemplate the type of voice which should be used to put over your message. For example, a breathless one speaking faster and faster as he or she tries to mention all of your products in time might be both humorous *and* effective, especially if topped and tailed with a contrasting, cool and rather amused voice reminding listeners of the name and address of your well-stocked shop. Similarly, a kind but authoritative voice could be most appropriate for a logically approached recruitment advertisement, informing job hunters of the reasons why they should apply for this vacancy and encouraging them to do so. Should you want to have two characters chatting, perhaps about your products, try to see these people in your mind, giving them names, personalities and a reason for the conversation. This will help you to write a real dialogue, and enable the stations to interpret your wishes more accurately. See the 'Box' radio script on page 180. Miranda Richardson's voice is just perfect for this advertisement.

Think about the background music and sound effects that might be added to your advertisements to support your key points. As an example, fast

and furious music could be played alongside that swift-speaking voice to under-
line the vast range of goods that need to be referred to within the 30 seconds or
so, and to make it sound even funnier. For the job advertisement, the noise of a
busy office, full of people going about their tasks, might be fitting, making
would-be applicants want to work there. Do not be afraid of silence though. It is
not always relevant to fill your advertisements with music and sound effects. A
clear, well-spoken voice putting across your points may be sufficient, and could
stand out from the hurly-burly of the loud advertisements around it. The Irish
music and soft, warm voice of Donald Sutherland combine to great effect in the
advertisement on page 181, 'Wind'.

End advertisements by attempting to inspire the listeners to act, whether
to pick up the telephone and place an order with you or to come to your shop
when they're in town. Having stated the reasons why they should buy from you,
apply for the job or whatever, make them feel that they must do something *now*,
perhaps by indicating that stocks are limited, a sale will end soon or that there
is a closing date for job applications. Then help them to respond by reminding
them of your firm's name, telling them where you are and what your telephone
number is. Give them a contact name as well, if appropriate. Close off the advertisements by repeating the opening piece of music, sound effect or whatever, to
separate them from the following ones. Check out how the radio advertisement
on page 178, 'Cracker' ends – it's very effective!

Do write down all of your thoughts and ideas about your advertisements
so that they can be passed to the production departments of the radio stations.
Better still, tape an advertisement, doing the voice yourself and adding music
and sound effects if you are able to. This may make you feel self-conscious, but
it is worthwhile. Playing back the tape, you can judge the voice, the message,
music and sound effects for yourself, deciding if they are all suitable. You may
conclude that 30 seconds is not long enough to put over your message, or perhaps you are trying to convey too many points. However amateurish it may
sound, it will also be of great help to the production team, enabling them to produce what you want to hear, and at the first attempt.

Keeping within the law

It is important that your advertisements comply with the Radio Authority's
Code of Advertising Standards and Practice (and Programme Sponsorship).
This Code applies to all advertisements transmitted on radio stations licensed
by the Authority, and contains a number of over-riding principles. Radio advertising must be legal, decent, honest and truthful. Advertisements have to adhere
to the law in every respect. Advertising rules referred to in the Code should be
applied in spirit as well as by the letter. The Code is divided into three parts.
Section A covers the standards for the presentation of advertisements. Section

B deals with the contents of advertisements and is followed by appendices looking at key categories of some concern to the Authority. Section C considers programme sponsorship, which is less relevant to you.

You need to be aware of the rules and guidelines concerning the presentation of your advertisements, as set out within Section A of the Code. In particular, advertisements must be clearly distinguishable from programming. For example, you should avoid using sound effects associated with news bulletins which could cause confusion. Various types of advertisement must not be broadcast during certain programmes. Typically, advertisements for contraceptives are not to be transmitted in or around children's programmes. Advertisements for some products and services must not be broadcast at all. As examples, cigarettes, pornography and escort agencies cannot be promoted on air. Station presenters must not endorse or recommend advertisers' goods. Therefore, you could not employ these personalities to praise your products. Other, less significant rules are that radio stations must not discriminate for or against any advertisers, and product placements within programmes are prohibited.

Of course, the contents of advertisements are of equal concern, and you should thus be familiar with the rules and guidelines noted in Section B of the Code. Of key relevance, advertisements must not mislead. For example, you should not state that a product will restore hair growth, if it does not. Advertisements must not offend against good taste or decency, or be offensive to public feeling. Typically, you should not use profane language or make remarks about minority groups. Advertisements must not unfairly attack or discredit other products. As an example, competitors' goods should not be described using a denigratory tone of voice. Advertisements must not use sound effects likely to create a safety hazard to drivers. It would therefore be unwise to incorporate the sounds of sirens or screeching tyres within your advertisements.

Some advertising receives special attention from the Radio Authority and its Code incorporates appendices containing additional, detailed rules and guidelines on such advertisements. These appendices cover the do's and don'ts of financial advertising, alcoholic drink advertising, children and advertising, medicines, treatments and health, charity advertising, environmental claims and religious advertising. If your advertisements fall into any of these categories, it is absolutely essential that you not only study and understand Sections A and B of the Code but also read the appropriate appendix carefully. Section C of the Code relating to the sponsorship of programmes need not be looked at, unless and until this becomes an area of interest to you.

Sensible though it is to be conversant with the Code and its relevant sections, radio stations will act as a censor if you unintentionally breach the rules or guidelines. They are authorized by the Radio Authority to approve or reject most advertisements, although others such as those involving financial services, alcohol and so on are referred to the Association of Independent Radio Companies Limited for clearance prior to transmission. If in doubt, approach the radio stations, AIRC or the Radio Authority itself for advice and guidance. See Appendix D: 'Code of Advertising Standards and Practice', page 331, and 'Useful contacts, page 385.

Writing mailshots

Now that you know how to possess accurate and up-to-date mailing lists, it is sensible to think about creating quality mailshots that can be sent to your customers and prospects, whether businesses or members of the public. You need to evaluate envelopes, look at letters and contemplate adding inserts such as product samples and sales materials. It is also wise to know how to adhere to the standards of practice which have been set by the industry. Mixing your hands-on knowledge of your business, market and budget with a growing awareness of the basic do's and don'ts of successful direct mailing will enable you to pull together valuable ideas about your mailshots. Then, you will be ready to brief those firms or individuals who will produce your mailings, and can go on to run effective activities.

Evaluating envelopes

The envelope is your first point of contact with the recipient and should therefore be given due thought and consideration. Ideally, it ought to seize the recipient's attention in some way, making him or her want to lift it from the pile of letters on the desk or doormat, open it and study its contents. The reader should be in a positive mood towards the letter before he or she starts looking at it, so that it has a better chance of doing its job of persuading the reader to take the required action: to request a product demonstration, make an enquiry or place an order. At the very least, the envelope must avoid being shuffled to the bottom of the pile or, even worse, being mistaken for junk mail, to be consigned automatically to the wastepaper basket without a second glance.

Hundreds and thousands of different envelopes are available to choose from, and can be grouped into various types. Plain manilla envelopes are inexpensive and used often, but tend to be rather drab and nondescript. They are most likely to be read last and could be mistaken for bills to be left unopened until a final demand arrives. Coloured envelopes stand out, are not too costly and are increasingly popular nowadays, with businesses selecting colours to reflect their activities. An accountancy firm may use grey, a nursery goods store could choose pink and blue, and so on. You can choose envelopes with or without windows: those with windows are time-saving and convenient to use as the recipient's name and address can show through from the letter inside rather than being reprinted on the envelope too. They are slightly more expensive though, and you need to be careful that the name and address will not be jiggled out of sight during delivery. Envelopes without windows are cheaper but take time to be addressed. It all adds up!

A company logo and/or slogan can be rubber-stamped or printed onto the envelope. These can help to identify the mailshot to existing customers who may be keen to open the envelope to discover what you are writing to them about. Prospects could be intrigued by the eye-catching logo or puzzling slogan, and equally enthusiastic to find out exactly what is inside the envelope. Some businesses take the concept of individualized envelopes even further, producing special mailshots which border on works of art, ranging from images of a new £10 or £20 note to an illustration of the sun setting over the horizon. Clearly, these leap out of a pile of letters and can inspire curiosity, but are expensive and are often mistaken for junk mail, to be disposed of.

Naturally, the approach you take – manilla, coloured, with or without windows, with or without logos, slogans and pictures – depends upon your individual situation. Consider your firm, products, services and goals. For example, you may feel that your business is a traditional one which is held in high esteem, and that standard, low-key envelopes help to maintain and foster this image. Conversely, you might be planning to introduce a new product which will revolutionize the industry and want to make an impact with bright and colourful envelopes. Think about your customers, competitors and the marketplace. From talking to your customers, you may know the types of envelope which attract them. Your trade might always use the same style of envelope, which could make you want to make a different choice. Contemplate your budget too: there is little point in spending excessive sums on envelopes if this means you have to cut back elsewhere.

Whatever your decision, you need to adhere to various do's and don'ts which apply to all envelopes, plain or gaudy. They should be of good quality, not simply the cheapest available. You own a first-class firm making a fine offer to a valued customer: the envelope must reflect this. Accordingly, it should be neat and clean – the name, address, logo, slogan, stamp or franked postmark must all be placed carefully and not be smudged or grubby. It is up to you whether you write out the name and address by hand or have them typed or affixed by sticky label. Handwriting helps to personalize the letter but takes up time, is uneconomic for larger mailings and the details may not be as legible as they ought to be. The choice between a stamp or franked postmark involves similar pros and cons concerning personalization and the time involved. The name, address and postcode must be accurate. The wrong title or initials or a misspelt surname can irritate or offend. An inaccurate address or omitted postcode may delay delivery, or make it impossible.

Envelopes must be practical, sufficiently large to carry all of the contents and strong enough not to burst open during delivery. An envelope full of squashed and battered items will not create a good impression on the recipient and if it is returned because it has come apart is simply a waste of your money. It is sensible to choose envelopes which fall into the Royal Mail's recommended range of sizes, and are suited to its sorting equipment and delivery system. These range from 9 centimetres by 14 centimetres up to a maximum of 12 centimetres by 24 centimetres for first- and second-class deliveries. They ought to be oblong with the longer side 1.4 times the length of the shorter one. They should be made of paper, weighing at least 63 grams per square metre. Only certain parts ought to be printed, with other (rather obvious) spaces reserved for stamping, franking and addressing. The Royal Mail will provide further technical advice, on request.

Looking at letters

Your letter is the key part of your mailing and will make or break your success far more than the envelope and any inserts will do. It is the letter which persuades the reader to enquire, place an order, part with his or her hard-earned money or throw the whole mailshot away. Before writing anything down, have your typical customer fixed in your mind. Imagine he or she is real and you are addressing that one person, whether an executive in a dynamic, expanding concern or a housewife bringing up two young children in a three-bedroomed semi. You know him or her well from your earlier research – who he is, what she does, his likes and dislikes, habits, opinions and so on. Everything you write, the way that you phrase it and the layout of your letter must all be geared up to him or her, and what he wants to know, what she likes to read, what he wishes to see and so forth.

Knowing exactly who you are addressing, you can move on to decide what you want to put in the letter. This should be relatively straightforward if you are as familiar with your concern, products, services and objectives as you ought to be. Perhaps you wish to promote your firm as the best supplier in the trade or as the ideal place to come to for a family holiday. From those preliminary notes which you accumulated so conscientiously, jot down the main features of your business and the benefits which make it so attractive to customers. Similarly, you might be seeking to sell as many goods and services as you can to existing accounts. Accordingly, make a note of their varied characteristics and selling points as far as your customers are concerned. (Always remember to sell the benefits, not the features. All readers want to know 'What's in it for me?')

It is then necessary to sort these jotted comments into the right sequence so that the reader becomes more and more convinced that you are the top supplier, the best place for a family holiday or whatever, and places an order or makes a booking. Grab his or her attention immediately, perhaps by taking the main, over-riding benefit and turning it into a bold headline, a question or anything else which will leap off the page. As the recipient opens the envelope and unfolds the letter, he or she must be seized and drawn into wanting to read on, whether fascinated by that headline or puzzled by the question. The reader should recognize that there is something in this for him or her – the answer to supply difficulties or a good holiday – and wants to find out more.

Next, the reader's attention has to be turned into interest, maintained and built up, step by step. In your first paragraph, you may choose to take and elaborate upon that key benefit, so the recipient understands it inside and out. You might outline the wide range of products stocked by your firm, or the different ways in which families are made so welcome at your concern. Subsequent paragraphs could then deal with other benefits one after another, possibly covering your prompt delivery service, low prices, credit terms and so forth or the number of rooms, facilities available, proximity and easy access to the seafront and so on.

This increasing interest has to be transformed into desire, which hopefully will be generated as these selling points unfold before the reader's eyes. Always try to back up any statements made with proof, such as testimonials or research findings. Mentioning refund opportunities, money back and product guarantees can be helpful too, all working towards the conviction that this is a marvellous firm, product or offer. Attempt to limit your offer in some way at this stage, possibly referring to imminent price rises, the seasonal nature of some products, the clearance of various stocks, the shortage of rooms and the like. This will introduce a nagging worry and doubt, creating the fear that the recipient may miss out, which is likely to boost his or her desire further.

The reader's desire must be translated into action, and you should try to initiate this in your final paragraph. It is vitally important that he or she acts now, to obtain the product while stocks last and for you since a set aside letter is less likely to be responded to later on. Make it easy for the reader to take action. You might give your telephone number, including the dialling code, the extension number and a contact name. If you are inviting the recipient to visit you, attach a detailed map and mention it. Should you be expecting a reply, enclose an order, membership or subscription form and a reply-paid card or envelope, as appropriate. Refer to them here. If you wish the reader to pay for goods, state the wide range of payment methods available: cheque, postal order, credit card and so on. Add another nudge to round off the letter – a discount if he or she replies within 14 days or a discount and free gift if they get in touch within seven days.

Knowing what you want to put and its order, you must now think about how you ought to express yourself. Never forget that you are addressing one person, not a crowd. You also know the person. If you shut your eyes, you can almost see and hear him or her talking. Thus, you should strike a personal tone as though the letter has been written just for that person. Always make sure it is personalized with the accurate name and address at the top of the page, and the correct greeting, whether Dear Mr Singh, Mrs Rose or Ms Gayther. Be careful not to go over the top though, avoiding the constant 'Yes you, Mr Munglani' and 'That's right, Mrs Mason' which litter so many irritating, second-rate mailshots. Be subtle and discreet, topping it with their name and tailing it with your own, and a *real* signature whenever possible. This adds that little extra touch.

Be friendly, talking *to,* not *at* the recipient. You are equals, so steer away from talking down or patronizing him or her, as this is the swiftest way of having your letter shredded. Use the language the reader is familiar with. Technical phrases and trade jargon alienate members of the public who want to read clear and simple words and expressions which they can understand. Likewise, over-simplistic language should not be used to specialists in this field who will feel equally offended and patronized. Do be especially wary of in-house slang that is bandied about between colleagues and employees, and which is often meaningless and confusing to an outsider.

Write naturally, as though you are talking to the reader face-to-face, rather than writing a stiff and formal letter to an unknown person over a hundred miles away. Write as you would speak. Keep everything short and to the point, using clear and concise words, sentences, phrases and paragraphs. Whether a stressed business executive or an overworked housewife, he or she wants it to be an easy-to-read pleasure rather than a word-by-word struggle, full of lengthy phrases and garbled expressions. Make it simple for them to read on to the end, without having to think things over. The easier it is to read, the more successful it will be.

Give your letter some life as well. Show that you are enthusiastic about your firm, goods, services and the offer you are making. If you are half-hearted about the message, the reader will inevitably respond in the same, disinterested manner. Dot your text with positive words and phrases but be careful not to be excessive as a continual stream of 'Brilliant', 'Marvellous', 'Unbelievable', 'Once in a lifetime', 'This is what you've been waiting for' offers tends to annoy very quickly indeed. It can also be counter-productive – the more you stress, the less you are believed. So be subtle, with a nudge here and a shove there so that they appear to reach the conclusion for themselves.

As a rule – and rules concerning creativity are meant to be broken now and then – be wary of being humorous in your letter, unless it is absolutely relevant to your business, goods, services and goals: even then it is a notoriously difficult approach to handle successfully. Your sense of humour may not match your reader's, which might be non-existent. Also, a comment or aside which sounds hilarious to you and your colleagues when you are brainstorming ideas could seem very different when written down and read by someone else a few weeks later on. Genuinely funny statements and jokes may detract from the main thrust of your letter. In general, stick to facts, not funnies.

Fully conscious of its contents and phrasing, you can now go on to actually write the letter. Ensure that it is written on quality paper, preferably matching the envelope, which further conveys the first-rate image you wish to put across. Watermarked sheets are a wise choice, albeit rather costly for mass mailings. Make certain the paper is big enough for you to complete your letter over perhaps one or two sides without appearing cramped or running on and on over many pages which is offputting for a would-be reader who wants to finish it as soon as possible. The standard A4 (297 x 210mm) or the smaller A5 paper (210 x 148mm) are popular choices, depending on how much you have to write.

The layout of your letter will vary according to your personal preferences: there are no fixed rules. Typically, your letterhead will cross the top of the paper incorporating your firm's name, address, telephone and fax numbers, e-mail address and a logo. References, the date, the recipient's name and address and a greeting will be set down the left side of the page. Including a reference can help you to check and assess responses to your mailings. The date makes the letter feel topical and fresh. Always ensure the name and address are totally correct, and use 'Dear Mr Hicks' or 'Dear Mrs Barham'; not 'Dear Business Colleague', 'Dear Householder' or the vaguely unsettling 'Dear Sir or Madam'. Your bold headline or teasing question may follow thereafter.

You then arrive at the main section of the letter – the paragraphs which contain details of your product's qualities etc. Try to give these some variety rather than setting out one dull-looking paragraph after another. Indent them and vary widths and lengths. Play around with capitals to stress key benefits, or think about underlining them instead. Perhaps have sub-headings to break up text, or use bullet points to emphasise sections. Consider adding handwritten comments in the margins to highlight certain phrases. End the letter with 'Yours sincerely' or the less formal 'Kind Regards' or 'Best Regards'. Add a clear and readable signature, your name and 'Enclosures', as appropriate. Examples of winning mailshots are shown on pages 192 and 193.

Adding inserts

You ought to include a reply device of some kind in your mailshot, either a pre-addressed postcard or an envelope in which a proposal, order, membership or subscription form can be placed and returned to you. Incorporating such an item appears courteous and should also encourage and make it that much easier for the recipient to respond in the hoped-for manner. Your overall response rate ought to rise accordingly. The inclusion of an addressed card or envelope

Mrs T Maitland
16 Barton Close
Whiston
Suffolk
IP14 6JA

15305

**<u>Get 10% off all your direct
dialled calls with Option 15</u>**

Dear Mrs Maitland,

I'd like to introduce you to a new BT service that will save you money on your phone calls.

It's called **Option 15** and it's designed for people, like you, whose quarterly call bills are usually more than £40. Which means you can benefit immediately without making any more calls than you usually do.

You can enrol on Option 15 for a quarterly fee of just £4. In return, we'll take 10% off every direct dialled call you make – and the more calls you make the more you'll save.

It means that £100 of direct dialled calls at the basic unit rate will cost you only £94, £200 will cost you only £184 and so on.

What's more, both the £4 charge <u>and</u> your discount will be clearly shown on your bill, so you can see at a glance exactly how much you're saving.

You'll find full details of the discounts in the enclosed brochure. All you have to decide is whether your quarterly call bills are likely to exceed £40 over the coming year.

If so, I suggest you sign and return the Enrolment Form today and join the thousands of BT customers who are already paying less with Option 15.

Yours sincerely,

Ian Ash
Director of Marketing
Personal Communications

P.S. Details of the savings are shown on the attached form. But if you have any further questions, just call our free Helpline on 0800 800 862.

All prices quoted above are inclusive of VAT at 17.5%.

0013050   BT, FREEPOST BS6295, BRISTOL BS1 2BR.
© British Telecommunications plc. Registered Office: 81 Newgate Street, LONDON EC1A 7AJ. Registered in England no. 1800000. PHME 13126.

Mr I Maitland
16 Barton Close
Whiston
Suffolk
IP14 6JA

Now in Cambridge, Coventry and Manchester...

Dear Iain

Here's a fascinating new conference, which could bring more profit to your business. I'm getting together a few of our members and delegates from past seminars. People like yourself who want to get a lot more from your marketing budget.

I will present a vast amount of new material — ideas you haven't heard before from any seminar I've ever done. I'll put in many marketing ideas that have helped me make a lot of money (yes, they truly did make me financially independent). I'll even show you the actual materials I used and the results I got. So you can use them too.

What's more, I'll do something really strange — I'll give you a personal promise that, if you haven't heard enough in the first 90 minutes to enthral you, just come up to me in the first coffee break and say "Nick, you're a lovely man (etc) but I want a refund!" And I'll give it you all back, not just the money you've paid, *but 10% on top as well* — to repay you for your inconvenience. And you'll get it.

If I was to make that offer to you, would you find it useful?

Let me repeat what you'll get: a whole day, 9am to 5pm packed full of new ideas. Plus the chance to network with dozens of fellow marketers, who may well include several possible clients for you. You get lunch as well. Plus unlimited use (within the day) of my own brain (not an offer I idly make). And I'll charge you just £195, all in.

Does that sound reasonable?

I truly don't know. So I'm asking you to tell me. I've set it all out in the enclosed odd little brochure. It doesn't look like a brochure. Does it? **The events are in Cambridge (15th March), Coventry (22nd March) and Manchester (29th March).**

Frankly, I'm not sure if this idea will work. So will you tell me — by booking now? I'll let the brochure spell out the details. But just now, could you let me know — by booking now, under that odd "110% guarantee" as soon as possible?

Kindest regards
NICK

PS: Book **three** paying people, *and you can come along free.* But please do it quickly, or there may not be space for *you* too...

1 Houghton Court, Houghton Regis, LU5 5DY, Beds. England
Telephone: 01582 861556   Facsimile: 01582 864913
The Marketing Guild Ltd

000440

further ensures that the reply is sent back to the correct address, which is not always guaranteed if the recipient completes the envelope for himself or herself. You can use all of these returns to build up your mailing list, and keep it accurate too.

Of course, you may boost the response rate further still, and in several ways. Providing a stamped, business reply-paid or freepost card or envelope inevitably generates a larger and faster return as some waverers decide to reply and genuinely interested recipients do not have to search around or queue at the post office or corner shop for stamps. A prompt reponse may be important if you wish to send in sales representatives to demonstrate a product or explain a service before enthusiasm wanes or is redirected elsewhere. However, bear in mind that a significant proportion of the additional responses are likely to be from half-hearted readers who will not actually hand over their money when it comes to the crunch. The extra costs must be taken into account too.

Every part of the pre-paid, addressed card or envelope which needs to be filled in by the recipient ought to be easy to complete. Make sure the item can be written on in ballpen, and is not too glossy for a felt-tipped pen. Instructions should be clear and simple to understand. If the back of the card consists of an order form, then the types, numbers, costs and total costs ought to be easy to fill out. Giving an example can be helpful. Questions must be concise and unambiguous. If the reverse side of a postcard comprises a membership application form, have Yes/No responses to be deleted, together with and/or boxes to be ticked. Should the recipient be expected to add comments or complete his or her name and address, ensure there is sufficient room, and that they do not have to abbreviate details or omit the postcode. Whenever possible, fill in data such as the name and address on the recipient's behalf. It all helps to encourage a larger and speedier reaction.

You may also wish to incorporate other items in your mailshot in addition to the envelope, letter and reply device. A product could be included, perhaps a swatch to show the quality of your materials and range of colours and patterns, a sachet containing tea, coffee, powdered milk or a whole host of smaller items as diverse as clothes labels, buttons and zips to pens, pencils and rubbers. Forwarding a product to the reader can be a good idea. It is hard to ignore a mysterious shape within an envelope; people like to receive a free item however small and inexpensive and can study and examine it at their own pace, reaching their own conclusions. Nevertheless, these pluses need to be weighed against the cost of the goods, the expense of a larger and stronger envelope (if appropriate) and packaging time and efforts.

Sales literature is a popular alternative to samples, especially when a product is too large to be posted or services are offered. You might include a catalogue, brochure and leaflets as well as a price list and order form (although these could be incorporated onto your reply-paid card to save money). Full of pictures and text, your sales material can illustrate and explain your goods and services in some detail, and certainly in more depth than a letter. Many business executives and members of the public like to be given catalogues and brochures to mull over at their leisure when making their choices. Again, the costs involved need to be taken into consideration. Also, there is the danger of overkill, inundating the recipient with so much information that he or she does not need to respond to find out more, or is simply bewildered by it all.

Other inserts – and you can really put in anything which you personally feel is suitable – might include discount vouchers, money-off coupons, bingo cards, scratch-and-sniff cards and a whole host of gimmicks to attract and interest the reader. In their favour, these do appeal to many members of the public who enjoy cutting out and using coupons and playing with games to see if they have won a free product, trial subscription, no-obligation demonstration or some similar freebie. However, you need to be mindful that such novelties can, and do, annoy others such as busy business executives, and may lessen your credibility and cheapen your overall image.

The purpose of any additions is to substantiate and enhance your message, and increase the number and speed of responses. Thus, a product sample may verify the wide range of colours or the new improved taste that was mentioned in the letter, and could make the recipient want to find out more. Similarly, sales literature might help to prove the breadth of services available, and inspire the reader to apply for a demonstration. Vouchers may make him or her wish to try a product, and before the expiry date. Too often though, inserts simply confuse the message, muddle the recipient and raise nothing but the costs involved. The sachet of coffee never seems to taste as good as it does from the jar, the brochure is full of products which are not of interest and the bingo card does not seem to bear any connection to the message. Usually, simplicity – a smart envelope, concise letter and reply card – is best. Examples of successful inserts from recent years are illustrated on pages 196 to 207. Decide for yourself how good these are.

Adhering to standards

It is absolutely essential that you are fully familiar with the two self-regulatory codes of practice which govern the advertising and direct mail industries, namely The British Code of Advertising Practice and The British Code of Sales Promotion Practice. With regard to BCAP, which is a wide-ranging and lengthy code running to some hundred pages, you must ensure that your envelope, letter and inserts are legal, decent, honest and truthful. Two of the most common complaints in this area concern the use of 'Private and Confidential' and 'Urgent' on envelopes when the contents suggest they are not, and exaggerated and unsubstantiated qualities attributed to products offered to recipients.

If you'd like 10% off your phone calls, this is for you

Here's how much Option 15 could be saving you

CALLS PER QUARTER AT BASIC RATE OF 4.935p*	CALLS PER QUARTER WITH OPTION 15 (INC £4 CHARGE)*	THE DIFFERENCE PER QUARTER WITH OPTION 15 OVER THE BASIC RATE*
£75.00	£71.50	£3.50
£100.00	£94.00	£6.00
£150.00	£139.00	£11.00
£200.00	£184.00	£16.00
£250.00	£229.00	£21.00
£300.00	£274.00	£26.00

*All figures are approximate and inclusive of VAT. Customers who choose not to take Option 15 will still automatically receive the lower discounts available through Standard Call Charges.

Option 15 – your questions answered

Q. When is it worth applying for Option 15?

A. If your quarterly direct dialled call bill is consistently over £40, Option 15 will save you money. That's because you'll save enough each quarter to pay for the quarterly £4 fee.

Q. Can I cancel Option 15 at any time?

A. Yes. Just write to your local BT office giving seven days notice of your cancellation.

Q. What's the difference between Standard Call Charges and Option 15?

A. With Standard Call Charges, you receive no discount between £0.00 and £88.13 (inc VAT), a 5% discount between £88.13 and £293.75 (inc VAT), and an 8% discount for all calls made over £293.75 (inc VAT).

With Option 15, on the other hand, you get a 10% discount on *all* your direct dialled calls.

Q. Why do I have to pay an Option charge?

A. Customers already receive automatic discounts under Standard Call Charges when their quarterly direct dialled call bill exceeds £88.13 (inc VAT). The Option charge enables customers to benefit from the enhanced discounts available through Option 15, which apply to all direct dialled calls.

Q. When will I start receiving discounts?

A. Your discounts will appear on the first phone bill you receive after your application has been processed.

Q. Do the Option 15 discounts apply to any other charges on my phone bill?

A. Option 15 offers you discounts on all your direct dialled calls, but not to line rental and other phone charges.

Q. Is there any reason why I shouldn't join Option 15?

A. If you expect your call bill to remain over £40 in the future, it will certainly pay you to join.

Q. Will I receive a discount on all my calls?

A. For a £4 quarterly charge, you'll save money on every direct dialled call you make from that phone line.

Q. How do I apply for Option 15?

A. Once you've read the Terms and Conditions, simply fill in your enrolment form and return it to us in the reply-paid envelope.

Q. Who do I call if I have any questions or queries?

A. Simply call our free Helpline on **0800 800 862**. We'll be pleased to help you.

Terms and Conditions for Option 15

About these Terms and Conditions

These are the Terms and Conditions that apply to Option 15. They vary BT's Standard Conditions for Telephone Service which still apply in all other respects. These Terms and Conditions apply from the date that Option 15 is effective on your line.

What does Option 15 apply to?

Option 15 is only available on all direct dialled calls made on BT residential lines. You will not receive discounts on calls made:

- through the Operator

- with a BT Chargecard or credit card

- through a cardphone or pay-on-answer coinbox

- on lines not rented from BT

Prices

These are the charges that apply to Option 15. They are correct at the time of going to print but may vary from time to time. Changes will be published in our Price List at least two weeks before the changes take effect.

Option 15 is calculated as follows:

Option 15 charge per line

£4 a quarter (inc VAT).

Option 15 unit fee

4.442p per unit (inc VAT) with your 10% discount, instead of the Basic Unit Rate of 4.935p (inc VAT) per unit.

Offices in Europe, North America, Japan and Asia Pacific.

© British Telecommunications plc 1993.
Registered office:
81 Newgate Street, London EC1A 7AJ.

Acquire over 200 fresh powerful ways to make your business more profitable more quickly - at less cost, *now*

Would you like to make <u>your</u> business super-profitable with fresh marketing ideas tailored just to you - plus acquire <u>over 200</u> other practical new ways to get much, much more from your budget?

And take home all that power-packed information - after just one day? Under a pledge that guarantees you will be delighted - or 110% your money back at once?

Announcing the Marketing Super-Conference - now in Cambridge, Coventry and Manchester!

Then let me share with you a wealth of fresh, unusual marketing ideas that work. How do I know? They brought me total financial independence at the early age of 43. Plus the freedom to run precisely the business I love - the Marketing Guild - without ever needing to "work" again!

And many are totally <u>"new"</u> ideas - you've never heard them on any Guild conference before. They can be yours - in explicit step-by-step detail - in just a few stimulating hours. I'll also reveal the actual, often dramatically successful materials I've used myself. Take them. Adapt them. Put them to work at once, in your business. Or for your own profit....

Nor probably anywhere else!

> <u>In fact, I guarantee your total satisfaction or 110% your money back!</u> (That's no misprint. I'll return you 110% your fee if, having paid and attended, you don't agree these ideas could lift your profits dramatically.)

You will explore dozens of new low-cost ways to get sales... to make your organisation far, far better known and respected among your potential customers... to get referrals effortlessly.... and to win successful meetings with those influential decision-makers who elude your normal sales process. The ones who can, quite literally, double your sales...

You will discover ingenious strategies which launch your new products or services with maximum "payback" at minimum risk and cost... which create high quality sales leads (and convert them quickly to sale)... and which do so continually, month after month.

Plus you'll enjoy a bonus session - **How to advertise on the Internet to up to 40 million people at virtually no cost - ethically!**

Now I've taken the best ideas from the Guild's 400-plus workshops - from its 213 newsletter editions, its many tapes, books and manuals - and from my own 14 years' experience as Chairman till recently of one of Britain's most profitable marketing consultancies (in the top 15).

I've also added dozens of successful strategies that have helped my businesses make £000,000s over the years, and that I've never revealed to anyone, on any conference or in any newsletter, manual or book, ever before! What's more...

I've distilled them for you into an intensive "one of a kind" experience:

** THE MARKETING GUILD *SUPER*-CONFERENCE **

I am inviting you personally - and mailing only a very, very limited number of invitations - because I know that you have a strong interest in sharpening your business profits. How can I possibly know? Because you are a Guild member. Or you ordered or enquired after one of our manuals or services, or you bought a marketing book from our friends at Wyvern Business Library, a fellow Guild member. That's a select list!

Let me show you just a few of these so-rarely applied techniques you will take home... that I've proven work. (I was going to call your day "How to gain BIGGER results than you ever imagined on LESS money than you thought possible". It's true and I'll prove it to you!)

8.30am. Registration & welcome... Coffee/tea. Start 9am

How *your* advertising and mailings can win you market dominance - even in a small, local or niche market

An easy way to spot the "opportunity gap" in your market - any market - and fill it profitably. ** How to carry out a revealing audit of your competitors' marketing strategy (or lack of one) - and create your own campaign that exploits their weaknesses.

The Conference is worth it for this session alone!

Is your price "too high"... or your product or service less than spectacular... or your name unknown? Four clever ways your low-budget advertising and mailers can still fight big-budget competitors - and win.

Plus BONUS SESSION: 7 ethical ways to advertise to up to 40 million people on the Internet, at virtually no cost. (I'll reveal the Guild's own findings).

How to pack sales appeal into your ads - instantly.

The 5 basic "musts" in laying out any advertisement. ** How to identify "winner" and "loser" ideas for ads before you even put pen to paper. ** How you can improve any ad (even, or especially, your agency's ad).

10.30 - 10.45am. Mid-morning "blood sugar" break... fruit, coffee

Now there's a good idea

Three simple questions to ask, to improve results from your ads. ** Plus... 10 practical ways to sharpen your ad's credibility. (Use all 10 and watch your response soar!)

A 5-step plan that makes writing your ad more fun, less pain, and easily overcomes "writers block". ** How you can build "power words" plus the most powerful of all human motivators into your ads - to make your prospects respond!

Turn your directory and classified ads into gold.

1pm. Superb lunch - and a business ideas exchange. Start 2pm

Five methods to minimise your risk - and maximise your profits - by testing your ad, before you run it. ** A 3-second way to test an ad "concept". ** A 10-second test, that tells at once if your ad will pull response. ** A 30-minute test to avoid "howlers".

Plus... a totally original way to know precisely which of several alternative ad concepts will pull best for you in any given journal, before you run that ad. (Ad agencies don't know this. And wouldn't dare use it if they did...)

Yes, it's true!

Pack more power into your brochures and proposals

The most important thing to achieve in your brochure - why most brochures fail - and how you can ensure your brochure brings you business.

One simple move you can make, to improve the "sales appeal" of your brochure or technical spec sheet.

How to build proven "response devices" into your sales literature. The golden rules for designing brochures that work.

30 ways to cut your print costs. (Just one could repay your investment in this seminar many times over!)

How to as much as double the conversions-to-sale from response to your ad or mailer.

A winning approach for your written estimate or sales proposal.

3.30pm. Your mid-noon "lift". Fruit, coffee

Direct marketing for success

No, you haven't heard this one before!

How your direct mail can overcome barriers: Disinterest, Censorship (the secretary barrier), and Delay ("I'll get round to it later"). ** A magic ingredient which invariably multiplies your response - and ten ways you can use it, in any market.

Where to find your best possible mailing lists, and even get them free. ** Entirely new ways to mail the private mailing list of your closest competitor, ethically.

What to do if there are no suitable lists available to you. ** How to identify the worst lists before you waste money on them. ** A mailing list secret that even professional list brokers don't seem to know - that can multiply your response.

It's so clever, yet so simple

How to test lists - even tiny ones. ** A breathtakingly simple way to mail your own list - no matter how small - which can often double your response.

A step-by-step plan for writing a letter which stays out of the wastebin. ** How to use copy dynamics and action design to make your package pull more and better response. ** An easy, but little known way to gain at least 150% more response for virtually any mailing (I'll show you the Guild's own results).

Plus 22 proven mail order ideas you can steal, adapt and put to work immediately to lift your profits.

5pm. No need to go home yet - it's "Mission Impossible" time

Bar's open! Now you can share your marketing problems, and discover new solutions, informally with fellow delegates.

I promise you, not one moment at the Conference is academic theory. Every technique you acquire is based on current active experience. The Conference is studded with case studies from named organisations very like your own. They're using these ideas right now to build more profitable sales - often against more powerful competition - and with minimal resources. Here are just two examples:

** A small/*previously* little-known food company created a £100 million industry, gained shelf space in supermarkets nationwide - and achieved the accolade of a front cover in Marketing Week - without any conventional advertising whatsoever.

** A tiny company marketing advanced office systems used one approach - costing just 0.2% the advertising spend of its largest competitor. In under six months, it logged over 2000 valid sales leads with several of its £10,000-plus systems already sold.

Value for money? An amazing <u>97% of delegates</u> to the Guild's one day conferences reported they were "Good" or "Excellent". Listen to just one delegate:

> "One of the best conferences I have ever attended. Packed from start-to-finish with practical what-to-do-because-it-works advice. Strongly recommended to anyone who wants to get results." Michael Herbert, Managing Director, Wyvern Business Library.

I have set a strict ceiling on the numbers we will accept for this conference, to ensure you have the maximum opportunity to enjoy a personal role. But I know from the experience of our two immensely successful Super-Conferences at Heathrow in January 1995, our bookings will come in fast! So please reserve a place <u>quickly</u> for yourself and your colleagues.

And here's an offer you shouldn't miss... book three paying delegates on the Conference, and you can come free! Every fourth booking is "no charge".

I look forward to meeting you personally in March.

With every good wish

Nick Robinson

PS: I nearly forgot to tell you - every delegate receives a full workbook crammed with ideas and sources, plus a free copy of several *profit-packed Guild Reports*. Their fresh ideas are worth the Conference fee in themselves!

**PPS: YOU NEED SEND NO MONEY NOW -
WE WILL INVOICE YOUR ORGANISATION.**

YOUR "QUICK GLIMPSE" AGENDA

1. You may wish to arrive the night before and enjoy the chance to relax for an early start.

    Although the Conference is not residential, you may care to make a hotel booking for the prior night. Garden House Hotel, Cambridge: 0223 63421 (mention the Marketing Guild conference and gain a special rate of £80 incl breakfast); Novotel, Coventry: 0203 365000; Novotel, Worsley, Manchester: 061 799 3535. Do make your reservations early.

2. Perhaps you have already contacted some of your fellow attendees - because you'll have received a delegate list the week before. It's the perfect start to your "personal network" of business contacts (that's a valuable idea in itself!).

    We make it easy!

    |(You'll find it simple to develop this network throughout the Conference (if you wish).

3. You start early to get a fast start on a very full programme - the day packs in over 200 ideas! You'll join fellow delegates for coffee and Registration from 8.30am - a quiet time to browse through your Welcome Pack before the prompt 9am start.

4. Now you're on the fast track - making rapid notes and taking in more ideas per minute than on any conference you've attended before.

    The pace slackens only for a 10.30am coffee break and for the many surprises - and entertaining "mini exercises" - which challenge your skills. But whether or not you participate is always your choice.

5. From 1pm, you'll enjoy an excellent buffet, and the chance to network with even more delegates.

We'll have a separate table for them

   Now is your chance, if you wish, to exchange ideas, brochures and business cards (you will bring a modest stock of them all, won't you?).

6. It's 2pm, and the pace changes again with your marketing "mini clinic". Now there are prizes galore for your winning marketing ideas!

7. Relax! It's 3.30pm and time for a brief "blood sugar" break - fresh fruit, coffee, tea... then it's back into another idea-packed session.

8. Suddenly it's 5pm, and that will be...

   ...only the beginning. You have started a whole new approach to your marketing programme, taking with you hundreds of fresh ideas you can use at once.

   You have renewed your relationship with the Marketing Guild, and its vast treasury of ideas and resources to help bring more profit to your marketing.

   And of course, you will have met many new colleagues who may prove invaluable friends to both you and your organisation in the future.

9. Safe journey... and we hope to see you again very soon!

YOUR 110% GUARANTEE OF VALUE

"I personally promise you can only gain from this event. Over 97% of our prior delegates rated the Guild's one-day conferences as "Good" or "Excellent" value. I am so positive you will agree that I offer you this extraordinary guarantee: if after listening to the first 90 minutes you don't agree this is a superb investment of your time, simply come up to me or Julie in the first coffee break at 10.30am. Say "Nick, I'm leaving! This is not the best use of my time". I will arrange to refund you the full conference fee - plus a further 10% (£19.70) as a small token to compensate you for your time.

"It means you can book with total confidence, and be assured of a superbly rewarding day."

Nick Robinson

(This Guarantee applies, of course, only if you have attended, and paid beforehand...)

YOUR CONFERENCE DIRECTOR

Nick Robinson MA (Oxon) MIPR is author of The Marketing ToolKit (on sale worldwide in four languages), Persuasive Business Presentations, Strategic Customer Care and many other sales and marketing "ideas" books and manuals. For 14 years, he was founding director of Datanews, one of Britain's top 15 regional marketing consultancies. Over 15,000 delegates have attended his 400-plus full day seminars and mini-conferences. With over 26 years' marketing experience, he now chairs the Marketing Guild

A LITTLE ABOUT THE MARKETING GUILD

The Guild helps businesses gain more from their assets, through the astute use of unconventional marketing ideas. Established 1987, it publishes three practical newsletters, innovates seminars, reports and resource materials, and facilitates joint venturing among its many thousands of members and delegates. These range from agencies to professional services, consultants to manufacturers and resellers - businesses of every size and kind. From The Times Top 100 companies, to one-person operations.

But all have the same urgent need - to make their marketing money go much further.

WHAT, WHERE, WHEN, HOW MUCH & HOW?

The Marketing Guild Super-Conference:

Wednesday 15th March 1995: **Garden House Hotel, Cambridge** (superb City centre hotel overlooking the Cam)

Wednesday 22nd March 1995: **Novotel, Coventry** (at J3/M6)

Wednesday 29th March 1995: **Novotel, Manchester West, Worsley** (at J13/M62)

Ample free parking at all hotels. Map provided.

Register 8.30am for 9am. End 5pm.

Fee only £197 + VAT (£34.48): Total £231.48

Fee includes coffee/tea, full buffet lunch, and detailed workbook.

Post or fax your completed acceptance form to:

The Marketing Guild Ltd, 1 Houghton Court, Houghton Regis, Beds LU5 5DY. HelpLine: 01582 861556. Fax: 01582 864913.

YOU NEED SEND NO MONEY NOW - WE WILL INVOICE YOUR COMPANY

A PERSONAL MESSAGE TO YOU FROM DEBBIE CLIFTON

SUBJECT: Everything Nick didn't tell you!

Hello, I'm Debbie Clifton, the Conference Registrar. I thought it would be a good idea to give you my impressions of what we have in store for you at the Conference, even if you hadn't planned to come. Perhaps I can change your mind!

First of all, I'm new to the company so I sat in on one of Nick's mini-conferences recently. I was honestly amazed at how fast the time went - how really entertaining it was - and how much the delegates seemed to get out of it.

Having worked for other marketing organisations before, I can tell you this Conference is completely unlike anything you've attended before. (Nobody has a chance to fall asleep - there's just so much packed in!)

In fact, I have in front of me right now a pile of written testimonials from delegates ten inches deep - over 1000 of them! I open the post so I see all the genuinely unsolicited and kind letters that attendees write to us afterwards. Many delegates come back time and again.

If I still haven't persuaded you, then you must have a question Nick and I haven't answered here! So please give me or Julie Rogers a ring on 0582 861556 and we'll try to convince you to book. Hope to see you at one of the Conferences in March!

Debbie

The Marketing Guild
Super-Conference

YES, I would like to acquire *many* tested, fresh ways to build my business profits more quickly and reliably. I understand my booking includes full buffet lunch and practical workbook. I have the right to leave after the first 90 minutes and gain a 110% refund of my fees paid if I do not agree this is a superb investment of my time. Please register the following at £197+VAT (£231.48) per person:

☐ **Wed 15th March 95:** Garden House Hotel, Cambridge (City centre)

☐ **Wed 22nd March 95:** Novotel, Coventry (J3/M6)

☐ **Wed 29th March 95:** Novotel, Manchester West, Worsley (J13/M62)

Register 8.30am for 9am. End 5pm. Ample *free* parking. Map provided.

☐ **My cheque is enclosed, made payable The Marketing Guild Ltd**
☐ Please invoice my organisation
☐ **Debit my Access/Visa/Amex card No:**

[_____] Expiry: [_____]

Card in name of: Signature:
Statement address (if different from below):

☐ **I am booking three paid delegates below and claim my fourth place FREE. My name is:** _____

1. **Surname**   1st name   **Dr/Mr/Mrs/Ms**
    Job title
2. **Surname**   1st name   **Dr/Mr/Mrs/Ms**
    Job title
3. **Surname**   1st name   **Dr/Mr/Mrs/Ms**
    Job title
Organisation
Address
Postcode   Phone   Fax

You need send no money now - we will invoice your organisation.

Post or fax to The Marketing Guild Ltd, 1 Houghton Court, Houghton Regis, Beds LU5 5DY.
HelpLine (24 hours): 01582 861556. Faxed bookings: 01582 864913
You will receive a VAT receipt and map. No delegate will be permitted to attend without prior payment.
If you do not wish to receive marketing-related offers in future other than from the Guild, please tick box ☐

The Marketing Guild Ltd
FREEPOST LOL 2052
Unit 1, Houghton Court
Houghton Regis
Beds LU5 5UX
England

No
stamp
required
if posted
in UK

FOLD AS SHOWN

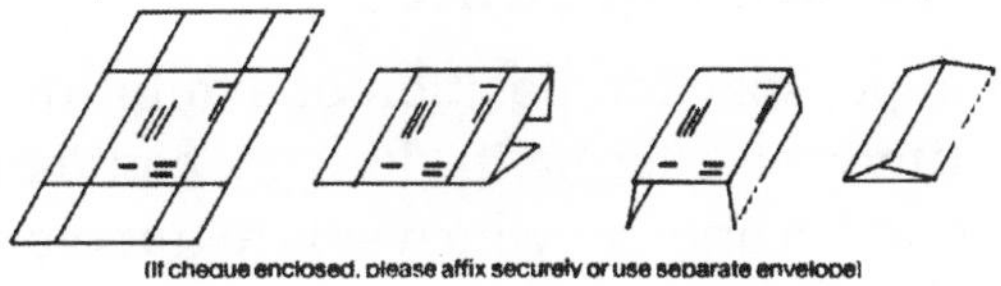

(If cheque enclosed, please affix securely or use separate envelope)

Also, your mailshot has to be prepared with a sense of responsibility to consumers and to society. For example, advertisers must not play on fear or excite distress without good reason. Thus, if a direct mailer followed a description of his or her safety item with a graphic colour photograph of an accident to imply that it could have been avoided if only the product had been used, then this might well constitute a breach of the Code. Equally important, your mailing must conform to the principles of fair competition as generally accepted in business. Should a direct mail advertiser compare the prices of his or her goods with those of relatively dissimilar products stocked by rivals, it could again be in breach of the BCAP.

The British Code of Sales Promotion Practice, BCSPP, covers similar ground to its sister code, but from a promotional viewpoint. All sales promotions have to be legal, decent, honest and truthful and should uphold the principles of fair competition in business. As examples of typical guidelines, advertisers must ensure that promotional mailings are not sent to individuals who are registered with the Mailing Preference Service and who do not wish to receive them. Alcohol ought not to be included as a promotional item in any offer addressed to the under-18s. Advertisers should not attempt to lead recipients into over-estimating the quality of the goods and services available.

Avoid breaching BCAP and BCSPP guidelines in any way. If you do, the regulatory body known as the Advertising Standards Authority Limited can ask you to amend or stop sending your mailshots. Should you continue, you will undoubtedly receive negative publicity from the Authority's monthly report and could find that the Royal Mail refuses to deliver your mail. You might even be expelled from your trade association. Read these two codes from cover to cover to ensure that you adhere to them, in letter *and* in spirit. The ASA – and its Committee of Advertising Practice – will provide advice and guidance on specific cases, on request. See Appendix C: 'The British Code of Advertising Practice', page 317 and Appendix E: 'The British Code of Sales Promotion Practice', page 363, and 'Useful contacts', page 385.

Designing exhibition stands

Whatever the type, size and position of exhibition stand planned, you need to spend some time considering its design – contemplate its appearance and contents and compose a brief for whoever is to turn your thoughts into reality. Realistically, the design and subsequent construction of your stand will be carried out by specialists in this field – typically a freelance designer and a contractor nominated by the exhibition organizer – but you ought to have a broad idea of what you want before approaching them for professional help and guidance.

Contemplating appearance

You should not try to design your exhibition stand yourself, unless you possess hands-on knowledge and genuine expertise in this area. Even the personalization of a shell unit should be referred to an experienced stand designer, or at least be carried out following his or her extensive advice and suggestions. Too many exhibitors adopt a DIY approach because they naively believe that they have a flair for colour co-ordination, can stack a pile of goods in an imaginative way and (not least) will save money. As a consequence, they 'design' an amateurish hotch-potch of a stand which conveys a poor impression and leaves customers unmoved or alienated. Take an administrative rather than an artistic role, deciding what you would like prior to going to an expert.

Your stand should perform several functions, and will do if it is designed properly. It ought to create and put across the desired image of your firm. Be clear about what message you want to convey to visitors and customers. It may be that you wish to tell them you are a wholesaler who can supply any and every item they could conceivably need to run and maintain their business equipment without interruption. Alternatively, you might want to confirm that you are a well-established, leading manufacturer in your particular industry. Think how these (and other images) may be conveyed to the outside world, perhaps by the difficult task of displaying every single product stocked or through having a glossy stand decked out in your firm's familiar logo and colours.

Your stand also needs to be attractive enough to draw visitors to it and to make them come and talk to staff, pick up a brochure or whatever. Again, consider what can be done to achieve this aim: have some ideas to put to the designer. Perhaps a banner or a flag showing your logo and colours may be attached to the top of your stand to attract people from afar. Similarly, a matching fascia might tug at those visitors who are a little closer to you. When walking by, an out-of-reach new product, an intriguing photograph, a heard but not seen audio-visual display, even the simple attraction of a cup of tea and a sit-down could entice them.

The stand is also a working environment, where customers and staff meet to establish contact, build a rapport, place and take orders and so forth. This should never be overlooked and everything possible ought to be done to ensure that they can do this in a comfortable and convenient manner. Contemplate and prepare some suggestions for the designer. You may feel an office area with desks and chairs is needed, perhaps closed off if confidential deals are to be made. You could decide that your staff want product samples, information files and technical and promotional literature at hand to support them. Customers will want to feel relaxed and at ease in a place which is neither too brightly lit, hot, cold nor loud.

With many thoughts in your head, you may begin to believe that you and/or your colleagues are enormously creative and feel that you are itching to design the stand yourself. Resist this understandable temptation, however powerful it is. Unless you are well qualified, you are no more likely to be able to create a winning stand than you are to design a car that drives itself. This is a highly complex, specialized field, too often tackled by amateurs with half-baked ideas and unlimited confidence – and it invariably ends with disastrous consequences. Stick to what you do best, and employ others to carry out remaining work on your behalf.

Selecting contents

Although your chosen designer will be responsible for overall display tactics, you must select those products that should be exhibited on the stand. In many instances, this will be a relatively straightforward choice: a new range of goods is being launched onto the market, a set of products has been refined and repackaged for a different sector, seasonal goods are available for a limited period only and so on. Your selection will simply reflect and enhance the activities and goals of your firm, whether to sell a certain volume or value of goods in a given region or time, or whatever.

On other occasions, your choice may be less obvious. Some products might be too large and heavy to display at this venue (although you should therefore question whether this is the right event for you). Various goods may not be ready to be displayed, demonstrated and examined by customers, which might suggest you are not yet in a position to exhibit. You could wish to show all of your stock to prove you are the best wholesaler in the region, but only have a limited and insufficient amount of space available to do this. You may want to convey the impression that you are the market leader and just do not know which products will help to strengthen this image.

In these and similar situations you are faced with a difficult dilemma, and need to think carefully about what to do. Even if they are big and cumbersome, try to display the items that you want to sell though this may involve taking a larger stand. Photographs, illustrations and the like do have a role to play on a stand but there is little point in attending an exhibition to show a picture of a product that could just as easily be seen in a brochure or catalogue. Always make certain that displayed goods can be handled and tested, and will perform as expected. Prototypes and models are poor replacements. If you are unable to decide between products, you may wish to pick a blend of your best-sellers, new goods and those items that cannot be promoted effectively by other means, perhaps because they are too big to be loaded into a sales agent's car and so on.

Visual display items can be incorporated on the stand as well, to back up your exhibits. Photographs, diagrams and illustrations with clear and concise captions may be placed on the inside or outside of your unit, on ceilings, walls or even floors. They could possibly show different parts of a product and how they are assembled together or might illustrate how your services are carried out on a step-by-step basis. It is sensible to have these materials produced especially for the show. As an example, a photograph in a catalogue may not be of a sufficiently high quality when blown up to the size required for an exhibition stand. Talk to the Association of Illustrators, British Institute of Professional Photography, British Printing Industries Federation, and the Society of Typographic Designers for advice. See 'Useful contacts', page 385.

Audio-visual displays may be a beneficial addition to your stand too, whether in the form of a slide show, film or video presentation. Think about whether these will substantiate and further your message, help to promote your goods and services and maintain a quality working environment. Sometimes, you may feel that the distraction from face-to-face contact, the noise levels and the time and effort involved with setting up and running such displays are not worthwhile. Also, the organizer's rules and regulations often limit or even forbid these activities if they are a nuisance to your neighbours, possibly by causing crowds to build up and block gangways. Gather your thoughts and ideas together before chatting about them to a designer.

Composing a brief

Knowing roughly what you want, you now need to compile a brief for whoever will have to translate your ideas into a finished product, usually a freelance designer, followed by an on-site contractor. The brief must incorporate all of the information required by the designer to design an appropriate stand for you. Clearly, the details needed will vary according to individual circumstances but might be grouped under the various and familiar headings of the firm, the market, the show and the stand.

With regard to your firm, you may wish to provide background information about its organization, especially its marketing and advertising policies, the desired image and a who's who of contact names and responsibilities; products and services, with descriptions and comments on good and bad features; objectives, outlining how attending this event will help to achieve them; and budget, with a breakdown of how monies are allocated. Concerning the market, you could decide to put down data about your: customers, describing their characteristics and habits; rivals, with special emphasis on those exhibiting at the show; and marketplace, explaining your position within it.

In relation to the show, you ought to cover: the event itself with dates, opening times and reasons for its selection; the venue, including a floor plan, and comments on its positive and negative aspects and flow patterns; the organizer, with a copy of their rules and regulations; exhibitors, particularly those close to and/or in direct competition with your firm; and visitors, with notes on their numbers and types. For the stand, you should explain its: type, whether a shell scheme or free-build unit; size, incorporating its height, width and depth; site, with its stand number, key features and proximity to other units and facilities, such as restaurants and toilets.

In addition, you must set down: the message you wish your stand to convey to the outside world, such as being the biggest stockist or leading manufacturer in the trade; thoughts about its appearance, perhaps incorporating banners and flags; ideas about its working environment, possibly including an office area, desks, chairs and so forth; exhibit details, with data about their numbers, dimensions, weights, pros, cons, special features and so on; display material details, incorporating photographs, drawings and so forth; audio-visual suggestions, such as videos; staff names, numbers, positions, roles and responsibilities whilst on the stand.

Hopefully, you will sketch out all of this information now – for clarification of your own intentions as much as anything else – and have it to hand when you go out to seek and commission a stand designer. Naturally, he or she will confirm the precise details that are required from you and the order and layout in which they should be presented for his or her use. You can then attend to this task in a rapid and efficient manner.

Commissioning a designer

You can obtain design services from one of several sources, typically a freelance designer, design house or a contractor. A freelance designer who has managed to survive and prosper through recessionary times is likely to be imaginative, helpful and should have a broad-based knowledge of and expertise in various aspects of exhibition stand design and construction techniques. However, a small-business person may lack a depth of experience in certain, key areas and with limited resources might not be able to take his or her stand design all the way through to supervising its assembly on the exhibition floor.

Design houses may offer similar benefits; but with numerous departments and employees, ranging from estimators through to project controllers, should also be in a position to provide extensive, hands-on expertise in all areas. Obviously, their charges are significantly higher and they tend to be cost-effective only for more substantial projects, such as a free-build stand at larger trade and popular consumer shows. It is likely that they will not be suitable for you on this occasion.

Many contractors offer stand design services for a limited or even no fee (although a 'free' service is invariably built into the overall construction package price). Obviously, it can appear to be inexpensive and convenient to employ the same organization to design and build your stand, especially if it is the on-site contractor nominated by the organizer. Nevertheless, there are drawbacks. A standardized design using at-hand materials may be produced, more suited to the contractor's requirements than your own. By commissioning a contractor, you may be tied to using their construction services too, which you may not necessarily want to do. Also, it is not unknown for contractors to subcontract design services to a freelance designer or design house, so you will effectively be paying over the odds in some instances.

Before approaching anyone – possibly a freelance designer – you must decide what qualities ought to be possessed by this particular specialist. He or she should be sufficiently talented and imaginative enough to design a stand that conveys the right image, is attractive and provides a quality working environment, all in a fresh and original fashion. You do not want a rehash of 1,001 other stands. The designer must be fully experienced in exhibition stand design rather than in related (but quite different) design fields so that he or she knows what works and does not work at a show. Ideally, he or she should also have some specific experience of your type of firm, products, services, customers, rivals, marketplace, exhibition and stand, as preparing a design for a nuts and bolts wholesaler at a local show is different from one for a house builder at an international event. The more hands-on experience that he or she has in your territory, the better the results will probably be.

You will wish to see that the designer is reputable, will disclose rival commissions to you and maintain confidentiality at all times: you do not want details of your revolutionary new product to be leaked before it is unveiled on the opening day of the event. Similarly, you wish to be sure that you are receiving independent and impartial advice which is right for you, and is not being given because the designer wants to palm you off with rejected ideas from another commission or materials left over from the previous job. Compatibility is important too. As in any professional relationship, it is necessary for you, your team, the designer and his or her team to work together well, with everyone pulling in the same direction.

Financial stability has to be taken into account, especially when operating in difficult trading conditions. You do not want to commission a designer only to find that the business subsequently runs into financial problems or even ceases trading during the run-up to the exhibition. As a consequence, your plans could be ruined. Likewise, you need to be certain that you will receive value-for-money services, and will not be exploited because of your inexperience in the field. Typically, fees are set by an hourly rate or as a percentage of the total, estimated production costs and should be agreed upon commission. Often, they become payable in stages, perhaps on commission, after the design is accepted and at the end of the show. Expenses – for telephone calls, travel and so on – are usually added to the final bill as well.

Knowing what you want, you then need to draw up a list of perhaps three to six designers whom you can approach to discuss your requirements before formally providing your choice with a brief and commissioning him or her to work on your behalf. You can prepare such a shortlist by contacting the trade body known as The Chartered Society of Designers which maintains a register containing detailed information about its members and their areas of expertise; see 'Useful contacts', page 385. These designers abide by the Society's code of conduct, which is good news for their clients. Alternatively, or better still as well, approach the exhibition organizer, trade associations such as the Agricultural Show Exhibitors Association, British Exhibition Contractors Association and the National Exhibitors Association plus personal contacts for recommendations. Refer again to 'Useful contacts', page 385.

Whether meeting shortlisted designers on your or their premises (or preferably both on successive occasions), you need to tell them all about yourself. Talk of and show them around the firm, encouraging them to sit in on discussions, perhaps concerning budgets, marketing and advertising strategies and goals. Introduce them to key colleagues, outlining roles and responsibilities. Let them see products used and services performed, examining and testing goods, as appropriate. Chat about customers and competitors too, possibly giving them the opportunity to meet and talk to some of the customers, if relevant. Discuss the show, the venue, the organizer and the anticipated exhibitors and visitors, sharing the information which you have with them so that they develop as detailed an understanding of everything as you possess.

Question the designers about themselves to see how they match the qualities required. As and when appropriate, you might raise such queries as: Do you belong to your trade organization? When did you begin trading? How is your business organized? Who are the owners and key employees? What are their backgrounds? What qualifications do they possess? What are their areas of expertise? Who else have you worked for? What other commissions do you have at the moment? Do you act on behalf of any of my rivals? These and other questions which arise naturally during the course of your conversations should enable you to go some way towards deciding whether the designers are experienced, reputable and so forth.

Further thought can be directed towards how far the designers match your various requirements by visiting them at their offices, to assess the working environment, their staff and so on. Seeing them on their home ground may enable you to ascertain whether they are busy and professional in their approach, and if the atmosphere towards you is warm or frosty. You can watch them in action, checking their work and discussing their backgrounds, experiences and expertise with them in some depth. Hopefully, firm conclusions can be reached about their talents, imagination and all-round suitability for you.

You then need to work through your workload and what you want a designer to do on your behalf. Obviously, you will talk about the proposed type, size and site of your stand, with your ideas for its appearance, contents and working areas. Perhaps you wish the designer to produce a scale drawing and explanation of the stand as well as a scale model for clarification, and to avoid confusion and misunderstandings later on. Typically, you will also wish him or her to forward the agreed design to the organizer for permission, attend to any necessary amendments, employ a contractor and supervise the construction of the stand for you. In return, the designers will talk to you about work schedules and likely fees and expenses.

With a clear idea in your mind of who you want to commission, you should ask for the names and telephone numbers of their past and present clients so that you can contact these people for reference purposes. Telephone rather than write to them for off-the-record comments. Raise questions such as: How pleased were you with their work? Was it fresh and original? Was it well suited to your individual needs? Did they act in a professional and efficient manner? If not, what happened? Did you like and trust them, and their advice? Did they complete their work on time? Was it in budget? Did their work represent value for money? Would you use them again? If not, why not?

Hopefully, you can then make your choice, forwarding your detailed brief to the favoured designer. It is always wise at this stage to have everything agreed and noted down in writing, referring any written agreement to a solicitor if necessary. Whether in a letter or a formal contract, you and the designer should set out the precise brief, workload and schedule, fees, likely expenses and payment arrangements, before signing the document. Other designers who were under consideration ought to be thanked and rejected politely.

Employing a contractor

It is likely that your selected designer will take charge of employing a contractor to build your stand under his or her instruction and supervision. Nevertheless, you should be aware of what the process ought to involve, if tackled properly. As with choosing a designer, it is wise to identify the qualities which should exist in the winning contractor. You might want to pick one who is sufficiently talented, fully experienced in stand design, specifically experienced in your field, reputable, compatible, financially stable and cost-effective, all for much the same reasons.

Again, a shortlist of contractors should be compiled. Contact the British Exhibition Contractors Association which can supply details of its members who must abide by its code of conduct and recommended conditions of contract. See pages 217 to 219. This is reassuring news for you. In addition, talk to the exhibition organizer and other trade associations such as the Agricultural

Show Exhibitors Association and the National Exhibitors Association. See 'Useful contacts', page 385.

It is then usual for you – or more probably your designer – to approach the listed contractors, submitting documents and asking them to tender for the contract. Depending upon the complexity of the task – varying from adding display panels to a shell scheme to constructing a complex, free-build stand – you would provide working drawings to illustrate the work, specifications to describe it and a set of the exhibition organizer's rules and regulations (see pages 152 to 157). On receipt of tenders, you may wish to arrange meetings to discuss your requirements along similar lines as before, prior to taking up references, making your choice and rejecting the other contractors.

In many cases, exhibitors and contractors operate with 'gentlemen's agreements' based upon correspondence, discussions and handshakes. Clearly, this is naive as it creates opportunities for confusion at best, and exploitation at worst. It is advisable to have everything written down and signed by both parties before work commences. Typically, acceptance of a contractor's quote binds you to any terms and conditions that are printed on the reverse side, unless otherwise agreed in writing. Hence, this small print should be viewed as a starting point, to be read by you and a solicitor, with alterations, deletions and additions to be made to it. Hopefully, your contractor belongs to the British Exhibition Contractors Association and adheres to those fair and reasonable recommended conditions of contract. Even so, these conditions should be the beginning, not the end of the matter.

Make sure that roles and responsibilities are well defined, so both sides know who has to do what. Often, certain tasks are subcontracted by the contractor to outside specialists. Be certain the contractor remains responsible to you for *all* of the work carried out, including (and perhaps especially) those duties allocated to others. Ensure that the lines of communication are clear. For example, instructions and confirmations must pass through the designer, and changes and amendments should be put in writing. Have everything timetabled, so both parties know what has to be done, and by when. Be particularly careful to set a completion date. Make sure ownership of goods and materials is understood, and everyone is aware of what happens to them after the show. You do not want your reusable items to be junked. Be clear about fees, and payment arrangements too.

GENERAL CONDITIONS

1 INTERPRETATION

1.1 In these Conditions
'The Contractor' means the Member of the British Exhibition Contractors Association which agrees to perform the Contract Work.
'Contract Work' means any or all of the work which the Contractor agrees to perform and/or the services which the Contractor agrees to provide including the provision of Goods on hire or by sale.
'Goods' means all goods of whatsoever description including but not limited to materials, plant, equipment. machinery and fittings.
'Customer' means the person, firm or corporate body who agrees to purchase Contract Work.
'Contract' means any contract between the Contractor and the Customer for the carrying out of Contract Work.
1.2 Any reference in these Conditions to any provision of a statute shall be construed as a reference to that provision as amended, re-enacted or extended at the relevant time.
1.3 The headings in these Conditions are for convenience only and shall not affect the interpretation of a Contract.

2 ORDERS AND SPECIFICATIONS
2.1 These Conditions shall apply to every Quotation and Contract. The Contractor shall not be bound by any terms or conditions which may be inconsistent with these Conditions.
2.2 No variation of, or addition to, these Conditions shall be effective unless in writing and signed by the Contractor.
2.3 Any advice or recommendation given by the Contractor or its employees or agents to the Customer concerning Contract Work prior to the making of the Contract to which it relates, which is not confirmed in writing by the Contractor when such Contract is made, is followed or acted upon entirely at the Customer's own risk and the Contractor shall not be liable for any such advice or recommendation.
2.4 Any typographical or clerical error or omission in any Quotation, price list, acceptance, invoice or other such document issued by the Contractor shall be subject to correction without any liability on the part of the Contractor.
2.5 All specifications, descriptions, drawings, designs, measures or other information provided by the Contractor in relation to Contract Work and/or Goods are approximate, howsoever provided, shall not form part of a Contract and, with relation thereto, the Contractor reserves the right to incorporate modifications or amendments in Contract Work.

2.6 No Contract shall be created unless the Contractor has accepted in writing a Quotation acceptance or order placed by the Customer, irrespective of how such Quotation acceptance or order is expressed and whether it results from a prior quotation or arises otherwise.
2.7 The Customer shall be responsible to the Contractor for ensuring the accuracy of the terms of any order or other material (including any applicable specification) submitted by it or on its behalf and for giving the Contractor any necessary information relating to Contract Work within a sufficient time to enable the Contractor to perform the Contract in respect thereof in accordance with its terms.
2.8 The Customer shall be responsible to the Contractor for obtaining all necessary Licences and other permissions whatsoever for the performance of Contract Work.
2.9 The Customer shall be responsible for ensuring that every building, path, private road, open space or other property to be used in the performance of Contract Work is safe and suitable for the intended use and, without limitation of the foregoing, is adequately served with all required public utilities.
2.10 The Customer may not cancel a Contract unless the Contractor agrees in writing and then on the terms that the Customer shall indemnify the Contractor in full against all loss including loss of profit, costs (including the cost of all labour and materials used), claims, actions, damages, charges and expenses incurred by the Contractor as a result of cancellation.
2.11 The Contractor shall have and retain the property, copyright and all other intellectual or industrial property rights in drawings, designs, plans, models, specifications and/or estimates prepared by the Contractor.
2.12 Where the Customer is to supply goods ('Customer's Property') to the Contractor in connection with the Contract Work, risk in Customer's Property will remain in the Customer. The Contractor will not be liable to the Customer for loss of or any damage to Customer's Property unless caused by the negligent act or omission of the Contractor.
2.13 If any part of Contract Work is to be performed elsewhere than on the Contractor's premises, the Customer shall be responsible to the Contractor for insuring the place of performance of such Contract Work and shall indemnify the Contractor against liability for any damage to the place of performance of such Contract Work, however caused.

3 PRICES
3.1 The Contractor will quote for Contract Work only after the Contractor has received a written specification from, or on behalf of, the Customer.
3.2 The Contractor's Quotation shall be open for acceptance within either the period stated therein or, if none is stated, within three calendar months of its date.
3.3 The Contractor reserves the right by giving notice to the Customer at any time before completion of Contract Work to increase the price of the applicable Contract in the following circumstances:
3.3.1 Where additional work is performed at the Customer's request; and/or
3.3.2 to reflect any increase in the cost to the Contractor which is due to any factor beyond the Contractor's control (such as, without limitation, any foreign exchange fluctuation, currency regulation, alteration of duties, increase in the cost of labour, materials or other costs of performance) or any failure of the Customer to give the Contractor adequate information or instructions; and/or
3.3.3 without prejudice to the generality of condition 3.3.2 above, to reflect any increase in the general index of retail prices compiled by the United Kingdom Department of Employment and published in the United Kingdom in the monthly digest of statistics by the Central Statistical Office or any index substantially replacing it.
3.4 Prices are exclusive of VAT and, where applicable, any additional or substitute taxes, levies, imposts, duties, fees or charges whatsoever and wherever payable, all of which shall be paid by the Customer

4 TERMS OF PAYMENT
The Customer shall pay one half of the price of a Contract when it is made and shall pay the balance (including any extra sums due under Condition 3.3 above) on completion of Contract Work as notified by the Contractor or, where Contract Work relates to an exhibition, on the opening of the exhibition if earlier. Time for payment shall be of the essence. Receipts for payment will be issued only on request.
4.1 If the Customer fails to make any payment on the due date then, without prejudice to any other right or remedy available to the Contractor, the Contractor shall be entitled, at its option at any time thereafter to
4.1.1 terminate the relevant Contract and suspend further performance of Contract Work; and
4.1.2 require the immediate return of any Goods hired to the Customer and
4.1.3 full payment, without deduction, of the total amount due and/or which would have

become due under the relevant Contract but for termination, together with interest (both before and after any judgement) on the amount overdue from time to time at the rate of 4% per annum above Midland Bank base rate from time to time until payment in full is made.
4.2 Property in Goods supplied by way of sale under a Contract shall not pass until payment by the Customer of all sums due under the Contract under which the Goods were delivered; until property in such Goods passes the Customer shall hold them as bailee for the Contractor, shall store them separately from all other property of the Customer or any third party, marked so as to be clearly identifiable as belonging to the Contractor, shall keep them insured against all usual risks in their full invoice value and if any of the events referred to in clause 9 occurs, the Customer shall place such Goods at the disposal of the Contractor and the Contractor shall be entitled to enter upon any premises of the Customer, or any other premises where such Goods are kept, for the purpose of removing them.

5 WARRANTY
Provided that notice is given as soon as reasonably possible, and in any event within seven days of the defect being discovered and Provided Always that in the case of goods such notice must be given within the period of hire, where supplied on hire, or within 12 months of the date of delivery where supplied by way of sale, if the Customer gives notice of a defect in Contract Work, and the Contractor is satisfied that a defect exists and was not caused in whole or in part by any matter, action or occurrence outside the Contractor's control the Contractor shall in its sole discretion either remedy the defect or refund to the Customer a reasonable proportion of the price of the Contract.

6 LIABILITY
6.1 The terms of Condition 5 are in lieu of all conditions warranties and statements of whatever nature in respect of Contract Work whether express or implied by statute, trade, custom or otherwise and any such condition, warranty or statement is hereby excluded.
6.2 The Contractor shall not be liable for any defect in Contract Work arising directly or indirectly from compliance with any drawing, design, specification or order of the Customer.
6.3 Without prqudice to the terms of Conditions 6.1 6.2 and 6.4 the Contractor will accept liability for any loss or damage sustained by the Customer as a direct result of any breach of a Contract or of any liability of the Contractor (including negligence) in respect of the perfor-

mance of a Contract provided that such liability shall be limited to payment of damages not exceeding the invoice value of the Contract in question.

6.4 Subject to the terms of Condition 6.6, the Contractor shall not be liable for the following loss or damage howsoever caused (even if foreseeable or in the Contractor's contemplation):

6.4.1 Loss of profits, business or revenue whether sustained by the Customer or any other Person; and/or

6.4.2 special, indirect or consequential loss or damage, whether sustained by the Customer or any other person; and/or

6.4.3 any loss arising from any claim made against the Customer by any other Person.

6.5 The Customer shall indemnify the Contractor against all claims, actions, costs, expenses (including court costs and legal fees) or other liabilities whatsoever in respect of:

6.5.1 Any liability arising under the Consumer Protection Act 1967 unless caused by the negligent act or omission of the Contractor in the manufacture and/or supply of Goods; and/or

6.5.2 any claim for breach of industrial and/or intellectual property rights arising out of compliance with any drawings, designs, specifications or order of the Customer; and/or

6.5.3 any breach of Contract or negligent or wilful act or omission of the Customer in relation to a Contract.

6.6 These Conditions do not purport to exclude or restrict any liability the exclusion or restriction of which is prohibited by Sections 2(1) and 6(1) of the Unfair Contract Terms Act 1977.

NOTHING IN THESE CONDITIONS SHALL AFFECT THE STATUTORY RIGHTS OF A CONSUMER

7 HIRED GOODS

7.1 Unless specifically provided by way of sale, all Goods used or supplied by the Contractor in connection with Contract Work shall be deemed to be on hire to the Customer.

7.2 The Customer shall indemnify the Contractor against the loss of and/or damage to hired Goods howsoever caused.

7.3 The Customer shall keep hired Goods in his possession and/or under his control at all times and shall not remove them from the place where they are installed by the Contractor without the latter's prior written consent .

7.4 Upon expiry of the period of deemed hire, or upon the earlier termination of the relevant Contract, the Customer shall no longer be in possession of hired Goods and the Contractor may at any time without notice, retake possession of

such hired Goods and the Contractor shall be entitled to enter the premises of the Customer and/or any other place of performance of Contract Work, for such purposes.

8 FORCE MAJEURE

The Contractor shall be entitled, without liability on its part and without prejudice to its other rights to terminate a Contract or any unfulfilled part thereof or at its option, to suspend or give partial performance under it, if performance by the Contractor or by its suppliers is prevented, hindered, or delayed whether directly or indirectly by reason of any cause whatever beyond the Contractor's or its suppliers' reasonable control, whether such cause existed on the date when the Contract was made or not .

9 INSOLVENCY

If the Customer, being an individual, or being a firm, if any partner in the Customer is the subject of a petition for a bankruptcy order or of an application for an interim order under Part VIII of the Insolvency Act 1986, or if the Customer, being a company, compounds with its creditors or has a receiver or manager appointed in respect of all or any part of its assets or is the subject of an application for an administration order or of any proposal for a voluntary arrangement under Part I of the Insolvency Act 1986; or enters into liquidation whether compulsorily or voluntarily otherwise than for the purpose of amalgamation or reconstruction, or if the Contractor reasonably believes that any of the above events is about to occur, then the Contractor shall be entitled immediately, and at any time thereafter, to terminate forthwith any Contract or any unfulfilled part thereof.

10 GENERAL

10.1 No waiver by the Contractor of any breach of Contract by the Customer shall be construed as a waiver of any subsequent breach of the same or any other provision.

10.2 If any provision of these Conditions is held by any competent authority to be invalid or unenforceable in whole or in part the validity of the other provisions of these Conditions and the remainder of the provision in question shall not be affected thereby.

10.3 Any dispute arising under or in connection with these Conditions or the work done by the Contractor shall be referred to arbitration by a single arbitrator appointed by agreement or (in default) nominated on the application of either party.

10.4 This Contract shall be governed by the Laws of England.

Summary

- There are three main types of press advertisement – display advertisements, classified advertisements and semi-display advertisements.

- Potential press advertisers should choose a type of advertisement and an approach, layout and copy that reflects the message that they want to put across to their target audience. They need to comply with the law, ensuring advertisements are legal, decent, honest and truthful.

- Radio advertisements should be devised by the advertisers but created and produced by the station's experts. It is a specialist area.

- Would-be radio advertisers should pick an approach and contents that attract attention among their customer base, then create a desire and inspire listeners to act, whether telephoning, visiting or placing an order for products or services. Advertisements should comply with the Radio Authority's Code of Advertising Standards and Practice.

- Winning mailshots comprise three, key ingredients – an envelope, a letter and inserts; typically a pre-paid envelope and an order form or similar.

- Prospective direct mailers should follow the A-I-D-A principle: attention, interest, desire and action. Mailshots should comply with the British Code of Advertising Practice and the British Code of Sales Promotion Practice.

- There are two main types of exhibition stand – 'shelves' and 'free-standing' stands. It is wise to employ a designer and a constructor to create and erect these.

- Likely exhibitors should concentrate on creating an appearance that attracts visitors and selecting contents that interest them; products to buy and visual and audio-visual displays that help to promote those goods and enhance the atmosphere.

Notes

6 Running your advertising campaign

YOU ARE NOW READY to put together your press, radio, direct mail and exhibition activities and run an advertising campaign. It is important that you do this on a step-by-step basis – first the press, then the radio, and so on – so that you can monitor what is happening and make changes where necessary as you go along.

Buying press space

You should know how to purchase spaces within the newspapers, magazines and miscellaneous publications which you have chosen to use. It is important that you can read a rate card properly and are able to negotiate with the representatives who have been sent along by advertisement managers, subsequently dealing with the various titles in a correct and efficient manner. Only then can you hope to be successfully involved with advertising activities in this medium.

Reading the rate card

The rate card which lists advertising costs and other relevant data about a title is the basis for your discussions with representatives and publications. It is wise to be aware of the trade jargon used within it, perhaps concerning the type and size of advertisements. Some words and phrases will already be familiar to you, namely 'display', 'classified' and 'semi-display' advertisements, 'linage', single column centimetre' or 'SCC' and 'double-page spread' or 'DPS'. Others are self-explanatory, including 'quarter', 'half', 'whole' and 'full-page'. A number may be unknown to you though. An 'advertorial' is a promotional feature that accompanies an advertisement. An 'insert' is an advertising item such as a leaflet which is loosely placed within or bound into a publication. A 'gatefold' is a sheet with folded-in leaves. The 'type area' is the part of the page taken up with editorial and advertising matter. 'Bleed off' means extending an advertisement off the edge of a page for maximum impact.

You also need to be able to recognize the different terms which relate to the positioning of advertisements. 'Inside front cover' or 'IFC', 'first left-hand page' or 'first LHP', 'first right-hand page' or 'first RHP', 'inside back cover' or 'IBC' and 'outside back cover' or 'OBC' are all self-evident. Others may be less obvious. 'Title cover', 'ear', 'ear pieces' or 'ear specs' refer to the spaces to the sides of the front page title. 'Run of paper', 'run of press' or 'ROP' indicate that advertisements will be located anywhere in the publication at the publisher's discretion. 'Run of week', 'run of month' and 'run of year' – 'ROW', 'ROM', and 'ROY' respectively – mean that advertisements will be printed at a date selected by the publisher. A 'special position' guarantees a certain space for an advertisement, as chosen by the advertiser. A 'solus position' ensures that an advertisement is the only one on the page. An 'island position' indicates that an advertisement will be surrounded by editorial text. 'Facing matter' or 'FM' and 'next matter' or 'NM' mean that advertisements will be sited facing or next to editorial copy.

The remaining jargon is usually associated with technical and mechanical data which will normally not concern you, as the publications will handle the production of your advertisements. Nevertheless, it is sensible to be conscious of the most frequently used language on the card. 'Mono' means black and white, with 'spot colour' or 'single spot' referring to a colour which may be added to highlight parts of an advertisement. 'Colour' suggests that a full range of varied colours is available to enhance advertisements, albeit of mixed quality in newspapers and some miscellaneous publications. 'Copy' usually relates to the text of an advertisement, although the word often encompasses 'artwork' too, which describes illustrative matter such as drawings and photographs. 'Camera ready' means that copy is ready to be passed to the production department. A 'block' is a plate with an illustration etched onto it and is used during printing. A 'bromide' is a photographic print on bromide paper. 'Letterpress', 'litho' and 'gravure' are different printing methods.

The terms and conditions of acceptance of advertisements are printed on the reverse or at the back of the rate card. You ought to study these before tackling representatives and publications. Although the order and phrasing of clauses may vary from one card to another, their contents are very similar, if not identical in many instances. Expect to see statements such as: 'all advertisements must conform to the Consumer Credit Act of 1974, the Sex Discrimination Act of 1975, the Business Advertisements (Disclosure) Order of 1977, the Trade Descriptions Act of 1986 and the British Code of Advertising Practice; orders have to be confirmed in writing no later than so many days or weeks before the publication; artwork and other material must be submitted so many days or weeks ahead of publication; the publisher cannot be held responsible for the loss of or damage to the advertiser's property.'

Also: 'the publisher reserves the right to refuse, amend or withdraw advertisements even if previously accepted and paid for; cancellations have to be notified in writing no less than so many days or weeks prior to publication; the advertiser must check and return 'proofs' – draft copies of (parts of) pages – no later than so many days or weeks before publication. No changes may be made at this stage except to correct spelling and grammatical mistakes and facts which differ from the advertiser's original copy; the publisher is not liable for any loss or damage resulting from a failure to publish or distribute the title; if omissions, errors or misprints occur which materially affect advertisements, the publisher shall either adjust the cost, provide a reasonable refund up to the price of the advertising space or reinsert the advertisements at a later date. All omissions, errors and misprints must be notified to the publisher in writing within so many days of publication; payment has to be made with the initial order/on receipt of the invoice/on receipt of the monthly statement; voucher copies – complimentary issues of a title – are available upon written request by the advertiser.'

Negotiating with representatives

Having studied numerous rate cards in some detail, you should be ready to meet representatives of the publications in which you want to advertise. The representatives of chosen titles will normally visit you at your shop, office or factory within a day or so of your telephone calls, and are worth talking to in depth. If they are good at their work, they will know all about their publications and may offer general and specific guidance concerning schedules, advertisements and the do's and don'ts of space buying for the particular titles. The representatives act as hands-on sources of information and advice, and work as intermediaries between you and the departments which exist in their newspapers, magazines and/or miscellaneous publications.

When meeting a representative for the first time, probably on an informal basis during a coffee or tea break, you ought to seize the opportunity to learn as much as possible from him or her. You should ask about the title, seeking to confirm and expand (or perhaps adjust) your understanding of its characteristics, departments, staff and workings, circulation, readership and advertising rates, production methods and capabilities, rival media and their strengths or weaknesses plus its relationships with advertisers. Similarly, a representative who is dedicated to doing his or her job properly – by selling only the type, size and amount of space which is suitable for you – will question you about your firm, products and services, goals, customers, competitors, market and proposed budget. From your answers, he or she should be able to study and comment upon the viability of your planned schedule and its timing, frequency, duration and so on as well as your advertisements and their approaches, layouts and copy.

Establishing a rapport with representatives who carry out their duties in a conscientious and thorough manner, you ought to listen to their knowledge-able (albeit biased) opinions, amending your schedule and/or advertisements accordingly. It is then tempting to book, and even pay for, all advertisements for the forthcoming quarter, six months or year, especially as discounts of up to 20 per cent may be readily offered or made available on demand. Whatever deals can be negotiated – and you should always push hard for price reductions for first-time orders, for series of advertisements, at quiet times and for payments in advance – only make verbal bookings for the initial few insertions with remaining ones being pencilled in by both parties. It is sensible to continue to adopt a measured, step-by-step strategy to advertising, testing your ideas, spotting flaws and rectifying mistakes at an early stage before committing yourself to long-term expenditure.

Dealing with publications

Your opening orders with the various titles must be confirmed in writing as soon as possible after your meetings with the representatives, and certainly before the deadlines imposed in the respective rate cards. Addressing your letters to the Classified or Display Advertisement Managers – unless representatives are act-ing as go-betweens for you and the different departments – you should simply state the advertisement sizes, positions, dates, agreed costs and discount terms and conditions. Follow this correspondence by sending in your copy, illustra-tions and photographs for the advertisements, if not already taken by the repre-sentatives. Ensure that they arrive in good time – delivering them in person if necessary – particularly if advertisement and production staff need to work on them on your behalf prior to publication. Retain the originals or satisfactory copies in case your submitted material is lost, which happens in busy and chaotic offices.

Some titles will automatically supply you with the proofs of your advertisements ahead of publication although others will need to be asked well in advance to forward these to you. Always request, obtain and look at these, making certain that the advertisement and production teams have interpreted your thoughts and suggestions properly, any changes which may have been made meet with your approval and advertisements are free of typo-graphical and factual errors. Although amendments at this stage are expensive for the publication, you should not hesitate to notify them of mistakes which are their or the printer's responsibility. Left uncorrected, those flawed adver-tisements could reflect badly on you and may obscure or detract from your advertising message.

On publication, copies of each of the titles which carried your advertise-ments ought to be posted or brought to you by the representatives, but may have to be requested if the publications are poorly organized or the representatives are half-hearted at their work. Time-consuming though it is, check carefully to see that the advertisements were the right sizes (half, not quarter pages and so on), in the correct positions (displays not semi-displays and so forth) and were printed on the appropriate days or at satisfactory times if booked as run of week or run of month. Assess their overall appearance (quality of reproduction, enlargement, reduction and so on) and the positive and negative features of the surrounding material (the appeal of editorial copy, presence of rivals' advertisements etc.).

You must immediately contact the appropriate titles if any errors have occurred and/or you have genuine grievances, re-negotiating costs and/or seeking refunds. Read through invoices submitted to you, ensuring that they relate to the correct advertisements, that costs and discounts are duly noted and agreed payment terms and conditions are incorporated within them. Always pay promptly to maintain good relations. Based on your experiences so far – of the representatives, publications and their treatment of you and your advertisements – you may choose to cancel some subsequent bookings, giving the required notice in writing and rearranging your schedule as necessary.

Administering a trial run

You need to step back and contemplate the opening stages of your schedule and the early press advertisements. You have to find out if you are moving along the right lines before spending any more of your advertising appropriation. It is wise to prepare for this tricky (and sometimes almost impossible assessment) by setting questions about the make-up of your schedule which you will subsequently attempt to answer. In particular, you will want to try to discover whether suitable publications are being used and if appropriately sized advertisements are being well located and published at relevant times.

Also, you should list assorted questions concerning the component parts of your various advertisements. Typically, you will wish to find out whether you are choosing the right kinds of advertisement in this instance and if your selected approach is fitting in the circumstances. Then, your thoughts ought to turn to the layout and contents of your advertisements, seeking to ascertain whether they are appropriate or not. If they are not, they may be having little or even no impact, thus wasting your funds.

You need to attempt to judge how far and how well the opening part of your schedule and initial batch of advertisements are helping you to fulfil your objectives. Depending on your various goals, you may be wondering whether independent retailers and consumers in the county are beginning to become aware of your new goods and their benefits, if a contacts list of potential retail stockists is starting to be built up and whether you are generating the targeted turnover.

Monitoring responses

In order to appraise the quality of your schedule and advertisements and how they are helping you to achieve your goals, you must monitor the responses to each of your press advertisements. You need to evaluate the enquiries received if you are trying to develop a contacts list, build up a customer base or recruit staff. It is necessary to measure sales should you be attempting to sell direct, adjust demand, generate turnover or clear out stock. You have to assess changing moods and opinions if you are seeking to increase product recognition, reassure, remind or notify developments to customers or uphold the firm's reputation.

Evaluating the enquiries which derive from individual advertisements is a relatively straightforward process. You can deduce which advertisement initiated a response by inserting a different 'key', or identifying mark, into each of your advertisements. You might ask readers to write to varied addresses (20–30 Windmill Road may become 20a, 20b, 21a, 21b onwards), departments, desks or rooms (Department SE for the *Sunday Express*, SE1 for the first advertisement in that paper, and so on) or people (Sophie Louise Jones could be Ms S. Jones, Ms S. L. Jones, S. Jones and other variations). Alternatively, you may suggest that they quote a reference number when corresponding with or telephoning you, perhaps NW3A for the advertisement which appeared in the *News of the World* on 3 April. Responses can then be logged alongside the appropriate advertisements.

Often, you can measure sales in the same manner, simply noting down addresses on letters, references on orders and so forth, and matching them to the advertisements in which they originally appeared. Naturally, this task has to be tackled carefully, especially if sales do not arise immediately but are spread out over several months following the advertisement, and perhaps after initial enquiries too. If orders are not sent direct to you, sales and the effects of your schedule and advertisements upon them may be harder to judge. You could need to conduct audits of opening stock levels, plus/minus deliveries and closing stock levels at distribution and retail outlets, comparing figures with previous periods whilst making allowances for different and ever-changing internal and external scenarios.

In many instances when you are evaluating enquiries and measuring sales, you can make further value-for-money assessments between advertisements, similar to those which you made when you selected the titles to go into your schedule. Dividing the price of an advertisement by the number of enquiries received from it gives you a comparable cost-per-enquiry figure. Similarly, if you divide the cost of the advertisement by the quantity of sales generated by it, you will be left with a cost-per-sale figure. Clearly, you must also bear in mind the number of enquiries which turn into sales and the amounts of each sale before reaching any firm conclusions.

Assessing developing moods and opinions – possibly of stockists and/or consumers – is extremely difficult as they cannot be quantified in terms of the number of enquiries or orders, although those who do enquire or order goods could be considered to have been reminded and reassured of products and services. You have to interview customers (or whoever you are trying to influence) before and after advertisements have been published, questioning them about their knowledge of the firm, goods and services plus their opinions on any recent changes that you have implemented. Questions could also be raised about their purchase and usage of products to further measure or check upon estimated sales.

Knowing about the enquiries, sales and changes of opinion which are attributable to each keyed advertisement may now enable you to answer some of the questions that you posed about your early schedule and advertisements. Perhaps advertisements in one title produced far fewer responses than those in others. Possibly, advertisements with a particular mix of contents did far better than other ones. Of course, you cannot expect to answer every query as fully as you would wish to, given the modest amount of advertising carried out so far. Nevertheless, you should be able to put together a rough and ready impression of what seems to work, and not to work. Take a look at the 'Media assessment' form on page 229 at this point. It may assist you in your activities.

Making changes

Mindful of your initial impressions, you should then set about revising your schedule and press advertisements accordingly, dropping one or two titles that failed to generate any replies, concentrating on display rather than semi-display advertisements, shifting your approach and so on. You may decide to cancel several outstanding insertions which have been booked, if you are sure that they are unlikely to stimulate the number and type of responses which you are seeking. Make certain you adhere to the cancellation terms and conditions on the individual rate cards.

It is imperative that you continue with your advertising activities step by step, possibly placing one month's advertisements at a time. Always be conscious that your early opinions cannot be complete and may even be inaccurate on occasions. You could have deduced that one advertisement initiates more responses than another, does better in this rather than that title and on one particular day compared to others; but never forget that you are working on limited data. Don't be in too much of a hurry to hand over your money until you have a more substantial body of evidence and have filled in any gaps in your knowledge, perhaps about frequency and duration.

Also, internal and external factors can alter as time passes. Internally, your business may contract or expand, with differing strengths and weaknesses

MEDIA ASSESSMENT FORM

	Campaign:		Number:
	Media:		Date:

Media	Cost incurred (£)	Number of enquiries	Cost per enquiry (£)	Number of orders	Cost per order (£)	Total sales	Average sale per enquiry (£)	Average sale per order (£)	Comment

Media assessment form

becoming apparent. Products and services could come and go. You might amend your short-, medium- and long-term goals. Externally, new customers and rivals may come into the market, as others leave. Political, social and other influences could affect your marketplace, for better or for worse. These developments can all have knock-on effects upon your campaign. Hence, you need to pursue a hands-on approach at all times, analysing yourself, your market, schedule, advertisements and their results, over and again, never being afraid to make amendments as required, even to long-held practices.

Purchasing radio time

Having also adopted an extremely thorough, step-by-step approach towards this particular medium, you should be more than capable of running winning advertising activities over the airwaves. Your careful and conscientious build-up will have given you both the knowledge *and* the confidence to go on to purchase airtime, conduct a trial run in order to assess your initial activities, and amend your schedule in a way which puts you in a position to mount a successful campaign.

Getting on air

With your proposed schedule and advertisement notes to hand, you can telephone the radio stations (or sales houses) in turn to talk to and arrange to meet their sales executives. Some of these go-betweens are good at their work, others less so. Some know the radio world inside out, understand their station and what it has to offer advertisers and will recognize your needs and try to fulfil them to your satisfaction. They are a mine of valuable information and hands-on assistance. Others seem to be employed only for their looks and are capable of doing little more than smiling sweetly and writing down your order. Nevertheless, you do need to meet sales executives as you cannot expect to post your schedule and advertising ideas to the station in the hope that someone correctly interprets your requirements.

Usually, a sales executive will call on you at your shop, office or factory within a day or so of your telephone conversation. It is a good idea to encourage the exchange of views and opinions during a chat over tea or coffee. Establish a rapport, if you can. Talk generally about radio advertising and its pros and cons. Perhaps the executive will tell you something you do not know or may stress an advantage or disadvantage you have not thought about thoroughly. Discuss who's who at the station so that you are aware of who will be doing what for you. Chat about radio bodies and advertising organizations too, updating your knowledge of the industry.

Talk over your small business, your goods and services, goals, customers, rivals and the marketplace. Clarify your thoughts if necessary, and see whether the sales executive has any valid comments or suggestions to make. Outline the budget that you have allocated to your radio advertising activities, the minimum and maximum amounts, and what you feel able to spend via the radio station. Discuss your proposed schedule and the timing, length, frequency and duration of your advertisements, and the reasons behind your choices. Find out if the executive agrees with them. Explain your advertisement ideas, and why you believe this approach and these contents are right for your firm. Hear what the sales executive has to say about them.

Of course this valuable, two-way exchange may not be possible if you are faced with an executive who simply agrees with everything you say because he or she just wants to sell you as much airtime as possible. Even so, you will both still need to cover your proposed schedule in some depth, thrashing out the prospective number of advertisements allocated to the particular station, their respective lengths and possible dates and times, whether rotated evenly at the radio station's discretion or planned for specific periods or special breaks. Clearly, you have to discuss your wishes and see what is available before reaching agreement on the numbers and types of advertisements to be scheduled.

Again, you will both have to discuss your thoughts in some considerable detail. You need to outline the approach that you think is most suitable for your firm, products and services. The planned contents of your advertisements have to be talked through as well, with you explaining what it is you want to say to your customers and describing the types of voices, music and sound effects that are required to put over your message in the most effective manner. Once more, you have to decide whether – and if so, how far – your ideas can be translated into reality by the radio station.

It is very tempting to book your entire schedule at once, perhaps to take advantage of the discounts stated in the rate card or even to impress the sales executive, as some foolish small-business owners and managers seek to do. This is wholly unwise, and at odds with the steady and measured build-up which you have adopted to date. Do no more than book an initial batch of advertisements – possibly for the first week, fortnight or month at most – with the remaining ones being pencilled in for subsequent confirmation, adjustment or cancellation, as appropriate. You need to be able to appraise various aspects of your schedule and radio advertisements – timing, frequency, duration and so forth – and measure their effects before settling upon or amending your plans as necessary.

Having discussed your schedule and advertisements together, you then have to finalize the costs and any other terms and conditions associated with the booking. Always push for discounts, whether first time, payment in cash or bulk discounts, on the basis of what you intend to spend with the station over the coming year. Never forget that the radio world is growing rapidly and more and more stations are competing to attract the same number of advertisers in the marketplace, so take advantage of this as far as you can. Whatever the costs indicated on the rate card, tough bargaining should ensure these are reduced by between 10 and 25 per cent.

Make sure other terms and conditions are worked through and understood by both parties at this stage to avoid confusion and disagreements later on. The rate card will have stated the basic terms and conditions which advertisers are deemed to have accepted upon placing an order. You may wish to try to have these varied or added to, when relevant. In particular, do insist that the executive arranges to supply you with a tape of the advertisements produced for you by the station, well before they are due to be transmitted. You must be able to check and approve these in advance. Also, avoid paying up front. You have to be absolutely happy with the advertisements and satisfied with the station's performance before handing over your money. Make this an unbreakable rule.

Following your meeting with the sales executive, confirm your agreement in writing, sending it to him or her at the radio station. Do this in good time, and well before your advertisements are due to be produced and transmitted on air. Set out the numbers, lengths, dates and times of your first advertisements. Write down the agreed approach to, and contents of, your advertisements, including an accompanying cassette containing your prepared example. Note the costs, discounts and other terms and conditions that were negotiated between you. Remind him or her to pencil in subsequent advertisements to be decided upon, one way or the other. Keep a copy of your letter, in case the original goes astray.

If necessary, chase up the executive thereafter to obtain copies of the advertisements which have been prepared on your behalf by the station's production team. Check that your thoughts and ideas have been interpreted correctly, and the approach and contents are what you wanted. Make certain the voices, music and sound effects are how you imagined them to be, and put over your message in as effective a manner as possible. Listen for errors such as a mispronounced name, an incorrect dialling code or an incomplete telephone number, which can and do crop up surprisingly often. Do not hesitate to demand changes as and when necessary. Your reputation and money are at risk if you do not.

Conducting trial activities

You must view your initial batch of radio advertisements as a trial run, and an opportunity to test your schedule and advertisements, measure the responses and adjust your plans if this seems sensible. You have to try to discover if you are advertising via the right radio stations. It is important to find out whether you are promoting yourself at the best times and as frequently and for as long as you ought to do. You need to learn if the approach to and contents of your advertisements are correct, and are as successful as they could be. In short, you must feel sure – or at least as certain as you can be – that you are on the right lines, before you go further with your campaign.

Attempt to hear all of your advertisements as they are transmitted – which may not be an easy task if you have booked perhaps 28 advertisements to be spread out over one week. Nevertheless, the more you listen to, the better. You ought to make your own preliminary judgements of your schedule and advertisements, and can only do this by tuning in. Check to see that advertisements were broadcast at the agreed times, if appropriate. If timings were left to the radio station, see that they were transmitted at relevant times for your particular target audience. As an example, those which are broadcast in the early hours of the morning may be wasted if your audience comprises housewives with young children.

On hearing your advertisements as they are transmitted, decide for yourself whether they really are the right length. Imagine that you are the targeted customer, and calculate if you would be able to absorb the message in such a short time; or possibly the advertisements now seem too long, seeking to put across too much information to the audience. Advertisements always sound different when they are played on air. Contemplate the frequency of your advertisements, working out to your own satisfaction whether they are well spaced out, too close together or too far apart. It is not unknown for advertisements which are supposed to be rotated evenly over one week to be grouped on one or two days at the end of that period.

Think about the advertisements themselves in more detail. Hearing them again over the airwaves, you may feel that the overall approach is rather low-key or too upbeat for your specific message. The contents could be too brief or overly detailed. You may believe that the voices, music and sound effects do not convey your message in the appropriate manner. Check to ensure that any changes you had demanded – from an incorrectly quoted telephone number to quieter sound effects – were implemented. Be sure the advertisements were transmitted in full, and that the beginnings and ends were not cut off or talked over as sometimes happens. Listen to what else is transmitted around your advertisements. Quite rightly, you could feel that advertisements from rival firms may detract from yours. Similarly, a discussion about mad cow disease may not be the best time to promote your meat pies, sausages and related foodstuffs.

Do not hesitate to contact the radio station if you are unhappy with any aspect of your schedule or advertisements, whether timings, lengths, frequency or whatever. If the station is at fault – transmitting advertisements at inappropriate times, leaving notified errors uncorrected, presenters chatting over your advertisements and so on – then it should remedy the matter immediately and be prepared to adjust your subsequent invoice accordingly. Should you have changed your mind, perhaps about the length of the advertisements, the voices, music, sound effects and so forth, it is not too late to make changes. Never forget that radio is an instant medium, and advertisements can be re-recorded in hours and broadcast within minutes.

In addition to your own judgements concerning your schedule and advertisements, it is wise to try to assess your customers' responses to them so that you can see which times, lengths and other factors generate the best results. In theory, you can spot which advertisements initiated responses by including a 'key' into each and every advertisement transmitted. Listeners may be asked to telephone a specific person, write to a different address or quote a particular reference number when placing an order, buying a product or applying for a job. Recruitment advertisements in the mornings could ask listeners to telephone Alan Smith, with those in the afternoons calling Jenny Taylor. Thus, responses can be recorded, attributed to advertisements and conclusions drawn.

However, this method is difficult to operate in practice via the radio except on a very limited basis such as comparing and contrasting the success rates of advertisements broadcast in the mornings and afternoons, weekdays and weekends. Trying to evaluate many variable factors alongside each other becomes impossible as innumerable versions of the same advertisement have to be produced with Alan Smith quoted for morning advertisements, Jenny Taylor for afternoons, Tom Reynolds for 20-second advertisements, Jane King for 40-second advertisements and so on. This is time-consuming and costly to do and, even then, there is no guarantee that listeners responding to the advertisements will mention the specific name.

It is more sensible to talk to as many customers who enquire about, place orders for or buy your goods and services as possible. Ask them whether they heard your advertisements, which ones, what they thought of them and if these advertisements inspired them to call, write to or visit you. As a small-business owner or manager dealing with a relatively limited number of customers on a day-to-day basis, you ought to be able to speak to them all and draw conclusions from their various comments and suggestions.

If enquiries, orders and sales are not always channelled through you, it may be harder still to assess responses to your schedule and advertisements. You could need to ask sales representatives to act for you, posing questions to the customers on your behalf. Should your goods be sold through numerous outlets, you may have to content yourself with conducting audits of opening stock levels, deliveries and closing stock levels and comparing figures with previous periods whilst making allowances for changing circumstances. This will at least allow you to conclude that radio advertising has had an overall, worthwhile effect, or not.

Make a point of reading through the invoices that are subsequently sent to you by the radio stations or delivered by the sales executives. Mistakes are commonplace, so do be sure that they are correct, with the right numbers and types of advertisements listed, discounts given and so forth, before handing over your money. Often, the invoices will be brought to you by the executives who will want to know your opinions of the advertising to date, and whether you wish to take or cancel the other advertisements which have been pencilled in. You then have to decide whether your radio advertising has been successful or not. Hopefully, it will have been, and you will want to carry on, albeit with some amendments to your trial activities. 'Conducting a trial run: an action checklist' on page 236, and the 'Media assessment' form on page 229 may enable you to reach valid conclusions.

Amending your schedule

Conscious of your personal views and the responses of your customers towards your schedule and advertisements, you can then set about making amendments to them, as and where necessary. You may decide to reduce or increase the number of radio stations you use, if it seems that your target audience is covered excessively or inadequately. You might concentrate on one station rather than another from now on if one is noticeably more successful than the other. It may be apparent that advertising in the mornings produces significantly better responses than in the afternoons, so you can thus adjust your schedule as a consequence of this. You could feel that your advertisements need to be lengthened to have a greater impact upon your existing and would-be customers.

It may be wise to add to or to cut back upon the number of advertisements that are being transmitted over the airwaves, so the target audience hears them enough times to absorb your message but not so much that they become bored, and ignore what you are saying to them. Similarly, you could decide to close up or widen the gaps between each advertisement transmitted. You might conclude that the approach and/or contents of your advertisements to date need to be amended for the future, perhaps replacing a strident voice which irritated your customers and prospects with a softer one, and changing music or sound effects accordingly.

However minor or major your amendments may be, it is essential that you proceed with your advertising activities in a slow and careful manner. Book no more than one month's advertisements at a time, analysing them and the responses as you go along and prior to booking any more. Do bear in mind that your judgements to date are based upon short-lived knowledge and experience,

When conducting a trial run on the radio, it is sensible to assess advertisements personally in the first instance. Ask yourself if the following points are satisfactory or not. Hopefully, all your answers will be 'Satisfactory'.

	Satisfactory	Unsatisfactory
Timings	❑	❑
Lengths	❑	❑
Frequency	❑	❑
Approach	❑	❑
Contents	❑	❑
Preceding advertisements	❑	❑
Subsequent advertisements	❑	❑
Programmes	❑	❑

Conducting a trial run: an action checklist

and simply may not be valid: only time will tell. Similarly, responses have been derived from a limited number of advertisements and probably are sufficient enough for you to conclude that radio advertising has been worthwhile, but no more than that. Detailed and accurate assessments about timings, lengths, frequency and so on, build up over a lengthy period of time.

Furthermore, circumstances change as months and quarters pass by, necessitating further amendments to schedules and advertisements. The radio industry will continue to expand, with increasing numbers of stations transmitting across the United Kingdom on a local, regional and national basis. You will have more choice, which may be reflected in your upcoming schedules. The Radio Authority's Code of Advertising Standards and Practice will be updated further to meet developing situations, and might influence what you advertise and how you promote your goods and services much more than it does at the moment. Radio Joint Audience Research figures may differ dramatically from one year to the next – often diminishing and affecting your selection of those radio stations which will be given your advertising.

Your small business might expand into new trading areas, leading you to promote yourself via regional or national rather than local radio stations. You may diversify into other products and services, with the approach to and contents of your advertisements affected as a consequence of these developments. Your objectives could shift and alter over a period of time with similar adjustments being made to your advertising patterns. Customer habits might change, with people tuning in to more diverse stations catering for increasingly specialized needs. Rival firms may promote themselves on one station but not another, thus affecting your plans. Anything can happen, and you must adopt an ongoing, hands-on approach to your radio advertising activities if you are to become – and remain – a winner.

Producing mailshots

If you have approached direct mail in a scrupulous and detailed manner, you will now be ready and able to launch and run a highly successful campaign through the post. It is your lengthy and in-depth background work (which so many unsuccessful direct mail advertisers hurry through or overlook completely) that will enable you to be a winner in this medium. You must now take your mailing lists, your creative thoughts and ideas, and go into production, testing your activities, measuring responses and making constant amendments to these activities throughout this and subsequent, winning campaigns.

Going into production

As a small-business owner or manager probably undertaking mailing activities for the first time, it is likely that this initial campaign will be a very low-key affair, possibly involving no more than a hundred or so letters, sent to known customers and solid prospects. In many respects, you just want to test the medium to see how appropriate it is for you, and will not wish to commit more time and money until you are fairly convinced that it is well suited to your circumstances. Thus most, if not all, of the production work will be carried out by you, buying stationery from a local stationers or stationery wholesaler, using a word processor and compatible printer to run off self-devised letters and adding inserts which you already use in your business activities. It is very much a hands-on, learn-as-you-go operation.

Even so, talk at length to stationers and wholesalers about stationery before purchasing envelopes, paper and so on. Seek their advice, look at what they have to offer and take notice of their suggestions prior to obtaining quotations and making your choice from what is available to you. If you need to employ a printer to produce letterheaded paper, additional brochures, or new leaflets, draw up a shortlist of perhaps four or five by approaching the trade bodies known as the British Printing Industries Federation and the Society of Typographic Designers. Also, contact fellow-traders for word-of-mouth recommendations. See 'Useful contacts', page 385, for addresses and telephone numbers.

Meeting each of the shortlisted printers in turn, spell out your requirements to them – what you want them to produce, whether a booklet or leaflet, the amounts, the sizes and number of pages, the contents (perhaps text alone or text and pictures), the type, size and colour of the paper used and any miscellaneous requests such as incorporating folds so that the items are ready for insertion into the envelopes. Sketch out rough and ready examples of letterheads and leaflets, so that they can see what you have in mind. Explain when the job needs to be completed and where items should be delivered to you, if appropriate.

Try to appraise the printers in each of these areas, listening to what they have to say *and* looking at work they have produced for other customers like yourself. Consider whether they have the skills and experience to produce the material you want to the necessary standards and in the quantities required. Make sure they have printed something like it before. Be certain that they will complete the job by the set deadline so that you will be able to post out your mailshots on time. Get in touch with their other customers to see what they have to say about the printers, and the quality and speed of the work.

Check out the terms and conditions involved with working with the printers. For your part, ensure that all of the work will be carried out in-house rather than being passed on to other specialists, as this will increase costs for you. Make certain that payment is to be made on delivery only, and that appropriate discounts will apply, or the contract cancelled, if your deadline is not met by the printers. Obtain quotations from each of the printers, comparing and contrasting these before reaching your decision about which one you will commission on this occasion.

Having made your choice, you must then set out an achievable schedule leading up to the distribution of your mailshots. This needs to be set down, and make sure that everyone involved is aware of its various details. These would include listing when you will buy stationery, hand over your sketched-out ideas to the printer, collect proofs, check proofs, return amended proofs to the printer and pick up finished items. Then you need to calculate timings for folding letters, adding inserts, stamping, franking and addressing envelopes and delivering the mailshots to the post office. Always allow for delays and mistakes within your timetable – these can and do arise from time to time.

Testing your activities

Whether your direct mail activities involve sending out hundreds or thousands of items, it is sensible to test various aspects of your campaign before committing yourself to delivering all of the mailshots and spending your entire budget. To all intents and purposes, you can test just about each and every aspect of your activities, from the quality of one mailing list against another right down to whether 'Kind regards' produces better responses than 'Yours sincerely'. Whatever you choose to test, you need to weigh the time and expense involved with testing alongside the likely gains which will be derived from those changes made as a result of your test findings. As a basic example, if it costs £200 to discover that 'Kind regards' produces orders totalling £20 more than those generated by 'Yours sincerely', then it is an uneconomic and pointless exercise.

As a rule, it is wise to test only the key aspects of your campaign; mailing lists for example. You may wish to compare an internal list against an external one or to find out which sexes, age groups and geographical segments within a particular list are most responsive to your direct mail. Equally important, you might want to test your message, to discover which product qualities seem to draw the best responses, what offers are most popular and which prices achieve the highest-quality results. You could wish to test the timing of your mailshot, to see which season, month, week or day pulls in the best results. Less relevant aspects – the size of the words in the letter, the pros and cons of underlining some phrases and not others and so on – should be left to your subjective assessment, which will become increasingly valid as your knowledge and experience grow.

To test mailing lists accurately, or at least as accurately as you can without bringing in statisticians and a wealth of complex mathematical formulae, you must simply select a sample of names from each list which share the same characteristics. For example, both samples might consist of 50 per cent males, 50 per cent females, 10 per cent 15- to 24-year-olds, 15 per cent 25- to 34-year-olds and so forth. Send the mailshot to each of them, and await their responses to decide which list is most effective. Similarly, to test different mailings – perhaps one with a particular offer, another with an alternative one – you need to deliver them to two, identically matched samples, and wait for the replies to arrive so that you can judge them. To test timings, you just send the same mailshot to comparable samples, but at different times. Once more, you can reach conclusions based upon responses.

The key to successful and accurate testing – whether of lists, messages, timings or whatever – is linked closely to your chosen samples. Not only must they match each other in any tests, but they also have to be representative of your total audience. If you send alternative mailings to two samples made up of 60 per cent men/40 per cent women and so on, you can tell which mailshot generates the greatest responses. However, this is of little long-term practical use if your overall audience is 10 per cent male/90 per cent female. Think about the size of your sample too, which must be large enough to be representative of the total audience. It is notoriously difficult to establish the 'right' number to be approached. Even statisticians argue over different percentages. As a very approximate rule of thumb, a figure of between 2 and 7 per cent of the total is usually chosen, with the lower the expected response rate, the higher the figure selected.

Measuring replies

Your instinctive reaction to any test mailings or direct mail activities is whether or not you have made an overall profit (although this clearly should not be of sole concern when you are testing). Profitability is, or ought to be, easy to ascertain if you maintain scrupulous and up-to-date records. You should know precisely how many mailshots have been sent out and will record the number of enquiries and orders, total sales and the average sale per enquiry and order. Against these facts and figures you can set the costs of list purchase or rental, envelopes, letters, reply devices, added inserts and so forth to tot up your total expenses. Deducting these from total sales leaves you with your profit, which hopefully will be in line with your original budget.

Naturally, you will want more details than this so that you can fine-tune your current and future activities in order to maximize the effectiveness of your campaigns. Instead of taking a blanket look at the overall profitable or unprofitable response, you need to break it down in depth. If you sent out only a few hundred mailings, you can study the returns one by one, but if you delivered thousands then you will need to insert 'keys', or identifying elements, into your mailshots so that you can subsequently separate out the responses for analysis. You might do this by asking customers and prospects to telephone various extension numbers and people (Mr Harrison for one tested list, Ms Johnson for another) or write to alternative departments and addresses (18–24 Hamilton Road for one message, 20–24 for the other). Similarly, series of letters and numbers can be printed on reply cards and envelopes, order, membership and subscription forms, or these might even be produced in varying colours (light grey for March mailshots, a darker grey for April).

This then provides you with the data required for individal assessment purposes. You can take two, three, four or more lists, messages, and so on, and compare and contrast the results of each of them alongside of the others. Again, you may look at the number of mailshots sent out per list, the number of enquiries, the number of orders, the sales revenue and the average sale for each enquiry or order. Dividing up the total expenses of the overall mailings proportionately between list A and list B, allows you to study the profit or loss for all of them, and to reach your conclusions. Completing the 'Media assessment form' on page 229 may help you to clarify your findings.

Implementing amendments

Aware of your initial test findings (and look upon them as broadly accurate rather than absolutely precise) you can set about amending your overall direct mail activities accordingly. You may decide to use one external list in preference to the other, and to concentrate on certain segments of that list which seem to produce the best responses. It could appear sensible to adjust your sales message to stress one particular quality and to settle upon a specific price which tends to generate most sales. You might conclude that January and February produce few responses and are to be avoided, whereas March and April are much better.

It is wise to proceed with your direct mail campaign one step at a time, sending out mailshots and monitoring them carefully. Always remain aware that the tests which you carried out are inevitably rather limited and rough and ready by nature, rarely reveal the whole picture and could be inaccurate. Freak results are not unknown. Do not be too anxious to deliver all of your remaining mailshots in one go unless and until you have built up a clearer understanding and have accumulated more hands-on knowledge and experience.

Also, be conscious that circumstances change monthly, weekly or even daily. Your firm may grow, and might wish to promote new qualities. Products and services could fade in popularity, with replacements needing to be advertised. Your goals may alter, as the medium term draws near. Customers might come and go, moving from job to job and house to house. Rivals could start using direct mail, giving you fresh ideas for mailshots. The market may develop, with codes of practice and laws being updated and introduced. You must stay aware of shifting scenarios and adjust your mailing activities to keep abreast of them. In effect, you have come full circle to begin the process of assessing your business, viewing the marketplace again, but with a track record behind you this time around. Hopefully you will become better at direct mailing, improving on a continual, ongoing basis.

Having a successful exhibition

If you have approached exhibiting at a consumer, trade or private show in a careful and thorough way, you should now be able enough to go on and become a successful exhibitor at your first event. Working in close collaboration with your designer and/or your contractor, you must set about maintaining your schedule, running the stand and evaluating results which will hopefully all combine to bring your activities to a winning conclusion.

Maintaining your schedule

Having previously sketched out a list of activities that needed to be attended to up and beyond the exhibition and with some of these tasks already completed, you must now consider the remaining activities again. Having regrouped the various tasks from beneath the headings of the stand, exhibits, staff, promotional and other activities into a new order based on deadlines, you should set about tackling them properly and on time.

Several tasks will be handed over to your designer and/or contractor. These might include filling in forms in good time to obtain workers' passes from the exhibition organizer, hiring or buying display items on your behalf and arranging for exhibits and display materials to be lifted into place, assembled and installed under supervision. Also, they should book electricity, gas and other services from the organizer, supervise the erection of the stand and ensure that all of the services required are provided as agreed.

Other tasks will be dealt with by you. A significant proportion of them are mundane and can be carried out smoothly, assuming that they are approached early and in a co-ordinated fashion. You may have to reserve accommodation for yourself and your staff in a comfortable and conveniently sited hotel. Do this as soon as possible, as the most popular hotels and rooms are always booked some time ahead of an event. It may be necessary to complete forms in plenty of time to receive badges, exhibitor's passes, invitations to entertainments such as a dinner dance and car parking tickets from the organizer. Make sure that you ask for sufficient numbers of them to avoid petty wranglings and squabbles later on.

Substantial stocks of technical and sales literature should be kept on the stand for staff to refer to and hand out to customers. Submit orders for these well in advance. Similarly, ensure stationery is readily available, including notepads, enquiry forms, business cards, order books and sales invoices. Exhibits and other display items must be made, examined and be ready for transporting to the contractor or (more likely) the exhibition on the agreed dates. You will need to make or confirm travel arrangements for yourself and your staff, deciding whether to use individual cars or to hire a minibus for everyone.

Often overlooked – and bitterly regretted afterwards – is the insurance of your staff, exhibits, display items and stand when in transit and at the event. Also protect yourself against the possibility that the show may be postponed or cancelled, with the potential loss of significant expenditure. Arrange temporary cover by adapting your existing policy through your insurance broker or company. Check beforehand though to see what insurance has been taken out by your designer, contractor, organizer and venue owner to make certain that you do not duplicate cover, adding unnecessarily to your expenses.

Some activities which you must tackle are less routine and require careful thought and consideration. You have to appoint a stand manager to administer and run the stand. In all probability, you will take this supervisory role. If not, whoever is chosen must be as familiar with your firm, products and services, goals and so on as you now are. You also need to select the right numbers of stand staff. Too many, and they may crowd out visitors and have little to do. Too few, and they could be overrun and miss sales leads.

Contemplate the type of stand staff required. Pick sales employees who know the goods inside out, are familiar with selling techniques and who are able to talk to people from the most junior to senior visitor. Balance out the numbers with technicians who can deal with technical queries, public relations employees to handle customer complaints and media enquiries, and other staff as appropriate, such as cleaners, caterers and interpreters at an international event. It is wise to seek a blend of individual specialists working together in harmony rather than non-specialist staff who have to do everything and usually do so with mixed results. Decide whether to dress staff in uniforms which can help them to stand out from the crowd and convey a co-ordinated image of your firm.

A staff rota has to be drawn up well before the event, indicating who is on the stand and when. Employees need to be at their best to do their job properly and being on show for lengthy periods can be extremely stressful and tiring, so it is sensible to allow a 30-minute break after being on duty for three hours or more. Also, be careful to ensure that both the numbers and types of staff on the stand remain above or at certain minimum levels at all times, as leaving the stand undermanned or without key specialists especially at busy periods can be harmful to the business, in terms of weakened image and missed sales opportunities.

Your staff ought to be briefed prior to the exhibition. Fill in all the background details about the firm, products and services, goals, customers, rivals, market and budget, as relevant to them. Invite questions and provide answers about appropriate topics such as production schedules, delivery times, how the show fits in to your overall objectives and so on. Then talk about: the venue and its location, layout and facilities; the organizer and their plans; the show with dates and opening times; the stand, outlining its type, size, site, the exhibits, display materials and so forth; the other exhibitors, particularly your rivals; miscellaneous, personal information, such as hotel and travel arrangements, uniforms, rotas, stand do's and don'ts and so on. Provide written notes of the main points in a folder, for subsequent reference and use.

You may wish to offer additional training too. This could simply involve reading relevant books or watching videos on exhibiting and related topics such as handling customers on a face-to-face basis. Alternatively, you might arrange for them (and indeed you) to attend training courses such as those linked with the National Exhibitors Association and the Incorporated Society of British Advertisers Limited. Do so in good time. Refer to 'Useful contacts', page 385.

Promotional and advertising activities must be carried out as well. You should compile a prospects list of key, existing and would-be customers, arranging for direct mail shots to be sent to them publicizing your presence at the show and inviting them along. Enclose complimentary tickets to the show and associated entertainments, if appropriate. Send press releases to the media, especially any contacts that you have in the local, regional or trade press who might give you a good write-up. Sales agents should be instructed to spread the news of your imminent attendance at the exhibition, and what may happen there.

Also, you must submit your free entry to the show catalogue by the deadline set by the organizer, otherwise your details will be added to the addendum sheets which are usually lost or thrown away. Use all of your allocated number of words, outlining your firm, products and services, telephone and fax numbers, e-mail addresses and a contact name, perhaps your own. Typically, these catalogues are only glanced at during the exhibition to help visitors find the exhibitors they want to see. However, they are usually then kept as a reference guide, being dipped into on and off until the next event is staged. Hence, concentrate on conveying an image of your business and what it does, rather than on what you are exhibiting at this show.

Compile press kits – perhaps comprising press releases about your firm, goods, services and goals plus photographs of your stand, staff and exhibits – for distribution to the media as and when required. Give them what they want to know, making it easy for them to write favourable features about you. Do not overlook your other advertising activities in the press, radio and other media during the build up, possibly drawing in references to your attendance at the exhibition, and your plans thereafter.

Various other duties will need to be carried out after the show has ended and ought to be thought about and planned in anticipation. Your designer and/or contractor will normally have to make certain that the stand, exhibits and all other items are dismantled, removed and returned to the appropriate places within a day or so of the exhibition. You must ensure they have been instructed clearly to do this. Also, you should compile further press releases announcing the winning of an award, signature of a large contract or whatever. Contacts made at the show ought to be followed up with direct mail shots being sent out, telephone calls made and sales visits arranged. Staff should be debriefed, with a full review of the exhibition taking place.

Managing the stand

As stand manager, you, or a well-briefed colleague, should act in an administrative and advisory capacity. It is your overall role to make certain that staff follow the do's and don'ts of stand success, to ensure the stand is maintained in a fit and proper manner and to attend to those after-show duties. It is important to restrict yourself to supervisory and co-ordinating responsibilities only, pulling everyone and everything together. Leave sales, technical and public relations duties to fellow, appropriately qualified personnel.

You need to draw your stand staff's attention to several do's, some of which are probably familiar or instinctive to sales people, but are less so to others. Do have plenty of sleep beforehand, to sustain you through a long and tiring day. Do wear the agreed clothes and badges as planned and at all times, to convey a unified, professional image of the firm. Familiarize yourself with the flow patterns on and around the stand, taking up strategic positions during quieter moments. Greet visitors with a smile and a nod, while allowing them time to breathe and establish their interest before approaching them.

Open by asking a question such as 'What do you like about ... ?' or 'How does this compare to ... ?', which should elicit a full response that can be developed into a conversation. Be polite and interested in the visitor and what he or she has to say. Look and sound enthusiastic about the business, products, show and so on. If you are not, you cannot expect the visitor to be either. Stick to what you know, passing the visitor over to a colleague if he or she is better informed on a particular (sales, technical or public relations) subject. Note the numbers and types of visitors, take business cards, record enquiries, write down orders, sales and so forth on a regular basis.

Remain alert to spot would-be vandals and thieves who appear at many exhibitions, especially if small goods, product samples, alcohol and food are on the stand. Lock away valuables, taking them out and returning them to storage as and when required. Notify security staff whenever assistance is needed. Take regular breaks to refresh yourself. Be careful about what you eat and drink during these times. Try to take a walk outside the venue to clear your mind, ease the pressure and recharge your batteries. You, and your staff, can probably think of other do's to share with each other.

Of course, there are various don'ts that have to be pointed out to stand personnel, time and again if necessary. Don't overeat or drink too much the night before if you want to survive the next day. Don't wear tight clothes or new shoes which will make you feel extremely uncomfortable as time passes. Never eat, smoke, drink, swear, read books or newspapers within sight or sound of a visitor, all of which will harm your polished, quality image. Wait until your next break to do any of these. Only sit down if it is to talk to a visitor. Avoid looking bored or redundant. Busy yourself instead by tidying up the surroundings.

Do not stand around in groups; this is offputting to visitors. Similarly, avoid 'Roll up! Roll up!' stances or guard-like positions which are both unappealing. Never block entrances or obscure exhibits or display materials: visitors have not come to see what you look like. Be careful not to work in pairs, which can appear threatening and may alienate visitors. Try not to hover, trail or chase a visitor across the stand – you will simply drive him or her away. When starting a would-be discussion, don't say 'Can I help you?' 'No' ends the conversation before it even began.

During a talk, steer clear of patronizing the visitor, either by using technical jargon or over-simplified phrases. Find out who the person is and adjust your language accordingly. Don't tell him or her about what interests you. Discover what he or she wants to know and pass on the information in a clear and concise manner. Talk about whatever interests them. Never become flustered if you cannot answer a question yourself. Be ready to refer to a colleague, technical or promotional literature when appropriate. End on a positive note, by handing out a catalogue and price list or exchanging business cards which can be followed up. You, and other stand personnel, may be able to list more don'ts to be discussed between you.

The stand itself must be maintained in good order for the duration of the show if it is to continue to put across the right image, attract visitors to it and provide a first-rate working environment for everyone at all times. The organizer will typically be in charge of keeping the surrounding areas clean and tidy while you take responsibility for your own individual stand, although you may have arranged for stand cleaning to be provided before or after the day's activities; this is very sensible.

Whatever the cleaning arrangements, a busy stand will soon acquire a grubby, well-worn appearance unless everyone involved makes a positive and ongoing effort to keep it looking neat and tidy throughout the day. You and your staff should: hang up coats out of sight; put briefcases, bags and other personal possessions away in cupboards; remove dirty cups from view; pick up rubbish; straighten stationery and literature, disposing of dog-eared and scribbled-on copies; top up stationery and literature supplies as necessary; check for damage to the stand, exhibits and display items, contacting the on-site contractor or replacing as appropriate; keep entrances, chairs, floors and exits free from obstructive articles.

Do remember the after-show activities that you are responsible for. Tell newspapers, magazines and other media about any good news which happened at or was generated by the exhibition. Publicize the 'Product of the Year' award, the huge export order from overseas and so on. If you do not promote yourself, you cannot expect anyone else to do it on your behalf. Follow through on all leads. Study notes made, enquiry forms completed and business cards taken to decide which contacts should be telephoned, written to or visited by a sales agent. The show does not – or at least should not – end on the final day. The successful exhibitor chases up visitors, turning casual and definite interests alike into hard sales.

Staff should be debriefed after the exhibition while it is still fresh in their minds. Try to ensure that everyone attends – you, sales, technical, public relations and other staff plus the designer and/or contractor if possible. In much the same way that you previewed the venue, organizer, show, exhibitors, visitors, stand and so on, you now need to review them in the light of your actual participation. Ask and listen to what everyone has to say about these many and varied aspects.

Judging the results

Naturally, you ought to measure and evaluate the results of exhibiting at your first show to see how far it has helped you towards achieving your goals. It is wise to refresh your memory if necessary and set out again exactly what your objectives were. You may have wanted to achieve a certain volume and/or value of sales, could have sought information about a new marketplace or might have wished to have changed or improved the image of your firm. In all probability, you had a mix of different goals.

It is relatively easy to measure how far you have moved towards achieving your financial objectives through your exhibiting activities if you and your staff recorded faithfully the numbers and types of visitors to your stand, enquiries and the volume and values of orders taken and sales made. You can simply add up visitors, enquiries, orders and sales and subsequently compare them alongside your targets. You may then decide for yourself how successful it was and whether your attendance was worthwhile.

You can place your findings into a more significant context by judging visitors, enquiries, orders and sales in relation to the cost of exhibiting. You should now be in a position to calculate the actual rather than the estimated expenses involved with your stand, exhibits, promotional and other activities and be able to total up the final bill. From here it is simple to work out the cost per visitor, enquiry, order and sale of attending the show. If you keep similar records for sending out mailshots, advertising in the press and radio, having sales agents on the road and so forth, you can draw more conclusions about the viability of exhibitions as a sales medium.

Any assumptions that are made must take full account of the particular circumstances of this first show. For example, as a new exhibitor, it would be surprising if mistakes were not made and opportunities missed, whereas you may be more experienced in using other media. Also, numerous influences – bad weather, a transport strike, even a bomb scare – could have had knock-on effects. Consider the specific characteristics of exhibitions too. As an example, many visitors come to look and learn, and sales may follow on weeks or even months later; credit needs to be given to the show, when these eventually arrive.

Of course, other results are less easy to measure and put into context. It is difficult to judge how much data you have learned about a market or how far your image has changed in the minds of your customers. It is equally hard to value the other benefits to be derived from exhibiting, especially those that are less prominent in other media: the establishment of a warm rapport with an existing or new customer, the receipt of a snippet of information about a niche that can be exploited and so on. You need to take account of these too.

Much of this evaluation process into your objectives can be conducted by you, working in association with your stand staff, designer and/or contractor. Additional useful details during your assessments can sometimes be provided by the show organizer who may commission a general exhibition survey, subsequently selling its findings to exhibitors. For an appropriate fee, you can have questions inserted into this survey. As an example, you might wish visitors to be asked about their knowledge and views of your goods before and after the event.

Alternatively, you could employ a specialist company such as Exhibition Surveys Limited to act on your behalf. Using a mix of face-to-face interviews, telephone conversations and postal questionnaires they can find out abut visitors' interests, reactions to and opinions of the show, their recall of exhibitors, memories of the stands etc. If you are unable to evaluate key goals by yourself, consider employing an independent expert to assist you. The expense involved is a small price to pay to establish the success or failure of your exhibition activities.

Summary

- Successful press advertisers know how to read a rate card, negotiate the best possible deal with representatives and deal efficiently with publications.

- Effective radio advertisers are able to work closely with sales executives and other members of the radio station to ensure that their advertisements go on air as they imagined them.

- Winning direct mailers are familiar with their mailing lists and liaise with other specialists to make certain that their mailshots are produced and distributed according to plan.

- Successful exhibitors timetable their workload and work closely to it; paying particularly close attention to managing the stand and its personnel effectively.

- The best advertisers approach advertising on a careful, step-by-step basis – always testing, measuring responses and amending, now *and* on an ongoing basis.

Notes

Notes

Conclusion

HOPEFULLY, YOUR FIRST CAMPAIGN will be a winner and you will want to continue advertising via the press, radio, direct mail and exhibitions. Before doing this though, step back and review your activities so far. Learn from your past successes and failures, to boost your chances of an even better campaign next time. Looking at each medium in sequence, you should be able to answer all of these questions in a positive manner. If you cannot, you will know that you have more work to do for the future.

Your press checklist

Types of publication

❏ Were you totally familiar with the characteristics of and the similarities and dissimilarities between national daily and Sunday newspapers as well as regional dailies, Sundays, paid-for and free (bi-)weeklies?

❏ Did you know about the pros and cons of advertising in papers?

❏ Were you wholly aware of consumer and business magazines, especially their key, comparable and contrasting features?

❏ Did you recognize their benefits and drawbacks so far as advertisers are concerned?

❏ Have you taken full account of miscellaneous publications such as directories, brochures, in-house journals, timetables, maps and guidebooks?

❏ Did you appreciate the advantages and disadvantages which they offer you?

Who's who in the press

❏ Were you conscious of the different departments and employees within a publication along with their work and the ways in which they interact with each other?

❏ Have you found out about the trade organizations in the press industry and how they can help you with your campaign?

❏ Did you know of the advertising bodies that may be involved with press advertising and understand what they do?

Analysing yourself

❏ Were you completely conversant with your own business and its distinctive blend of strengths and weaknesses?

❏ Have you studied the types of goods and services which you sell and verified their main features and plus and minus points?

❏ Were your short-, medium- and long-term objectives absolutely clear to you?

❏ Have you compiled detailed notes about your firm, products, services and goals for hands-on use during your advertising campaign?

Knowing your market

❏ Did you know everything about your existing and potential customers, especially their characteristics and their perceptions of you and your goods?

❏ Have you taken stock of all your present and possible rivals, assessing them in the same areas and ways in which you examined your own concern?

❏ Were you up-to-date about the internal workings of and external influences upon the market in which you operate or plan to operate?

❏ Have you carried out as much research as you can into your customers, competitors and marketplace, recording information to subsequently assist you throughout your advertising activities?

Establishing a budget

❏ Were the various methods used to calculate a suitable advertising budget familiar to you?

❏ Have you reviewed the past, looked at the present and anticipated the future before setting the appropriation?

❏ Did you keep abreast of changing and developing circumstances, making amendments to your budget whenever necessary?

Bringing in experts

❏ Have you ascertained the roles and services on offer from a full service agency, à la carte agency and a media independent?

❏ Were you aware of how to select such a specialist to administer or support you with your activities?

❏ Have you weighed up the possibilities of commissioning other experts to work on your behalf, namely a market research agency, an illustrator, a photographer, a copywriter and a typesetter?

❏ Did you know how to set about making the right choice for you?

Planning your schedule

❑ Did you draw up a shortlist of useable titles by reading through *British Rate and Data* and listening to recommendations from valid sources?

❑ Were media packs, rate cards and copies of the most recent issues always obtained and scanned from cover to cover?

❑ Did you compare and contrast each publication's audience with your own, retaining only those titles with similar profiles and in-depth penetration into your customer base?

❑ Have you thought about the timing, frequency and duration of your advertising activities, discarding the publications which do not enable you to promote yourself when you want to?

❑ Have you decided which sizes and positions are best for your advertisements and calculated the value-for-money costs of advertising in various titles?

❑ Did you constantly draft and redraft your schedule until it matches your allocated budget?

Creating your advertisements

❑ Were you conscious of the main features, pros and cons of display, semi-display and classified advertisements?

❑ Have you familiarized yourself with the multitude of approaches which can be adopted towards advertising, and settled upon one which seems suitable in your given situation?

❑ Have you thought about the layout of your advertisements?

❑ Have you considered the text of your advertisements?

❑ Did your advertisements remain within the law, being legal, decent, honest and truthful?

❑ Were they prepared with a sense of responsibility to your customers and competitors?

Buying advertising space

❑ Have you mastered the rate card, being able to translate all of its jargon?

❑ Were the terms and conditions of advertising in the press known to you?

❑ Were you capable of handling representatives properly, negotiating the best possible deals with them?

❑ Did you know how to work with the various titles to achieve success?

Conducting your activities

❏ Was a trial run always carried out to test your schedule and advertisements?

❏ Did you monitor responses to your advertising activities on an ongoing basis, using appropriate measurement techniques?

❏ Were changes made to your schedule and advertisements as and when necessary, even if it means admitting that firmly held beliefs are incorrect?

❏ Were you an effective press advertiser?

Your radio checklist

Types of radio

❏ Did you learn about the characteristics of radio stations across the United Kingdom?

❏ Were you fully familiar with the advantages of advertising on air?

❏ Were you wholly aware of the disadvantages of advertising over the airwaves?

❏ Did you compare and contrast these characteristics, pros and cons with regard to your own situation?

Who's who in radio

❏ Did you find out about the departments and employees within a radio station, and what each of them do?

❏ Were you conversant with the trade bodies in the radio industry and their respective roles?

❏ Were you conscious of the professional organizations in the advertising world and their activities?

❏ Did you ask these various bodies for information and guidance as and when appropriate?

Evaluating your business

❏ Did you look at your concern and its mix of positive and negative features?

❏ Did you study your goods and services, spotting their particular pluses and minuses?

❏ Were you able to clarify your targets in the short, medium and long term?

❏ Were detailed notes taken for use during your campaign?

Understanding the marketplace

❏ Did you consider your customers, finding out as much as possible about them?

❏ Did you think about your rivals, identifying their strengths and weaknesses?

❏ Did you view the market and discover the influences upon it?

❏ Were you able to fill in the gaps in your knowledge by conducting further research, as required?

❏ Were in-depth notes prepared for use with your advertising activities?

Fixing an appropriation

❏ Did you analyse your sales in the past, during the present and for the future?

❏ Did you appraise your profits for previous, current and forthcoming years?

❏ Did you contemplate other influential factors before setting your appropriation?

❏ Was a suitable budget allocated for your radio advertising campaign?

Planning your activities

❏ Did you approach radio stations after composing a shortlist on the grounds of where you wanted to promote yourself?

❏ Did you peruse rate cards, separating key information about audiences, advertising rates and conditions from out-and-out sales hype?

❏ Did you assess each radio station's audience in relation to your own targeted audience?

❏ Did you calculate costs on a 'cost per thousand' basis, making as many detailed, value-for-money judgements as possible?

❏ Did you prepare a schedule of advertisements which was right for your unique circumstances?

Composing advertisements

❏ Did you select the best approach for your advertisements on this occasion?

❏ Did you choose the right contents for your advertisements, with voices, music and sound effects conveying your message in the most appropriate way?

❏ Did you comply with the law in this field, reading and adhering to the Radio Authority's Code of Advertising Standards and Practice?

Running your campaign

❏ Did you purchase airtime only after discussing your schedule and advertisements with sales executives, and in as much depth as possible?

❏ Did you conduct a trial run to test your schedule and advertisements, measuring the responses to them in order to work out their plus and minus features?

❏ Was your schedule amended in the light of these findings, and updated continually to keep abreast of changing and developing circumstances?

❏ Were you a successful radio advertiser?

Your direct mail checklist

Types of direct mail

❏ Were you wholly aware of the main characteristics of business-to-business and consumer mail?

❏ Did you discover the benefits of advertising through direct mail?

❏ Did you find out about the possible drawbacks of using direct mail?

❏ Did you weigh up the advantages and disadvantages next to each other, mindful of your own circumstances?

Who's who in direct mail

❏ Did you learn about the key participants in the industry, and their various roles?

❏ Were you conscious of the trade bodies, and what they could do for you?

❏ Were you familiar with the regulatory organizations, and how they affected your activities?

❏ Were you aware of the advertising organizations, and the ways in which they could assist you?

❏ Did you seek information and advice from anyone and everyone in the direct mail and advertising industries?

Assessing your business

❏ Did you analyse your organization, recognizing its individual blend of strengths and weaknesses?

❏ Did you investigate your products and services and appreciate their positive and negative features?

❏ Did you set short-, medium- and long-term objectives, to provide a framework to work within and towards?

❏ Did you draw up detailed notes about your firm, goods, services and goals for later reference?

Viewing the marketplace

❏ Did you think about your customers, especially their characteristics, opinions and habits?

❏ Did you contemplate your competitors, particularly their organizations, products, services and advertising activities?

❏ Were you able to understand your market, and the many internal and external influences upon it?

❏ Did you complete your knowledge of the marketplace by carrying out additional research, as appropriate?

❏ Did you compile more in-depth notes concerning your customers, rivals and market?

Calculating an appropriation

❏ Did you recognize all of the potential costs related to mailing activities?

❏ Did you appraise those costs that most applied to your situation?

❏ Were you able to establish the likely expenditure involved with your direct mail campaign?

Using mailing lists

❏ Did you build up your own lists, from your records and easily accessible, published material?

❏ Did you obtain other, external lists as necessary, making certain that they were clean and relevant in your circumstances?

❏ Did you maintain accurate and up-to-date lists at all times?

❏ Did you comply with the law throughout your activities?

❏ Were you totally familiar with the Data Protection Act 1984 and its principles, reading them carefully?

Creating direct mail

❏ Did you evaluate envelopes, before choosing ones which suited your specific situation?

❏ Did you look at letters and mull over the do's and don'ts prior to writing your mailshots?

❏ Did you contemplate possible supporting material, before adding inserts?

❏ Did you adhere to the standards of practice expected by the direct mail and advertising industries?

❏ Were you fully conversant with the British Codes of Advertising and Sales Promotion Practice, studying them from cover to cover?

Conducting your campaign

❏ Did you go into production with the help of your local stationers, printer and other specialists, to transform your creative thoughts and ideas into mailshots?

❏ Did you test various aspects of your mailing activities, before sending out all of your mailshots and spending your entire budget?

❏ Did you measure the responses to your numerous tests, reaching conclusions about the different approaches taken?

❏ Did you make amendments in the light of these findings, and continue to alter your activities in response to changing and developing circumstances?

❏ Were you a successful direct mail user?

Your exhibition checklist

Types of exhibition

❏ Were you fully aware of the characteristics of consumer, trade and private exhibitions?

❏ Did you recognize the potential benefits of exhibiting at a show, whether a consumer, trade or private event?

❏ Were you conscious of the possible drawbacks of attending a consumer, trade or private exhibition?

❏ Did you compare and contrast these various characteristics, pluses and minuses in relation to your own firm and circumstances?

Who's who at exhibitions

❏ Did you know about the key participants at a show, and how they all work together?

❏ Were you familiar with the representative bodies in the exhibition industry, and what they can do to help you?

❏ Were you up to date with the other organizations associated with the industry, and how they might assist you?

❏ Did you contact anyone and everyone for advice and guidance?

Thinking about yourself

❏ Did you possess a complete understanding of your own concern, and its distinctive mix of positive and negative features?

❏ Were you wholly conversant with your goods and services, and their specific strengths and weaknesses?

❏ Were you in touch with your short-, medium- and long-term, business goals?

❏ Did you compose notes about your firm, products, services and objectives for later reference?

Recognizing your market

❏ Did you discover as much as you could about your customers and their characteristics, habits and opinions?

❏ Were you aware of your competitors and their goods, services and exhibition activities?

❏ Did you understand your market, and any changes and developments that were occurring within it?

❏ Did you conduct additional research as and where required, to fill in any gaps in your knowledge of the marketplace?

❏ Did you compile notes about your customers, rivals and market for subsequent use?

Setting a budget

❏ Did you appreciate all of the possible costs that could be incurred when exhibiting at an event?

❏ Did you know which expenses were most relevant to you in your given situation?

❏ Were you conscious of the total expenditure involved in attending a show?

Choosing exhibitions

❏ Did you prepare a shortlist of potentially suitable exhibitions by studying a lengthy list of shows alongside your extensive background notes?

❏ Did you obtain as much detailed material as you could from the organizers of the various events?

❏ Did you analyse all aspects of each exhibition, seeking advice from many sources before making your choice?

❏ Were you familiar with the different types of stand, and how to select the right size and site for your business?

❏ Did you check the organizer's rules and regulations with the help of a solicitor, prior to booking space?

❏ Did you draft a timetable of activities leading up to and beyond the show so you knew what to do and when?

Designing a stand

❏ Were you aware of the key functions of an exhibition stand, and how these might be best achieved?

❏ Did you select exhibits and display items which were appropriate for the occasion?

❏ Did you sketch out a full and detailed brief for the person responsible for designing your stand?

❑ Were you wise enough to avoid adopting a D-I-Y approach to designing the exhibition stand?

Using specialists

❑ Did you consider the different types of designer who exist, and the key qualities that they ought to possess?

❑ Did you investigate your possible choices carefully, to see that they had all of the required qualities?

❑ Was everything agreed in writing before commissioning your designer?

❑ Did you contemplate your chosen contractor in the same way, and in as much depth?

❑ Did you obtain external advice and assistance before employing your contractor?

❑ Did you study any contract with your solicitor, before signing it?

Having a successful exhibition

❑ Did you keep to your schedule, completing all of the tasks on or before the set deadlines?

❑ Did you and your staff follow the do's and don'ts of stand success?

❑ Was your stand maintained in a fit and proper manner?

❑ Did you attend to the after-show activities, adopting a swift and effective approach?

❑ Did you evaluate how far your goals were achieved, seeking outside help and guidance as necessary?

❑ Were you an effective exhibitor?

Appendix A: Media pack

INTRODUCTION

Welcome to the East Anglian Daily Times Company's Media Pack.
It has been prepared to help you understand the values of the
premier advertising media in the region.

As a company we realise fully that we are in business to help you grow your
businesses. To that end all our products and services are designed to help you
capitalise on the development of the region. The ranges of advertising vehicles and
services we provide ensure the maximum coverage of target markets within our
trading area.

The following information contains details gathered from a comprehensive study of
the media habits and readership patterns in our trading area. This was conducted
by BJM Research and Marketing Consultancy Limited in the spring of 1993.
Conforming fully to market research industry standards generally and the
specification of the Joint Industry Committee for Regional Press Research (JICREG)
in particular, the sample was based on interviews among over 1,000 adults in the
key circulation or distribution areas of the titles. As JICREG calculations of total
readership for each newspaper are based on the whole circulation or distribution
area, they include all readers outside the researched areas.

Much more information than is contained here is available to help maximise
the effectiveness of your media or market planning
- just ask your representative for full details.

With our range of newspapers, the audiences they deliver, the editorial
environments they provide and the creative opportunities they offer, you can be
assured we deliver the most flexible and cost-effective use of your promotional
budgets.

EAST ANGLIAN DAILY TIMES COMPANY LIMITED

THE EAST ANGLIAN DAILY TIMES COMPANY

Our company trades in Suffolk and North Essex, an area wholly within East Anglia. This area's economy has grown rapidly in the recent past yet it has retained the rural character which is one of its main attractions.

The prosperity of the potential marketplace is evidenced by the fact that East Anglia as a whole has now the highest Gross Domestic Product (GDP) per head outside of the South East and, despite the early 1990's recession, has the lowest rate of unemployment in the country.

Furthermore the area is forecast to resume its growth in GDP, consumer expenditure, industrial production, employment and population from the end of 1993 and to overtake the UK averages by 1995. As a consequence, this area was found to be the "Best of British" in terms of a Quality of Life survey carried out by The Economist in June 1993.

Publications and services offered to consumers in the area are -

The East Anglian Daily Times which has served the area every morning for nearly 120 years. It provides undisputedly the best coverage of its circulation area with its unique source of international, national, regional and local news and sport. The circulation area stretches through Suffolk from south Norfolk to south Essex and the three daily editions (East, West, Essex) ensure that the total of 151,618* adults who read the title in an average day receive their local national daily.

The Evening Star which is the evening paper for Ipswich and the surrounding area, is proud to cover its community. Published since 1885, it today has a direct freshness for campaigns, local as well as national and international news and sport delivered in a vigorous style to encourage interaction with its readers.

The total of 85,622 adults* who read the Evening Star in an average day are responsive and interested in their community - as evidenced by the high levels of entries to competitions, coupon redemptions on offers, readers' letters received and of course in the very high levels of response to advertising.

The Suffolk Mercury Series of free weekly newspapers which offer advertisers coverage of the whole county or, by buying combinations of the editions within the East or West Suffolk Mercury, specific coverage of distinct parts of Suffolk.
In an average week some 263,442 adults read a copy of the Suffolk Mercury.

Anglian Direct, the service for inserting pre-printed material into any edition of an East Anglian Daily Times Company daily or weekly publication and our **Business Magazines** division completes the range of coverage opportunities available to our advertisers.

Notes: HMSO Regional Trends 1993
Financial Times 13.8.93
*Joint Industry Committee for Regional Press Research, 1994

EAST ANGLIAN DAILY TIMES
ABC January - June 1994 49,494

The East Anglian Daily Times gives unrivalled media coverage of an area which spans the whole of Suffolk and North Essex in three daily editions. It caters for all sections of the region's population and is recognised as an important source of advertising information by its readers.

Independent market research has shown that:

* in an average day the East Anglian Daily Times is read by more than 137,000 adults - a higher readership figure than any other daily paper in the area;

* each copy of the East Anglian Daily Times is seen by at least 3 adults ensuring high coverage each day;

* more than half of the readers of the East Anglian Daily Times (54%) do not read any national newspaper - showing the influence of the title;

* on average readers spend 29 minutes reading their copy of the East Anglian Daily Times;

* the East Anglian Daily Times has a broad-based appeal and the readership profile is in line with that of the population as a whole;

* readership by day is balanced and the daily content ensures high interest throughout the week -
     Monday: Sports coverage in depth
     Tuesday: Job Centre ads, Regional News Round-Ups
     Wednesday: Essex/Anglian Business Scene
     Thursday: Recruitment, Property
     Friday: Motors
     Saturday: 48 Hours;

* 210,000 adults read at least one issue of the East Anglian Daily Times in an average week. An advertisement in 6 issues has the opportunity to be seen by 53% more adults than a single insertion - an extra 73,000 adults;

* the East Anglian Daily Times is the premier advertising medium in its area - more adults turn to it first for details about major purchases, property, jobs, local entertainment and second-hand items than to any other newspaper.

Notes: Research conducted by BJM Ltd., April 1993
   5%+ household penetration sample area (Base 1,017 adults)
   Readership = average issue readership, those reading for
   2 or more minutes in the issue period, ie yesterday.

EAST ANGLIAN
DAILY TIMES

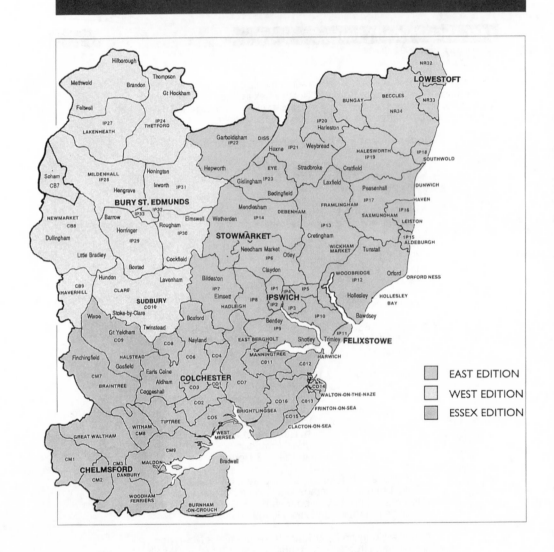

EAST EDITION

WEST EDITION

ESSEX EDITION

ABC   January - June 1994 49,494

EAST ANGLIAN
DAILY TIMES

| ABC | Average Daily Sales JAN-JUNE 1994 — 49,494 |

The East Anglian Daily Times offers advertisers the most effective vehicle for covering Suffolk and North Essex.

RATES
ROP (PER S.C.C.) £6.40
PAGE 3 ....25% Surcharge
Other Premium Positions ......15% Surcharge
Front Page Solus...........................£450.00
Title Corners ......Front £84.00, Back £47.00
Full Page.....................................£1612.80
Half Page....................................£806..40

COLOUR CHARGES
Single Spot ....20% Extra
Multi Spot ....30% Extra
Full Process ....40% Extra

All rates subject to VAT

CLASSIFIED MARKET ADVERTISEMENT RATES

| ABC | Average Daily Sales JAN-JUNE 1994 — 79,630 |

Classified Advertisements are published in the East Anglian Daily Times and the Evening Star.

RATES   (PER S.C.C.)
Display
Situations Vacant £14.25
Motors £8.50
Property £8.25
Others £10.40
Public Notices/Tenders £11.00
Auctions £8.25
(Box Numbers ....£10.00)

LINAGE   (PER LINE)
Private/Trade £2.21
Situations Vacant £2.70
(Box Numbers Charged at 4 Lines)
All rates are subject to VAT

SUPPLEMENTARY INFORMATION

TECHNICAL DATA

Column length 360 mm; screen 35 per cm.
7 columns per page display,
8 columns per page classified.
Production —
Photosetting, artwork, bromides or
original photographs required.
Blocks or mats not acceptable.
Printed web offset. Studio design
and artwork service available
at no extra charge.

COLUMN WIDTHS (mm)

Columns	Display (7 cols. per page)	Classified (8 cols. per page)
1	36	31
2	75	65
3	115	100
4	154	134
5	194	168
6	233	203
7	273	237
8	-	272

DEADLINES (CLEAR WORKING DAYS)
Colour
Full Colour......10 Days
Multi Spot........5 Days
Spot Colour......2 Days

ORDER & COPY (MONO)

East Anglian Daily Times   } 48 hours prior
Evening Star   } to publication.

PROOFS

3 full days must be given
for any proof requests.
See Item 13 Terms & Conditions

EAST ANGLIAN DAILY TIMES COMPANY
Head Office: Press House, 30 Lower Brook Street, Ipswich IP4 1AN
Telephone: (01473) 230023 Telex: 98172 Fax: (01473) 232529 Ad Doc: Dx 3261 Ipswich

Branch Offices -
BURY ST. EDMUNDS Lloyds Bank Chambers, Buttermarket. Tel: (01284) 702588 Fax: 702970
FELIXSTOWE 120 Hamilton Road. Tel: (01394) 284109 Fax: 284994
STOWMARKET 1 Market Place. Tel: (01449) 674428 Fax: 774301
SUDBURY 1 King Street. Tel: (01787) 72242 Fax: 79157
HALESWORTH 16 Thoroughfare. Tel: (01986) 872202 Fax: 875338
LEISTON 72 High Street. Tel: (01728) 830472 Fax: 832187
COLCHESTER Dugard House, Moss Road, Stanway. Tel: (01206) 769212 Fax: 577857
WOODBRIDGE Barton House, 84 The Thoroughfare. Tel: (01394) 385353 Fax: 387025

AMRA
London Office: Park Place, 12 Lawn Lane,
Vauxhall, London SW8 1UD
Tel: 0171 820 1000. Fax: 0171 820 0304/5
Ad Doc: Dx 2327 Victoria.
Manchester Office: Byrom House,
Quay Street, Manchester M3 3HG
Tel: 0161 834 2050. Fax: 0161 835 2781
Ad Doc: Dx 18157 Manchester 3

Rates Effective from 3rd October 1994

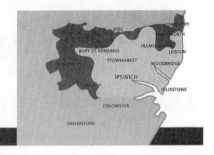

EVENING STAR

ABC January - June 1994 30,136

The Evening Star has the highest readership penetration of any daily paper in its area and is followed in penetration by its sister paper the East Anglian Daily Times. Readership of the national dailies in the area is depressed by the presence of such strong evening and morning titles.

Independent market research has shown that:

* in an average day the Evening Star reaches 71,000 adults - 40% of the total population aged over 15 in the survey area. When total readership is included, this figure rises to 86,000 adults who read the Evening Star on an average day;

* each copy of the Evening Star is read by 2.8 readers - ensuring high daily coverage;

* a very high proportion of readers (6 in 10) have their Evening Star delivered to their homes, showing the commitment of readers to the title;

* the Evening Star has a particular appeal for those aged 45-64, the C2DE social grades and women. Unlike many regional / local dailies it has a better penetration of non-working than working people;

* readership by day is constant and the daily content ensures high interest throughout the week -
  Monday: Weekend Sports Round-Up
  Tuesday: Job Centre ads
  Wednesday: Commercial Property
  Thursday: Recruitment, Property
  Friday: Motors
  Saturday: Weekender;

* in an average week 94,000 adults read at least one issue of the Evening Star. This means that the potential audience of a series of six consecutive insertions rather than one stand-alone advertisement is increased by one third;

* on average each reader spends 29 minutes reading the Evening Star - evidence of a "well-read" paper;

* the Evening Star is a major source of advertising information with more adults turning to it first for details of jobs, property, major purchases, second-hand items and local entertainment than to any other newspaper in its area.

Notes: Research conducted by BJM Ltd., April 1993
10%+ household penetration sample area (Base 503 adults)
Readership = average issue readership, those reading for
2 or more minutes in the issue period, ie yesterday.

Evening Star

ABC   January - June 1994 30,136

Evening Star

ABC Average Daily Sales
JAN-JUNE 1994 — 30,136

First with local news, sport and
entertainment, the Evening Star covers
Ipswich and the surrounding area.

RATES
ROP (PER S.C.C.)..............................£5.50
PAGE 3.............................25% Surcharge
Other Premium Positions .....15% Surcharge
Front Page Solus...........................£315.00
Title Corners......Front £47.00, Back £19.00
Full Page......................................£1386.00
Half Page.......................................£693.00

COLOUR CHARGES
Single Spot..............................20% Extra
Multi Spot ....30% Extra
Full Process ....40% Extra

All rates subject to VAT

CLASSIFIED MARKET ADVERTISEMENT RATES

ABC Average Daily Sales
JAN-JUNE 1994 — 79,630

Classified Advertisements are
published in the East Anglian Daily Times
and the Evening Star.

RATES	(PER S.C.C.)
Display	
Situations Vacant	£14.25
Motors	£8.50
Property	£8.25
Others	£10.40
Public Notices/Tenders	£11.00
Auctions	£8.25
(Box Numbers	£10.00)

LINAGE	(PER LINE)
Private/Trade	£2.21
Situations Vacant	£2.70

(Box Numbers Charged at 4 Lines)
All rates are subject to VAT

SUPPLEMENTARY INFORMATION

TECHNICAL DATA

Column length 360 mm; screen 35 per cm.
7 columns per page display,
8 columns per page classified.
Production —
Photosetting, artwork, bromides or
original photographs required.
Blocks or mats not acceptable.
Printed web offset. Studio design
and artwork service available
at no extra charge.

COLUMN WIDTHS (mm)

Columns	Display (7 cols. per page)	Classified (8 cols. per page)
1	36	31
2	75	65
3	115	100
4	154	134
5	194	168
6	233	203
7	273	237
8	-	272

DEADLINES (CLEAR WORKING DAYS)

Colour
Full Colour......10 Days
Multi Spot........5 Days
Spot Colour...... 2 Days

ORDER & COPY (MONO)

East Anglian Daily Times } 48 hours prior
Evening Star } to publication.

PROOFS

3 full days must be given
for any proof requests.
See Item 13 Terms & Conditions

EAST ANGLIAN DAILY TIMES COMPANY
Head Office: Press House, 30 Lower Brook Street, Ipswich IP4 1AN
Telephone: (01473) 230023 Telex: 98172 Fax: (01473) 232529 Ad Doc: Dx 3261 Ipswich

Branch Offices -
BURY ST. EDMUNDS Lloyds Bank Chambers, Buttermarket. Tel: (01284) 702588 Fax: 702970
FELIXSTOWE 120 Hamilton Road. Tel:(01394) 284109 Fax: 284994
STOWMARKET 1 Market Place. Tel: (01449) 674428 Fax: 774301
SUDBURY 1 King Street. Tel: (01787) 72242 Fax: 79157
HALESWORTH 16 Thoroughfare. Tel: (01986) 872202 Fax: 875338
LEISTON 72 High Street. Tel: (01728) 830472 Fax: 832187
COLCHESTER Dugard House, Moss Road, Stanway. Tel: (01206) 769212 Fax: 577857
WOODBRIDGE Barton House, 84 The Thoroughfare. Tel: (01394) 385353 Fax: 387025

AMRA
London Office: Park Place, 12 Lawn Lane,
Vauxhall, London SW8 1UD
Tel: 0171 820 1000. Fax: 0171 820 0304/5
Ad Doc: Dx 2327 Victoria.
Manchester Office: Byrom House,
Quay Street, Manchester M3 3HG
Tel: 0161 834 2050. Fax: 0161 835 2781
Ad Doc: Dx 18157 Manchester 3

Rates Effective from 3rd October 1994

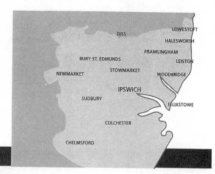

THE CLASSIFIED SECTION

EAST ANGLIAN DAILY TIMES AND EVENING STAR

Carried within both daily titles the Classified Section of the East Anglian Daily Times and Evening Star provides a major attraction and focal point to both newspapers.
Duplicate readership of both papers is very small (3% of all adults) as very few adults read both in an average day. Together the East Anglian Daily Times and Evening Star reach more than 205,000 adults in an average day.

Categories covered daily include -

    Auctions
    Business and Finance, Office Equipment
    Agricultural, Farming, Plant & Machinery, Poultry & Livestock
    Recruitment, General Vacancies, Hotel & Catering, Part-time, Training Courses
    Property, Accommodation to Let, Commercial, Building Land, Overseas
    Motors, New & Used, Accessories, Spares, Service, Vehicle Hire
    Leisure, Hobbies, Boating & Yachting, Holidays, Caravans, Horse & Rider
    General and Home Services, Personal, Dental, Catering, Builders, Landscape Gardening
    Miscellaneous Sales, Pets, Musical, Articles for Sale/Wanted
    Public and Legal Notices, Tenders & Contracts

Each week there are special supplements dedicated to Property (Thursday); Motors (Friday); as well as comprehensive coverage of all Recruitment advertisements on Thursdays.

The Classified advertising sections in both the East Anglian Daily Times and Evening Star reach significant proportions of the population - more than 299,000 adults in an average year .

* 126,000 readers of the East Anglian Daily Times read the
  Classified Section at least once a week, 187,000 read it at all;

* 57,000 readers of the Evening Star read the Classified Section
  at least once a week, 90,000 read it at all;

* 60,000 adults placed an advertisement in the East Anglian
  Daily Times in the last year - 96,000 responded;

* 37,000 adults placed an advertisement in the Evening Star
  in the last year - 60,000 responded.

Notes: Research conducted by BJM Ltd., April 1993
        5%+ household penetration area (Base 1,017 adults)
        Readership = average issue readership, those reading for
        2 or more minutes in the issue period, ie yesterday.

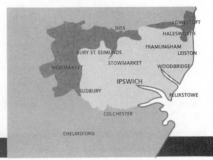

SUFFOLK MERCURY SERIES

VFD January - June 1994:
Whole series - 157,122
East - 110,284 (Ipswich 86,041; Stowmarket 12,219; North 12,024)
West - 46,838 (Bury St. Edmunds 27,219; Sudbury 19,619)

Covering the major areas of Suffolk, the Suffolk Mercury series has high levels of penetration and readership each week. Specific editions for individual areas ensure that Suffolk Mercury editorial is relevant to readers.

Independent market research has shown that:

* 76% of adults aged 15 or over read the Mercury in an average week - some 265,000 adults;

* 182,000 adults read the East Suffolk edition (75% penetration) and 84,000 adults read the West Suffolk edition (78% penetration);

* the Mercury overall has 1.7 readers per copy - a good figure for a free newspaper (East Suffolk Mercury 1.6, the West Suffolk Mercury 1.8 readers per copy);

* a high proportion of adults, 88% receive the Mercury every or most weeks, proof of the effective distribution system;

* the sex profile of readers exactly matches the profile of the area as a whole and generally readers are likely to be slightly older and less upmarket than the total population in the area;

* on average readers spend 16 minutes reading the Mercury - 15 minutes the East Suffolk Mercury and 17 minutes the West Suffolk Mercury.

Notes: Research conducted by BJM Ltd., April 1993
10%+ household distribution sample area (Base 810 adults)
Readership = average issue readership, those reading for 2 or more minutes in the issue period, ie last 7 days.

Mercury

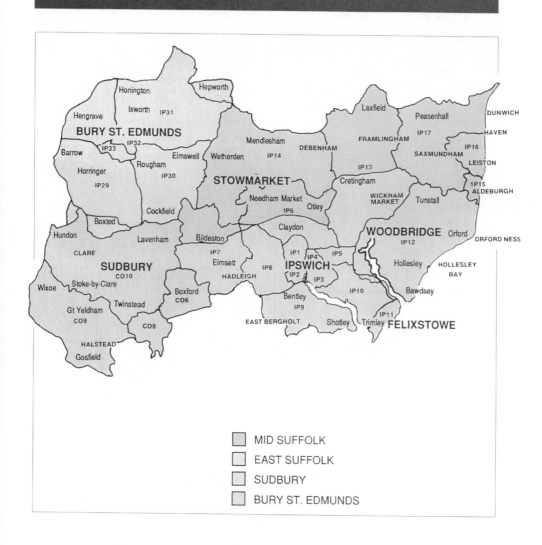

MID SUFFOLK

EAST SUFFOLK

SUDBURY

BURY ST. EDMUNDS

VFD January - June 1994 157,122

Mercury

 VFD East Suffolk Mercury 110,284
West Suffolk Mercury 46,838
Jan-Jun 1994

The Mercury series are the leading free weekly
newspapers. They are divided into East and
West Suffolk and offer advertisers the most
comprehensive coverage of the area.

RATE (P.S.C.C.)	EAST		WEST	
ROP	£6.60		£3.80	
Guaranteed Position	25% Surcharge		25% Surcharge	
	Display	Linage	Display	Linage
Situation Vacant	£16.20	—	£6.75	—
Motors	£5.66	—	£4.12	—
Property	£5.66	—	£4.12	—
Others	£6.20	—	£3.95	—
Public Notices	£11.55	—	£4.65	—
Box Numbers	£10.00 (4 Lines)		£10.00 (4 Lines)	

Separate Edition Rates on request.

All rates subject to VAT.

The separate editorial editions ensure that
each area has its own local news and stories
relevant to its distribution area. Thus
advertisers have a variety of unique vehicles
by which to convey a sales message.

The East Suffolk Mercury, operating from the
Ipswich Head Office, has two advertising
editions, East Suffolk and Mid Suffolk
(including North Suffolk and Stowmarket).
Tel. 01473 230023.

The West Suffolk Mercury, situated in
Bury St. Edmunds itself, has two editions,
(Bury and Sudbury).
Tel. Sudbury 01787 72242
Tel. Bury St. Edmunds 01284 702588

SUPPLEMENTARY INFORMATION

TECHNICAL DATA

Column length 360 mm; screen 35 per cm.
7 columns per page display,
8 columns per page classified.
Production —
Photosetting, artwork, bromides or
original photographs required.
Blocks or mats not acceptable.
Printed web offset. Studio design
and artwork service available
at no extra charge.

COLUMN WIDTHS (mm)

Columns	Display (7 cols. per page)	Classified (8 cols. per page)
1	36	31
2	75	65
3	115	100
4	154	134
5	194	168
6	233	203
7	273	237
8	-	272

DEADLINES (CLEAR WORKING DAYS)

Colour
Full Colour......10 Days
Multi Spot........5 Days
Spot Colour......2 Days

ORDER & COPY (MONO)

East Suffolk Mercury } Orders Friday prior
West Suffolk Mercury } to publication. Copy
Monday 12 noon
prior to publication.

PROOFS

3 full days must be given
for any proof requests.
See Item 13 Terms & Conditions

EAST ANGLIAN DAILY TIMES COMPANY

Head Office: Press House, 30 Lower Brook Street, Ipswich IP4 1AN
Telephone: (01473) 230023 Telex: 98172 Fax: (01473) 232529 Ad Doc: Dx 3261 Ipswich

Branch Offices -
BURY ST. EDMUNDS Lloyds Bank Chambers, Buttermarket. Tel: (01284) 702588 Fax: 702970
FELIXSTOWE 120 Hamilton Road. Tel: (01394) 284109 Fax: 284994
STOWMARKET 1 Market Place. Tel: (01449) 674428 Fax:774301
SUDBURY 1 King Street. Tel: (01787) 72242 Fax: 79157
HALESWORTH 16 Thoroughfare. Tel: (01986) 872202 Fax: 875338
LEISTON 72 High Street. Tel: (01728) 830472 Fax: 832187
COLCHESTER Dugard House, Moss Road, Stanway. Tel: (01206) 769212 Fax: 577857
WOODBRIDGE Barton House, 84 The Thoroughfare. Tel: (01394) 385353 Fax: 387025

AMRA
London Office: Park Place, 12 Lawn Lane,
Vauxhall, London SW8 1UD
Tel: 0171 820 1000. Fax: 0171 820 0304/5
Ad Doc: Dx 2327 Victoria.
Manchester Office: Byrom House,
Quay Street, Manchester M3 3HG
Tel: 0161 834 2050. Fax: 0161 835 2781
Ad Doc: Dx 18157 Manchester 3

Rates Effective from 3rd October 1994

SERVICES FOR ADVERTISERS

The following services have been developed to help our advertisers maximise their investments in advertising. This list does not cover every need or indeed every service we can provide. If you would like more information about how we can enhance your marketing effort please talk to your representative.

Campaign Planning: our advertising staff are trained to help increase the effectiveness of clients' campaigns and are able to assist in planning the most effective use of local media to achieve both marketing and media objectives.

Partnership Marketing: involves both retailers and manufacturers in the funding of advertisements to further the advertising and promotion of goods for sale. Supported by the Newspaper Society the EADT Company is able to identify suppliers who will provide financial or creative support for local advertising.
Contact : 01473 282340

Anglian Direct: caters for clients wishing to use Leaflets, Brochures or Coupons to promote their goods or services and offers precise targeting or blanket coverage throughout Suffolk and North Essex.

Leaflets or other suitable material can be inserted directly into any of the newspapers for maximum impact. Alternatively leaflets can be delivered in the traditional manner for precisely defined areas.
Contact : 01473 282215

Creative Services: our Design studio can give help on the design, layout and content of advertisements. Creative ideas can be carried through to full artwork.

Box Numbers: we offer a private and confidential advertisement reply service where all responses can be forwarded to advertisers or collected in person from our Ipswich office.

Research and Marketing Data: our consumer research data and information covering details about markets, the area, its inhabitants and their media habits are available to clients to help in the planning, accomplishment and evaluation of advertising campaigns.

The information ranges from our own commissioned research to market reports and government information - including the 1991 census - and also includes MOSAIC - a geo-demographic classification system.

CONDITIONS OF ACCEPTANCE FOR ADVERTISEMENTS

1 We reserve the right to refuse to insert any advertisement even though accepted and paid for and to make any alterations we deem necessary to maintain our standards.

2 The publisher shall not be liable for any loss or damage occasioned by any total or partial failure (however caused) of publication or distribution of any newspaper or edition in which any advertisement is scheduled to appear.

3 In the event of any error, misprint or omission in the printing of any advertisement or part of an advertisement the publisher will either re-insert the advertisement or relevant part of the advertisement as the case may be or make a reasonable refund or adjustment to the cost. No re-insertion, refund or adjustment will be made where the error, misprint or omission does not materially detract from the advertisement. In no circumstances shall the total liability of the publisher for any error, misprint or omission exceed the amount of a full refund of any price paid to the publisher for the particular advertisement in connection with which liability arose or the cost of a further or corrective advertisement of a type and standard reasonably comparable to that in connection with which liability arose.

4 Advertisements which do not conform to the Trade Descriptions Act, 1968, the Sex Discriminations Act, 1975, the Business Advertisements (Disclosure) Order, 1977 and other relevant legislation will be refused.

5 We do not accept liability for any loss or damage incurred by advertisers allegedly arising in respect of loss, damage or non-receipt of box number replies, save where such loss or damage has arisen directly as a result of our negligence.

6 Advertisers cancelling advertisements will be given a Stop Number which must be quoted in subsequent inquiries. Cancellation of "till discontinued" bookings must be confirmed by a letter addressed to the General Advertisement Manager.

7 Mistakes that arise in the course of publication must be notified to us within one week of insertion. After that time claims for credit cannot be considered.

8 Participation in advertisement features and supplements does not imply any editorial mention.

9 Advertisers placing pre-paid classified advertisements are responsible for checking that the published advertisement matches the charge made. Requests for adjustments, accompanied by the official receipt, should be made to branch or head offices.

10 We do not hold ourselves responsible for the loss of artwork or photographs supplied.

11 Advertisements ordered for the Classified Section will appear in both the East Anglian Daily Times and the Evening Star except on Public Holidays when they could appear in one title only and normal rates will apply.

12 Cancellations: No cancellations to bookings will be accepted for special positions or features within 10 clear working days of publication and for all other advertisements 2 clear working days prior to publication.

13 Proofs: No alterations to proofs will be made other than for spelling, grammar or factual information that differs from the copy supplied.

14 The quality of our reproductions is dependent upon the quality of the original material, photographs, artwork or bromides which are supplied. Should there be any doubt regarding the suitability for reproduction of any of these prior to publication advice can be obtained from our staff.

15 We reserve the right to open or withhold any box number correspondence should it be deemed necessary in the public interest.

SPECIAL NOTICE

All gross advertising rates (except classified lineage and semi-display) are subject to a 0.1% Advertising Standards Board of Finance surcharge payable by advertisers, to help finance the self-regulatory control system administered by the Advertising Standards Authority.

ADVERTISING RATES (effective 8.10.95)

Daily titles: *East Anglian Times and Evening Star*

Classified Market	Display	Linage
Recruitment	£15.50 per scc	£3 per line
Motors	£8.80 per scc	£2.30 per line
Property	£8.55 per scc	£2.30 per line
Others	£10.75 per scc	£2.30 per line
ROP		
(EA)	£6.65 per scc	
(ES)	£5.70 per scc	
Legal Notices	£11.40 per scc	

Weekly titles:	*East Suffolk Mercury*	*West Suffolk Mercury*
	Display	**Display**
Recruitment	£17.50	£7.10
Motors	£5.90	£4.30
Property	£5.90	£4.30
Others	£6.45	£4.15
ROP	£6.85	£3.95

All charges exclude VAT; all display charges per scc; min. sizes 3cms or 3 lines.

SERVICES AVAILABLE INCLUDE:

Campaign planning;
Partnership marketing;
Anglian Direct – leaflet distribution;
Creative services;
Research and marketing

Appendix B: Rate cards

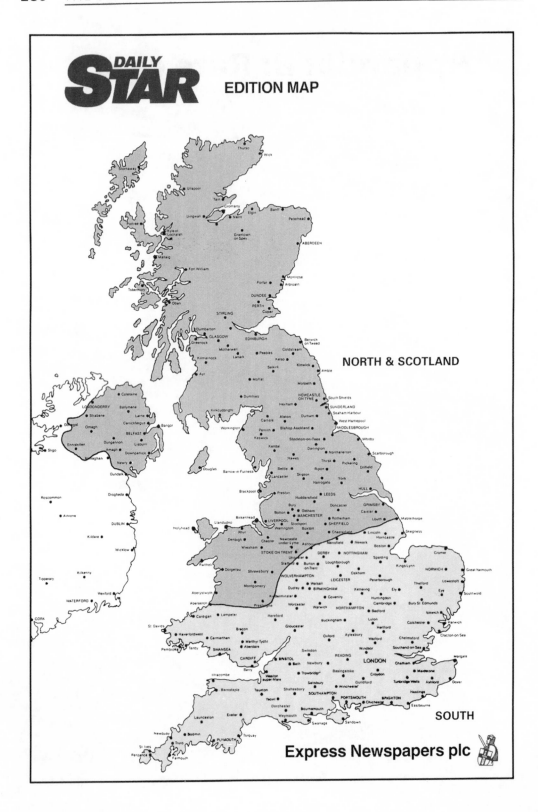

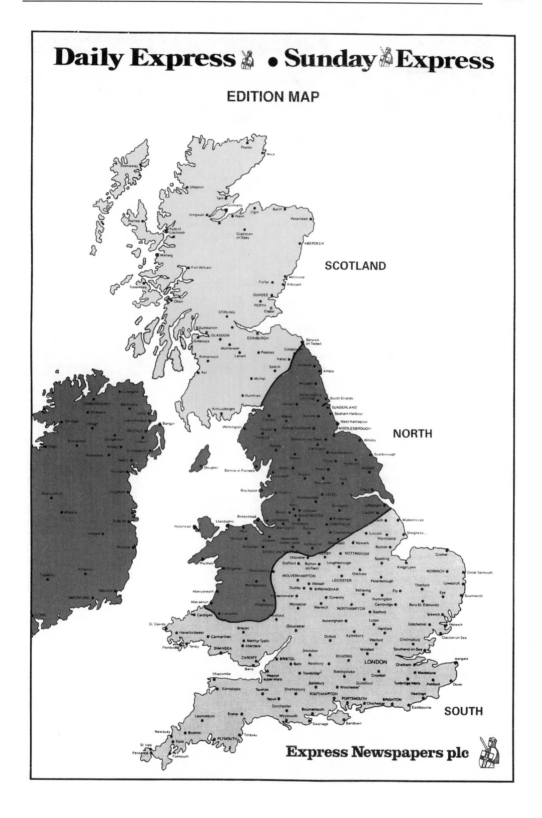

Daily Express • Sunday Express

EDITION MAP

SCOTLAND

NORTH

SOUTH

Express Newspapers plc

(All numbers act as direct lines if
prefixed by 0171-922 or as
extensions off the main switchboard)

Advertisement Controller
Howard Warren   2720
Advertisement Manager
Philip Snowdon   2770
Group Heads
Harry Torrance   2766
Janey Pilkington   2755
Travel
Keith Cartwright   2814
Financial
Paul Reynolds   2733
Mail Order
Terry O'Connor   2773
Advertisement Features
Ian Hockridge   2747
Heather Murphy   2792
Inserts
Mike Winston   2797
Research
Stuart Corke   2862

EXPRESS GROUP

Advertisement Director
Christine Costello   2727
Deputy Advertisement Director
Julie France   2754
Research & Sales Support Director
Iain McLellan   2868
Client Sales Controller
Patrick Chaundy   2803
Contracts Controller
Mike Baker   2704
Financial Advertisement Manager
Peter Thompson   2732
Travel Advertisement Manager
Glynis Jeffery   2779
Regional Advertisement Manager
Chris Skinner   2788

DAILY STAR ADVERTISEMENT RATES

DISPLAY MONO (Minimum 3scc's)	**scc**
Firm Day	£44.00
Run of Week	£38.50
(Page Size - 35cm x 7 columns = 245cm)	
DISPLAY OTR COLOUR	
Page	£15,092
FEATURES (Minimum 3scc's)	**scc**
Holidays & Travel, Gardening, Postal Bargains	£38.50
SPECIAL POSITIONS	
Back Page Solus (up to 15cm x 2 columns)	£1,320
(Other special positions and A/B and North/South copy splits subject to 10% surcharge)	
REGIONAL	**scc**
Scotland	£10.00
North (excluding Scotland)	£27.50
South	£22.00
London and the South East	£15.00
ADVERTISEMENT FEATURES	**page**
Mono	£13,475
OTR Colour	£18,865
Sponsorship Rates	On application

1 column width	37mm	5 column width	197mm
2 column width	77mm	6 column width	237mm
3 column width	117mm	7 column width	275mm
4 column width	157mm		

Total Page Area   345mm x 275mm

MAKE-UP

(All numbers act as direct lines if prefixed by 0171-922 or as extensions off the main switchboard)

**Group Advertisement
Make-up Manager**
Steve Sherer   2832
Colour Production Manager
Karen Miller   7255

COLOUR SPECIFICATION

Material supplied for colour advertisement reproduction in the Daily Star must be either artwork and transparencies, CMYK separated data or RGB data and artwork (or disk).

All colour advertisement material should be sent to Digital Partnership Limited at the Express Newspapers address.

All colour advertisement material must be supplied at least 72 hours prior to publication.

For more information please contact Digital Partnership Limited on 0171-922 7374 or Express Newspapers Colour Production Manager on 0171-922 7255.

Express Newspapers plc
Ludgate House
245 Blackfriars Road
London SE1 9UX
Tel: 0171-928 8000
Fax: 0171-620 1646

**Ratecard effective from
October 1995**

Daily Express

NAMES & EXTENSIONS

(All numbers act as direct lines if
prefixed by 0171-922 or as
extensions off the main switchboard)

Advertisement Controller
Georgina Crace   2782
Daily Express
Advertisement Manager
Charles McCrostie   2784
This Week
Advertisement Manager
Chris Morris   2706
Group Heads
Jo Fullbrook   2916
Neil McQuillan   2830
Fiona Nobles   2929
Travel
Keith Cartwright   2814
Financial
Simon Haque   2735
Mail Order
Terry O'Connor   2773
Advertisement Features
Ian Hockridge   2747
Heather Murphy   2792
Inserts
Mike Winston   2797
Research
Stuart Corke   2862

EXPRESS GROUP

Advertisement Director
Christine Costello   2727
Deputy Advertisement Director
Julie France   2754
Research & Sales Support Director
Iain McLellan   2868
Client Sales Controller
Patrick Chaundy   2803
Contracts Controller
Mike Baker   2704
Financial Advertisement Manager
Peter Thompson   2732
Travel Advertisement Manager
Glynis Jeffery   2779
Regional Advertisement Manager
Chris Skinner   2788

DAILY EXPRESS ADVERTISEMENT RATES

DISPLAY MONO (Minimum 3scc's)	**scc**
Firm Day	**£97.00**
Run of Week	**£85.00**
(Page Size - 35cm x 7 columns = 245cm)	
DISPLAY OTR COLOUR	
Page	**£31,500**
FEATURES (Minimum 5scc's)	**scc**
Holidays & Travel, Gardening, Postal Bargains	**£85.00**
Express Money	**£97.00**
SPECIAL POSITIONS	
Back Page Solus (20cm x 2 columns)	**£4,250**
Express Money Front Page Earpiece (4cm x 1 column)	**£500**
(Other special positions and A/B and North/South copy splits subject to 10% surcharge)	
REGIONAL	**scc**
Scotland	**£19.00**
North (excluding Scotland)	**£36.50**
South	**£60.50**
London and the South East	**£55.00**
ADVERTISEMENT FEATURES	**page**
Mono	**£29,706**
OTR Colour	**£39,375**
Sponsorship Rates	On application

THIS WEEK ADVERTISEMENT RATES

DISPLAY COLOUR	**page**
Run of Paper	**£27,500**
Outside Back Cover	**£32,000**
Inside Front/Back Cover	**£30,000**
ADVERTISEMENT FEATURES	
Page	**£34,375**
Sponsorship Rates	On application

INSERTS
(Loose or stitched available by ISBA region)

Under 100,000	**£30** (per 1,000)
Over 100,000	**£25** (per 1,000)

16 pages or above subject to 20% surcharge
Minimum volume 25,000
Special printing facilities ie fragrance and gummed cards on request

Daily Express

MAKE-UP

(All numbers act as direct lines if prefixed by 0171-922 or as extensions off the main switchboard)

Group Advertisement
Make-up Manager
Steve Sherer   2832
Colour Production Manager
Karen Miller   7255

DAILY EXPRESS MECHANICAL DATA

1 column width	37mm	5 column width	197mm
2 column width	77mm	6 column width	237mm
3 column width	117mm	7 column width	275mm
4 column width	157mm		

Total Page Area   345mm x 275mm

COLOUR SPECIFICATION

Material supplied for colour advertisement reproduction in the Daily Express must be either artwork and transparencies, CMYK separated data or RGB data and artwork (or disk).

All colour advertisement material should be sent to Digital Partnership Limited at the Express Newspapers address.

All colour advertisement material must be supplied at least 72 hours prior to publication.

For more information please contact Digital Partnership Limited on 0171-922 7374 or Express Newspapers Colour Production Manager on 0171-922 7255.

THIS WEEK MECHANICAL DATA

	Depth Width
Full page (Trimmed)	367 x 270mm
Double Page Spread (Trimmed)	367 x 540mm
Page (Untrimmed Bleed)	377 x 280mm
Double Page Spread (Untrimmed Bleed)	377 x 550mm
Page (Type Area)	335 x 245mm
Double Page Spread (Type Area)	335 x 511mm

COLOUR SPECIFICATION
Refer to Express Newspapers' Colour Specification Guidelines or contact Karen Miller.
Inserts
Refer to Express Newspapers' Inserts Guidelines or contact Karen Miller.

Express Newspapers plc
Ludgate House
245 Blackfriars Road
London SE1 9UX
Tel: 0171-928 8000
Fax: 0171-620 1646

Ratecard effective from
October 1995

NAMES & EXTENSIONS

(All numbers act as direct lines if prefixed by 0171-922 or as extensions off the main switchboard)

Advertisement Controller
Simon Young   2721
Advertisement Manager
Shalene Perkins   2808
Group Heads
David Rossiter   2810
Gaby Fireman   2713
Travel
Keith Cartwright   2814
Financial
Mark Finney   2734
Mail Order
Terry O'Connor   2773
Advertisement Features
Ian Hockridge   2747
Heather Murphy   2792
Inserts
Mike Winston   2797
Research
Stuart Corke   2862

EXPRESS GROUP

Advertisement Director
Christine Costello   2727
Deputy Advertisement Director
Julie France   2754
Research & Sales Support Director
Iain McLellan   2868
Client Sales Controller
Patrick Chaundy   2803
Contracts Controller
Mike Baker   2704
Financial Advertisement Manager
Peter Thompson   2732
Travel Advertisement Manager
Glynis Jeffery   2779
Regional Advertisement Manager
Chris Skinner   2788

DISPLAY MONO (Minimum 3scc's)   scc
Firm Day   £116.00
2 Week Option   £105.00
(Page Size - 35cm x 7 columns = 245cm)
(Large sizes, above 25cm high and/or 5 columns, and guaranteed positions subject to 10% surcharge)

Half Page Horizontal   £16,916
Full Page Firm Day   £30,960
Full Page 2 Week Option   £29,864

DISPLAY OTR COLOUR
Full Page Front Half   £40,725
Full Page Back Half   £38,623

SPECIAL POSITIONS
First Right/Left Hand Page   £37,670
Second Right Hand Page   £35,713
Back Page Solus (15cm x 2 columns)   £7,700
(Other special positions subject to 10% surcharge)

FINANCIAL
Full Page Firm Day   £30,960
Full Page 2 Week Option   £29,864

REGIONAL   scc
Scotland   £11.00
North (excluding Scotland)   £37.00
South   £85.00
London and the South East   On application
North/South Copy Splits   £500

ADVERTISEMENT FEATURES   page
Mono   £32,156
OTR Colour   £50,906
Sponsorship Rates   On application

1 column width	37mm	5 column width	197mm
2 column width	77mm	6 column width	237mm
3 column width	117mm	7 column width	275mm
4 column width	157mm		

Total Page Area 345mm x 275mm

MAKE-UP

(All numbers act as direct lines if prefixed by 0171-922 or as extensions off the main switchboard)

Group Advertisement Make-up Manager
Steve Sherer   2832
Colour Production Manager
Karen Miller   7255

COLOUR SPECIFICATION

Material supplied for colour advertisement reproduction in the Sunday Express must be either artwork and transparencies, CMYK separated data or RGB data and artwork (or disk).

All colour advertisement material should be sent to Digital Partnership Limited at the Express Newspapers address.

All colour advertisement material must be supplied at least 72 hours prior to publication.

For more information please contact Digital Partnership Limited on 0171-922 7374 or Express Newspapers Colour Production Manager on 0171-922 7255.

Express Newspapers plc
Ludgate House
245 Blackfriars Road
London SE1 9UX
Tel: 0171-928 8000
Fax: 0171-620 1646

Ratecard effective from October 1995

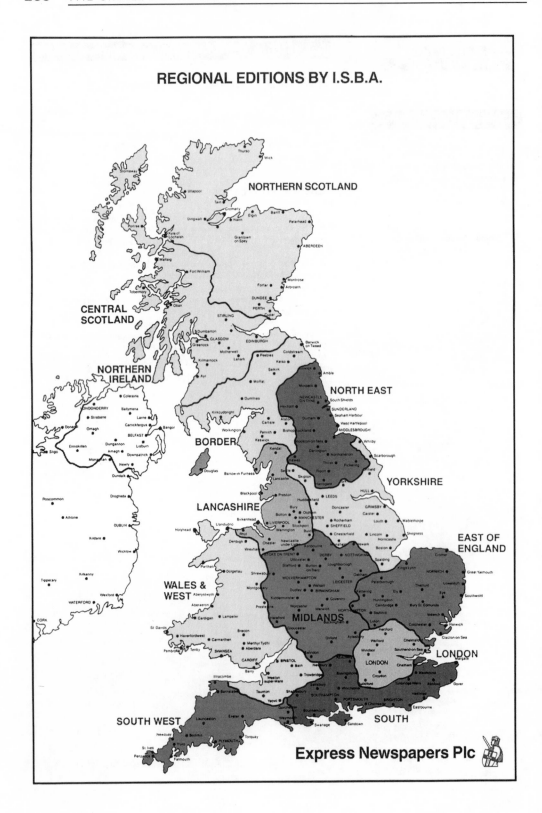

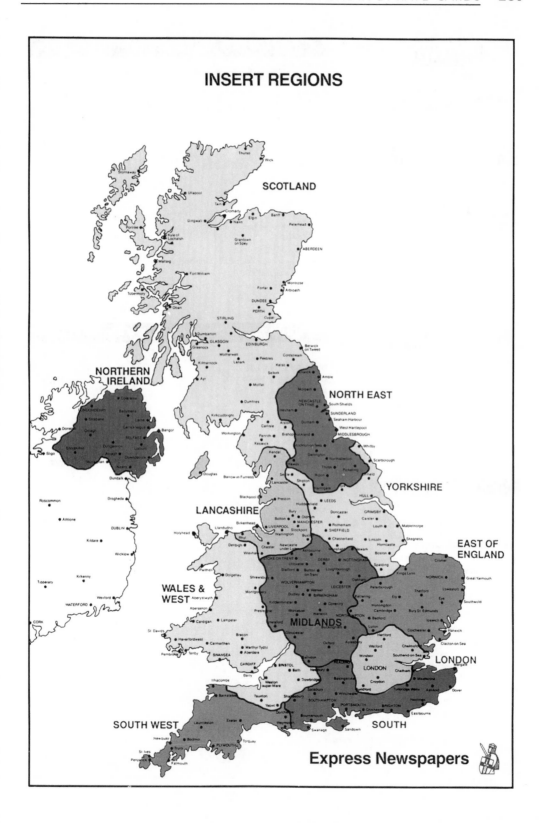

INSERT REGIONS

Express Newspapers

magazine

NAMES & EXTENSIONS

(All numbers act as direct lines if prefixed by 0171-922 or as extensions off the main switchboard)

Advertisement Controller	
Simon Young	2721
Advertisement Manager	
Andy Farthing	2724
Group Heads	
Kieran Kelly	2726
Alan Totten	2758
Travel	
Keith Cartwright	2814
Financial	
Mark Finney	2734
Advertisement Features	
Ian Hockridge	2747
Heather Murphy	2792
Inserts	
Mike Winston	2797
Research	
Stuart Corke	2862

EXPRESS GROUP

Advertisement Director	
Christine Costello	2727
Deputy Advertisement Director	
Julie France	2754
Research & Sales Support Director	
Iain McLellan	2868
Client Sales Controller	
Patrick Chaundy	2803
Contracts Controller	
Mike Baker	2704
Financial Advertisement Manager	
Peter Thompson	2732
Travel Advertisement Manager	
Glynis Jeffery	2779
Regional Advertisement Manager	
Liz Mathams	2798

SUNDAY EXPRESS CLASSIC ADVERTISEMENT RATES

DISPLAY COLOUR	**page**
Run of Magazine	**£30,000**
Special Positions	
Outside Back Cover	**£35,000**
Inside Back/Front Cover	**£32,500**

ADVERTISEMENT FEATURES	
Page	**£37,500**
Sponsorship Rates	On application

INSERTS
(Loose or stitched available by ISBA region)

Under 100,000	**£30** (per 1,000)
Over 100,000	**£25** (per 1,000)

16 pages or above subject to 20% surcharge
Minimum volume 25,000
Special printing facilities ie fragrance and gummed cards on request

SUNDAY EXPRESS MAGAZINE ADVERTISEMENT RATES

DISPLAY COLOUR	
Run of Magazine, Page	**£22,400**
Run of Magazine, Half Page	**£13,600**
Quarter and Eighth Pages/Mono Pages	On application

Special Positions	**page**
Outside Back Cover	**£36,050**
Inside Back Cover	**£30,000**
Inside Front Cover	**£34,600**
First Spread	**£58,100**

(Other special positions subject to a 10% surcharge)

ADVERTISEMENT FEATURES	
Page	**£28,000**
Sponsorship Rates	On application

INSERTS
As above

magazine

MAKE-UP

(All numbers act as direct lines if prefixed by 0171-922 or as extensions off the main switchboard)

Group Advertisement Make-up Manager
Steve Sherer   2832
Colour Production Manager
Karen Miller   7255

SUNDAY EXPRESS CLASSIC MECHANICAL DATA

	Depth Width
Full Page (Type Area)	332 x 235mm
Full Page (Untrimmed Bleed)	373 x 276mm
Full Page (Trimmed Bleed)	367 x 270mm
Half Page Across (Type Area)	163 x 235mm
Half Page Across (Untrimmed Bleed)	186 x 276mm
Half Page Across (Trimmed Bleed)	180 x 270mm
Half Page Upright (Type Area)	332 x 114mm
Half Page Upright (Untrimmed Bleed)	373 x 137mm
Half Page Upright (Trimmed Bleed)	367 x 131mm
Half Page Spread (Type Area)	163 x 504mm
Half Page Spread (Untrimmed Bleed)	186 x 546mm
Half Page Spread (Trimmed Bleed)	180 x 540mm
Double Page Spread (Type Area)	332 x 504mm
Double Page Spread (Untrimmed Bleed)	373 x 546mm
Double Page Spread (Trimmed Bleed)	367 x 540mm

SUNDAY EXPRESS MAGAZINE MECHANICAL DATA

	Depth Width
Full page (Type Area)	259 x 200mm
Full Page (Untrimmed Bleed)	292 x 231mm
Full Page (Trimmed Bleed)	286 x 225mm
Double Page Spread (Gutter Bleed)	259 x 422mm
Double Page Spread (Untrimmed Bleed)	292 x 456mm
Double Page Spread (Trimmed Bleed)	286 x 450mm

COLOUR SPECIFICATION
Refer to Express Newspapers' Colour Specification Guidelines or contact Karen Miller.
Inserts
Refer to Express Newspapers' Inserts Guidelines or contact Karen Miller.

Express Newspapers plc
Ludgate House
245 Blackfriars Road
London SE1 9UX
Tel: 0171-928 8000
Fax: 0171-620 1646

Ratecard effective from June 1995

The Franchise Magazine

The UK's fastest selling Franchise publication and the accepted leader for franchisee recruitment, *The Franchise Magazine's* consistent high standard of professional editorial makes it today's most eagerly awaited and relevant publication. Totally dedicated to promoting new and currently available franchise opportunities, keenly read by those seeking to own and operate a franchise. Available from W.H.Smith, John Menzies, all leading newsagents and every Franchise Exhibition. Bulk subscribers include Armed Forces, Re-Settlement Centres, Job Centres, Accountants, Banks and Professional Advisors. Promoting your franchise opportunity to *The Franchise Magazine's* 100,000 nationwide readership by means of advertising and commissioned editorial is the most efficient and cost-effective way of achieving a constant flow of serious and well qualified prospects. Franchisors receive an excellent return on investments, often far exceeding their own expectations!

The FDS Publications Division

Since 1981 Franchise Development Services Ltd. has been producing award winning informative publications to the mutual benefit of both Franchisor and Franchisee

COPY DEADLINE DATES						
	Jan/Feb	Mar/Apr	May/Jun	Jul/Aug	Sept/Oct	Nov/Dec
COMMISSIONED EDITORIALS	6 NOV	6 JAN	6 MARCH	6 MAY	6 JULY	6 SEPT
NEWS EDITORIALS	13 NOV	13 JAN	13 MARCH	13 MAY	13 JULY	13 SEPT
ADVERTISEMENTS (ready film)	20 NOV	20 JAN	20 MARCH	20 MAY	20 JULY	20 SEPT
ON SALE	24 DEC	24 FEB	24 APRIL	24 JUNE	24 AUGUST	24 OCT

DIMENSIONS AND MECHANICAL DATA

FULL PAGE — 190 x 270mm

HALF PAGE LANDSCAPE — 190 x 132mm

HALF PAGE PORTRAIT — 92 x 270mm

	Bleed (mm)	Trim (mm)	Type (mm)
A4 Size Perfect Bound			
Double Page Spread	426 x 303	420 x 297	400 x 270
Full Page	213 x 303	210 x 297	190 x 270

GUARANTEED MINIMUM PRINT RUN - 25,000 Copies per Edition

N.B. I f presenting copy other than in film and proof form, please allow an extra 5 working days of copy deadline and note that there will be a conversion and assembly charge.

If supplying a double page as one film, please allow a total of 5mm in the centre of the film to allow for binding
Film Positives - Emulsion side down, right reading, 150 screen for work to be produced on machine stock of 60gsm.
Web proofing sequence - Magenta, Cyan, Black, Yellow.
Dot Gain - Art paper: allow 12%, Cartridge: allow 17%, WSOP: allow 21%
Formats accepted - Macintosh: Microsoft Word, Quark Xpress, Pagemaker. All scans to be saved as EPS file, CMYK mode for download into Photoshop 4.0. Disks accepted: SyQuest 44/88MB, SyQuest ezflyer, Zip.

1998 / 1999 Advertising Rates And Information

The Franchise Magazine is published BI-MONTHLY in January/February - March/April - May/June - July/August - September/October - November/December

PUBLISHERS: Franchise Development Services Ltd.
Rouen House, Rouen Road, Norwich NR1 1RB
Tel: 01 603 620 301 Fax: 01 603 630 174
e-mail: fdsltd@norwich.com Web Site: http://www.franchise-group.com

All charges below are per insertion. They exclude VAT, which is chargeable at the standard rate.

FULL COLOUR

Size	6 Editions £	3/4/5 Editions £	1/2 Editions £
Double Page Spread	2995	3215	3575
Full Page	1995	2225	2475
Half page	1395	1495	1675

BLACK AND ONE COLOUR (SPOT)

Full Page	1895	1975	2195
Half page	1195	1275	1425

BLACK AND WHITE (MONO)

Full Page	1765	1875	2085
Half page	1195	1275	1425

SPECIAL POSITIONS

1st Double Page	3735	3955	4395
Outside Back Cover	2795	2965	3295
Inside Front Cover	2335	2475	2750
Inside Back Cover	2235	2365	2635

All other guaranteed positions + 10%

COMMISSIONED EDITORIAL

You may commission our editorial team to conduct research, interview principals and produce a professional feature on your company and to attract the ideal candidates for the opportunity available. These features secure reader interest and produce excellent results.

Commissioned Editorial First Page	£2475
Additional Pages Thereafter	£2225

FRONT COVER PACKAGE

Consisting of six pages: Front cover in Full Colour plus a four page editorial feature with colour photographs and one full page colour advertisement or agreed variation. The front cover design and production is entirely in the control of the publisher.
Single bookings only and no repeat for 1 year. Additional pages may be taken at appropriate rates.

FRONT COVER PACKAGE: £9,975

NATIONAL SHOWCASE

An attractively designed quarter page promotion in full colour with 150 words to describe your opportunity. This high profile service links to our database and provides a continual flow of well qualified prospects from our readership. Upon initial   registration, a backlog of prospects for your category will be available.

	5/6 EDITIONS £	2/3/4 EDITIONS £	ENTRY COST £
Showcase Half Page	1595	1775	1975
Showcase Quarter Page	995	1125	1250

SPECIAL PACKAGES

Talk to us about your franchisee recruitment requirements for the next 12 months.
Special packages have proved of immense value to franchisors in the past and continue to provide an excellent return on investment. We can pre-qualify prospects to meet your various criteria, i.e. capital available, age, skills, geographical area etc. Further details on request

INSERTS

Looseleaf inserts produce a fast response. They add impact to any campaign carried in the publication and can also stand alone effectively.

Full run £125 per 1,000 for A4 80GSM - first 10,000

ADVERTISING ARTWORK

The publisher can produce artwork and film.
Quotations available on request.

TERMS

All prices are per insertion and exclude Agency commission. Following booking confirmation and final acceptance by publisher, all payments must be received **prior to the relevant copy deadline date** . ADVERTISEMENTS NOT PAID FOR BY THIS DATE WILL BE AUTOMATICALLY WITHDRAWN. This is company policy and there are no exceptions. This is also a safeguard to our readers. Cancellations for advertisements must be made 20 (twenty) working days prior to publication.

To discuss your campaign, call your Account Executive on:

Tel: 01 603 620 301   **Fax: 01 603 630 174**

Other Leading Publications From

The United Kingdom *franchise* Directory

Every purchaser of this publication is a good prospect! Lists every known franchisor in the UK, currently over 750 companies. This award winning annual publication is now in its 14th successful year. *The United Kingdom Franchise Directory* is also distributed nationwide to all Job Centres and Libraries, guaranteeing an enormous readership of individuals actively looking for the right franchise. Your promotion in *The United Kingdom Franchise Directory* will ensure a continual flow of enquiries from qualified prospects.

FRANCHISE INTERNATIONAL

The only publication totally dedicated to promoting and selling Master Franchise Rights worldwide. Distributed to 180 countries worldwide Plus all British and American Embassies and more than 25 Global Franchise Exhibitions. *Franchise International* is the perfect publication for achieving international expansion goals.

NEW! *WORLDWIDE FRANCHISE DIRECTORY*
The first *Worldwide Franchise Directory* is now available on the Internet. See our web site:

http://www.franchise-group.com

THE IRISH FRANCHISE MAGAZINE

To meet the ever increasing demand for information on opportunities in franchising for Ireland, The Irish Franchise Magazine has been launched. Distributed to all prospective investors in Single Unit and Master Franchise Rights plus, on sale at all leading Irish news outlets.

1998/1999 ADVERTISING INFORMATION

FULL COLOUR	
DOUBLE PAGE SPREAD	£2500
FULL PAGE	£1750
HALF PAGE	£1250

SPOT COLOUR	
FULL PAGE	£1650
HALF PAGE	£1150

SPECIAL POSITIONS	
1ST DOUBLE PAGE	£2950
OUSIDE BACK COVER	£2750
INSIDE FRONT/BACK COVER	£2250

COMMISSIONED EDITORIAL	
COMMISSIONED EDITORIAL 1ST PAGE	£1995
ADDITIONAL PAGES THEREAFTER	£1950

FRONT COVER PACKAGE

SIX PAGES: FRONT COVER, FOUR PAGE EDITORIAL AND ONE PAGE FULL COLOUR AD. £5500

IRISH FRANCHISE DIRECTORY

FULL COLOUR QUARTER PAGE PROMOTION WITH 150 WORDS AND COLOUR PHOTOGRAPH.
DIRECTORY QUARTER PAGE: £995

TO ADVERTISE IN THE IRISH FRANCHISE MAGAZINE PLEASE CONTACT CHRIS DAVIES ON 01603 620 301

CLASSIFIED RATES

Single column cm = £12   Minimum 3 cm = £36

All rates subject to VAT 15%   Series discounts on application

Lineage - 32p per word, minimum £10.   Extras - **BOLD** 80p per word

Cancellations: six weeks prior to booking deadline

EXAMPLE SIZES

Single Column cost £48.00

Single Column cost £72.00

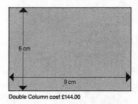

Double Column cost £144.00

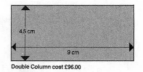

Double Column cost £96.00

CONDITIONS

REMITTANCES: Cheques should be crossed and made payable to AGB Specialist Publications Ltd and sent to Car Mechanics Classified, AGB Specialist Publications Ltd, Audit House, Field End Road, Eastcote, Ruislip, Middlesex HA4 9LT.

IMPORTANT: Whilst every effort is made to ensure that advertisements appear correctly, the Publishers will not be responsible for the consequences arising from errors or delay in publication. It is the advertisers responsibility to check that the first insertion of every series is published correctly and corrections must be notified in time for the second insertion, otherwise the Publishers will not accept liability or offer any reduction in charges.

THE LAW: Advertisers must comply with the Trade Descriptions Act (particularly the description of goods offered for sale) and The Business Advertisements (Disclosures) Order 1977 which requires all advertisements which seek to sell goods in the course of a business to make that fact clear. Readers should be able to tell whether an advertisement relates to a sale by a trader or private seller. It is the responsibility of the advertiser to comply with the order.

MECHANICAL DATA

Whole Page		273×190mm
Half Page		273×92mm or 130×190mm
Quarter Page		130×92mm or 63×190mm
Eighth Page		63mm×92mm
Column Length	266m	Column Width 44mm
Untrimmed WP		306×216mm
DPS type area		273×400mm
WP Bleed		306×216mm
½ page bleed		210×148mm
DPS Bleed		306×432mm
DPS trimmed size		300×213mm
Screen, mono — 100 (40/48 metric) 4 col — 133 (54 metric)		
Positives right reading, emulsion side down		
Web fed, saddle stitched		

DISPLAY RATES

MONO	1	6	12
Full Page	995	945	896
Full Page FM	1095	1040	985
Half Page	533	506	480
Half Page FM	586	557	528
Quarter Page	278	264	250
Eighth Page	139	132	125

TWO COLOUR			
Full Page	1478	1404	1330
Full Page FM	1626	1545	1463
Half Page	761	723	685
Half Page FM	837	795	753

FOUR COLOUR			
Full Page	1995	1895	1796
Full Page FM	2195	2085	1975
DPS	3990	3791	3591
First DPS Amongst Matter	4190	3980	3771
Half Page	1111	1055	1000
Half Page FM	1222	1161	1100

SPECIAL POSITIONS			
Facing Contents	2294	2180	2065
Outside Back Cover	2294	2180	2065
1st RH Colour	2294	2180	2065
Page 2/3 DPS	4389	4170	3950

INSERT DATA

Loose Cost per thousand subject to checking sample.
Minimum quantity: 40,000.
Print run, maximum 70,000 depending on issue.
Area dictation runs available at extra cost. Ring for quotation.

Bound-in Quotation on request.
Minimum weight of paper for single loose-leaf insert — 135gsm. A sample of the proposed insert is necessary to check with printers.
Size — not larger than magazine: 295x210mm.
Preferred size no larger than 270x185mm.
Insert can be folded, but if more than one fold, we must have a sample for checking.
Bound-in inserts must be folded. If fold is off-centre, the shorter 'leaf' must be at least 75mm wide (i.e. minimum guard 75mm).
Inserts must be delivered to:

Binder Manager, Chase Web Offset,
Eastern Wood Road, Language Industrial Estate, Plympton, Plymouth PL7 5ET, Devon. Tel: 0752 345411

Delivery must be at least 20 days before the publication date (our production department will advise). Parcels need to be clearly marked with the client's name, magazine to be inserted in and issue date.

CAR
MECHANICS

SPOT DURATION

60 SECONDS	+80%
50 SECONDS	+65%
40 SECONDS	+30%
20 SECONDS	-20%
10 SECONDS	-50%

The rates quoted are for a 30 second duration spot.
Other spot lengths are available and their costs, in relation to
the 30 second spot rate, are seen above.
Commercials longer than 60 seconds will be pro rata to the
60 second rate.

R A T E

RATES PER 30 SECONDS FOR

AVAILABILITY LEVEL		4
0000-2400	A	£ 3
0600-2400	B	£ 4
0600-1800	C	£ 6
0600-1200	D	£ 10
1200-1800	E	£ 5
1800-2400	F	£ 1

Rates effective from 1st October 1995 and are exclusive of VAT. Any three hour D E or F timeb
200%. End of week advertising (Thursday, Friday, Saturday) may be selected at a 25% surcha

SGR FM

At SGR FM, we are dedicated to giving our audience the best. We play 'the best mix of music' from
the last twenty years or so, featuring the best of today's quality hits and the great records of the 80's
and early 90's with classic hits from the 70's.

SGR is designed for younger adults in the key 20 to 40 age group, but it reaches everybody. The style of
presentation is accessible, innovative, fresh and fun. But SGR is more than just the best music, it's great
entertainment. Our listeners stay tuned for exciting competitions with great prizes, for the latest local,
national and world news, regular sports news updates and the most up-to-date travel and weather reports.

And that's why SGR has become one of the top local radio stations in the country since it relaunched just
over 3 years ago. Simply the best, that's the SGR promise on 96.4 FM and 97.1 FM.

WEEKLY PROFILE

15-34	172,000
34-44	80,000

ALL ADULTS	504,000
MEN	247,000
WOMEN	257,000

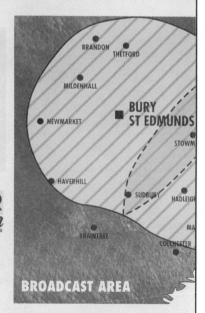

BROADCAST AREA

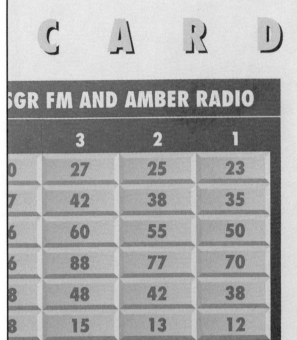

AVAILABILITY LEVELS

All airtime orders will be made at the availability level in force at the time of booking. The levels vary due to the limited availability of commercial airtime. The more demand, the less airtime available, therefore, increasing the availability level. Booking your airtime well in advance enables you to enjoy the benefits of a much lower rate. Weekly availability levels will be issued upon request.

COMMERCIAL SCHEDULING

All spots will be evenly spread throughout the time segments of the campaign booked in order to reach the maximum number of listeners possible. Subject to availability, advertisers preferences will be considered but cannot be guaranteed.

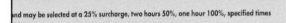

...and may be selected at a 25% surcharge, two hours 50%, one hour 100%, specified times ...ge.

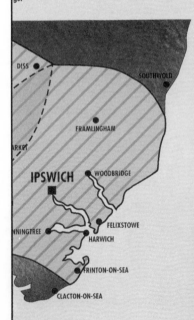

AMBER RADIO

AMBER RADIO puts you in touch with an older adult audience. It's 'easy-gold' music format is aimed at the over-40's but appeals to all ages who appreciate classic all-time hits from the past.

AMBER is a radio station for the 90's but brings back the musical memories with those great golden hits. It's Classic Hit Radio, with popular, familiar music of the last 35 years. From the Rock 'n' Roll years, through the 60's and 70's to the choice records of the 80's and 90's. All-time hits that all have that special quality that stands the test of time.

Quality presentation adds to the great entertainment. AMBER is warm and friendly, bright and alive, with a superb mix of music and information - offering an up to the minute service of news, weather, sport and travel reports 24 hours a day. AMBER RADIO - a mature sound for a sophisticated audience.

WEEKLY PROFILE

35-44	80,000
45-54	85,000
55+	166,000
ALL ADULTS	504,000
MEN	247,000
WOMEN	257,000

TOTAL EAST ANGLIAN RADIO AREA

SGR FM, BROADLAND FM and AMBER RADIO together form East Anglian Radio, one of the most successful commercial radio groups in the UK.

SGR IPS & BURY	504,000
SGR COLCHESTER	132,000
BROADLAND FM	572,000
EAR TOTAL AREA	1,155,000
AMBER TOTAL	1,050,000

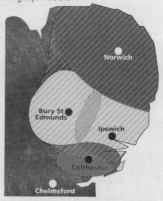

SGR IPSWICH & BURY **Radio House Alpha Business Park Whitehouse Road**
Ipswich Suffolk IP1 5LT Tel: 01473 461000 Fax: 01473 741200

SGR COLCHESTER **Abbeygate 2 9 Whitewell Road Colchester CO2 7DE**
Tel: 01206 575859 Fax: 01206 561199

BROADLAND FM **St George's Plain Colegate Norwich NR3 1DB**
Tel: 01603 630627 Fax: 01603 666353

AMBER RADIO **Radio House Alpha Business Park Whitehouse Road**
Ipswich Suffolk IP1 5LT Tel: 01473 461000 Fax: 01473 741200

VOLUME DISCOUNT

A series of volume discounts are available to advertisers who spend a minimum of £6,000 per annum and who give notice of annual expenditure in writing, in advance. Any shortfall in the agreed expenditure will lead to the airtime being re-invoiced at the actual level of discount achieved.

Please ask your representative for further details.

SPONSORSHIP AND PROMOTIONS

A number of sponsorship and promotional opportunities exist. These include - traffic and travel; weather and sports reports; tea and coffee breaks and the SGR FM and AMBER RADIO Roadshow. Full details are available on request.

CONDITIONS OF BOOKING

The general terms and conditions of contract for acceptance and broadcast of advertisements is available on request. All prices quoted are subject to VAT. This rate card applies only to outlets whose sole area of business is within the SGR FM and AMBER RADIO marketing area.

PRE-PAYMENT

Pre-Payment is required from all new and non-account clients.

CANCELLATION

Subject to the provision of the general terms and conditions (available on request) any bookings may be cancelled provided that notice in writing is given not less than 28 days before the scheduled broadcast date. Bookings may be cancelled within 28 days of broadcast subject to the following terms:

- 14 working days from date of broadcast, 10% of the total airtime value cancelled will be invoiced.

- 7 working days from date of broadcast, 20% of the total airtime value cancelled will be invoiced.

- 3 working days from date of broadcast, 40% of the total airtime value cancelled will be invoiced.

Unless a booking is cancelled in accordance with these conditions, an advertiser who fails to deliver advertisement copy will remain liable to pay in full whether or not any advertisement is broadcast.

96.4 & 97.1 RADIO

Great music - golden memories
1152 - 1170 - 1251 AM/MW

Why do so many companies who advertise on Capital Radio come back time and time again? It's simple, Capital Radio works.

**95.8
CAPITAL
FM**

L O N D O N

R A T E C A R D

RATECARD

A STEP BY STEP GUIDE TO ADVERTISING ON 95.8 CAPITAL FM

Why do so many companies who advertise on Capital Radio - from the largest international businesses to single retail outlets - come back time and time again? It's simple; Capital works!

LONDON

London is a city with a population and affluence that other cities, indeed, some other countries, would find difficult to match. It's also home of the most desirable consumer group in the UK, with income per capita an astonishing 21% above the national average.

95.8 CAPITAL FM

95.8 Capital FM is London's most popular radio station and commands tremendous loyalty from its millions of listeners. It serves an area containing nearly 10 million adults; more than one fifth of the UK population. 95.8 Capital FM is particularly successful at reaching London's 15-34 year olds, with a high percentage of its audience in the ABC1 social class. Millions of Londoners couldn't imagine starting the day without the legendary Chris Tarrant's Breakfast Show. 95.8 Capital FM keeps London buzzing with its unique blend of chart music, entertainment, news and information, 24 hours a day, every day.

THE CAPITAL SERVICE

Whether you're a seasoned media veteran or have never advertised on radio before, you'll find that Capital's back-up service is second to none. Below we've outlined just some of the ways in which we can help you make the most of advertising on 95.8 Capital FM.

PLANNING

Our knowledge of when and where your target audience is listening to radio is unsurpassed. We have a sophisticated and proven planning system which will enable you to optimise your budget. You can buy individual spots based on our Ratecard Segments and Standard Rates (listed below) or, as most people do, book a series of commercials. In either case, our sales team will be happy to guide you through the process and ensure you reach your target audience effectively.

MAKING AN AD

Our professional, award-winning Commercial Production team can help with everything from recommending personalities for voice-overs, to writing, producing and recording an appropriate commercial. For more information, ring the team on 0171 608 6270.

RATECARD SEGMENTS			
Time Segment	Monday-Friday	Saturday	Sunday
P1	0700-1100	0700-1200	0900-1300
P2	0600-0700	-	-
	1100-1600	-	-
A	1600-2000	1200-1800	0700-0900
			1300-1900
B	2000-2400	1800-2400	1900-2400
C	0000-0600	0000-0700	0000-0700
	(M-F am)	(am)	(am)

STANDARD RATES						
	10"	20"	30"	40"	50"	60"
Ratio	(50)	(80)	(100)	(130)	(165)	(180)
P1	£1000	£1600	£2000	£2600	£3300	£3600
P2	£450	£720	£900	£1170	£1485	£1620
A	£325	£520	£650	£845	£1075	£1170
B	£150	£240	£300	£390	£495	£540
C	£25	£40	£50	£65	£83	£90

All prices shown are per spot and are exclusive of VAT at the prevailing rate. Spots in excess of 60 seconds can be bought in increments of 10 seconds and are charged pro-rata to the 60 second rate.

MARKET DATA

We have a wealth of general marketing data, which tells you about the potential of the market you're addressing and how 95.8 Capital FM can help your advertising exploit that potential.

DIRECT RESPONSE

For direct response advertising we can organise call-handling to collect names and addresses of customers, dispatch brochures or samples and provide further marketing data by building consumer profiles.

CAMPAIGN EVALUATION

We can organise pre- and post-awareness research for you, to show you exactly how much impact your campaign had, and to maintain optimum effectiveness for your future campaigns.

WHAT'S MORE...

We're committed to developing business in the Capital Radio area. For instance, we offer special rates to Local Advertisers and to those businesses or products new to radio and testing the effectiveness of the medium. In addition, our Sponsorship Department can help you make the most of the opportunities in this exciting area. Please ring us for more details of these and other incentives.

OUR PLEDGE TO YOU

We want your advertising to work! Here at Capital Radio London Sales we have unrivalled experience of planning radio. Above all, we appreciate the importance of responding with innovative plans and ideas that are unique to your brand or product. We'd be delighted to talk to you about your particular requirements so ring the Sales Department today.

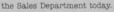

0171 388 6801

CANCELLATION

Written cancellation or postponement requests for campaigns within 28 clear days before the scheduled broadcast date shall be considered by the Company and may be accepted at the company's absolute discretion subject to the following cancellation charges:

up to 28 clear days before the date of broadcast	40%
up to 14 clear days before the date of broadcast	60%
up to 8 clear working days before the date of broadcast	80%
day of broadcast	100%

COPY DEADLINES

Where advertisement copy is received less than 8 clear working days before the scheduled broadcast date, or is deemed not to have been so received as a result of failure to comply with the Company's technical requirements or submission or other procedure, the acceptance of such advertisement copy shall be at the absolute discretion of the Company and shall be subject to a surcharge of £75 per copy. In these circumstances the advertiser shall remain liable to pay in full for the advertising time whether or not it is broadcast.

TERMS AND CONDITIONS Our service is offered subject to our Standard Terms and Conditions, copies of which are available on request.

Why do so many companies who

advertise on Capital Radio come

back time and time again?

It's simple, Capital Radio works.

1548 AM
CAPITAL
GOLD

L O N D O N

RATECARD

A STEP BY STEP GUIDE TO ADVERTISING ON 1548 AM CAPITAL GOLD

Why do so many companies who advertise on Capital Radio - from the largest international businesses to single retail outlets - come back time and time again? It's simple; Capital works!

LONDON

London is a city with a population and affluence that other cities, indeed, some other countries, would find difficult to match. It's also home of the most desirable consumer group in the UK, with income per capita an astonishing 21% above the national average.

1548 AM CAPITAL GOLD

With a transmission area that extends for over 30 miles in every direction from the centre of London, 1548 AM Capital Gold can be heard by nearly 10 million adults - that's more than one fifth of the UK population. Right from its launch in November 1988, 1548 AM Capital Gold has enjoyed tremendous popularity and success. The unbeatable combination of classic hits and live sporting action has made 1548 AM Capital Gold second only to its sister station 95.8 Capital FM, as London's most popular commercial radio station. All the greatest hits from the 60s, 70s, and 80s are presented by such household favourites as Tony Blackburn and Mike Read. What's more, the passionate coverage and commitment of Capital Gold Sport's service has made it the number one choice for true sports fans in the South East.

THE CAPITAL SERVICE

Whether you're a seasoned media veteran or have never advertised on radio before, you'll find that Capital's back-up service is second to none. Below we've outlined just some of the ways in which we can help you make the most of advertising on 1548 AM Capital Gold.

PLANNING

Our knowledge of when and where your target audience is listening to radio is unsurpassed. We have a sophisticated and proven planning system which will enable you to optimise your budget. You can buy individual spots based on our Ratecard Segments and Standard Rates (listed below) or, as most people do, book a series of commercials. In either case, our sales team will be happy to guide you through the process and ensure you reach your target audience effectively.

RATECARD SEGMENTS

Time Segment	Monday-Friday	Saturday	Sunday
P1	0700-1100	0700-1200	0900-1300
P2	0600-0700	-	-
	1100-1600	-	-
A	1600-2000	1200-1800	0700-0900
			1300-1900
B	2000-2400	1800-2400	1900-2400
C	0000-0600	0000-0700	0000-0700
	(M-F am)	(am)	(am)

STANDARD RATES

	10"	20"	30"	40"	50"	60"
Ratio	(50)	(80)	(100)	(130)	(165)	(180)
P1	£375	£600	£750	£975	£1238	£1350
P2	£250	£400	£500	£650	£825	£900
A	£108	£172	£215	£280	£355	£387
B	£30	£48	£60	£78	£99	£108
C	£10	£16	£20	£26	£33	£36

All prices shown are per spot and are exclusive of VAT at the prevailing rate. Spots in excess of 60 seconds can be bought in increments of 10 seconds and are charged pro-rata to the 60 second rate.

MAKING AN AD

Our professional, award-winning Commercial Production team can help with everything from recommending personalities for voice-overs, to writing, producing and recording an appropriate commercial. For more information, ring the team on 0171 608 6270.

MARKET DATA

We have a wealth of general marketing data, which tells you about the potential of the market you're addressing and how 1548 AM Capital Gold can help your advertising exploit that potential.

DIRECT RESPONSE

For direct response advertising we can organise call-handling to collect names and addresses of customers, dispatch brochures or samples and provide further marketing data by building consumer profiles.

CAMPAIGN EVALUATION

We can organise pre- and post-awareness research for you, to show you exactly how much impact your campaign had, and to maintain optimum effectiveness for your future campaigns.

WHAT'S MORE...

We're committed to developing business in the Capital Radio area. For instance, we offer special rates to Local Advertisers and to those businesses or products new to radio and testing the effectiveness of the medium. In addition, our Sponsorship Department can help you make the most of the opportunities in this exciting area. Please ring us for more details of these and other incentives.

OUR PLEDGE TO YOU

We want your advertising to work! Here at Capital Radio London Sales we have unrivalled experience of planning radio. Above all, we appreciate the importance of responding with innovative plans and ideas that are unique to your brand or product. We'd be delighted to talk to you about your particular requirements so ring the Sales Department today.

0171 388 6801

CANCELLATION

Written cancellation or postponement requests for campaigns within 28 clear days before the scheduled broadcast date shall be considered by the Company and may be accepted at the company's absolute discretion subject to the following cancellation charges:

up to 28 clear days before the date of broadcast	40%
up to 14 clear days before the date of broadcast	60%
up to 5 clear working days before the date of broadcast	80%
day of broadcast	100%

These charges apply to the value of the airtime booked at the time of the cancellation request.

COPY DEADLINES

Where advertisement copy is received less than 3 clear working days before the scheduled broadcast date, or is deemed not to have been so received as a result of failure to comply with the Company's technical requirements or submission or other procedures, the acceptance of such advertisement copy shall be at the absolute discretion of the Company and shall be subject to a surcharge of £75 per copy. In these circumstances the advertiser shall remain liable to pay in full for the advertising time whether or not it is broadcast.

TERMS AND CONDITIONS

Our service is offered subject to our Standard Terms and Conditions, copies of which are available on request.

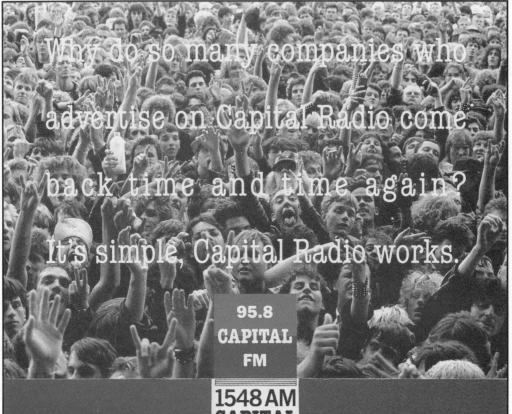

CAPITAL RADIO AND THE LONDON MARKET

London continues to be the country's most dynamic and exciting radio market, with Londoners having a greater choice of radio stations than anywhere else in the UK. We are delighted that the latest RAJAR results confirm 95.8 Capital FM and 1548 AM Capital Gold as London's favourite radio stations. This book features a selection of some of the most popular demographics to give you an idea of the size and quality of the audiences of both FM and Gold. If you'd like information on a specific target market please contact Capital Radio London Sales on **0171 388 6801**.

If you've got a product or service you want to advertise to Londoners then Capital FM and Capital Gold offer unrivalled numbers of listeners in all the important target demographics. It's simple, Capital Radio works.

95.8 CAPITAL FM AND 1548 AM CAPITAL GOLD

Capital Radio broadcasts to a huge area stretching 30 miles around Central London, covering over 12 million individuals - more than one fifth of the UK population. Every week almost 4.5 million Londoners, aged 4 years and over, choose to tune to either Capital FM or Capital Gold (a large proportion listen to both). What's more, these listeners spend an astonishing total of nearly 58 million hours tuned to Capital Radio.

1548 AM CAPITAL GOLD / **95.8 CAPITAL FM LONDON**

	ADULTS	CHILDREN 4 - 14	MEN	WOMEN	ADULTS 15 - 34	ADULTS 15 - 54	ABC1S	HOUSEWIVES	HWS WITH KIDS	ABC1S 20 - 44
POPULATION 000s	9,829	1,694	4,773	5,057	3,845	7,018	5,391	5,077	1,466	2,779
WEEKLY REACH %	38	43	40	37	53	49	37	34	47	49
WEEKLY REACH 000s	3,761	733	1,903	1,858	2,054	3,429	2,020	1,717	688	1,361
AVERAGE HOURS	13.8	8.2	15.0	12.6	13.2	14.0	11.8	13.2	14.0	12.9
TOTAL HOURS 000s	51,979	5,996	28,625	23,354	27,067	48,052	23,871	22,647	9,651	17,546
SHARE OF LISTENING %	28.6	53.9	30.2	26.9	46.7	40.1	24.8	23.7	42.6	39.5

95.8 CAPITAL FM

In survey after survey 95.8 Capital FM remains the market leader. The brilliant mix of hit music, competitions, award winning news and entertainment has made it London's favourite since 1990. 95.8 Capital FM is central to the lives of millions of Londoners who wake up to the legendary Chris Tarrant's Breakfast Show and continue to tune in during the day. As the figures clearly show, FM has a huge and dedicated following amongst both London's kids and the important 15-34 age break. And you can't ignore the station's strong performance against upmarket ABC1s.

95.8 CAPITAL FM LONDON

	ADULTS	CHILDREN 4 - 14	ADULTS 15 - 24	MEN 15 - 34	WOMEN 15 - 34	ABC1S	ABC1 MEN 20 - 44	HOUSEWIVES
POPULATION 000s	9,829	1,694	1,581	1,945	1,899	5,391	1,373	5,077
WEEKLY REACH %	33	39	52	48	53	32	46	29
WEEKLY REACH 000s	3,211	660	819	934	1,007	1,746	631	1,449
AVERAGE HOURS	12.3	8.4	11.4	13.3	11.6	10.3	11.8	11.8
TOTAL HOURS 000s	39,656	5,559	9,362	12,432	11,715	18,012	7,457	17,163
SHARE OF LISTENING %	21.8	50.0	45.0	39.2	44.7	18.7	30.8	17.9

ry's audience measurement system and uses methodology adopted by both Independent Radio and the BBC.

1548 AM CAPITAL GOLD

Since its launch in 1988 Capital Gold has been a success, attracting a large and loyal audience. Results from its first audience survey confirmed Gold's place as London's second largest commercial station and that's where it has stayed ever since. Gold's audience is concentrated among London's 25-54s who can't get enough of the station's classic hits from the 60's, 70's and 80's, presented by DJ's like Tony Blackburn, Alan Freeman and Mike Read. And for sports fans, Jonathan Pearce heads up the Capital Gold sports team delivering comprehensive live sporting action coverage in its own unique way.

1548 AM CAPITAL GOLD LONDON

	ADULTS	CHILDREN 4 - 14	MEN 25 - 54	WOMEN 25 - 54	HOUSEWIVES	HWS WITH KIDS	C1C2s	C1C2s 25-54
POPULATION 000s	9,829	1,694	2,733	2,705	5,077	1,466	5,367	3,029
WEEKLY REACH %	15	11	23	18	13	19	18	23
WEEKLY REACH 000s	1,482	183	624	477	685	278	944	689
AVERAGE HOURS	8.3	2.4	9.9	8.6	8.0	7.8	8.9	10.7
TOTAL HOURS 000s	12,323	436	6,184	4,112	5,484	2,173	8,422	7,351
SHARE OF LISTENING %	6.8	3.9	11.0	9.7	5.7	9.6	8.5	12.9

AUDIENCE PROFILES

The tables below illustrate the sex, age and class profiles of the weekly audiences to Capital FM and Capital Gold, alongside those of the population of Capital's transmission area.

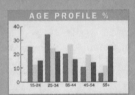

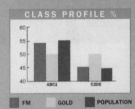

IN-CAR LISTENING

Talk about a captive audience! Radio, like no other medium, has the ability to reach and stimulate an audience whilst that audience is listening in-car. This is great news for advertisers, as the graphs below prove. They show the proportion of the adult audience to both Capital FM and Capital Gold that is listening in-car across an average weekday.

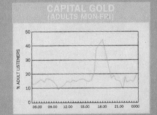

Source: All figures are taken from the Radio Joint Audience Research (RAJAR) survey covering the first quarter of 1995. Fieldwork took place over the twelve weeks between 2nd January - 26th March. RAJAR is the UK radio industry

PRODUCTION MENU

STARTERS
Our attentive staff will be happy to discuss your brief, quote for production, recommend appetisers for your audience or search for the right ingredients.

MAIN COURSES

Sound Bite -   Plain and simple. This filling treat contains a professional voice over, studio, script and materials. Very often it provides the basis for a more satisfying creation.
Cost: £400

Music Feast -   Using a Sound Bite base, the Music Feast spices up a more straight-forward advertisement with your choice of library music. Our extensive collection will have something to sate any appetite.
Cost: £500

Sound Supreme - A real mouthful. The Supreme includes two professional voice over artists, who'll not only deliver your script but savour every nuance of it. It is accompanied by a selection of hand picked musical instruments, making this a good choice for anyone with a huge appetite for success.
Cost: £700

CHOOSE AN EXTRA!

A wide selection of extras are available to spice up your production. Additional toppings include:

Music - from £100 per track per ad.
Sound Effects - £10 each
Celebrity voice overs or jingles - price on application

Capital Radio Commercial Production - serving from 8.30am weekdays.
For reservations, call Gail, Phil or Jo on 0171 608 6270.

All prices quoted are exclusive of VAT @17.5% and are based on one commercial being transmitted on one IR station. Further usage fees may apply if the campaign extends beyond three consecutive calendar months, and in a small number of cases may apply after one month.

95.8
CAPITAL
FM

LONDON

1548 AM
CAPITAL
GOLD

LONDON

"Immac's 1994 advertising campaign consisted of TV, radio and press. The total advertising awareness for Immac, amongst Capital and Kiss FM listeners, rose to a very satisfactory 66%. Additionally, over 27% of consumers said that the advertising made them think about trying the brand. This is the first time we have run a radio campaign for Immac and we hope to be able to build on it in the future."

Sue Brown
Brand Manager

CAPITALRADIOWORKS

BACKGROUND

Immac had previously used TV and press successfully. This time Immac wanted to test the effectiveness of radio in reaching its broad target market of women aged 18-34, and particularly in targeting young girls aged 12-16, to encourage them to try Immac as they were starting to think about hair removal.

It was felt that 95.8 Capital FM and Kiss FM could work powerfully with the young press titles Mizz, Big and Just 17, a theory which was put to the test by independent research carried out following the advertising.

THE CAMPAIGN

The main purpose of the campaign was to encourage young girls to sample the product on the basis that it was a more effective and longer-lasting method of hair removal than shaving.

Three commercials were produced taking humorous situations where legs treated with Immac proved to be vastly superior to legs that had been shaved. All three featured the strapline "no stubble, no trouble".

A total of 181 spots ran on 95.8 Capital FM achieving 640 Radio Ratings across 6 weeks, reaching 38% of 12-16 year old girls with an average of 17 opportunities to hear.

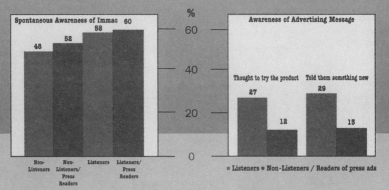

RESULTS

The research was conducted just after the campaign finished by Continental Research, using a sample of females aged 12-16.

- Spontaneous awareness of Immac as a hair removing product, at 58% amongst 95.8 FM Capital listeners, was 10 percentage points higher than amongst non-listeners (48%). Listeners who were also press readers scored higher still at 60%. However, amongst press readers who had not listened to Capital it was considerably lower at 52%.
- The difference in spontaneous awareness was even more marked amongst 12-14 year olds - 50% amongst Capital listeners as against 36% amongst non-listeners.
- Total awareness of Immac was 87% amongst listeners and 77% amongst non-listeners.
- Again, this difference was especially marked in the 12-14 year old group, with 83% awareness amongst Capital listeners but 66% amongst non-listeners.
- Perhaps even more significantly, the research showed that the radio advertising had had far more impact than the press. 27% of Capital listeners said that the radio ads had made them think about trying the product and 29% said that the ads had told them something new. However, the response from non-listeners who had read the press was much lower with 12% and 13% respectively.
- 44% of Capital listeners had received the message that Immac was more effective than shaving, with 59% understanding that legs would be smoother for longer.

CONCLUSION

The research showed that radio had achieved a substantial increase in awareness for the product and had played a crucial role in increasing the effectiveness of the press advertising.

Radio had also proved to be particularly effective in conveying the key messages of the campaign. There was a significant increase in the number of people intending to sample the product and the longer-lasting effect had been communicated well.

CAPITAL RADIO
L O N D O N

EUSTON TOWER · EUSTON ROAD · LONDON NW1 3DR · TEL: 0171 388 6801 · FAX: 0171 608 6150

"The Woolwich has always used radio in the advertising mix and we are happy to see the positive effects of a solus radio campaign. Increases in awareness were both through Continental's research and movement on the Gallup monitor. We certainly plan to continue to use radio, both through Capital and the rest of the independent radio network."

Chris Byrom
Marketing Manager

CAPITALRADIOWORKS

L O N D O N

CAPITALRADIOWORKS

BACKGROUND

The building society market is extremely competitive, with many of the major organisations promoting similar products. The product ranges themselves can often seem complex and confusing, making the market as a whole seem unappealing to consumers. This makes for a tough environment for brand building.

The Woolwich was planning a campaign to promote mortgage services to first time buyers aged 20-29, and savings schemes to 30-40 year olds, targeting ABC1C2s in particular in both age groups. The campaign objective was to promote the products in a simple and memorable way while at the same time positioning The Woolwich uniquely as an approachable, friendly building society.

The Woolwich is one of the biggest supporters of commercial radio in the financial sector and was confident of Capital's ability to achieve broad coverage of the target market, so it was natural that Capital would form a substantial part of the media mix. In this case, it was decided to use this opportunity to quantify whether a new campaign could be successfully established on radio and subsequently transferred to other media.

THE CAMPAIGN

Monty Python's Eric Idle was chosen to make two light-hearted commercials of 60 seconds each, one for mortgage services and the other for savings schemes. Although the commercials had different lyrics and dialogue they both used the same creative approach.

The campaign ran for 3 weeks with 183 spots on 95.8 Capital FM and 1548 AM Capital Gold, achieving a 46% reach of ABC1C2 15-44s with a frequency of 7.9. Additional airtime was bought on LBC and JFM.

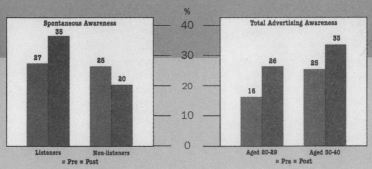

RESULTS

The results from Continental Research's panel of ABC1C2 adults aged 20-40 in London showed:

- Spontaneous awareness of The Woolwich as a provider of mortgage services increased from 27% to 35% among listeners and fell from 25% to 20% among non-listeners.

- Spontaneous awareness for the savings campaign among adult listeners aged 30-40 increased from 30% to 36%.

- Total advertising awareness among Capital listeners aged 20-29 increased from 16% to 26%, while awareness among listeners aged 30-40 increased from 25% to 33%.

CONCLUSION

The campaign was so successful that a second burst of advertising was placed on Capital and the creative treatment was extended to TV, thus achieving its important objective of establishing a new advertising theme initially on radio.

CAPITAL RADIO
L O N D O N

EUSTON TOWER · EUSTON ROAD · LONDON NW1 3DR · TEL: 0171 388 6801 · FAX: 0171 608 6150

Appendix C:
The British Code of
Advertising Practice

Principles
2.1   All advertisements should be legal, decent, honest and truthful.
2.2   All advertisements should be prepared with a sense of responsibility to consumers and to society.
2.3   All advertisements should respect the principles of fair competition generally accepted in business.
2.4   No advertisement should bring advertising into disrepute.
2.5   Advertisements must conform with the Codes. Primary responsibility for observing the Codes falls on advertisers. Others involved in preparing and publishing advertisements such as agencies, publishers and other service suppliers also accept an obligation to abide by the Codes.
2.6   Any unreasonable delay in responding to the ASA's enquiries may be considered a breach of the Codes.
2.7   The ASA will on request treat in confidence any private or secret material supplied unless the Courts or officials acting within their statutory powers compel its disclosure.
2.8   The Codes are applied in the spirit as well as in the letter.

Substantiation
3.1   Before submitting an advertisement for publication, advertisers must hold documentary evidence to prove all claims, whether direct or implied, that are capable of objective substantiation. Relevant evidence should be sent without delay if requested by the ASA. The adequacy of evidence will be judged on whether it supports both the detailed claims and the overall impression created by the advertisement.
3.2   If there is a significant division of informed opinion about any claims made in an advertisement they should not be portrayed as universally agreed.
3.3   If the contents of non-fiction books, tapes, videos and the like have not been independently substantiated, advertisements should not exaggerate the value or practical usefulness of their contents.
3.4   Obvious untruths or exaggerations that are unlikely to mislead and

incidental minor errors and unorthodox spellings are all allowed provided they do not affect the accuracy or perception of the advertisement in any material way.

Legality
4.1   Advertisers have primary responsibility for ensuring that their advertisements are legal. Advertisements should contain nothing that breaks the law or incites anyone to break it, and should omit nothing that the law requires.

Decency
5.1   Advertisements should contain nothing that is likely to cause serious or widespread offence. Particular care should be taken to avoid causing offence on the grounds of race, religion, sex, sexual orientation or disability. Compliance with the Codes will be judged on the context, medium, audience, product and prevailing standards of decency.
5.2   Advertisements may be distasteful without necessarily conflicting with 5.1 above. Advertisers are urged to consider public sensitivities before using potentially offensive material.
5.3   The fact that a particular product is offensive to some people is not sufficient grounds for objecting to an advertisement for it.

Honesty
6.1   Advertisers should not exploit the credulity, lack of knowledge or inexperience of consumers.

Truthfulness
7.1   No advertisement should mislead by inaccuracy, ambiguity, exaggeration, omission or otherwise.

Matters of opinion
8.1   Advertisers may give a view about any matter, including the qualities or desirability of their products, provided it is clear that they are expressing their own opinion rather than stating a fact. Assertions or comparisons that go beyond subjective opinions are subject to 3.1 above.

Fear and distress
9.1   No advertisement should cause fear or distress without good reason. Advertisers should not use shocking claims or images merely to attract attention.
9.2   Advertisers may use an appeal to fear to encourage prudent behaviour or to discourage dangerous or ill-advised actions; the fear likely to be aroused should not be disproportionate to the risk.

Safety
10.1   Advertisements should not show or encourage unsafe practices except in the context of promoting safety. Particular care should be taken with advertisements addressed to or depicting children and young people.
10.2   Consumers should not be encouraged to drink and drive. Advertisements, including those for breath testing devices, should not suggest that the effects of drinking alcohol can be masked and should include a prominent warning on the dangers of drinking and driving.

Violence and antisocial behaviour
11.1   Advertisements should contain nothing that condones or is likely to provoke violence or anti-social behaviour.

Political advertising
12.1   Any advertisement whose principal function is to influence opinion in favour of or against any political party or electoral candidate contesting a UK, European parliamentary or local government election, or any matter before the electorate for a referendum, is exempt from clauses 3.1, 7.1, 14.3, 19.2 and 20.1. All other rules in the Codes apply.
12.2   The identity and status of such advertisers should be clear. If their address or other contact details are not generally available they should be included in the advertisement.
12.3   There is a formal distinction between government policy and that of political parties. Advertisements by central or local government, or those concerning government policy as distinct from party policy, are subject to all the Code's rules.

Protection of privacy
13.1   Advertisers are urged to obtain written permission in advance if they portray or refer to individuals or their identifiable possessions in any advertisement. Exceptions include most crowd scenes, portraying anyone who is the subject of the book or film being advertised and depicting property in general outdoor locations.
13.2   Advertisers who have not obtained prior permission from entertainers, politicians, sportsmen and others whose work gives them a high public profile should ensure that they are not portrayed in an offensive or adverse way. Advertisements should not claim or imply an endorsement where none exists.
13.3   Prior permission may not be needed when the advertisement contains nothing that is inconsistent with the position or views of the person featured. Advertisers should be aware that individuals who do not wish to be associated with the advertised product may have a legal claim.
13.4   References to anyone who is deceased should be handled with particular care to avoid causing offence or distress.

13.5   References to members of the Royal Family and the use of the Royal Arms and Emblems are not normally permitted; advertisers should consult the Lord Chamberlain's Office. References to Royal Warrants should be checked with the Royal Warrant Holders' Association.

Testimonials and endorsements

14.1   Advertisers should hold signed and dated proof, including a contact address, for any testimonial they use. Testimonials should be used only with the written permission of those giving them.

14.2   Testimonials should relate to the product being advertised.

14.3   Testimonials alone do not constitute substantiation and the opinions expressed in them must be supported, where necessary, with independent evidence of their accuracy. Any claims based on a testimonial must conform with the Codes.

14.4   Fictitious endorsements should not be presented as though they were genuine testimonials.

14.5   References to tests, trials, professional endorsements, research facilities and professional journals should be used only with the permission of those concerned. They should originate from within the European Union unless otherwise stated in the advertisement. Any establishment referred to should be under the direct supervision of an appropriately qualified professional.

Prices

15.1   Any stated price should be clear and should relate to the product advertised. Advertisers should ensure that prices match the products illustrated.

15.2   Unless addressed exclusively to the trade, prices quoted should include any VAT payable. It should be apparent immediately whether any prices quoted exclude other taxes, duties or compulsory charges and these should, wherever possible, be given in the advertisement.

15.3   If the price of one product is dependent on the purchase of another. the extent of any commitment by consumers should be made clear.

15.4   Price claims such as 'up to' and 'from' should not exaggerate the availability of benefits likely to be obtained by consumers.

Free offers

16.1   There is no objection to making a free offer conditional on the purchase of other items. Consumers' liability for any costs should be made clear in all material featuring the offer. An offer should only be described as free if consumers pay no more than:
   a) the current public rates of postage
   b) the actual cost of freight or delivery
   c) the cost, including incidental expenses, of any travel involved if consumers collect the offer.

Advertisers should make no additional charges for packing and handling.
16.2   Advertisers must not attempt to recover their costs by reducing the quality or composition or by inflating the price of any product that must be purchased as a pre-condition of obtaining another product free.

Availability of products

17.1   Advertisers must make it clear if stocks are limited. Products must not be advertised unless advertisers can demonstrate that they have reasonable grounds for believing that they can satisfy demand. If a product becomes unavailable, advertisers will be required to show evidence of stock monitoring, communications with outlets and the swift withdrawal of advertisements whenever possible.
17.2   Products which cannot be supplied should not normally be advertised as a way of assessing potential demand.
17.3   Advertisers must not use the technique of switch selling, where their sales staff criticise the advertised product or suggest that it is not available and recommend the purchase of a more expensive alternative. They should not place obstacles in the way of purchasing the product or delivering it promptly.

Guarantees

18.1   The full terms of any guarantee should be available for consumers to inspect before they are committed to purchase. Any substantial limitations should be spelled out in the advertisement.
18.2   Advertisers should inform consumers about the nature and extent of any additional rights provided by the guarantee, over and above those given to them by law, and should make clear how to obtain redress.
18.3   'Guarantee' when used simply as a figure of speech should not cause confusion about consumers' legal rights.

Comparisons

19.1   Comparisons can be explicit or implied and can relate to advertisers' own products or to those of their competitors; they are permitted in the interests of vigorous competition and public information.
19.2   Comparisons should be clear and fair. The elements of any comparison should not be selected in a way that gives the advertisers an artificial advantage.

Denigration

20.1   Advertisers should not unfairly attack or discredit other businesses or their products.
20.2   The only acceptable use of another business's broken or defaced products in advertisements is in the illustration of comparative tests, and the source, nature and results of these should be clear.

Exploitation of goodwill

21.1   Advertisers should not make unfair use of the goodwill attached to the trade mark, name, brand, or the advertising campaign of any other business.

Imitation

22.1   No advertisement should so closely resemble any other that it misleads or causes confusion.

Identifying advertisers and recognising advertisements

23.1   Advertisers, publishers and owners of other media should ensure that advertisements are designed and presented in such a way that they can be easily distinguished from editorial.

23.2   Features, announcements or promotions that are disseminated in exchange for a payment or other reciprocal arrangement should comply with the Codes if their content is controlled by the advertisers. They should also be clearly identified and distinguished from editorial (see clause 41).

23.3   Mail order and direct response advertisements and those for one day sales, homework schemes, business opportunities and the like should contain the name and address of the advertisers. Advertisements with a political content should clearly identify their source. Unless required by law, other advertisers are not obliged to identify themselves.

ALCOHOLIC DRINKS

46.1   For the purposes of the Codes, alcoholic drinks are those that exceed 1.2% alcohol by volume.

46.2   The drinks industry and the advertising business accept a responsibility for ensuring that advertisements contain nothing that is likely to lead people to adopt styles of drinking that are unwise. The consumption of alcohol may be portrayed as sociable and thirst-quenching. Advertisements may be humorous, but must still conform with the intention of the rules.

46.3   Advertisements should be socially responsible and should not encourage excessive drinking. Advertisements should not suggest that regular solitary drinking is advisable. Care should be taken not to exploit the young, the immature or those who are mentally or socially vulnerable.

46.4   Advertisements should not be directed at people under eighteen through the selection of media, style of presentation, content or context in which they appear. No medium should be used to advertise alcoholic drinks if more than 25% of its audience is under eighteen years of age.

46.5   People shown drinking should not be, nor should they look, under twenty five. Younger models may be shown in advertisements, for example in the context of family celebrations, but it should be obvious that they are not drinking.

46.6 Advertisements should not feature real or fictitious characters who are likely to appeal particularly to people under eighteen in a way that would encourage them to drink.

46.7 Advertisements should not suggest that any alcoholic drink can enhance mental, physical or sexual capabilities, popularity, attractiveness, masculinity, femininity or sporting achievements.

46.8 Advertisements may give factual information about the alcoholic strength of a drink or its relatively high alcohol content but this should not be the dominant theme of any advertisement. Alcoholic drinks should not be presented as preferable because of their high alcohol content or intoxicating effect.

46.9 Advertisements should not portray drinking alcohol as the main reason for the success of any personal relationship or social event. A brand preference may be promoted as a mark of the drinker's good taste and discernment.

46.10 Drinking alcohol should not be portrayed as a challenge, nor should it be suggested that people who drink are brave, tough or daring for doing so.

46.11 Particular care should be taken to ensure that advertisements for sales promotions requiring multiple purchases do not actively encourage excessive consumption.

48.12 Advertisements should not depict activities or locations where drinking alcohol would be unsafe or unwise. In particular, advertisements should not associate the consumption of alcohol with operating machinery, driving, any activity relating to water or heights, or any other occupation that requires concentration in order to be done safely.

46.13 Low alcohol drinks are those that contain 1.2% alcohol by volume or less. Advertisers should ensure that low alcohol drinks are not promoted in a way that encourages their inappropriate consumption and should not depict activities that require complete sobriety.

CHILDREN

47.1 The way in which children perceive and react to advertisements is influenced by their age, experience and the context in which the message is delivered. The ASA will take these factors into account when assessing advertisements.

47.2 Advertisements and promotions addressed to or featuring children should contain nothing that is likely to result in their physical, mental or moral harm:

a) they should not be encouraged to enter strange places or talk to strangers. Care is needed when they are asked to make collections,

enter schemes or gather labels, wrappers, coupons and the like
b) they should not be shown in hazardous situations or behaving danger-
ously in the home or outside except to promote safety. Children
should not be shown unattended in street scenes unless they are old
enough to take responsibility for their own safety. Pedestrians and
cyclists should be seen to observe the Highway Code
c) they should not be shown using or in close proximity to dangerous
substances or equipment without direct adult supervision. Examples
include matches, petrol, certain medicines and household substances
as well as certain electrical appliances and machinery, including agricultural equipment
d) they should not be encouraged to copy any practice that might be
unsafe for a child.

47.3   Advertisements and promotions addressed to or featuring children
should not exploit their credulity, loyalty, vulnerability or lack of experience:
a) they should not be made to feel
inferior or unpopular for not buying the advertised product
b) they should not be made to feel that they are lacking in courage, duty
or loyalty if they do not buy or do not encourage others to buy a particular product
c) it should be made easy for them to judge the size, characteristics and
performance of any product advertised and to distinguish between
real-life situations and fantasy
d) parental permission should be obtained before they are committed to
purchasing complex and costly goods and services.

47.4   Advertisements and promotions addressed to children:
a) should not actively encourage them to make a nuisance of themselves
to parents or others
b) should not make a direct appeal to purchase unless the product is one
that would be likely to interest children and that they could reasonably afford. Mail order advertisers should take care when using youth
media not to promote products that are unsuitable for children
c) should not exaggerate what is attainable by an ordinary child using
the product being advertised or promoted
d) should not actively encourage them to eat or drink at or near bedtime,
to eat frequently throughout the day or to replace main meals with
confectionery or snack foods
e) should not exploit their susceptibility to charitable appeals and
should explain the extent to which their participation will help in any
charity-linked promotions.

47.5   Promotions addressed to children:
a) should not encourage excessive purchases in order to participate
b) should make clear that parental permission is required if prizes and

incentives might cause conflict between children and their parents. Examples include animals, bicycles, tickets for outings, concerts and holidays

c) should clearly explain the number and type of any additional proofs of purchase needed to participate

d) should contain a prominent closing date

e) should not exaggerate the value of prizes or the chances of winning them.

MOTORING

48.1 Advertisements for motor vehicles, fuel or accessories should avoid portraying or referring to practices that encourage antisocial behaviour.

48.2 Advertisers should not make speed or acceleration claims the predominant message of their advertisements. However it is legitimate to give general information about a vehicle's performance such as acceleration statistics, braking power, roadholding and top and mid-range speeds.

48.3 Advertisers should not portray speed in a way that might encourage motorists to drive irresponsibly or to break the law.

48.4 Vehicles should not be depicted in dangerous or unwise situations in a way that would encourage irresponsible driving. Their capabilities may be demonstrated on a track or circuit provided it is clearly not in use as a public highway.

48.5 Care should be taken in cinema advertisements and those in electronic media where the moving image may give the impression of exceptional speed. In all cases where vehicles are shown in normal driving circumstances on the public road they should be seen not to exceed UK speed limits.

48.6 When making environmental claims for their products, advertisers should conform with the Specific Rules on Environmental Claims.

48.7 Prices quoted should correspond to the vehicles illustrated. For example, it is not acceptable to feature only a top-of-the-range model alongside the starting price for that range.

48.8 Safety claims should not exaggerate the benefit to consumers. Advertisers should not make absolute claims about safety unless they hold evidence to support them.

ENVIRONMENTAL CLAIMS

49.1 The basis of any claim should be explained clearly and should be qualified where necessary. Unqualified claims can mislead if they omit significant information.

49.2 Claims such as 'environmentally friendly' or 'wholly biodegradable' should not be used without qualification unless advertisers can provide convincing evidence that their product will cause no environmental damage. Qualified claims and comparisons such as 'greener' or 'friendlier' may be acceptable if advertisers can substantiate that their product provides an overall improvement in environmental terms either against their competitors' or their own previous products.

49.3   Where there is a significant division of scientific opinion or where evidence is inconclusive this should be reflected in any statements made in the advertisement. Advertisers should not suggest that their claims command universal acceptance if it is not the case.

49.4   If a product has never had a demonstrably adverse effect on the environment, advertisements should not imply that the formulation has changed to make it safe. It is legitimate, however, to make claims about a product whose composition has changed or has always been designed in a way that omits chemicals known to cause damage to the environment.

49.5   The use of extravagant language should be avoided, as should bogus and confusing scientific terms. If it is necessary to use a scientific expression, its meaning should be clear.

HEALTH & BEAUTY PRODUCTS AND THERAPIES
General

50.1   Medical and scientific claims made about beauty and health-related products should be backed by trials, where appropriate conducted on people. Substantiation will be assessed by the ASA on the basis of established scientific knowledge.

50.2   Advertisers should not discourage people from having essential treatment; medical advice is needed for serious or prolonged ailments and advertisers should not offer medicines or therapies for them.

50.3   Advice, diagnosis or treatment of any serious medical condition should be conducted face-to-face. Advertisers inviting consumers to diagnose their own minor ailments should not make claims that might lead to a mistaken diagnosis.

50.4   Consumers should not be encouraged to use products to excess and advertisers should not suggest that their products or therapies are guaranteed to work, absolutely safe or without side-effects for everyone.

50.5   Advertisements should not suggest that any product is safe or effective merely because it is 'natural' or that it is generally safer because it omits an ingredient in common use.

50.6   Advertisers offering individual treatments, particularly those that are physically invasive, may be asked by the media and the ASA to provide full details together with information about those who will supervise and administer them. Where appropriate, practitioners should have relevant and recognised qualifications. Consumers should be encouraged to take independent medical advice before committing themselves to significant treatments.

50.7   References to the relief of symptoms or the superficial signs of ageing are acceptable if they can be substantiated. Unqualified claims such as 'cure' and 'rejuvenation' are not generally acceptable.

50.8   Claims made for the treatment of minor addictions and bad habits should make clear the vital role of willpower.

50.9   Advertisers should not use unfamiliar scientific words for common conditions.

Medicines

50.10 The Medicines Act 1968 and its regulations, as well as regulations implementing European Community Directive 92/28/EEC, govern the advertising and promotion of medicines and the conditions of ill health that they can be offered to treat. Guidance on the legislation is available from the Medicines Control Agency (MCA).

50.11 Medicines must be licensed by the MCA before they are advertised and any claims made for products must conform with the licence. Unlicensed products should not make medicinal claims. Advertisements should refer to the MCA, the licence or the EC only if required to do so by the MCA.

50.12 Prescription-only medicines may not be advertised to the public. Health-related claims in advertisements and promotions addressed only to the medical and allied professions are exempt from the Codes.

50.13 Advertisements should include the name of the product, an indication of what it is for, text such as 'Always read the label' and the common name of the active ingredient if there is only one. There should be no suggestion that any medicine is either a food or a cosmetic.

50.14 Advertisers must not use fear or anxiety to promote medicines or recovery from illness and should not suggest that using or avoiding a product can affect normal good health.

50.15 Illustrations of the effect or action of any product on the human body should be accurate.

50.16 Advertisements for medicines should not be addressed to children.

50.17 Advertisers should not use health professionals or celebrities to endorse medicines.

50.18 Advertisements for any medicine should not claim that its effects are as good as or better than those of another identifiable product.

50.19 Homeopathic medicinal products must be registered in the UK. Any product information given in the advertisement should be confined to what appears on the label. Advertisements should include a warning to consult a doctor if-symptoms persist and should not make any medicinal or therapeutic claims or refer to any ailment.

Vitamins, minerals and food supplements

50.20 Advertisers should hold scientific evidence for any claim that their vitamin or mineral product or food supplement is beneficial to health.

50.21 A well-balanced diet should provide the vitamins and minerals needed each day by a normal, healthy individual. Advertisers may offer supplements as a safeguard, but should not suggest that there is widespread vitamin or mineral deficiency or that it is necessary or therapeutic to augment a well-balanced diet. Advertisements should not imply that supplements will guard against deficiency, elevate mood or enhance performance. Supplements should not be promoted as a substitute for a healthy diet.

50.22 Certain groups of people may benefit from vitamin and mineral supplementation. These include people who eat nutritionally inadequate meals, the elderly, children and adolescents, convalescents, athletes in training, those who are physically very active, women of child-bearing age, lactating and pregnant women and dieters. In assessing claims the ASA will bear in mind recommendations made by the Department of Health.

50.23 Serious vitamin and mineral depletion caused by illness should be diagnosed and treated by a doctor. Self-medication should not be promoted on the basis that it will influence the speed or extent of recovery.

Cosmetics

50.24 Claims made about the action that a cosmetic has on or in the skin should distinguish between the composition of the product and any effects brought about by the way in which it is applied, such as massage. Scientific evidence should also make this distinction.

50.25 Some cosmetics have an effect on the kind of skin changes that are caused by environmental factors. Advertisements for them can therefore refer to temporarily preventing, delaying or masking premature ageing.

Hair and scalp

50.26 Advertisers should be able to provide scientific evidence, where appropriate in the form of trials conducted on people, for any claim that their product or therapy can prevent baldness or slow it down, arrest or reverse hair loss, stimulate or improve hair growth, nourish hair roots, strengthen the hair or improve its health as distinct from its appearance.

EMPLOYMENT AND BUSINESS OPPORTUNITIES

54.1 Advertisers should distinguish clearly between offers of employment and business opportunities. Before publication, media normally require full details of the advertisers and any terms and conditions imposed on respondents.

54.2 Employment advertisements must correspond to genuine vacancies and potential employees must not be asked to send money for further details. Living and working conditions should not be misrepresented. Quoted earnings should be precise; if a forecast has to be made this should not be unrepresentative. If income is earned from a basic salary and commission, commission only, or in some other way, this should be made clear.

54.3   An employment agency must make clear in advertisements that it is an employment agency.

54.4   Homework schemes require participants to make articles, perform services or offer facilities at or from home. Consumers should be given:

a) the full name and address of the advertisers

b) a clear description of the work; the support available to homeworkers should not be exaggerated

c) an indication of whether participants are self-employed or employed by a business

d) the likely level of earnings, but only if this can be supported with evidence of the experience of current homeworkers

e) no forecast of earnings if the scheme is new

f) details of any required investment or binding obligation

g) details of any charges for raw materials, machines, components, administration and the like

h) information on whether the advertisers will buy back any goods made

i) any limitations or conditions that might influence consumers prior to their decision to participate.

54.5   Advertisements for business opportunities should contain:

a) the name and contact details of the advertisers

b) where possible, a clear description of the work involved and the extent of investors' commitments, including any financial investment; the support available should not be exaggerated

c) no unrepresentative or exaggerated earnings figures.

54.6   Vocational training and other instruction courses should make no promises of employment unless it is guaranteed. The duration of the course and the level of attainment needed to embark on it should be made clear.

54.7   The sale of directories giving details of employment or business opportunities should indicate plainly the nature of what is being offered.

FINANCIAL SERVICES AND PRODUCTS

55.1   The rules that follow provide only general guidance. Advertisers, their agencies and the media must also comply with the numerous statutes that govern financial services and products including issuing advertisements, investment opportunities, credit facilities and the provision of financial information.

55.2   Offers of financial services and products should be set out in a way that allows them to be understood easily by the audience being addressed. Advertisers should ensure that they do not take advantage of people's inexperience or gullibility.

55.3   Advertisers asking for a commitment at a distance should make sure that

their full address is given outside any response coupon or other mecha-
nism.

55.4   Advertisements should indicate the nature of the contract being offered,
any limitations, expenses, penalties and charges and the terms of withdrawal. Alternatively, where an advertisement is short or general in its
content, free explanatory material giving full details of the offer should
be readily available before a binding contract is entered into.

55.5   The basis used to calculate any rates of interest, forecasts or projections
should be apparent immediately.

55.6   Advertisements should make clear that the value of investments is variable and, unless guaranteed, can go down as well as up. If the value of
the investment is guaranteed details should be included in the advertisement.

55.7   Advertisements should specify that past performance or experience
does not necessarily give a guide for the future. Any examples used
should not be unrepresentative.

**(Reproduced by kind permission of the Committee of Advertising Practice.
Further details about the Act can be obtained from: 2 Torrington Place,
London WC1E 7HW.)**

Appendix D: The Code of Advertising Standards and Practice

It is essential that you are familiar with the Radio Authority's code of advertising standards and practice, especially when you are composing advertisements. To help you find the sections that are most relevant to you, the code is divided up as follows:

Introduction
The code.
Advertising principles.
Sponsorship principles.
Copy clearance and pre-vetting.

Section A: Presentation of Advertisements
Identification.
Exclusion and distribution.
Prohibited categories.
Presenter-read advertisements.
Unreasonable discrimination.
Product placement.

Section B: Standards for Advertisements
Misleadingness.
Political, industrial and public controversy.
Taste and offence.
Protection of privacy and exploitation of the individual.
Superstition and appeals to fear.
Price claims.
Comparisons.
Denigration.
Testimonials.
Guarantees.
Use of the word 'Free'.
Competitions.
Premium rate telephone services.
Matrimonial and introduction agencies.

Sexual discrimination.
Racial discrimination.
Sound effects.
Direct marketing.

Appendix 1: Financial advertising.
Appendix 2: Alcoholic drink advertising.
Appendix 3: Advertising and children.
Appendix 4: Medicines, treatments and health.

You are advised to read the 'Practice Notes' particularly carefully as these set out the do's and don't's of writing acceptable radio advertisements.

Introduction

(a) The Broadcasting Act 1990 ('The Act') makes it the statutory duty of the Radio Authority ('The Authority') to draw up, and periodically review, a code ('The Code') which sets standards and practice in advertising and programme sponsorship on independent radio.

(b) This is the Radio Authority Code of Advertising Standards and Practice and Programme Sponsorship which the Authority has adopted under Section 92(1)(a) of the Act, after appropriate consultation. The Code applies to all advertisements and sponsorship on radio services licensed by the Authority.

(c) Radio Authority licensees are responsible for ensuring that any advertising and sponsorship they broadcast complies with this Code.

(d) The Authority advises licensees on interpretation of the Code and monitors compliance by investigating complaints. It may direct advertising and sponsorship which does not comply to be withdrawn. In the case of a breach of the Code, the Authority may impose any of a number of sanctions.

(e) The Broadcasting Act 1990 reserves the right of the Authority to impose requirements which go beyond the Code's rules. The Authority is empowered to give directions to exclude not only categories of advertisement and methods of advertising or sponsorship but also individual advertisements – either in general or in particular circumstances.

The code

(f) The rules are divided into three sections. Sections A and B deal with standards for the presentation and content of advertisements. They are followed by seven appendices which deal with categories of advertisement which require particular detail. Section C deals with programme sponsorship.

(g) The main code rules are followed by 'Practice Notes' which offer further guidance on practical implementation.

(h) Many of the advertising rules are derived directly from statute. As a minimum, licensees should be familiar with the provisions of the Broadcasting Act 1990 and relevant consumer protection legislation.

(j) Licensees may receive additional guidance on interpretation of the Code from the Authority's Advertising Regulation staff.

(k) Advertisers, advertising agencies, independent producers or potential sponsors seeking further clarification of any of the rules should approach the radio station on which they wish to advertise or sponsor programmes.

Advertising principles

1. **'Advertisement'** in this Code refers to any item of publicity, other than a sponsor credit, broadcast in return for payment or other valuable consideration to a licensee.

2. Radio advertising should be legal, decent, honest and truthful.

3. Advertisements must comply in every respect with the law, common or statute, and licensees must make it a condition of acceptance that advertisements do so comply.

4. The advertising rules are intended to be applied in the spirit as well as the letter.

Sponsorship principles

1. **'Sponsorship'** in this Code refers to any item of publicity, other than an advertisement, broadcast in return for payment or any other valuable consideration to a licensee.

2. Editorial control of sponsored programmes must remain with the licensee.

3. All sponsor involvement must be declared so that the listener knows who is paying/contributing and why.

4. The sponsorship rules are intended to be applied in the spirit as well as the letter.

Copy clearance and pre-vetting

ADVERTISEMENTS

(a) **'Local'** clearance applies to advertisements which are broadcast only by a radio station or stations servicing one particular locality. Copy may be approved for broadcast by relevant station staff who are responsible for ensuring that it complies with this Code. Exceptions to this are the 'special categories' detailed at (d) below.

(b) **'Regional'** clearance applies to advertisements which are broadcast by a number of radio stations in any one region out of the following five: Scotland and Northern Ireland; the North; Midlands and East Anglia; London; the South, West and Wales. Copy may be approved for broadcast by nominated regional clearance executives who are responsible for ensuring that it complies with this Code. (For details of the breakdown of stations per region and for the names and contact numbers of regional clearance executives, please contact the AIRC on 0171-727 2646). Exceptions to this are the 'special categories' detailed at (d) below.

(c) **'National'/'Central'** clearance applies to advertisements which are broadcast nationally or in more than one of the five regions detailed in (b) above. Copy must be submitted for advance clearance to an organisation or person approved by the Radio Authority, i.e. the Broadcast Advertising Clearance Centre (BACC).

(d) **'Special Categories'** of advertisement (whether for broadcast locally, regionally or nationally) need particular care and require advance central clearance as detailed in (c) above. They comprise:
Consumer credit, investment and complex financial advertising;
Alcoholic drink;
Medicines, treatments and health (includes contraceptives, feminine hygiene, slimming products);
Government advertising (e.g. COI campaigns, anti-AIDS, anti-drugs);
Advertisements containing references to political or industrial controversy or to public policy;
Advertisements claiming environmental benefits;
Charities;
Religion.

(e) For central clearance, advertisers or their agencies may submit five copies of preproduction scripts to the following address:
BACC, 200 Gray's Inn Rd., London WCIX 8HF. Tel: 0171-843 8265. Fax: 0171-843 8154.

(f) For all clearances, scripts should be accompanied by the following details:
Advertising agency or production house name, address and telephone number;
Name of agency or production house executive responsible for BACC negotiations;
Name of advertiser;
Name of product;
Reference number (if applicable);
Title and length of advertisement;
Recording date;
Date of script;
Transmission area(s);
First transmission date(s);
Name(s) of voiceover artist(s);
Precise description of sound effects.

(g) Supporting evidence must accompany scripts which include any factual claims, e.g. sales claims, price claims, consumer credit, guarantees, free or special offers, competition details, testimonials, etc.

(h) For central clearance, scripts are usually cleared within five working days and, if acceptable, stamped and returned with a BACC clearance form which notifies the licensee of any special requirements (e.g. scheduling restrictions).

(j) For regional clearance, scripts are usually cleared within three days. Two copies of the script need to be sent to the regional clearance executive, accompanied as relevant by the material listed in (f) and (g) above, and may be sent by facsimile. The script will be returned stamped 'approved', 'approved as amended' or 'rejected for reasons stated' as applicable.

(k) Licensees or their sales houses must hold photocopies of clearance forms and approved scripts prior to broadcast. This is their only means of knowing that scripts have been cleared. Final recorded versions of commercials need not normally be sent to the BACC. They must be checked against approved scripts by the licensee(s) concerned.

SPONSORED PROGRAMMES

(l) The Authority does not require sponsorship proposals to be cleared in advance.

(m) Licensees must ensure that their sponsored programmes comply both with this Code and with the Authority's Programme Codes.

(n) The Radio Authority's Advertising Regulation staff will give general guidance to licensees on sponsorship proposals if requested.

Section A:
Presentation of Advertisements

Rule 1: Identification
Advertising breaks must be clearly distinguishable from programming.

Practice Notes
Licensees must ensure that the distinction between advertising and programming is not blurred and that listeners are not confused between the two.
Advertisements which have a similar style and format to editorial must be separated from programming by other material such as a jingle/station ident or by scheduling in the middle of a break.
Particular care should be exercised if expressions and sound effects associated with news bulletins are used. Listeners must quickly recognise the message as an advertisement.
References to programmes in advertisements are only acceptable in advertisements for specific television or radio programmes and in advertisements placed by sponsors.

Rule 2: Exclusion and distribution
(a) EXCLUSION FROM SOME TYPES OF PROGRAMME
Advertisements must not be broadcast within coverage of a religious ser-

vice, a formal royal ceremony or occasion or a programme designed for reception in schools, unless the programme is over 30 minutes in length.

(b) DISTRIBUTION WITHIN SOME TYPES OF PROGRAMME
  i.   Licensees must exercise responsible judgements when scheduling cate-gories of advertisement which may be unsuitable for children and those listening to religious programmes. Particular care is required in the fol-lowing categories: sanitary protection products, family planning ser-vices, contraceptives, pregnancy-testing services/kits, anti-AIDS and anti-drugs messages and solvent abuse advice.
       [NB: For the purpose of this rule, the Authority considers that children are aged 15 and below. However, there may be exceptional circum-stances when advertising messages may be targeted at those aged 12–15 (e.g. anti-AIDS information or sanitary protection)].
  ii. Advertisements for alcoholic drinks, cigars, pipe tobacco, sensational newspapers/magazines or their content and violent or sexually explicit films must not be broadcast in or around religious programmes or pro-grammes/ features directed particularly at people under 18.
  iii. Advertisements by charity organisations must not be broadcast in immediate juxtaposition to programme appeals for donations or com-munity service announcements.
  iv. Advertisements by religious organisations for the purposes of categories (a), (b) and (d) of Rule 2 of Appendix 7 must not be broadcast in or around programmes principally directed at people under 18, or likely to be of particular appeal to them.

Practice Note
A sense of responsibility should be exercised where advertisements or their scheduling could be perceived as insensitive because of a tragedy currently in news or current affairs programmes, e.g. a commercial for an airline should be immediately withdrawn if a neighbouring news bulletin featured details of a plane crash.

Rule 3: **Prohibited categories**
Advertisements for products and services coming within the recognised char-acter of, or specifically concerned with, the following are not acceptable:
(a) breath-testing devices and products which purport to mask the effects of alcohol;
(b) the occult (excluding publications of general interest, e.g. newspapers or magazines whose editorial is unrelated to the occult but which includes regular horoscopes and/or occasional articles on the paranormal);
(c) betting and gaming (includes bookmakers, betting tips, gaming machines and bingo but excludes non-gaming machines and the social, non-gam-bling activities offered by organisations/clubs who may also hold gaming

licences. Also excluded are advertisements for football pools and lotteries permitted under the National Lottery etc Act 1993 and the Lotteries and Amusements Act 1976 as amended (this Act does not extend to Northem Ireland) provided that advertisements are neither directed at those under 16 nor broadcast in or around programmes likely to be of particular appeal to them).

(d) escort agencies and the like;

(e) cigarettes and cigarette tobacco;

(f) commercial services offering advice on personal, consumer or medical problems (excluding solicitors) which are not operating with the approval of their Local Authority/Local Health Authority or are not otherwise approved in a way acceptable to the Authority;

(g) guns and gun clubs (excluding shops which sell guns provided there is no mention of this);

(h) pomography (including 'topshelf' publications and the like);

(j) products for the treatment of alcoholism;

(k) hypnosis, hypnotherapy, psychology, psychoanalysis, psychotherapy or psychiatry (excluding certain types of publication approved in a way acceptable to the Authority);

(l) advertisements for investments in metals, commodities, futures and options, securities which are not readily realisable, volatile or complex investments such as swaps and currency or interest rate instruments, con-tracts based on market indices, and such other categories which the Authority may from time to time consider inappropriate;

(m)advertisements for the issue of shares or debentures (other than advertise-ments announcing the publication of listing particulars or a prospectus in connection with an offer to the public of shares or debentures to be listed on the Stock Exchange or dealt in on the Unlisted Securities Market);

(n) advertisements recommending the acquisition or disposal of an invest-ment in any specific company (other than an investment trust company listed on the Stock Exchange).

Practice Note
An advertisement for an acceptable product or service may be withdrawn if the Authority considers that a significant effect is to publicise indirectly an unacceptable product or service.

***Rule 4*: Presenter-read advertisements**
(a) GENERAL
Station presenters (excluding those involved in news and current affairs) may voice commercials provided that they do not:
i. endorse, recommend, identify themselves with or personally testify about an advertiser's products or services (however, presenters may refer to their own appearance(s) at an event run by an advertise

provided that the words used do not endorse or recommend the product or service which the event is designed to promote);

   ii. make references to any specific advertisement, (whether presenter-read or not), when in their presenter role;

   iii. feature in an advertisement for a medicine or treatment.

(b) PRESENTER-READ ADVERTISEMENTS WITHIN PRESENTERS' OWN PROGRAMMES

Station presenters (excluding those involved in news and current affairs) may voice commercials within their own programmes provided that:

   i. a proper distinction and clear separation is maintained between the programming material they deliver and the advertisements they read;

   ii. the form of words and style of delivery do not imply that the presenter is endorsing the product or service advertised.

Rule 5: Unreasonable discrimination
A licensee must not unreasonably discriminate either against or in favour of any particular advertiser.

Practice Notes
Rule 5 is derived from Section 92(2)(b) of the Broadcasting Act 1990. Licensees are entitled to refuse advertising they do not wish to carry for legal or moral reasons but they must not unreasonably discriminate against or in favour of an advertiser. For example, to accept a commercial from one advertiser and decline a commercial from another simply because their products are competitors would constitute unreasonable discrimination.

If an advertiser believes he has been unreasonably discriminated against and has been unable to negotiate a settlement with the radio station, he is entitled to approach the Radio Authority with all relevant and detailed information.

Rule 6: Product placement
Product placement in programmes is prohibited.

Practice Note
The gratuitous *mentioning of brand names in programmes constitutes a form of indirect advertising and is contrary to this Code.*

Section B:
Standards for Advertisements

Rule 7: Misleadingness
(a) Advertisements must not contain any descriptions, claims or other material which might, directly or by implication, mislead about the product or service advertised or about its suitability for the purpose recommended.

(b) Advertisements must clarify any important limitations or qualifications without which a misleading impression of a product or service might be given.
(c) Before accepting advertisements licensees must be satisfied that any descriptions and claims have been adequately substantiated by the advertiser.

Practice Notes
'The Control of Misleading Advertisements Regulations 1988' define an advertisement as misleading if '. . . in any way, including its presentation, it deceives or is likely to deceive the persons to whom it is addressed . . . and if, by reason of its deceptive nature, it is likely to affect their economic behaviour or . . . injures or is likely to injure a competitor of the person whose interests the advertisement seeks to promote'.

Under the Regulations the Radio Authority has a specifiduty to investigate complaints (other than frivolous or vexatious ones) about alleged misleading advertisements. The Authority will require the removal of an advertisement which it has found to be misleading and is empowered to regard a factual claim as inaccurate unless adequate evidence of accuracy is provided when requested.

Advertisements must not misleadingly claim or imply that the product advertised, or an ingredient, has some special property or quality which cannot be established. Scientific terms, statistics, quotations from technical literature, etc. should be used with a proper sense of responsibility to the unsophisticated listener. Irrelevant data and scientific jargon should not be used to make claims appear to have a scientific basis they do not possess. Statistics of limited validity should not be presented in such a way as to make it appear that they are universally true.

Simple 'puffery' is acceptable in descriptions of products and services, as listeners can easily recognise and accept it for what it is. Any factual claim, however, needs substantiation and advertisers should be encouraged to provide supporting written evidence if the claim is likely to be challenged. Particular care is needed with superlative claims, e.g. 'cheapest', 'best', etc.

Rule 8: Political, industrial and public controversy
(a) No advertisement may be broadcast by, or on behalf of, any body whose objects are wholly or mainly of a political nature, and no advertisement may be directed towards any political end.
(b) No advertisement may have any relation to any industrial dispute (other than an advertisement of a public service nature inserted by, or on behalf of, a government department).
(c) No advertisement may show partiality in matters of political or industrial controversy or relating to current public policy.

Practice Notes
(a) The term 'political' here is used in a wider sense than 'party political'. The prohibition precludes, for example, issue campaigning for the purposes of influencing legislation or executive action by local or national government.
(b) The term 'industrial dispute' here includes strikes, walkouts and withdrawals of labour by workers, lockouts by employers, disputes between managements and differences between rival trade unions, etc. which are connected with the employment, nonemployment or terms and conditions of employment of any individual group. It makes no difference whether a dispute is official or unofficial.
Whilst it is unacceptable for a trade union to advertise for support in a ballot, advertising for members is not prohibited provided the advertisement itself is not politically or industrially contentious.
The Radio Authority will normally regard an advertisement as having 'any relation to any industrial dispute' when it considers it to be in furtherance of an industrial dispute or expressing partiality in relation to such a dispute. Announcements of the resumption of normal working following agreement between management and unions, or those concerned with public safety during, for example, a gas strike are not precluded.
(c) The Act requires that advertisements do not contain any words or phrases which could create or reinforce public opinion on controversial political, industrial or public policy questions.
Advertisements for newspapers which have an editorial stance in political or industrial affairs and current public policies are acceptable, provided the copy does not give any impression that a partisan point of view is being expressed. In practice, such advertisements either state facts and/or pose questions, e.g. 'Read our four-page story on the coal strike' or 'Will hospital services improve or deteriorate under new proposed legislation?'.
Advertisements which include references to any political, industrial or public controversy should be submitted for central copy clearance.

Rule 9: Taste and offence
Advertisements must not offend against good taste or decency or be offensive to public feeling.

Practice Notes
Standards of taste are subjective and individual reactions can differ considerably. Licensees are expected to exercise responsible judgements and to take account of the sensitivities of all sections of their audience when deciding on the acceptability or scheduling of advertisements.
The following points may help to ensure that offence is minimal:
(a) references to minority groups should not be unkind or hurtful;
(b) references to religious or political beliefs should not be deprecating or hurtful;

(c) special precautions should be taken to avoid demeaning or ridiculing listeners who may suffer from physical or mental difficulties or deformities;
(d) advertisements should avoid salacious or indecent themes and should not include any sexual innuendo or stereotyping;
(e) advertisements must avoid offensive and profane language;
(f) productions with salacious titles and clips from them should be carefully considered. Although it is recognised that the use of audio clips from advertised productions should portray their true nature, particular care must be exercised when selecting such clips – those containing bad language or sexual innuendo must be avoided;
(g) care should be exercised when promoting songs which contain words and phrases not normally acceptable. Some record titles and extracts of songs could result in widespread offence.

Rule 10: Protection of privacy and exploitation of the individual
Individual living persons must not normally be portrayed or referred to in advertisements without their prior permission.

Practice Notes
Advertisements for books, films, and particular editions of radio or television programmes, newspapers, magazines, etc. which feature the person referred to in the advertisement do not need prior permission, provided the reference or portrayal is neither offensive nor defamatory.
In the case of generic advertising for news media, the requirement for prior permission may also be waived if licensees reasonably expect that the individual concerned would have no reason to object. Such generic advertising must, however, be withdrawn if individuals portrayed without permission do object. If impersonations or soundalikes of celebrities or well-known characters are to be used, it is strongly advisable for advertisers to obtain advance permission. References to, and portrayals of, people active in politics should be carefully worded; they can easily fall foul of the requirements of the Act that political matters must be treated impartially and that advertisements must not be directed towards any political end.

Rule 11: Superstition and appeals to fear
Advertisements must not exploit the superstitious and must not, without justifiable reason, play on fear.

Practice Note
An example of a 'justifiable reason' would be where the aim of the advertisement was to influence listeners to take action to improve their own and their families' safety or welfare. Creating the impression of a person under threat from fire could be acceptable, for example, if the advertisement's function was to persuade adult listeners to fit a smoke alarm in their homes.

Rule 12: Price claims

Advertisements indicating price comparisons or reductions must comply with all relevant requirements of the Consumer Protection Act 1987 (Section III) and Regulations made under it.

Practice Notes

Actual and comparative prices quoted must be accurate at the time of broadcast and must not mislead. Claims of 'lowest prices' must be supported by evidence from the retailer that none of his competitors sell the advertised product or service at a lower price. Claims of 'unbeatable prices' or 'you can't buy cheaper' must be supported by evidence from the retailer that his prices are as low as his competitors.

All prices quoted in the advertisement should include VAT except for business-to-business and professional services where it must be made clear in the advertisement that prices are exclusive of VAT.

Rule 13: Comparisons

Advertisements containing comparisons with other advertisers, or other products, are permissible in the interest of vigorous competition and public information provided that:

(a) the principles of fair competition are respected and the comparisons used are not likely to mislead the listener about either product;
(b) points of comparison are based on fairly selected facts which can be substantiated;
(c) comparisons chosen do not give an advertiser an artificial advantage over his competitor;
(d) they comply with Rule 14.

Rule 14: Denigration

Advertisements must not unfairly attack or discredit other products, advertisers or advertisements directly or by implication.

Practice Note

Advertisers must not discredit competitors or their products by describing them in a derogatory way or in a denigratory tone of voice. This is particularly important in comparative advertising. Whilst it is acceptable for an advertiser whose product has a demonstrable advantage over a competitor to point this out, care must be taken to ensure that the competitor product is not depicted as generally unsatisfactory or inferior.

Rule 15: Testimonials

(a) Testimonials must be genuine and must not be misleading.
(b) Licensees must obtain satisfactory documentary evidence in support of

any testimonial or claim before accepting it for inclusion in an advertisement.

(c) Celebrities must not personally testify about a medicine or treatment.

(d) Children must not testify about any product or service.

Practice Notes

An expression of view or statement of experience of a real person in an advertisement is regarded as a testimonial.

A person's professional status may be used to lend authority to his/her opinions, e.g. 'I'm Miss X, actress and model, and I use Y soap because I think it's the creamiest'.

Celebrities may testify about products and services they use but must not present, endorse, recommend or personally testify about any medicine or treatment. They may, however, be the voiceover in an advertisement for a medicine or treatment if they are merely playing a role or speaking commentary.

Station presenters may not testify on their own station about any products or services they use.

Fictional playlets (i.e. where characters express, in dramatised form, the claims of an advertiser) are acceptable, provided it is made clear that the situation and people depicted are not real.

Rule 16: Guarantees

Advertisements must not contain the words 'guarantee', 'guaranteed', 'warranty' or 'warranted', or words with similar meaning, unless the licensee is satisfied that the terms of the guarantee are available for inspection if required and are outlined in the advertisement or are made available to the purchaser in writing at the point of sale or with the products.

Practice Notes

It is illegal for any guarantee to diminish the statutory or common law rights of the purchaser. A guarantee must include details of the remedial action open to the purchaser.

Use of the word 'guarantee' etc. is valid in advertisements when a material remedial action is offered to the purchaser in addition to legal requirements or accepted trade practice.

The colloquial use of the word 'guarantee' may be acceptable in contexts where its meaning cannot be construed as being part of an advertiser's offer.

Rule 17: Use of the word 'Free'

Advertisements must not describe products or samples as 'free' unless they are supplied at no cost or no extra cost (other than postage or carriage) to the recipient.

Practice Note
A trial may be described as 'free' provided that any subsequent financial oblig-
ations of the customer are specified in the advertisement, e.g. the cost of
returning the products in the case of dissatisfaction or the cost of the products
at the end of the trial period.

Rule 18: Competitions
Advertisements inviting listeners to take part in competitions are acceptable,
subject to Part III of the Lotteries and Amusements Act 1976 (which excludes
Northern Ireland).

Practice Notes
Licensees must be satisfied that prospective entrants can obtain printed
details of a competition, including announcement of results and distribution
of prizes.
Under the 1990 Act, there are no limitations on prize values.
Please see also competition rules in Appendices 2, 3 and 4.

Rule 19: Premium rate telephone services
Advertisements for premium rate telephone services must comply with the
ICSTIS (Independent Committee for the Supervision of Standards of Telephone Information Services) Code of Practice.
In particular
(a) pricing information should be given as 'Calls cost xp per minute cheap rate
   and xp per minute at all other times' or as the total maximum cost of the
   complete message or service to the consumer;
(b) the identity of either the service provider or the information provider must
   be stated in the advertisement;
(c) the address of either the service provider or the information provider must
   be stated in the advertisement unless licensees keep on file the relevant
   address and broadcast the following announcement (at an appropriate
   time, twice a day) when advertisements for premium rate telephone services are being transmitted: 'Addresses of all premium rate telephone services advertised on (station name) are available to enquirers by
   telephoning (station number)'.
(d) advertisements for recorded message services which normally last over
   five minutes must include a warning that use of the service(s) might
   involve a long call;
(e) advertisements for live conversation services must state that conversations
   are being continuously recorded;
(f) advertisements should not encourage people under 18 to call live conversation services.

Rule 20: **Matrimonial and introduction agencies**
Advertisements from agencies who offer introduction services for adults seeking long-term companionship are acceptable, subject to the following conditions:
(a) before accepting advertisements licensees must establish that those wishing to advertise conduct their business responsibly and can provide a level of service commensurate with the claims in their advertising;
(b) the advertiser must conduct business from premises which clients, actual or potential, or other interested parties can visit. The full postal address, or published telephone number for that address must be included in all advertisements;
(c) licensees must obtain an assurance that the advertiser will not disclose data to a third party without the client's consent, and that the client's name will be promptly deleted on request;
(d) any quoted price must be the price at which the full service described in the advertisement is actually available and any qualification or supplementary charge must be made clear;
(e) advertisements must not:
  i.   exploit emotional vulnerability by dwelling excessively on loneliness, or suggest that persons without a partner are in some way inadequate or unfulfilled;
  ii. contain material which could be taken to encourage or endorse promiscuity.

Practice Note
Agencies with computerised records must provide an assurance that they comply with the requirements of the Data Protection Act 1984.

Rule 21: **Sexual discrimination**
It is illegal (with a few exceptions) for an advertisement to discriminate against women or men in opportunities for employment, education or training.

Practice Note
The Sex Discrimination Acts 1975 and 1986 make it unlawful to discriminate solely on the grounds of sex. The Acts apply mainly to employment, education and training opportunities. There are a few exceptions; full details of which can be obtained from the Equal Opportunities Commission on 0161-833 9244.

Rule 22: **Racial discrimination**
(a) It is illegal (with a few exceptions) for an advertisement to discriminate against ethnic minorities.
(b) Advertisements must not include any material which might reasonably be construed by ethnic minorities to be hurtful or tasteless.

Practice Note
The Race Relations Act 1976 makes it unlawful to broadcast an advertisement which indicates or implies racial discrimination. There are a few exceptions; full details of which can be obtained from The Commission for Racial Equality on 0171-828 7022.

Rule 23: Sound effects
Advertisements must not include sounds likely to create a safety hazard to drivers.

Practice Note
Caution should be exercised when considering distracting or potentially alarming sound effects such as sirens, horns, screeching tyres, vehicle collisions and the like; they may be dangerous to those listening whilst driving.

Rule 24: Direct marketing
Advertisements for products and services offered by direct marketing methods (e.g. mail order and direct response) are acceptable, subject to the following conditions:
(a) arrangements must be made for enquirers to be informed by the licensee concerned of the name and full address of the advertiser if this is not given in the advertisement – the address given to enquirers must be in a form which enables them to locate the premises without further enquiry;
(b) licensees must be satisfied that adequate arrangements exist at that address for enquiries to be handled by a responsible person available on the premises during normal business hours;
(c) samples of products advertised should be made available at that address for public inspection, if requested;
(d) licensees must be satisfied that the advertiser can meet any reasonable demand created by the advertising (e.g. via assurances of adequate stock);
(e) the advertiser must be able to fulfil orders within a certain delivery period which must be stated in the advertisement. This should normally be 28 days unless licensees are satisfied that there are particular circumstances where it is reasonable for the advertiser to state in the advertisement a delivery period in excess of 28 days;
(f) licensees must be satisfied that fulfilment arrangements are in operation whereby monies sent by consumers are only released to the advertiser on receipt of evidence of despatch (unless licensees are satisfied that adequate alternative safeguards exist);
(g) an undertaking must be received from the advertiser that money will be refunded promptly and in full to consumers who can show justifiable cause for dissatisfaction with their purchase(s) or with delay in delivery;
(h) advertisers who offer products and services by direct marketing methods must be prepared to demonstrate or supply samples of products to

licensees in order that they may assess the validity of advertising claims;

(j) advertisers who intend to send a sales representative to a respondent's home or place of work must ensure that this intention is made clear either in the advertisement or at the time of response and that the respondent is given an adequate opportunity of refusing such a call. In the case of such advertising:

  i. advertisers must give adequate assurances that sales representatives will demonstrate and make available for sale the articles advertised;

  ii. it will be taken as prima facie evidence of misleading and unacceptable 'bait' advertising for the purpose of 'switch selling' if an advertiser's sales representative disparages or belittles the article advertised, reports unreasonable delays in obtaining delivery or otherwise puts difficulties in the way of its purchase with a view to selling an alternative article.

Practice Notes
Licensees must obtain assurances that advertisers with computerised records of respondents comply with the requirements of the Data Protection Act 1984. Appendix 3, Rule 7 prohibits advertisements which invite children to purchase products by mail or telephone.

Appendix 1:
Financial Advertising

In this Appendix, 'investment', 'investment business', 'investment advertisement' and 'authorised person' have the same meanings as in the Financial Services Act 1986.

Advertisements for investment, complex finance and consumer credit should be submitted for central copy clearance.

Rule 1: Legal responsibility
It is the responsibility of the advertiser to ensure that advertisements comply with all the relevant legal and regulatory requirements.

Rule 2: Misleadingness
Advertisements must present the financial offer or service in terms which do not mislead whether by exaggeration, omission or otherwise.

Rule 3: Investment advertisements
(a) PERMITTED CATEGORIES

  The following may be broadcast:

  i. investment advertisements issued by an authorised person, or those whose contents have been approved by an authorised person;

  ii. advertisements issued in respect of the investment business of an

authorised person, which are not themselves investment advertisements;

iii. investment advertisements which by virtue of the Financial Services
Act 1986 do not require to be issued or approved by an authorised person.

Practice Note
*Licensees may need to seek legal advice if an advertiser claims an advertise-
ment should be considered:*
i.   not to be an investment advertisement;
or
*ii. an investment advertisement which does not require to be issued or
approved by an authorised person.*

(b) APPROVAL OF INVESTMENT ADVERTISEMENTS
Before accepting investment advertisements to which Section 57 of the
Financial Services Act 1986 applies, licensees must be satisfied that:
i.   the compliance officer (or equivalent) of the advertiser, or authorised
person issuing or approving the proposed advertisement, has confirmed
that the final recorded version of the advertisement is in accordance
with the Rules of the Securities and Investments Board (SIB) or the relevant recognised Self Regulating Organisation (SRO) or Recognised Professional Body (RPB);
ii. an investment advertisement or other advertisement in respect of
investment business proposed by an appointed representative has
been approved by the authorised person to whom that person is responsible.

Practice Note
*Licensees may need to consult the relevant SRO or RPB or refer to the SIB con-
cerning the compliance of any advertisement with Financial Services Act 1986
requirements.*

Rule 4: Advertisements for deposit and savings facilities
The following deposit and savings facilities may be advertised:
(a) local government savings and deposit facilities in the United Kingdom, the
Isle of Man and the Channel Islands;
(b) such facilities provided in accordance with the Building Societies Act
1986 by building societies authorised under that Act;
(c) such facilities provided by the National Savings Bank, and authorised
institutions within the meaning of the Banking Act 1987;
(d) building society and authorised institutions' 'appropriate personal pen-
sion schemes' as established in accordance with the Social Security Act
1986;

(e) such facilities provided by registered Credit Unions regulated by the Credit Unions Act 1979;

(f) such facilities, guaranteed by the national government of an EC country, in currencies other than sterling, provided that a warning statement is included as to the effects of exchange rate fluctuations on the value of savings.

Practice Notes
Acceptance of advertisements in connection with deposit facilities is subject to any regulations made under Section 32 of the Banking Act 1987.
Rule 4 does not authorise the issue of any investment advertisement.

Rule 5: Interest on savings
References to interest payable on savings are acceptable, subject to the following:

(a) they must be stated clearly and be factually correct at the time of broadcast;

(b) calculations of interest must not be based on unstated factors (e.g. minimum sum deposited, minimum deposit period, or minimum period of notice for withdrawal) which might affect the sum received by individuals or be capable of misunderstanding in any other way;

(c) it must be made clear whether the interest is gross or net of tax;

(d) interest rates relating to variables (e.g. a bank's base rate) must be so described.

Practice Note
Attention is drawn to the code on the conduct of the advertising of interest-bearing accounts adopted and implemented by the Building Societies Association, British Bankers' Association and the Finance Houses Association.

Rule 6: Insurance advertisements

(a) LIFE ASSURANCE AND DISABILITY INSURANCE POLICIES
Except with the prior approval of the Authority, such policies (not constituting investments) may only be advertised by:

   i. companies authorised to carry on long term business under the Insurance Companies Act 1982;

   ii. companies who have complied with Schedule 2F of the Insurance Companies Act 1982 in respect of carrying an insurance business or providing insurance in the UK;

   iii. registered friendly societies under the Friendly Societies Act 1974 or the Friendly Societies (Northern Ireland) Act 1970 and authorised under the Friendly Societies (Long Term Insurance Business) Regulations 1987.

(b) GENERAL INSURANCE COVER
Except with the prior approval of the Authority, such cover (e.g. for motor, household, fire and personal injury) may only be advertised by:

   i. insurance companies who carry on business under the Insurance Companies Act 1982, or have complied with Schedule 2F of that Act in respect of carrying on insurance business or providing insurance in the UK.

   ii. Lloyd's underwriting syndicates.

(c) INSURANCE BROKERAGE SERVICES

Except with the prior approval of the Authority, general insurance, sickness insurance and other forms of long term assurance which are not covered by the Financial Services Act 1986 may only be advertised by:

   i. brokers registered under the Insurance Brokers (Registration) Act 1977 or bodies corporate enrolled under that Act;

   ii. intermediaries who have undertaken to abide by the provisions of the Association of British Insurers Code for the Selling of General Insurance;

   iii. building societies empowered to offer such services in accordance with the Building Societies Act 1986.

Rule 7: Insurance premiums and cover

Subject to any applicable legal requirement:

(a) references to rates and conditions in connection with insurance must be accurate and must not mislead;

(b) when specifying rates of premium cover, there must be no misleading omission of conditions;

(c) in life insurance advertising, reference to specific sums assured must be accompanied by all relevant qualifying conditions, e.g. age and sex of the assured at the outset of the policy, period of policy and amount and number of premiums payable.

Rule 8: Lending and credit advertisements

(a) PERMITTED CATEGORIES

The advertising of mortgage, other lending facilities and credit services is acceptable from:

   i. Government and local government agencies;

   ii. building societies authorised under the Building Societies Act 1986;

   iii. authorised or permitted insurance companies;

   iv. registered Friendly Societies;

   v. authorised institutions under the Banking Act 1987;

   vi. registered Credit Unions regulated by the Credit Unions Act 1979;

   vii.those persons and bodies granted a licence under the terms of the Consumer Credit Act 1974.

Practice Note

Advertisers are reminded of the need for advertisements offering credit to comply with all relevant requirements of the Consumer Credit (Advertise-

ments) Regulations 1989. Where there is doubt about the applicability or interpretation of these Regulations, advertisers should be encouraged to seek guidance from their Local Trading Standards department.

(b) MORTGAGES AND RE-MORTGAGES

The following should be noted:

i. advertisements for mortgages and remortgages are credit advertisements and the requirements of the Consumer Credit (Advertisements) Regulations 1989 therefore apply. Particular note should be taken of the requirements in these Regulations for secured loans;

ii. advertisements for mortgages may, in some circumstances, also be considered as investment advertisements under the terms of the Financial Services Act 1986 and particular note should therefore be taken of the rules of the relevant SRO and RPB.

Rule 9: **Tax benefits**

References to income tax and other tax benefits must be properly qualified, clarifying what they mean in practice and making it clear, where appropriate, that the full advantage may only be received by those paying income tax at the standard rate.

Rule 10: **Direct remittance**

Advertisements are unacceptable if they directly or indirectly invite the remittance of money direct to the advertiser or any other person without offering an opportunity to receive further details.

Rule 11: **Financial publications**

(a) Advertisements for publications, including periodicals, books, teletext services and other forms of electronic publishing, on investments and other financial matters must make no recommendation on any specific investment offer.

(b) Advertisements for subscription services must be in general terms and make no reference to any specific investment offer.

Rule 12: **Unacceptable categories of advertisement**

Please see Section A, Rule 3.

Appendix 2:
Alcoholic Drink Advertising

Advertisements in this category should be submitted for central copy clearance.

These rules apply principally to advertisements for alcoholic drinks and low alcoholic drinks but the incidental portrayal of alcohol consumption in advertisements for other products and services must always be carefully considered to ensure that it does not contradict the spirit of these rules.

Rule 1: Distribution of advertisements for alcohol
Advertisements for alcoholic drinks must not be broadcast in or around religious programmes or programmes/features directed particularly at people under 18 (please see Section A, Rule 2).

Rule 2: Protection of the young
(a) Alcoholic drink advertising must not be directed at people under 18 or use treatments likely to be of particular appeal to them.
(b) Advertisements for alcoholic drinks must not include any personality whose example people under 18 are likely to follow or who have a particular appeal to people under 18.
(c) Advertisements for alcoholic drinks must only use voiceovers of those who are, and sound to be, at least 25 years of age.
(d) Advertisements for drinks containing less than 1.2% alcohol by volume must only use voiceovers of those who are, and sound to be, at least 18 years of age.
(e) Children's voices must not be heard in advertisements for alcoholic drinks.

Rule 3: Unacceptable treatments
(a) Advertisements must not imply that drinking is essential to social success or acceptance or that refusal is a sign of weakness. Nor must they imply that the successful outcome of a social occasion is dependent on the consumption of alcohol.
(b) Advertisements must neither claim nor suggest that any drink can contribute towards sexual success or that drinking can enhance sexual attractiveness.
(c) Advertisements must not suggest that regular solitary drinking is acceptable or that drinking is a means of resolving personal problems. Nor must they imply that drinking is an essential part of daily routine or can bring about a change in mood.
(d) Advertisements must not suggest or imply that drinking is an essential attribute of masculinity. References to daring, toughness or bravado in association with drinking are not acceptable.
(e) Alcoholic drinks must not be advertised in a context of aggressive, antisocial or irresponsible behaviour.
(f) Advertisements must not foster, depict or imply immoderate drinking or drinking at speed. References to buying rounds of drinks are unacceptable.
(g) Advertisements must not offer alcohol as therapeutic, or as a stimulant, sedative, tranquilliser or source of nourishment/ goodness. While advertisements may refer to refreshment after physical performance, they must

not give any impression that performance can be improved by drink.
(h) Advertisements must not suggest that a drink is preferable because of its higher alcohol content or intoxicating effect and must not place undue emphasis on alcoholic strength.

Rule 4: Safety
(a) Nothing in any advertisement may link drinking with driving or with the use of potentially dangerous machinery.
(b) Nothing in any advertisement may link alcohol with a work or other unsuitable environment.

Rule 5: Competitions and promotions
Alcoholic drink advertisements must not publicise competitions. Alcoholic drink advertisements must not publicise sales promotions which encourage or require multiple purchase.

Rule 6: Cut-price offers
References to 'cut-price/happy hour drinks', 'buy two and get one free', 'money-off coupons' and the like must be considered with extreme caution by licensees. Those references which encourage excessive or immoderate drinking are unacceptable. However, off-licences and alcoholic drink retailers may advertise price reductions for their stock.

Rule 7: Humour
Advertisements may employ humour but not so as to circumvent the intention of any of these rules.

Rule 8: Low alcohol drinks
Provided they comply with the generality of the Code and reflect responsible consumption and behaviour, advertisements for drinks containing less than 1.2% alcohol by volume will not normally be subject to rules 3(f), 4(b) and 5. However, if the licensee considers that a significant purpose of an advertisement for a low alcoholic drink is to promote a brand of stronger alcoholic drink or if the drink's low alcohol content is not stated in the advertisement, all the above rules are applicable.

Appendix 3:
Advertising and children

For the purpose of this Appendix, the Authority considers that children are aged 15 and below.

Rule 1: **Misleadingness**
Advertisements addressed to the child listener must not exaggerate or mislead about the size, qualities or capabilities of products or about the sounds they might produce.

Rule 2: **Prices**
Prices of products advertised to children must not be minimised by words such as 'only' or 'just'.

Rule 3: **Immaturity and credulity**
Advertisements must not take advantage of the immaturity or natural credulity of children.

Rule 4: **Appeals to loyalty**
Advertisements must not take advantage of the sense of loyalty of children or suggest that unless children buy or encourage others to buy a product or service they will be failing in some duty or lacking in loyalty.

Rule 5: **Inferiority**
Advertisements must not lead children to believe that unless they have or use the product advertised they will be inferior in some way to other children or liable to be held in contempt or ridicule.

Rule 6: **Direct exhortation**
Advertisements must not directly urge children to buy products or to ask adults to buy products for them. For example, children must not be directly invited to 'ask Mum' or 'ask Dad' to buy them an advertiser's product.

Rule 7: **Direct response**
Advertisements must not invite children to purchase products by mail or telephone.

Rule 8: **Competitions**
(a) References to competitions for children are acceptable provided that any skill required is appropriate to the age of likely participants and the values of the prizes and the chances of winning are not exaggerated.
(b) The published rules must be submitted in advance to the licensee and the principal conditions of the competition must be included in the advertisement.

Rule 9: **Free gifts**
References to 'free' gifts for children in advertisements must include all qualifying conditions, e.g. any time limit, how many products need to be bought, how many wrappers need to be collected, etc.

Rule 10: Health and hygiene
(a) Advertisements must not encourage children to eat frequently throughout the day.
(b) Advertisements must not encourage children to consume food or drink (especially sweet, sticky products) near bedtime.
(c) Advertisements for confectionery and snack foods must not suggest that such products may be substituted for balanced meals.

Rule 11: Children as presenters
(a) The participation of children in radio commercials is acceptable, subject to all relevant legal requirements.
(b) If children are employed in commercials, they must not be used to present products or services which they could not be expected to buy themselves. They must not make significant comments on characteristics of products and services about which they could not be expected to have direct knowledge.

Rule 12: Testimonials
Children must not personally testify about products and services. They may, however, give spontaneous comments on matters in which they would have an obvious natural interest.

Appendix 4:
Medicines, treatments and health

With the introduction of new or changed products, the diverse licensing requirements of the Medicines Act 1968 and changes in medical opinion on particular issues, this Appendix cannot provide a complete conspectus of required standards in relation to health claims or the advertising of particular products or classes of medicines and treatments. The general principles governing the advertising of medicines, treatments and health claims (including veterinary products and services) are set out below.
Advertisements in this category should be submitted for central copy clearance.

Rule 1: Legal responsibility
Advertisements for products subject to licensing under the Medicines Act 1968 must comply with the requirements of the Act, Regulations made under it and any conditions contained in the product licence.

Rule 2: Claims
Claims about any type of product or treatment which fall within this Appendix require very close scrutiny. Whenever a proper assessment of such claims

can only be made by a medically qualified expert, appropriate independent medical advice should be sought before acceptance. This includes claims relating to the nutritional, therapeutic or prophylactic effects of products such as food or toilet products.

Practice Note
The Radio Authority has access to a panel of eminent consultants* nominated by the leading medical professional bodies to advise it on health and medical aspects of advertising (*the Medical Advisory Panel – MAP). Medical claims in radio advertisements are referred by the Broadcast Advertising Clearance Centre (BACC) to members of this panel.

Rule 3: EC Council Directive 92/28/EEC
The above Directive concerns 'The Advertising of Medicinal Products for Human Use' and has been implemented in the UK by The Medicines (Advertising) Regulations 1994 and The Medicines (Monitoring of Advertising) Regulations 1994. The latter Regulations require the Radio Authority to investigate complaints about alleged breaches of Regulation 8 of The Medicines (Advertising) Regulations 1994 and take appropriate action if necessary. The requirements of Regulation 8 are incorporated in the Rules of this Appendix.

Rule 4: Prescription-only medicines
Advertisements for medicinal products or treatments available only on prescription are not acceptable.

Rule 5: Products without a product licence
Advertisements for products which do not hold a product licence under the Medicines Act 1968 must not include medical claims.

Rule 6: Mandatory information
Advertisements for medicinal products must include the following information:
(a) the name of the product;
(b) the name of the active ingredient, if it contains only one;
(c) an indication of what the product is for;
(d) wording such as 'always read the label' or 'always read the leaflet' as appropriate.

Rule 7: Unacceptable references
Advertisements must not refer to the fact that a medicinal product has been granted a product licence or contain any reference to the European Commission or the Medicines Control Agency (unless the MCA require such a reference).

Rule 8: **Medicines and children**
Advertisements for medicinal products and treatments must not be directed exclusively or principally at children (i.e. those aged 15 and below).

Rule 9: **Conditions requiring medical advice**
Advertisements must not offer any product for a condition for which qualified medical advice should be sought or give the impression that a medical consultation or surgical operation is unnecessary (this excludes advertisements for spectacles, contact lenses and hearing aids).

Rule 10: **Commercial services or clinics offering medical advice and treatments**
Advertisements are only acceptable if the organisation wishing to advertise provides an assurance that it is registered with its Local Health Authority or is otherwise approved following referral to the Medical Advisory Panel (MAP). Central copy clearance is required.

Rule 11: **Avoidance of impressions of professional support and advice**
The following are not acceptable:
(a) presentations by doctors, nurses, midwives, dentists, pharmaceutical chemists, veterinary surgeons, etc. which give the impression of professional advice or recommendation;
(b) statements which give the impression of professional advice or recommendation by people who feature in the advertisements and who are presented as being qualified to do so;
(c) references to approval of, or preference for, a product or its ingredients or their use by the professions listed at (a).

Rule 12: **Homoeopathic medicinal products**
Advertisements for homoeopathic medicines are acceptable, subject to all relevant requirements of EC Directive 92/73/EEC on homoeopathic medicinal products. In particular:
(a) advertisements are only acceptable for products which have been registered in the UK;
(b) product information must be confined to that which appears on product labelling (a statutory requirement). Advertisements may not, therefore, include medicinal or therapeutic claims or refer to a particular ailment;
(c) advertisements must include wording such as 'always read the label' or 'always read the leaflet' as appropriate.

Rule 13: **Celebrities**
Advertisements for medicines and treatments must not be presented by, or include testimonials from, persons well known in public life, sport, entertainment, etc.

Rule 14: **Cure**
Words or phrases which claim or imply the cure of any ailment, illness, disease or addiction as distinct from the relief of its symptoms are unacceptable. (Words such as 'help' or 'relieve' should be used.)

Rule 15: **Tonic**
Unless authorised by its product licence, the word 'tonic' is not acceptable in advertisements for products making health claims.

Rule 16: **Unacceptable descriptions**
Advertisements must not suggest that any medicinal product is a food stuff, cosmetic or other consumer product.

Rule 17: **Diagnosis, prescription or treatment by correspondence**
Advertisements must not contain any offer by correspondence (including post, telephone or facsimile) to diagnose, advise, prescribe or treat.

Rule 18: **Self-diagnosis**
Advertisements for medicinal products must not contain any material which could, by description or detailed representation of a case history, lead to erroneous self-diagnosis.

Rule 19: **Guarantee of efficacy**
Advertisements for medicinal products must not claim or imply that the effects of taking the product are guaranteed.

Rule 20: **Side effects**
Advertisements for medicinal products must not suggest that the effects of taking the product are unaccompanied by side effects. (It is acceptable to highlight the absence of a specific side effect, e.g. 'no drowsiness'.)

Rule 21: **'Natural' products**
Advertisements for medicinal products must not suggest that the safety or efficacy of the product is due to the fact that it is 'natural'.

Rule 22: **Claims of recovery**
Advertisements for medicinal products must not refer to claims of recovery in improper, alarming or misleading terms.

Rule 23: **Appeals to fear or exploitation of credulity**
(a) No advertisement may cause those who hear it unwarranted anxiety if they are suffering or may suffer (if they do not respond to the advertiser's offer) from any disease or condition of ill health.
(b) Advertisements must not falsely suggest that any product is necessary for

the maintenance of health or the retention of physical or mental capacities (whether by people in general or by particular groups) or that health could be affected by not taking the product.

Rule 24: Encouragement of excess
Advertisements must not imply or encourage indiscriminate, unnecessary or excessive use of any medicinal product or treatment.

Rule 25: Exaggeration
Advertisements must not make any exaggerated claims, in particular through the selection of testimonials or other evidence unrepresentative of a product's effectiveness, or by claiming that it possesses some special property or quality which cannot be substantiated.

Rule 26: Comparisons
Advertisements for medicinal products or treatments must not suggest that the effects of taking the product are better than, or equivalent to, those of another, identified or identifiable medicinal product or treatment.

Rule 27: Analgesics
A 'tension headache' is a recognised medical condition and analgesics may be advertised for the relief of pain associated with it. However, no simple or compound analgesic may be advertised for the direct relief of tension. In such advertisements there must be no references to depression.

Rule 28: Food and beverages
Advertisers must ensure that their advertisements comply with all relevant legislation, in particular The Food Labelling Regulations 1984 and The Food Safety Act 1990.

Rule 29: Generalised health claims for food
Generalised claims such as 'goodness' or 'wholesome' may imply that a food product or an ingredient has a greater nutritional or health benefit than is actually the case. In some instances, reference to the properties of a particular ingredient may give a misleading impression of the properties of the product taken as a whole. Such claims are unacceptable unless supported by sound medical evidence.

Practice Note
Particular attention should also be paid to the requirements of the Food Labelling Regulations 1984, especially the prohibited and restricted claims set out in Schedule 6.

Rule 30: **Dietary supplements**
(a) Advertisements for dietary supplements, including vitamins or minerals, must not state or imply that they are necessary to avoid dietary deficiency or that they can enhance normal good health.
(b) Restrained advertisements for vitamins or minerals related to the dietary requirements of growing children, pregnant or lactating women or the elderly may be accepted subject to qualified medical advice.

Rule 31: **Slimming products, treatments and establishments**
(a) Advertisements for slimming products, treatments and establishments must be submitted for central copy clearance.
(b) Advertisements for slimming products and treatments must make it clear that weight loss can only be achieved as part of a controlled diet.
(c) Advertisements for establishments offering slimming treatments are acceptable only if such treatments are based on dietary control, which must be specified in the advertisement. Licensees must have obtained acceptable independent medical advice that the treatments are likely to be effective and will not lead to harm; and satisfied themselves that any claims can be substantiated. Any financial and other contractual conditions must be made available in writing to customers prior to commitment.

Rule 32: **Sanitary towels and tampons**
(a) Particular care is required when scheduling advertisements for sanitary protection products (please see Section A, Rule 2).
(b) Central copy clearance for advertisements for sanitary protection products is required.
(c) Copy must not contain anything likely to embarrass or undermine an individual's confidence in her own personal hygiene standards.
(d) Care must be taken to ensure that any detailed description of the product avoids anything which might offend or embarrass listeners.
(e) No implication of, or appeal to, sexual or social insecurity is acceptable.
(f) References to sexual relationships are best avoided.
(g) Female voiceovers are more appropriate than male ones and men should not feature prominently in advertisements.
(h) Particular discretion is required where an advertiser wishes to communicate a product's suitability to very young women.
(j) Comparative advertising is acceptable but commercials must not disparage other products, either directly or by implication.
(k) Normal marketing techniques are acceptable, e.g. pack offers, samples, etc.

Rule 33: **Family planning services**
(a) Particular care is required when scheduling advertisements for family planning services (please see Section A, Rule 2).

(b) Central copy clearance for advertisements for family planning services is required.
(c) Advertisements are acceptable only from family planning centres approved by a Local Health Authority, the Health Education Authority or the Central Office of Information.

Rule 34: **Pregnancy-testing kits and services**
(a) Particular care is required when scheduling advertisements for pregnancy-testing kits and services (please see Section A, Rule 2).
(b) Central copy clearance for pregnancy-testing kits and services is required.

Rule 35: **Contraceptives**
(a) Particular care is required when scheduling advertisements for contraceptives (please see Section A, Rule 2).
(b) Central copy clearance for advertisements for contraceptives is required.
(c) Advertisements must not promote or condone promiscuity.

Rule 36: **Anti-AIDS and anti-drugs advertising**
(a) Particular care is required when scheduling anti-AIDS and anti-drugs messages (please see Section A, Rule 2).
(b) Central copy clearance for anti-AIDS and anti-drugs messages is required.
(c) Advertisements are acceptable only from bodies approved by a Local Health Authority, the Health Education Authority or the Central Office of Information.

Rule 37: **Refund of money**
Advertisements must not contain any offer to refund money to dissatisfied users of any product or service within the scope of this Appendix (other than appliances or therapeutic clothing).

Rule 38: **Sales promotions**
Advertisements for medicinal products or treatments must not contain references to sales promotions (includes competitions, premium offers, samples).

Rule 39: **Jingles**
Jingles may be used but must not incorporate any medical/health claim.

Rule 40: **Unacceptable categories of advertisement**
Please see Section A, Rule 3.

(Reproduced by kind permission of the Radio Authority. Further information about this code can be obtained from: Holbrooke House, 14 Great Queen Street, London WC2B 5DG.)

Appendix E:
The British Code of
Sales Promotion Practice

Introduction
26.1 The Sales Promotion Code should be read, where appropriate, in conjunction with the rules in the Advertising and Cigarette Codes. The Specific Rules and the sections headed Introduction, Legislation and How the System Works are common to both Codes.
26.2 The Sales Promotion Code is designed primarily to protect the public but it also applies to trade promotions and incentive schemes and to the promotional elements of sponsorships.
26.3 The Sales Promotion Code regulates the nature and administration of promotional marketing techniques. These techniques generally involve providing a range of direct or indirect additional benefits, usually on a temporary basis, designed to make goods or services more attractive to purchasers.

Principles
27.1 All sales promotions should be legal, decent, honest and truthful.
27.2 All sales promotions should be prepared with a sense of responsibility to consumers and to society; they should be conducted equitably, promptly and efficiently and should be seen to deal fairly and honourably with consumers. Promoters should avoid causing unnecessary disappointment.
27.3 All sales promotions should respect the principles of fair competition generally accepted in business.
27.4 No promoter or intermediary should bring sales promotion into disrepute.
27.5 Sales promotions must conform with the Codes. Primary responsibility for observing the Codes falls on promoters. Intermediaries and agents also accept an obligation to abide by the Codes.
27.6 Any unreasonable delay in responding to the ASA's enquiries may be considered a breach of the Codes.
27.7 The ASA will on request treat in confidence any private or secret material supplied unless the Courts or officials acting within their statutory powers compel its disclosure.
27.8 The Codes are applied in the spirit as well as in the letter.

Public interest

28.1 Sales promotions should not be designed or conducted in a way that conflicts with the public interest. They should contain nothing that condones or is likely to provoke violent or anti-social behaviour, nuisance, personal injury or damage to property.

Substantiation

29.1 Promoters must be able to demonstrate that they have complied with the Codes by submitting documentary evidence without delay when asked by the ASA. The adequacy of evidence will be judged on whether it supports the detailed claims, on the way in which the sales promotion is administered and on the overall impression created by the promotion.

Legality

30.1 Promoters have primary responsibility for ensuring that what they do is legal. Sales promotions should contain nothing that breaks the law or incites anyone to break it, and should omit nothing that the law requires.

Honesty

31.1 Promoters should not abuse consumers' trust or exploit their lack of knowledge or experience.

Truthfulness

32.1 No sales promotion should mislead by inaccuracy, ambiguity, exaggeration, omission or otherwise.

Protection of consumers and promoters

33.1 Promotions involving adventurous activities should be made as safe as possible by the promoters. Every effort should be made to avoid harming consumers when distributing product samples. Special care should be taken when sales promotions are addressed to children or when products intended for adults may fall into the hands of children. Literature accompanying promotional items should give any necessary safety warnings.

33.2 Promotions should be designed and conducted in a way that respects the right of consumers to a reasonable degree of privacy and freedom from annoyance.

33.3 Consumers should be told before entry if participants may be required to become involved in any of the promoters' publicity or advertising, whether it is connected with the sales promotion or not. Prizewinners should not be compromised by the publication of excessively detailed information.

33.4 Promoters and others responsible for administering sales promotions

should ensure that the way they compile and use lists containing personal information about consumers conforms to the Specific Rules on
List and Database Practice.

Suitability

34.1 Promoters should make every effort to ensure that unsuitable or inappropriate material does not reach consumers. Neither the sales promotions themselves nor the promotional items should cause offence.
Promotions should not be socially undesirable to the audience
addressed by encouraging either excessive consumption or inappropriate use.

34.2 Alcoholic drinks and tobacco products should not feature in sales
promotions addressed to people who are under eighteen and tobacco
promotions should be addressed only to existing smokers.

Availability

35.1 Promoters should be able to demonstrate that they have made a reasonable estimate of likely response and that they are capable of meeting that
response. This applies in all cases except prize promotions, where the
number of prizes available to be awarded should be made clear to participants.

35.2 Phrases such as 'subject to availability' do not relieve promoters of the
obligation to take all reasonable steps to avoid disappointing participants.

35.3 If promoters are unable to supply demand for a promotional offer
because of any unexpectedly high response or some other unanticipated
factor outside their control, products of a similar or greater quality and
value or a cash payment should normally be substituted.

Children

36.1 For the purposes of this Code, a child or young person is someone under
the age of sixteen.

Participation

37.1 Sales promotions should specify:
a) how to participate, including any conditions and costs
b) the promoters' full name and business address in a form that can be
retained by consumers
c) a prominent closing date if applicable; where the final date for purchase of the promoted product differs from the closing date for the submission of claims or entries, this should be made clear to participants
d) any proof of purchase requirements; this information should be
emphasised for example by using bold type, separating it from other
text or using a different colour

e) where it is not obvious, if there is likely to be a limitation on the availability of promotional packs in relation to any stated closing date of the offer

f) where applicable, geographical or personal restrictions, including whether permission is needed from an adult

g) any other factor likely to influence consumers' decisions or understanding about the promotion

h)that any deadline for responding to an undated mailing will be calculated from the date the mailing was received by consumers.

Administration

38.1 Sales promotions should be conducted under proper supervision and adequate resources should be made available to administer them. Promoters and intermediaries should not give consumers any justifiable grounds for complaint.

38.2 Promoters should allow ample time for each phase of the promotion: notifying the trade, distributing the goods, issuing rules where appropriate, collecting wrappers and the like, judging and announcing the results.

38.3 Promoters should fulfil applications within thirty days unless:
a) participants have been told in advance that it is impractical to do so
b)participants are informed promptly of unforeseen delays and are offered another delivery date or an opportunity to recover any money paid for the offer.

38.4 When damaged or faulty goods are received by consumers, promoters should ensure that they are either replaced without delay or that a refund is sent immediately. The full cost of replacing damaged or faulty goods should fall on promoters. If an applicant does not receive goods, promoters should normally replace them free of charge.

Free offers and promotions where consumers pay

39.1 In the case of free offers and offers where a payment is required, consumers should be informed if any other conditions apply.

39.2 There is no objection to making a free offer conditional on the purchase of other items. Consumers' liability for any costs should be made clear in all material featuring the offer. An offer should only be described as free if consumers pay no more than:
a) the current public rates of postage
b)the actual cost of freight or delivery
c) the cost, including incidental expenses, of any travel involved if consumers collect the offer.
Promoters should make no additional charges for packing and handling.

39.3 Promoters must not attempt to recover their costs by reducing the quality or composition or by inflating the price of any product that must be purchased as a pre-condition of obtaining a free item.

39.4 Promoters should provide a cash refund, postal order or personal cheque promptly to consumers participating in 'try me free' offers or those with a money-back guarantee.

Promotions with prizes

40.1 Promotions with prizes including competitions, free draws and instant win offers are subject to legal restrictions. Promoters should take legal advice before embarking on such schemes.

40.2 Before making a purchase, participants should be informed of:
a) the closing date for receipt of entries
b) any geographical or personal restrictions such as location or age
c) any requirements for proof of purchase
d) the need to obtain permission to enter from an adult or employer
e) the nature of any prizes.

40.3 Before entry, participants should be informed:
a) of any restrictions on the number of entries or prizes
b) if a cash alternative can be substitu-ted for any prize
c) how and when winners will be notified of results
d) how and when winners and results will be announced
e) of the criteria for judging entries
f) where appropriate, who owns the copyright of the entries
g) whether and how entries will be returned by promoters
h) of any intention to use winners in post-event publicity.

40.4 Complex rules should be avoided and promoters should not need to supplement conditions of entry with additional rules. If further rules cannot be avoided, participants should be informed how to obtain them; the rules should contain nothing that would have influenced consumers against making a purchase or participating. Participants should always be able to retain entry instructions and rules.

40.5 The closing date for entry to a prize promotion should not be changed unless circumstances outside the reasonable control of the promoters make it unavoidable.

40.6 A poor response or an inferior quality of entries is not an acceptable basis for extending the duration of a promotion or withholding prizes unless the promoters have announced their intention to do so at the out-set.

40.7 Promoters must either publish or make available on request details of the name and county of major prizewinners and their winning entries. They should make clear in promotional material how this will be done.

40.8 Unless otherwise stated in advance, prizewinners should receive their prizes no more than six weeks after the promotion has ended.

40.9 If the selection of winning entries is open to subjective interpretation, an independent judge, or a panel including one member who is independent of the competition's promoters and intermediaries, should be appointed. Those appointed to act as judges should be competent to judge the subject matter of the competition. The identity of judges should be made available on request.

40.10 Promoters should ensure that tokens, tickets or numbers for instant win and similar promotions are allocated on a fair and random basis. An independent observer should supervise prize draws to ensure that participants have an equal opportunity of winning.

40.11 Participants in instant win promotions should get their winnings at once or should know immediately what they have won and how to claim it without delay, unreasonable costs or administrative barriers.

40.12 When prize promotions are widely advertised, promoters should ensure that entry forms and any goods needed to establish proof of purchase are widely available.

40.13 The distinction between a prize and a gift should always be clear to consumers. Gifts offered to all or most participants in a promotion should not be described as prizes. If promoters offer a gift to all entrants in addition to giving a prize to those who win, particular care is needed to avoid confusing the two.

40.14 Promoters should avoid exaggerating the likelihood of consumers winning a prize.

Advertisement promotions

41.1   Advertisement promotions should be designed and presented in such a way that they can be easily distinguished from editorial.

41.2   Features, announcements or promotions that are disseminated in exchange for a payment or other reciprocal arrangement should comply with the Codes if their content is controlled by the promoters.

41.3   Publishers announcing reader promotions on the front page or cover should ensure that consumers know whether they will be expected to buy subsequent editions of the publication. Major qualifications that may influence consumers significantly in their decision to purchase the publication should appear on the front page or cover.

Charity-linked promotions

42.1   Promotions claiming that participation will benefit registered charities or good causes should:
a) name each charity or good cause that will benefit, and be able to demonstrate to the ASA that those benefiting consent to the advertising or promotion
b) when it is not a registered charity, define its nature and objectives
c) specify exactly what will be gained by the named charity or cause and state the basis on which the contribution will be calculated

d) state if the promoters have imposed any limitations on the contribution they will make out of their own
pocket

e) not limit consumers' contributions; any extra money collected should be given to the named charity or cause on the same basis as contributions below that level

f) not exaggerate the benefit to the charity or cause derived from individual purchases of the promoted product

g) if asked, make available to consumers a current or final total of contributions made

h) take particular care when appealing to children.

Trade incentives

43.1 Incentive schemes should be designed and implemented to take account of the interests of everyone involved and should not compromise the obligation of employees to give honest advice to consumers.

43.2 Promoters should secure the prior agreement of employers or of the manager responsible if they intend to ask for assistance from, or offer incentives to, any other company's employees. Promoters should observe any procedures established by companies for their employees, including any rules for participating in promotions. In the case of a trade incentive scheme that has been generally advertised rather than individually targeted, employees should be asked to obtain their employer's permission before participating.

43.3 It should be made clear to those benefiting from an incentive scheme that they may be liable for tax.

(Reproduced by kind permission of the Committee of Advertising Practice. Further information about this Code can be obtained from: 2 Torrington Place, London WC1E 7HN.)

Appendix F: The Data Protection Act 1984

Purpose of the Act

Computers are in use throughout society – collecting, storing, processing and distributing information. Much of that information is about people – 'personal data' – and is subject to the Data Protection Act 1984.

The Act is derived from the Council of Europe Convention for the Protection of Individuals with regard to Automatic Processing of Personal Data (European Treaty Series No.108) which was opened for signature on 28 January 1981. That Convention set out to maintain a 'just balance between the different rights and interests of individuals' and in particular between the freedom to process information on the one hand and rights of privacy on the other. Enacting the Data Protection Act allowed the United Kingdom to ratify Convention 108 so that data might flow freely between the United Kingdom and other countries with similar laws.

The Act gives rights to individuals about whom information is recorded on computer. They may find out information about themselves, challenge it if appropriate and claim compensation in certain circumstances. The Act places obligations on those who record and use personal data (data users). They must be open about that use (through the Data Protection Register) and follow sound and proper practices (the Data Protection Principles).

The Act has improved practices among computer users and raised public confidence in computing and continues to do so.

When interpreting the Act, the Data Protection Tribunal has taken the following approach:

'It is quite clear, from the Act as a whole and in particular from the Data Protection Principles set out in Schedule 1, that the purpose of the Act is to protect the rights of the individual about whom data is obtained, stored, processed or supplied, rather than those of the data user.'

What the Act covers

The Act only applies to automatically processed information – broadly speaking, information which is processed by a computer. The Act does not cover all computerised information but only that which relates to living individuals. It does not cover information on individuals which is held and processed manually – for example, in ordinary paper files.

The Act uses some unfamiliar words and phrases and it is important to grasp their meaning because they define how the Act works.

Personal data

Information recorded on a computer about living, identifiable individuals. Statements of fact and expressions of opinion about an individual are personal data but an indication of the data user's intentions towards the individual is not.

Data subject

An individual to whom personal data relate.

Data users

People or organizations who control the contents and use of a collection of personal data. A data user will usually be a company, corporation or other organization but it is possible for an individual to be a data user.

Computer bureaux

People or organizations who process personal data for data users or who cause – even indirectly – personal data to be processed for data users, or who allow data users to process personal data on their computer.

What kinds of personal data are exempt from the Act?

The Act does not apply to all personal data: data held for some purposes are exempt from the requirement to register. The Registrar cannot take enforcement action and individuals cannot exercise their rights under the Act in respect of such personal data. They cover the following situations:

- personal data held by an individual only in connection with personal, family or household affairs or for recreational purposes
- personal data used only for calculating and paying wages and pensions, keeping accounts or keeping records of purchases and sales in order to ensure that the appropriate payments are made. This exemption does not apply if the data are used for wider purposes – for example, as a personnel record or for marketing purposes
- personal data used for distributing articles or information to the data subjects – under this exemption only a very small amount of data can be held (usually only name and address). A data subject must be asked if he or she objects to the data being held for this purpose. If he or she does object the exemption does not apply to his or her data
- personal data held by an unincorporated members club (eg. a sports or recreational club which is not a registered company). All the data subjects must be members of the club and each person must be asked if he or she objects to the data being held for this purpose. If he or she does object the exemption does not apply to his or her data

- personal data which the law requires the user to make public for example, personal data in the electoral register kept by an Electoral Registration Officer
- personal data which are required to be exempt to safeguard national security. Whether this exemption is required is a question that a Government Minister decides.

Most exemptions are subject to strict conditions, particularly as to when and how information may be disclosed. In practice, many data users will find that since they cannot rely safely on the exemptions, they will need to register under the Act.

Information which is processed only for preparing the text of documents is also outside the Act's scope. This rule is sometimes referred to as the 'word processor exemption'. Its effect is that the Act does not apply to information entered onto a computer for the sole purpose of editing the text and printing out a document.

What is in the register?

Every data user who holds personal data must be registered, unless all the data are exempt. Applications for registration are made on forms DPR1 (the long form) or DPR4 (the short form). DPR4 is intended for use by small businesses. Both forms are available from the Registrar's office. There is a fee payable on an application for registration. The fee may change so you should check the current fee with the Registrar's Enquiry Service (Tel: 01625 535777) before sending in an application form.

The data user's register entry is compiled by the Registrar from the information given in the application. The entry contains the data user's name and address together with broad descriptions of:

- the personal data which the data user holds
- the purposes for which the data are used
- the sources from which the data user intends to obtain the information
- the people to whom the data user may wish to disclose the information, and
- any overseas countries or territories to which the data user may wish to transfer the personal data.

The Registrar can refuse registration applications – for example, if they contain insufficient information.

Computer bureaux which process or arrange the processing of personal data for others must also register. Their register entries will contain only their names and addresses.

Data users and computer bureaux may apply at any time to alter or cancel their register entries.

Data users and computer bureaux who should register but do not do so commit a criminal offence.

Registered data users commit a criminal offence if they knowingly or recklessly operate outside the descriptions contained in their register entries. So, for example, it would be an offence to hold personal data of a type not described in the register entry.

The Register is open to public inspection at the Registrar's office in Wilmslow. Inspection of the Register is free. Official copies of individual register entries (known as 'certified copies') are available from the Registrar's office. A fee of £2 per entry is payable.

The data protection principles

Registered data users must comply with the Data Protection Principles in relation to the personal data they hold. Broadly they state that personal data shall:

- be obtained and processed fairly and lawfully
- be held only for lawful purposes which are described in the register entry
- be used or disclosed only for those or compatible purposes
- be adequate, relevant and not excessive in relation to the purpose for which they are held
- be accurate and, where necessary, kept up to date
- be held no longer than is necessary for the purpose for which they are held
- be surrounded by proper security.

The Principles also provide for individuals to have access to data held about themselves and, where appropriate, to have the data corrected or deleted.

To enforce compliance with the Principles, the Registrar can serve three types of notice. They are:

- an enforcement notice, requiring the data user to take specified action to comply with the particular Principle. Failure to comply with the notice would be a criminal offence
- a de-registration notice, cancelling the whole or part of a data user's register entry. It would then be a criminal offence for the data user to continue to treat the personal data which are subject to the notice as though they were still registered in the same way
- a transfer prohibition notice, preventing the data user from transferring personal data overseas if the Registrar is satisfied that the transfer is likely to lead to a Principle being broken. Failure to comply with the notice would be a criminal offence.

A data user on whom a notice is served is entitled to appeal against the Registrar's decision to the Data Protection Tribunal.

What rights do individuals have?

The Act gives legal rights to individuals (data subjects) concerning personal data held about them.

Compensation

A data subject is entitled to seek compensation through the Courts if, after 11 September 1984, damage has been caused by the loss, unauthorised destruction or unauthorised disclosure of the personal data. If damage is proved, then the Court may also order compensation for any associated distress. 'Unauthorised' means without the authority of the data user or computer bureau concerned.

A data subject may also seek compensation through the Courts for damage caused after 10 May 1986 by inaccurate data. Again compensation for distress may be awarded if damage can be proved.

Correction or deletion

If personal data are inaccurate the data subject may complain to the Registrar or apply to the Courts for correction or deletion of the data.

Subject access

An individual is entitled, on making a written request, to be supplied by any data user with a copy of all the information which forms the personal data held about him or her. The data user may charge a fee of up to £10 for suppling this information from one register entry.

This right is called 'subject access'. Sometimes the right will not apply – for example, where giving subject access would be likely to prejudice the prevention or detection of crime. Usually a request for subject access must be responded to within 40 days. If it is not, the data subject is entitled to complain to the Registrar or to apply to the Courts for an order that the data user should give access.

Complaint to the Registrar

A data subject who considers there has been a breach of one of the Principles or any other provision of the Act is entitled to complain to the Data Protection Registrar. If the complaint raises a matter of substance, is made without undue delay and directly affects the complainant, the Registrar must consider it. If the complaint is justified and cannot be resolved informally then the Registrar may use the powers to prosecute or to serve one of the notices already mentioned. In any event, when the Registrar has considered the complaint, the complainant must be notified of any action which the Registrar proposes to take.

When may personal data be disclosed?

Provided that the Principles and the registration requirements are complied with, the Act does not prevent a data user from disclosing information about an individual if the data user wishes to do so. There is therefore no general right for the data subject to object to the disclosure of personal data relating to him or her. Disclosures may be made if either:

- the person to whom the disclosure is made is described in the disclosures section of the data user's register entry, or

- the disclosure is covered by one of the 'non-disclosure exemptions'. These include, for example, disclosures required by law or made with the data subject's consent.

However, the first Data Protection Principle does require data users to obtain and process information fairly and lawfully. They should be careful not to deceive or mislead anyone, even inadvertently, about the purpose for which the information is to be held, used or disclosed. They should also take care to ensure that in disclosing information they do not breach any duty of confidence, exceed their statutory powers or otherwise act unlawfully.

The compensation rules mentioned in section 6 above apply only to 'unauthorised' disclosures, meaning those made without the authority of the data user or computer bureau concerned. Unless a non-disclosure exemption applies, computer bureaux may only disclose personal data with the authority of the data user who controls the data.

What does the Data Protection Registrar do?

The Data Protection Registrar is an independent officer who is appointed by Her Majesty the Queen and who reports directly to Parliament. The Registrar's duties are to

- establish and maintain the Register of data users and computer bureaux and make it publicly available
- spread information on the Act and how it works
- promote compliance with the Data Protection Principles
- encourage, where appropriate, the development of Codes of Practice to help data users to comply with the Principles
- consider complaints about breaches of the Principles or the Act and, where appropriate, prosecute offenders or serve notices on registered data users and computer bureaux who are contravening the Principles.

The Data Protection Tribunal

The Data Protection Tribunal consists of a legally qualified Chairman together with lay-members. The lay-members are appointed to represent the interests of data users and of data subjects. The Tribunal's task is to consi-der appeals by data users or computer bureaux against the Registrar's decisions. Appeals may relate to the refusal of a registration application, or to the service of an enforcement, de-registration or transfer prohibition notice. The Tribunal can overturn the Registrar's decision and substitute whatever decision it thinks fit. On questions of law the data user or the Registrar may make a further appeal from the Tribunal to the High Court in England and Wales or to the Court of Session in Scotland.

(Reproduced with the kind permission of The Data Protection Registrar. Further details about the Act can be obtained from The Data Protection Registrar, Wycliffe House, Water Lane, Wilmslow, Cheshire SK9 5AF.)

Appendix G: Code of Practice Covering the Use of Personal Data for Advertising and Direct Marketing Purposes

1   General

1.1   This Code of Practice, covering the use of personal data for advertising and direct marketing under the Data Protection Act, is published by the Advertising Association.

1.2   The Association of Mail Order Publishers, the British Direct Marketing Association, the British List Brokers' Association, the Direct Mail Producers' Association, and the Mail Order Traders' Association have committed themselves to observe this Code both in letter and in spirit, and have made such a commitment a condition of membership of their respective associations. It enjoys the full support of the Post Office.

1.3   Other constituent bodies of the Advertising Association recommend the provisions of the Code in so far as they may apply to the advertising and direct marketing functions of their members.

1.4   The Code may be supplemented from time to time by the publication of specific guidelines to assist members with interpretation and technical problems as they arise.

2   Duties of the Data User

2.1   The Data Protection Act 1984 is a novel and far-reaching piece of legislation with implications in every sphere of activity where computers are employed to hold and use the names, addresses or other personal data of living persons.

2.2   The Act is therefore relevant to the direct marketing industry which depends on the use of personal data to mail out its offers, deal with response to advertisements, despatch goods, service accounts, and handle enquiries.

2.3   The Act gives significant new rights to data subjects. They have the right to claim compensation for damage and associated distress arising from the loss or unauthorised destruction or disclosure of personal data, or from the inaccuracy of such data; to have a copy of the information about themselves which is held in computers; to challenge the accuracy of information and, when appropriate, to have it corrected or erased.

2.4   At the same time, those holding the information now have the duty to register as data users and to indicate the types of persons on whom they hold data, the nature of the personal data held, the purposes for which they are held, the sources from which they are derived, and to whom they will be disclosed. The Data Protection Register ('the Register'), as it is called, is a document which is published and regularly updated, and thus constitutes the primary source of information about those holding and using data relating to individuals.

2.5 The Council of Europe *Recommendation on the protection of personal data used for the purposes of direct marketing*, whilst directed at protecting the privacy of the individual in the face of the growing use of data processing in direct marketing, also recognizes that the use of personal data is essential to the maintenance and development of direct marketing. The Data Protection Act does not prevent the use of personal data for legitimate direct marketing purposes provided that the data user is properly registered and complies with the Data Protection Principles. Nothing in this Code is intended to restrict the proper use of personal data for direct marketing. It is of the essence of this Code that its provisions are intended to safeguard the rights of data subjects in such a way that good customer relations and good business practice coincide.

2.6 Nowhere is this coincidence more clearly demonstrated than in the case of data subjects who do not wish to receive unsolicited marketing approaches as a consequence of their personal data being put to uses which they could not have foreseen at the time those data were collected, and to which they would have objected had they known. These are the very prospects data users will wish to pin-point in order to avoid.

2.7 Data users' duties to the data subject (as described in this Code) include therefore:

a) reminders at appropriate times of the existence of the Register and the Data Protection Act

b) particular care in cases where it is intended to pass personal data to third parties so as to give data subjects an opportunity to object

c) the installation and maintenance of facilities for recording and honouring objections to direct marketing approaches whether received direct or via the Mailing Preference Service.

PRINCIPAL PROVISIONS

3 The Principles

3.1 *The First Principle.* The information to be contained in personal data shall be obtained, and personal data shall be processed, fairly and lawfully.

3.1.1 The statutory interpretation of the First Data Protection Principle, in determining whether personal data have been collected fairly, lays stress on the method by which the information has been obtained.

3.1.2 It is therefore the duty of data users at all times to proceed with transparency in their collection and use of data for direct marketing purposes. One important ingredient of transparency is the disclosure of the identity of the data user(s) at the time that personal data are collected.

3.1.3 There are three classes of personal data which shall always, for the reasons given hereunder, be regarded as having been fairly obtained:

a) those required by law to be made public, which are exempt by virtue of S.34(1) of the Data Protection Act;

b) those obtained from a person who is 'required to supply (the personal data comprising the information) by or under any enactment' which shall be treated as having been fairly obtained by virtue of Sch. 1 . Part II Para. 2, of the Data Protection Act;

c) those obtained from published sources where notification will not normally be relevant.

3.1.4 If in the course of acquiring personal data from data subjects, data users materially misrepresent to these data subjects the purposes for which the data are to be held, used or disclosed, those data will be regarded as having been unfairly obtained.

3.1.5 Any use for direct marketing purposes of personal data obtained by data users as a result of enquiries from, or transactions with, data subjects will be regarded as unfair unless that use is clearly covered by a data user's registration.

3.1.6 As the Data Protection Register is the primary repository of information about data users, and their sources, uses, and disclosures of personal data, data users should wherever appropriate draw the attention of data subjects to the existence of the Register, which may be consulted on application to the Data Protection Registrar. While most direct marketing transactions are by their nature transparent and the information contained in the Register does not, in such cases, add anything of substance to the knowledge of the data subject, it is however to the data subject's advantage to be regularly reminded about the Register as the statutory source of information about data users, and that registration is a condition of holding personal data in computerized form.

3.1.7 There are however circumstances in which the requirement of fairness in the collection of personal data calls for additional measures. In such cases (see 3.1.8 below) data users to whom this Code applies should at an appropriate point in their communications, and subject to the conditions set out in 3.1.9 below, advise data subjects in general terms of the uses and/or disclosures that are intended to be made in the particular circumstances, and how data subjects may object thereto.

3.1.8 A statement as mentioned in Section 3.1.7 above must be made to data subjects in all cases in which, at the time that personal data are collected, data users intend to put their personal data to a significantly different use, namely

a) to disclose their personal data to third parties for direct marketing purposes; or

b) to use or disclose their personal data for any purpose(s) substantially different from the purpose(s) for which they were collected and which data subjects could not reasonably have foreseen and to which it is probable that they would have objected if they had known; or

c) in any other case in which, but for the making of such a statement, harm to data subjects would be likely to occur (see also Section 3.3.3 below).

3.1.9 For the purpose of the foregoing Section, an appropriate point will

a) in all cases be at the time of collection of the personal data; or

b) at any other time prior to the intended use or disclosure, provided that the notice is so served as to allow the data subject adequate opportunity to object to such use or disclosure.

3.1.10 Data users must comply with any objections from data subjects to their personal data being put to any significantly different use.

3.1.11 Fairness and lawfulness apply also to antecedent possession and collection, and data users should therefore, as far as is practicable, ensure that personal data they propose to acquire or to use comply with this Principle. In many cases, the data user will have to be satisfied with a formal warranty from the supplier that they do.

The warranty from the list owner should include undertakings that

a) he is registered as a data user;

b) the data were fairly and lawfully obtained (see also Sections 3.1.4 to 3.1.7 above);

c) the list was updated on a specified date or during a specified period (see Section 3.5.1 below). This undertaking should be accompanied by a statement of the respects in which the data have been updated;

d) requests from data subjects for the correction or deletion of data have been complied with;

e) received and disputed data have, where appropriate, been so marked;

f) the purpose or purposes for which the data are registered are compatible with their disclosure to the intending user and his proposed use of them (see Section 3.3 below);

g) the data have, where applicable, been collected, held and processed in compliance with this Code.

The warranty should also state whether the list has been MPS cleaned, and if so, during what period this was last done.

3.1.12 The supplier of any such list as aforesaid should in turn require from the prospective user undertakings that

a) the data will be used only for the purpose or purposes authorised by the supplier;

b) where the prospective user is required to be registered under the Act, those purposes are within the terms of the prospective user's registration;

c) no disclosure will be made to any third party, except as expressly permitted by the supplier, and provided always that any such disclosure is covered by the terms of the prospective user's registration;

d) any request for access, correction or deletion received by the prospective data user from a data subject will, when appropriate, be referred to the supplier.

3.2   ***The Second Principle.*** Personal data shall be held only for one or more specified and lawful purposes.

3.2.1   The Act requires data users not to hold personal data for any purpose that is not specified in the data user's Registration. If in registering, a data user has a choice as to how to specify a purpose, he should always choose that which will most clearly convey to ordinary individuals what he is using those data for. (See also Section 3.1.6.)

3.3   ***The Third Principle.*** Personal data held for any purpose or purposes shall not be used or disclosed in any manner incompatible with that purpose or those purposes.

3.3.1   Personal data will be regarded as disclosed in breach of this principle if the use for which they are disclosed is so dissimilar to the purpose, or one of the purposes, for which they were originally held as to make it probable that harm to the data subject would result from that use.

3.3.2   A prospective user shall not use for direct marketing purposes a list containing personal data unless there is a reasonable expectation that the category of data subjects on that list is likely to be interested in the product(s) the prospective user proposes to offer. A prospective user may also use a list for test purposes, provided that the aim of the test is to determine whether an interest of the foregoing kind exists, and provided always that this purpose is registered.

3.3.3   In any case where harm of any kind is likely to result from disclosure, such disclosure should not be regarded as acceptable unless the data subjects have been asked whether they object to such disclosure and have not objected. This Section does not apply to the disclosure of personal data to debt collection agencies in the course of securing or attempting to secure satisfaction of a debt or debts, provided that the requirements of S.40 of the Administration of Justice Act 1970 are not breached . This Section does not, furthermore, apply to disclosures constituting credit references, provided that the requirements of the Consumer Credit Act 1974 (S. 157 et seq.) are complied with.

3. 4   ***The Fourth Principle.*** Personal data held for any purpose or purposes shall be adequate, relevant and not excessive in relation to that purpose or those purposes.

3.4.1   Data users should at appropriate intervals review their operations with a view to establishing whether they might be able to accomplish their purposes by the use of fewer data.

3.4.2 Data users should also at appropriate intervals review the personal data they hold for the purpose of determining whether they are adequate and relevant for the purposes for which they are held and, if not, whether they could be supplemented by other data.

3.5 **The Fifth Principle.** Personal data shall be accurate and, where necessary, kept up to date.

3.5.1 In determining whether personal data need to be updated, data users should consider
a) whether the data subject would be likely to be harmed by the information being out of date;
b) whether their treatment of data subjects will be affected by the information being out of date;
c) whether a person to whom the personal data might be disclosed would treat the data subjects differently if the information were updated.
Where the answer to any of these questions is affirmative, list owners and list users should ascertain whether they can acquire personal data to update the information contained in their lists. They should take account of any such later information before making use of those lists, or, as the case may be, permitting any third party to do so. In the case of an affirmative answer to (a) above, and where it is not possible to acquire updating information, then that part of any list should not be used or disclosed.

3.5.2 Data users should amend their files if the accuracy of any personal data is challenged by a data subject, unless there are reasonable grounds for doubting the validity of any such challenge.

3.6 **The Sixth Principle.** Personal data held for any purpose or purposes shall not be kept longer than is necessary for that purpose or those purposes.

3.6.1 Data users should regularly review the data they hold with a view to ensuring that they do not hold personal data in breach of this principle. The frequency of such reviews will be related to the use that is made of the personal data, but only in exceptional circumstances will a period exceeding a year between reviews be acceptable.

3.6.2 The requirement in Section 3.6.1 above to review personal data regularly does not apply to personal data held solely for historical, statistical or research purposes.

3. 7 **The Seventh Principle.** An individual shall be entitled –
a) at reasonable intervals and without undue delay or expense
i. to be informed by any data user whether he holds personal data of

which that individual is the subject; and

    ii. to have access to any such data held by a data user; and

b) where appropriate, to have such data corrected or erased.

3.7.1 When a data user receives a request which states or implies that a data subject wishes to know whether the data user holds data on him, the user must treat this as a formal request by the applicant to be supplied with a copy of the information held on him (unless the applicant makes it clear that he wishes to know only whether the data user holds data on him).

3.7.2 Data users should appreciate that most enquiries from data subjects will constitute straightforward enquiries for specific pieces of information. It would needlessly inconvenience data subjects if data users were to treat questions such as 'How much do I owe you?' or 'Why did you send me this offer?' as subject access requests. Such questions should continue to be answered courteously and promptly when it is quite clear that the enquirer is interested only in the answers to them.

3.7.3 In the case of a formal subject access request the data user will need to satisfy himself that the person making the application is the data subject or is a person authorised to act on behalf of the data subject. He will also need to advise the applicant of the fee(s) required. In order to ensure that applications are dealt with speedily, and unnecessary correspondence avoided, a form has been designed which may be found useful. Use of it should in most cases establish the identity of the applicant while at the same time enabling him to let the data user know eactly what information he requires. It will also tell him what it will cost him.

3.7.4 When a data user holds data identifying a source who has supplied him with personal data relating to the applicant, the data user must disclose this to the applicant; provided, however, that the data user shall not be required to identify the source of the personal information if the source is a living individual who has not consented to his identity being disclosed. But the fact that the source is a private individual must be disclosed, unless this information would itself identify the individual.

3.7.5 Data users should acknowledge subject access requests as soon as possible, which other than in exceptional circumstances should not exceed 10 days after they have been received, and should at the same time indicate what delays, if any, might occur in supplying a copy of the information requested. Data users should aim to give applicants the information as soon as practicable after receiving the information they require under S.21 (4) (a) of the Act, and where applicable, any consent necessary under S.21 (4) (b). Only when it is impracticable to do otherwise should data users avail themselves of the maximum period of 40 days provided for in S.21(6) of the Act.

3.7.6 Data users should not make multiple registrations with the object of obstructing subject access applications.

3.7.7 Data users should not use any other provision of the Act (and in particular S.21 (4) (a)) to thwart data subjects' access requests.

3.7.8 Data users should review their procedures to ensure that in the time between the receipt of a subject access request and the production of a print-out of the information requested only routine updating takes place in accordance with the requirements of S.21 (7) of the Act.

3.7.9 When the data user and the data subject are unable to agree as to the correction or erasure of personal data, the data user should advise the data subject of the circumstances, under S.36(2) of the Act, under which the Data Protection Registrar may investigate an individual complaint.

3.8 *The Eighth Principle.* Appropriate security measures shall be taken against unauthorised access to, or alteration, disclosure or destruction of, personal data and against accidental loss or destruction of personal data.

3.8.1 Data users and bureaux need to be aware that security measures appropriate to routine personal data may not be adequate for systems containing sensitive data and should devise and implement their security systems accordingly.

3.8.2 Data users and bureaux should regularly review their security measures in the light of technological developments.

3.8.3 Data users and bureaux should regularly review their operations to ensure that access by their employees to personal data is limited to those who need to have access to such data in the performance of their duties.

3.8.4 Data users whose marketing lists contain sensitive personal data should, where appropriate, include access-markers to facilitate the investigation of suspected breaches of security. (See Section 4 below.)

4 **Sensitive Personal Data**
Data users who hold sensitive personal data, that is to say, data comprising information as to the racial origin of the data subjects, their political opinions or religious or other beliefs, their physical or mental health or their sexual life, or their criminal convictions, are expected to pursue means of compliance with the Data Protection Principles with exceptional rigour (see in particular Section 3.3.3 above; also Sections 3.8.1 and 3.8.4).

In particular, where sensitive personal data of this nature are collected, used or disclosed, data users should consider whether it is appropriate to seek express consent from the data subjects concerned.

(Reproduced by kind permission of The Advertising Association. Further information about this Code can be obtained from: Abford House, 15 Wilton Road, London SW1V 1NJ.)

Useful contacts

Advertising Association, Abford House, 15 Wilton Road, London SW1 1NJ. Telephone: 0171 828 2771.

Advertising Standards Authority Limited, 2–16 Torrington Place, London WC1E 7HW. Telephone: 0171 580 5555.

Agricultural Show Exhibitors Association, 7 Nursery Close, Chadwell Heath, Romford, Essex RM6 4LB. Telephone: 0181 597 1423.

Association of British Chambers of Commerce, Manning House, 22 Carlisle Place, London SW1P 1JA. Telephone: 0171 565 2000.

Association of British Market Research Companies, 67 Caledonian Road, London N1 9BT. Telephone: 0171 833 8251.

Association of Exhibition Organisers, 26 Chapter Street, London SW1P 4ND. Telephone: 0171 932 0252.

Association of Illustrators, 1st Floor, 32–38 Saffron Hill, London EC1N 8FW. Telephone: 0171 831 7377.

Association of Independent Radio Companies Limited, Radio House, 46 Westbourne Grove, London W2 5SH. Telephone: 0171 727 2646.

Association of Market Survey Organizations Limited, 16 Creighton Avenue, London N10 1NU. Telephone: 0181 444 3692.

Association of Media Independents Limited, 48 Percy Road, London N12 8BU. Telephone: 0181 343 7779.

Audit Bureau of Circulations Limited, Black Prince Yard, 207–209 High Street, Berkhamsted, Hertfordshire HP4 1AD. Telephone: 01442 870800.

British Business Press, Queens House, 28 Kingsway, London WC2B 6JR. Telephone: 0171 404 4166.

British Exhibition Contractors Association, Kingsmere House, Graham Road, London SW19 3SR. Telephone: 0181 543 3888.

British Exhibition Venues Association, Mallards, Five Ashes, Mayfield, Sussex TN20 6NN. Telephone: 01435 872244.

British Institute of Professional Photography, 2 Amwell End, Ware, Hertfordshire SG1 2HN. Telephone: 01920 464011.

British Printing Industries Federation, 11 Bedford Row, London WC1R 4DX. Telephone: 0171 242 6904.

Broadcasting Standards Council, 5–8 The Sanctuary, London SW1P 3JS. Telephone: 0171 233 0544.

Bulk Verified Services, 207 High Street, Berkhamsted, Hertfrodshire HP4 1AD. Telephone: 01442 870800.

CBD Research Limited, 15 Wickham Road, Beckenham, Kent BR3 2JS. Telephone: 0181 650 7745.

Central Statistical Office, Great George Street, London SW1P 3AQ. Telephone: 0171 270 3000.

Chartered Society of Designers, 32–38 Saffron Hill, London EC1N 8FW. Telephone: 0171 831 9777.

Committee of Advertising Practice, 2–16 Torrington Place, London WC1E 7HN. Telephone: 0171 580 5555.

Data Protection Registrar, Wycliffe House, Water Lane, Wilmslow, Cheshire SK9 5AF. Telephone: 01625 545745.

Department of Trade and Industry, 10–18 Victoria Street, London SW1H 0NN. Telephone: 0171 215 5000.

Direct Mail Accreditation and Recognition Centre, 5th Floor, Haymarket House, 1 Oxenden Street, London SW1Y 4EE. Telephone: 0171 766 4430.

Direct Mail Information Service, 5 Carlisle Street, London W1V 6JX. Telephone: 0171 494 0483.

Direct Marketing Association (UK) Limited, Haymarket House, 1 Oxenden Street, London SW1Y 4YZ. Telephone: 0171 321 2525.

Directory Publishers Association, 93a Blenheim Crescent, London W11 2EG. Telephone: 0171 221 9089.

Exhibition Audience Audits, 2 Clapham Road, London SW9 0JA. Telephone: 0171 582 5155.

Exhibition Venues Association, 115 Hartington Road, London SW8 2HB. Telephone: 0171 498 3306.

Exhibition Surveys Limited, PO Box 7, 7 Loughborough Road, Asfordby, Melton Mowbray, Leicestershire, LE14 3TP. Telephone: 01664 812481.

Her Majesty's Stationery Office, St Crispins, Duke Street, Norwich, Norfolk NR3 1PD. Telephone: 01603 622211.

Incorporated Society of British Advertisers Limited, 44 Hertford Street, London W1Y 8AE. Telephone: 0171 499 7502.

Independent Radio Sales, 163 Eversholt Street, London NW1 1BU. Telephone: 0171 388 8787. And at: 8th Floor, Trafford House, Chester Road, Manchester M32 0RS. Telephone: 0161 876 5880.

Institute of Direct Marketing, 1 Park Road, Teddington, Middlesex TW11 0AR. Telephone: 0181 977 5705.

Institute of Practitioners in Advertising, 44 Belgrave Square, London SW1X 8QS. Telephone: 0171 235 7020.

Institute of Sales Promotion, Arena House, 66-68 Pentonville Road, London N1 9HS. Telephone: 0171 837 5340.

Joint Industry Committee for National Readership Surveys, 44 Belgrave Square, London SW1X 8QS. Telephone: 0171 235 7020.

London Business School, Sussex Place, Regents Park, London NW1 4SA. Telephone: 0171 262 5050.

Maclean Hunter Limited, 33–39 Bowling Green Lane, London EC1R 0DA. Telephone: 0171 508 8000.

Mail Order Traders Association, 25 Castle Street, Liverpool L2 4TD. Telephone: 0151 227 4181.

Mailing Preference Service, Haymarket House, 1 Oxenden Street, London SW1Y 4EE. Telephone: 0171 766 4410.

Market Research Society, 15 Northburgh Street, London EC1V 0AH. Telephone: 0171 490 4911.

Marketing Society, Stanton House, 206 Worple Road, London SW20 8PN. Telephone: 0181 879 3464.

Media Audits Limited, 16 Dufors Place, London W1V 1FE. Telephone: 0171 734 4080.

Media Expenditure Analysis Limited, Register House, 4 Holford Yard, Cruickshank Street, London WC1X 9HD. Telephone: 0171 833 1212.

Media Sales and Marketing, 30 Leicester Square, London WC2H 7AL. Telephone: 0171 766 6200. And at: 9th Floor, Portland Tower, Portland Street, Manchester M1 3LF. Telephone: 0161 236 8386.

National Exhibitors Association, 29a Market Square, Biggleswade, Bedfordshire SG18 8AQ. Telephone: 01767 316255.

Newspaper Publishers Association, 34 Southwark Bridge Road, London SE1 9EU. Telephone: 0171 928 6928.

Newspaper Society, Bloomsbury House, Bloomsbury Square, 74–77 Great Russell Street, London WC1B 3DA. Telephone: 0171 636 7014.

Office of Fair Trading, Field House, 15–25 Breams Buildings, London EC4A 1PR. Telephone: 0171 211 8000.

Periodical Publishers Association, Queens House, 28 Kingsway, London WC2B 6JR. Telephone: 0171 404 4166.

Radio Advertising Bureau Limited, 77 Shaftesbury Avenue, London W1V 7AD. Telephone: 0171 306 2500.

Radio Authority, Holbrook House, 14 Great Queen Street, London WC2B 5DG. Telephone: 0171 430 2724.

Radio Joint Audience Research, 44 Belgrave Square, London SW1X 8QS. Telephone: 0171 235 7020.

Radio Sales Company, 32 Bedford Row, London WC1R 4HE. Telephone: 0171 242 1666.

Royal Mail Streamline, Direct Marketing Department, Beaumont House, Sandy
    Lane West, Oxford OX4 5ZZ. Telephone: 01865 780387.
Science Reference Library, 25 Southampton Buildings, Chancery Lane, London
    WC2A 1AN. Telephone : 0171 405 8721.
Scottish and Irish Radio Sales Limited, 55 Broadway, London SW8 1SJ. Tele-
    phone: 0171 587 0001.
Society of Typographic Designers, 21–27 Seagrave Road, London SW6 1RP.
    Telephone: 0171 381 4258.
Verified Free Distribution Limited, Black Prince Yard, 207 High Street,
    Berkhamsted, Hertfordshire HP4 1AD. Telephone: 01442 870800.

Recommended reading

Books

The Entrepreneur's Complete Self Assessment Guide by Douglas A. Gray. Published by Kogan Page, 120 Pentonville Road, London N1 9JN. Telephone: 0171 278 0433. This title makes fascinating reading for entrepreneurs planning to advertise to their customers. It enables you to evaluate yourself in different ways.

A Practical Guide to Project Planning by Celia Burton and Norma Michael. Published by Kogan Page, 120 Pentonville Road, London N1 9JN. Telephone: 0171 278 0433. A good introductory read for those business owners and managers who are planning a project, such as an advertising campaign. It provides a clear and concise overview.

Do Your Own Market Research by P. N. Hague and P. Jackson. Published by Kogan Page, 120 Pentonville Road, London N1 9JN. Telephone 0171 278 0433. Easy to read and understand, this text covers the basics of market research in a straightforward fashion. Study it to familiarize yourself with the do's and don'ts of investigating your marketplace.

Database Marketing by Robert Shaw and Merlin Stone. Published by Gower Publishing Group, Gower House, Croft Road, Aldershot, Hampshire GU11 3HR. Telephone: 01252 331551. This guide looks at developing a database system and using customer data effectively. Couched in language which is as non-technical as the subject will allow, it should be perused to see how relevant it is to your advertising activities.

Marketing Research for Managers by Sunny Crouch. Published by Butterworth Heinemann Limited, Linacre House, Jordan Hill, Oxford OX2 8DP. Telephone: 01865 311366. A first-class book, detailing the ins and outs of a complicated topic. Well worth a cover-to-cover read, making you a better buyer and user of research data.

Researching Business Markets edited by Ken Sutherland. Published by Kogan Page, 120 Pentonville Road, London N1 9JN. Telephone: 0171 278 0433. This is an excellent reference source for those who need to collect business data and wish to do so in the most effective way.

Budgeting by Terry Dickey. Published by Kogan Page, 120 Pentonville Road, London N1 9JN. Telephone: 0171 278 0433. This book is a useful and practical guide to financial planning and may help business owners and managers to budget more accurately – an essential skill for prospective advertisers.

Creative People by Winston Fletcher. Published by Century Books, Random Century House, 20 Vauxhall Bridge Road, London SW1V 2SA. Telephone: 0171-973 9670. A quality introduction to creative people, and the do's and don'ts of managing them. Study it if you intend to commission outside help to create and design your mailshots.

The Secrets of Successful Copywriting by Patrick Quinn. Published by Butter-worth Heinemann Limited, Linacre House, Jordan Hill, Oxford OX2 8DP. Telephone: 01865 311366. This book contains innumerable nuggets of valuable information on how to write copy for advertising purposes.

How to Perfect Your Selling Skills by Pat Weymes. Published by Kogan Page, 120 Pentonville Road, London N1 9JN. Telephone: 0171 278 0433. An informative guide, setting out the basics of selling. It should be read by salespeople on an exhibition stand, in particular.

Dealing with Demanding Customers by David M. Martin. Published by Pitman Publishing, 128 Long Acre, London WC2E 9AN. Telephone: 0171 379 7383. A useful book, explaining how to handle problem customers – especially useful for would-be exhibitors.

Law and the Media by Tom Crone. Published by Butterworth Heinemann Limited, Linacre House, Jordan Hill, Oxford OX2 8DP. Telephone: 01865 311366. This text is a practical, down-to-earth guide to the law with regard to the media. Work through it carefully *before* embarking on an advertising campaign.

Magazines

Campaign, £2 per copy. Published by Haymarket Campaign Magazines Limited, 22 Lancaster Gate, London W2 3LY. Telephone: 0171 413 4570. Published each week, this is widely regarded as the bible of the advertising industry and is read by everyone who wants to keep up-to-date on the latest news and developments.

Conferences and Exhibitions Fact Finder. Free within the conferences and exhibitions industries. Published by Batiste Publications, Pembroke House,

Campsbourne Road, London N8 7PE. Telephone: 0181 340 3291. Issued monthly, this magazine incorporates comments, features and up-to-date news on conferences and exhibitions, venues, services and so on. It is an interesting read.

Creative Review, £3.95 per copy. Published by Centaur Communications Limited, St Giles House, 50 Poland Street, London W1V 4AX. Telephone: 0171 439 4222. This is a monthly publication filled with information and guidance on creative matters. It may provide you with thoughts and ideas for your advertising activities.

Direct Response, £2.95 per copy. Published by Brainstorm Publishing Limited, 4 Market Place, Hertford, Hertfordshire SG14 1EB. Telephone: 01992 501177. Available on a monthly basis, this is *the* magazine for the direct marketing industry. Full of news, features, comments and advertisements, it is of real, hands-on interest to direct mail advertisers. If you read nothing else, read this.

Precision Marketing, £1.70 for a copy. Published by Centaur Publishing Limited, St Giles House, 50 Poland Street, London W1V 4AX. Telephone: 0171 439 4222. A weekly magazine filled with news, views and advertisements on direct marketing and promotions. This is a valuable read for prospective and established direct mail users.

Miscellaneous publications

British Rate and Data, £165 per copy. Published by Maclean Hunter Limited, 33 Bowling Green Lane, London EC1R 0DA. Telephone: 0171 505 8000. A 600-plus-page directory published every month, and which includes in-depth details about the media in the United Kingdom. This is a must if you are to gain a reference source for every prospective advertiser.

Conferences and Exhibitions Diary, £75 per annual subscription: four copies. Published by Themetree, 2 Prebendal Court, Oxford Road, Aylesbury, Buckinghamshire HP19 3EY. Telephone: 01296 428585. Published quarterly, this diary allows easy access to facts about forthcoming exhibitions planned in the United Kingdom and Europe, as well as details of organizers, services and so forth. An excellent, value-for-money source of reference.

Exhibition Bulletin, £15 per copy. Published by The London Bureau, 266–272 Kirkdale, London SE26 4RZ. Telephone: 0181 778 2288. This is a monthly brochure which lists upcoming exhibitions in the United Kingdom and overseas, and also includes an extensive directory of services.

The Exhibition Selector Pack. Free on request. Published by Target Response, 1 Riverside, Church Street, Edenbridge, Kent TN8 5BH. Telephone: 01732 866122. Available twice yearly, this pack consists of A4 colour sheets detailing manufacturers and suppliers of equipment and services which can help you to create a winning stand. Each sheet folds into a pre-paid envelope for the relevant advertiser.

Book prices are not given – shop around for the best deal. Other prices are believed to be accurate as at 1st August 1998, but are subject to change. Always ask for 'a review copy with a view to an annual subscription'. You should then receive one free copy of each relevant title.

Glossary

À la carte agency. Advertising agency which produces advertisements but does not usually participate in media planning, negotiating and purchasing. Also known as a 'creative agency'.

ABC Certificate. Audit Bureau of Circulation Ltd Certificate, verifying the average number of copies of a publication sold or distributed.

Accounts executive. A sales representative acting for an advertising agency or publication.

Advance booking discount. Price reduction on radio advertising packages booked some time ahead of transmission.

Advertorial. Article which appears to be written independently of a nearby advertisement, but is related to that advertising material.

Appropriation. Sum of money set aside for advertising activities. Better known as a budget.

Bleed off. Extension of text and/or illustrations to the edge of the page.

Block. Etched plate used during printing processes.

Bromide. Photographic print on bromide paper.

Budget. See 'Appropriation'.

Business exhibition. See 'Trade shows'.

Business-to-business mail. Mailshots sent to named individuals at firms.

BVS Certificate. Bulk Verified Services Certificate, verifying the average number of copies of a free publication distributed in bulk. See also VFD Certificate.

Camera ready. Text and illustrations ready for production.

Certificate of Attendance. Certificate verifying the numbers and types of visitors at an exhibition plus other miscellaneous data.

Circulation. The number of copies of an issue of a publication sold, delivered or handed out.

Classified advertisement. Line-by-line press advertisement beneath a general heading such as 'Employment Opportunities'. Relatively inexpensive.

Cold compilation. Building up of mailing lists by referring to existing sources of information such as directories and yearbooks rather than sales enquiries, responses to mailshots, and so on.

Combination discount. Price reduction available when radio advertisements are transmitted over two transmission areas.

Consumer exhibitions. Exhibitions of widespread appeal; attended by the trade and general public.

Consumer mail. Mailshots sent to members of the public at their homes.

Consumer-specific title. Magazine for special interest groups, such as sci-fi enthusiasts.

Contract discount. Price reduction given to radio advertisers who spend a certain amount on advertising over a period of time. Also called 'expenditure discount' and 'volume discount'.

Contractors. Those specialists responsible for building exhibition stands and other, associated duties such as painting and cleaning.

Controlled circulation. Method of circulation whereby titles are sent to a limited number of named individuals.

Copy. Another name for text. Often used to describe text and illustrations together.

Copy deadline. Date (and time) by which copy must be submitted for publication.

Copywriter. Creative person responsible for producing the text of advertisements.

Cost per thousand. The cost of reaching every thousand people of a medium's audience.

Creative agency. See 'À la carte agency'.

Demographics. Study of the make-up of a population, by age, sex, and so on.

Designers. Those experts who design exhibition stands, advise on display items, and supervise their construction, installation and removal from the exhibition.

Display advertisement. Bordered press advertisement, often large and relatively costly.

Double-page spread. Two, side-by-side pages. More often referred to as 'a DPS'.

Ear. Space to the side of the front page title of a publication. Also known as an 'ear piece' or 'ear spec', or referred to as the 'title cover'.

Ear piece. See 'ear'.

Ear spec. See 'ear'.

Expenditure discount. See 'Contract discount'.

Face. A type design.

Facing matter. The material facing a particular position in a publication. Sometimes abbreviated to 'FM'.

Fixing charge. Surcharge on radio advertisements transmitted at certain times.

Floor plan. Document showing the scale and layout of an exhibition and its stands. Also known as a hall plan.

Free-build stand. Individually designed stand.

Freepost. Pre-paid postage: free for the recipient of the mailshot as it is paid for by the sender.

Fulfilment house. Organization which deals with the responses to mailings on behalf of a direct mail advertiser. See 'Mailing house'.

Full service agency. Advertising agency able to plan and conduct an advertising campaign from beginning to end.

Gatefold. Sheet with folded-in leaves.

General consumer magazine. Publication of interest to most sectors of the population.

Gravure. Method of printing.

Insert. Item inserted into a publication, either loose or bound in. Or an item included in a mailshot to support the message. Typical inserts are brochures, price lists and order forms.

Island position. Distinctive but often expensive position surrounded by editorial text in a publication.

Junk mail. Unnamed and unaddressed advertising material.

Key. Identifying element specific to a particular advertisement or mailing enabling the response to it to be monitored accurately.

Letterpress. Method of printing.

Lettershop. Organization which specializes in taking mailshot components from direct mail advertisers, packaging and delivering them to recipents. Also known as Mailing houses.

Linage. The cost per line of a classified press advertisement. Also known as 'line rate'.

Line rate. See 'Linage'.

List broker. Organization or individual acting as an intermediary between list owners and direct mailers.

List compiler. Organization or individual who creates a mailing list for direct mail purposes.

List owner. Organization or individual who owns a mailing list, usually renting it out for a fee.

Litho. Method of printing.

Mailing house. See 'Lettershop'.

Mailsort. Range of services for large-volume mailings offered by the Royal Mail.

Marketing guide. Comprehensive information pack about a publication. Also called a 'Media guide' or 'Media pack'.

Media guide. See 'Marketing guide'.

Media independent. Advertising agency which deals with the planning and purchase of advertising space and time. It does not offer creative services.

Media pack. See 'Marketing guide'.

Mono. Black and white only.

Next matter. The material next to a particular position in a publication. May be abbreviated to 'NM'.

Package. Group of radio advertising spots purchased by an advertiser. A standard package would be 28 spots over a one-week period.

Pass-on readership. The total number of people who look at a copy of a publication.

Penetration. The extent to which a medium reaches an advertiser's target audience.

Private exhibitions. Self-organized exhibitions arranged for trade and/or public visitors.

Profile. The make-up of a medium's audience, by age, sex, social grade and so on.

Proofs. Copies of material produced for checking prior to amendments and production of the final version.

Public exhibitions. Events of interest mainly to the general public.

Rate card. Sheet or pamphlet listing advertising and other data about a medium.

Reach. Trade jargon for a radio station's estimated weekly audience.

Rep house. Independent sales organization which sells advertising time on behalf of radio stations. Services paid for by radio stations on a fee or commission basis. Also known as a 'sales house'.

Reply device. Item included in a mailshot to help initiate a response. Typical reply devices include pre-paid postcards and envelopes.

Run of paper. Arrangement whereby material will be placed anywhere within a newspaper, at the publisher's discretion. Also referred to as 'Run of press' or 'ROP'.

Run of press. See 'Run of paper'.

Run of week. Arrangement whereby material will be published at some time during a week, at the publisher's discretion. Also known as 'ROW'.

Sales executive. Representative of an advertising agency or medium.

Sales house. See 'Rep house'.

Semi-display advertisement. Display advertisement located in the classified section of a publication.

Shell scheme. Rented, standardized exhibition unit comprising ceiling, walls and floor.

Single column centimetre. Standard unit of sale in a publication, one column wide by one centimetre deep. Normally abbreviated to 'SCC'.

Single spot. One colour which may be added to a press advertisement, sometimes referred to as 'Spot colour'.

Social grades. Classification of the population based on the occupation of the head of the household.

Solus position. Arrangement whereby an advertisement is the only one on a page in a publication.

Space application form. Document used by exhibitors to book space at an exhibition. Better known simply as a booking form.

Special position. Guaranteed position for a press advertisement, as chosen by the advertiser.

Spot. Standard unit of radio advertising time, typically of 30 seconds duration.

Spot colour. See 'Single spot'.

Station-hop. Radio listeners' habits of retuning the radio from one station to another during advertisements.

Technical exhibitions. See 'Trade shows'.

Test market discount. Price reduction offered to first-time advertisers. Also called 'first-time discount'.

Trade shows. Exhibitions for a particular trade or industry; or specific groups of people working in different industries.

Volume discount. See 'Contract discount'.

Index